KT-370-969

ORGANIZATIONAL CHANGE

WITHDRAWN
FROM THE LIBRARY OF
UNIVERSITY OF ULSTER

100632052

PEARSON

At Pearson, we have a simple mission: to help people make more of their lives through learning.

We combine innovative learning technology with trusted content and educational expertise to provide engaging and effective learning experiences that serve people wherever and whenever they are learning.

From classroom to boardroom, our curriculum materials, digital learning tools and testing programmes help to educate millions of people worldwide – more than any other private enterprise.

Every day our work helps learning flourish, and wherever learning flourishes, so do people.

To learn more, please visit us at www.pearson.com/uk

WITHDRAWN FROM THE LIBRARY OF UNIVERSITY OF CHESTER

Fifth Edition

ORGANIZATIONAL CHANGE

Barbara Senior

Stephen Swailes

PEARSON

Harlow, England • London • New York • Boston • San Francisco • Toronto • Sydney
Auckland • Singapore • Hong Kong • Tokyo • Seoul • Taipei • New Delhi
Cape Town • São Paulo • Mexico City • Madrid • Amsterdam • Munich • Paris • Milan

100632052.
658.
406
SEN

Pearson Education Limited

Edinburgh Gate
Harlow CM20 2JE
United Kingdom

Tel: +44 (0)1279 623623
Web: www.pearson.com/uk

First published 1997 (print)
Second edition published 2002 (print)
Third edition published 2006 (print)
Fourth edition published 2010 (print and electronic)
Fifth edition published 2016 (print and electronic)

© Barbara Senior 1997, 2002 (print)
© Barbara Senior and Jocelyne Fleming 2006 (print)
© Barbara Senior and Stephen Swailes 2010, 2016 (print and electronic)

The rights of Barbara Senior and Stephen Swailes to be identified as authors of this work have been asserted by them in accordance with the Copyright, Designs and Patents Act 1988.

The print publication is protected by copyright. Prior to any prohibited reproduction, storage in a retrieval system, distribution or transmission in any form or by any means, electronic, mechanical, recording or otherwise, permission should be obtained from the publisher or, where applicable, a licence permitting restricted copying in the United Kingdom should be obtained from the Copyright Licensing Agency Ltd, Saffron House, 6–10 Kirby Street, London EC1N 8TS.

The ePublication is protected by copyright and must not be copied, reproduced, transferred, distributed, leased, licensed or publicly performed or used in any way except as specifically permitted in writing by the publishers, as allowed under the terms and conditions under which it was purchased, or as strictly permitted by applicable copyright law. Any unauthorised distribution or use of this text may be a direct infringement of the authors' and the publisher's rights and those responsible may be liable in law accordingly.

All trademarks used herein are the property of their respective owners. The use of any trademark in this text does not vest in the author or publisher any trademark ownership rights in such trademarks, nor does the use of such trademarks imply any affiliation with or endorsement of this book by such owners.

Contains public sector information licensed under the Open Government Licence (OGL) v3.0. http://www.nationalarchives.gov.uk/doc/open-government-licence/version/3/.

Contains Parliamentary information licensed under the Open Parliament Licence (OPL) v3.0. http://www.parliament.uk/site-information/copyright/open-parliament-licence/

Pearson Education is not responsible for the content of third-party internet sites.
ISBN: 978-1-292-06383-6 (print)
       978-1-292-06385-0 (PDF)
       978-1-292-14431-3 (ePub)

British Library Cataloguing-in-Publication Data
A catalogue record for the print edition is available from the British Library

Library of Congress Cataloging-in-Publication Data
Names: Senior, Barbara. | Swailes, Stephen.
Title: Organizational change / Barbara Senior, Stephen Swailes.
Description: Fifth Edition. | New York : Pearson, 2016. | Revised edition of
  Organizational change, 2010. | Includes bibliographical references and
  index.
Identifiers: LCCN 2015037702 | ISBN 9781292063836 (print) | ISBN 9781292063850
  (PDF) | ISBN 9781292063867 (eText)
Subjects: LCSH: Organizational change.
Classification: LCC HD58.8 .S456 2016 | DDC 658.4/06--dc23
LC record available at http://lccn.loc.gov/2015037702

10 9 8 7 6 5 4 3 2 1
20 19 18 17 16

Print edition typeset in 9.5/13 Stone Serif ITC Pro Medium by 76
Printed in Slovakia by Neografia

NOTE THAT ANY PAGE CROSS REFERENCES REFER TO THE PRINT EDITION

Contents

 Part One
THE CONTEXT AND MEANING OF CHANGE

**Part Two
CHANGING ORGANIZATIONS**

Part Three
STRATEGIES FOR MANAGING CHANGE

List of illustrations, figures and tables

Illustrations

Figures

Tables

About this book

Introduction

If you have worked in an organization then you might have witnessed how hard it can be to change even the smallest procedure or practice. You might think you hear words of support for a change but then notice that nothing happens; the same old situation keeps coming around again. Or you might encounter opposition to a change that seems so necessary and helpful. Why is it that your colleagues, who are all part of the same set-up, can show so much resistance to what looks like a simple change for the better?

At the other end of the scale, large organizations try to push through big changes to transform the ways in which they operate. It is difficult to get accurate figures because of the difficulty of using a consistent definition of 'change', but there is some evidence that executives think that only a small proportion of change initiatives are fully successful in meeting their objectives. Some projects achieve partial success but a lot of change initiatives fail to make any progress.

It is easy to find recipes to guide us through successful change initiatives. They make much sense at one level; who would not try to communicate a vision for the change, set some objectives and allocate responsibilities, for example? All organizations can do these things along with the other things but they are not enough to ensure successful change. Change initiatives do not fail because organizations fail to follow a recipe; that would be far too simple. There are simply too many factors involved for recipes to work.

In this book we consider the complexity of organizational change to try and understand why change is so difficult to manage. Indeed, after reading the book you might ask yourself whether 'managing change' is an illusion, a myth that can never be achieved. However, as you will see, in Part 3 of the book, a number of possibilities as to how change might be managed are discussed.

The aim of this book

The overall aim of this book is to discuss change in relation to the complexities of organizational life. The text takes both a theoretical and practical approach to organizational change and seeks to meet both the academic and applied aims of most business and management courses. Specifically this text aims to be:

- *Comprehensive* in its coverage of the significant ideas and issues associated with change from operational to strategic levels. Change is also examined in terms of its effects at the individual, group, organizational and societal levels.

- *Conceptual* in the way it explores and critiques theory and research on organizations and change.
- *Critical* through its recognition of the limitations of much of the change literature and its inclusion of critical management perspectives.
- *Practical* through descriptions and worked examples of different approaches to 'doing' change.
- *Challenging* through asking readers to undertake activities relating to their work contexts. Each chapter contains activities intended to personalize ideas from the text and to reinforce learning. End-of-chapter discussion questions, assignments and case examples invite longer and more detailed responses.
- *Balanced* in its use of case studies and examples, drawn from various types of organizations.

Who should use this book?

The book is intended for anyone interested in exploring organizational change and understanding how to make sense of it.

- *Undergraduate students* in the final year of business and management programmes should find the book gives a comprehensive and understandable introduction.
- *MBA students* who need to apply theory to the workplace will find the blend of theory and practice closely linked to the demands of their programme.
- *Students* on specialist Master's programmes should find sufficient practical examples to illustrate theory even if they have little practical experience of management and business.
- *Students on professional courses* that include organizational change.
- *Practising middle and senior managers* who wish to know more about change theory, models of change and its complexity in relation to how organizations behave.

Readers will benefit if they have some prior knowledge of organizational theory and behaviour and of experiencing at first hand the murky waters of change in organizations. However, we have tried to make the book accessible to readers without any prior working experience.

Distinctive features

- **Clear structure.** The book is in three parts. Part One considers the broader environmental contexts within organizations. The causes of change and different types of change are discussed. Part Two opens up the organization to explore issues that are crucial to an understanding of organizational change and how it happens. Part Three addresses the more practical considerations of designing, planning and implementing change.
- **Chapter summaries and learning objectives.** Each chapter begins with a short summary and the learning objectives.

- **Boxed illustrations and activities.** Illustrations that expand on or give examples of points made in the text are used throughout. They include summaries of research papers and short case examples. Each chapter contains several activities that invite readers to think about theory and practice in relation to their own experiences of change in organizations.
- **End of chapter discussion questions and assignments.** Each chapter ends with questions that are intended to promote a more lengthy consideration of issues raised in the text. Many of the questions can be used to prepare for assessments that might occur on a particular programme.
- **End of chapter case examples.** The chapters in Parts One and Two end with case example and case exercise, which helps readers apply concepts, theories and ideas introduced in the chapter to real examples. Case questions are intended as a guide to thinking about the different aspects of the case in relation to ideas and themes running through the book.
- **Indicative resources.** Further reading is suggested at the end of each chapter.
- **Website links.** At the end of each chapter several websites giving further information and support are provided.
- **Academic sources and references.** Full details of references used are given at the end of each chapter and in the author index.
- **Lecturer's Guide and PowerPoint slides.** A Lecturer's Guide is available, downloadable from **www.pearsoned.co.uk/senior**, to lecturers adopting this textbook. It includes commentaries on each chapter, in particular how to use the activities and the kinds of responses to be expected from students carrying out the activities and answering the discussion questions. Additional study work is suggested and PowerPoint slides are provided.

How to use this book

The book has a simple structure. Chapters in Part One are essential to readers new to organizational change. Readers with little knowledge of organizational behaviour will find Part Two especially important, and for those who have already studied organizational theory and behaviour Part Two explores power, culture and leadership with special reference to change. Part Three provides methodologies for planning and implementing changes and closes with a review of current trends and issues in change theory and research.

Activities distributed throughout all chapters embed ideas and concepts in the text. Sometimes they invite readers to reflect on their workplace; other times they invite application of concepts and ideas to work situations. A useful strategy is to read through a chapter quickly first then, on a second reading, carry out the activities.

Discussion questions, assignments and case examples enable readers to write at length on issues associated with organizational change. They are particularly useful as preparation for completing formal module assessments.

About the authors

Barbara Senior, BA (Hons), MA, D.Occ.Psych, C.Psychol

Barbara is Director of Highfield Consultants. She recently retired from supervising doctoral students for the Open University. She is a Chartered Occupational Psychologist and a Member of the Chartered Institute of Personnel and Development (CIPD). She also has a Doctorate in Occupational Psychology. Her past experience is varied. After working in administration and running her own dressmaking and tailoring business, she entered the academic world, researching, teaching and directing courses in organizational behaviour and change at Liverpool John Moores University, the Open University and the University of Northampton, where she was Director of the Postgraduate Modular Scheme. She is the author (with John Naylor) of two previous books on work and unemployment and has contributed to *Introduction to Work and Organisational Psychology*, by Nik Chmiel (Blackwell, 2000). She has published many papers on her research into teamworking and cross-cultural management.

Stephen Swailes B.Sc., DMS, M.Phil., MBA, PhD

Stephen is Professor of Human Resource Management at the University of Huddersfield and an Academic Fellow of the Chartered Institute of Personnel and Development. Starting his career in scientific research, Stephen worked in the water industry and later for a research and consulting organization. During this time he became interested in the study of management – trying to understand what was happening around him – and completed a Diploma in Management Studies and an MBA. After working in industry he moved into teaching and was awarded a PhD for research on employee commitment in organizations and how changes in the workplace influence the nature and expression of commitment. He has published over 40 papers, has contributed several book chapters on organization structure, teams and teamwork, and how organizations use technology. His main research interest now is on talent management and, in particular, what 'talent' means in organizations and how the idea of talent is constructed. He is a co-author of *Introduction to International Human Resource Management* published by Oxford University Process.

Acknowledgements

Barbara

This fifth edition of *Organizational Change* is dedicated to my late husband Gerry, without whom this project would not have happened. As always, my children David and Jayne, as well as various friends, have listened with patience to my accounts of researching, writing and checking. Their moral support has been important to me.

Stephen and I have tried to be true to the large amount of research and work already accomplished in the subject area of organizational change. Every effort has been made to trace and acknowledge ownership of copyright.

Stephen

Although Barbara and I have worked together for over 20 years I would like to take this opportunity of thanking her for inviting me to work with her again on the fifth edition of this popular book. I am also indebted to Elizabeth my wife for her patience and support while writing the fifth edition and to Thomas and Nicholas whose working lives will see change on a grand scale.

We are grateful to Dr Fiona Beddoes-Jones of The Cognitive Fitness Consultancy for contributing material on authentic leadership to Chapter 6 and to Dr Kae Reynolds of the University of Huddersfield for contributing material on servant-leadership, also to Chapter 6. We are also grateful to Jim Bamford of the University of Huddersfield for providing a practical illustration for Chapter 8.

Publisher's acknowledgements

We are grateful to the following for permission to reproduce copyright material:

Figures

Figure 2.1 from *Implementing Strategic Change*, London: Kogan Page (Grundy, T. 1993) p.25; Figure 2.3 from Radical Change Accidentally: the emergence and amplification of small change, *Academy of Management Journal*, Vol 50(3), pp.515–43 (Plowman, D.A., Baker, L.T., Beck, T.E., Kulkarni, M., Solansky, S.T. and Travis, D.V. 2007), Copyright © 2007, Academy of Management; Figure 2.4 from Evolution and Revolution as Organizations Grow, *Harvard Business Review*, July–August, p.41 (Greiner, L.E. 1972), Reprinted by permission of Harvard Business Review.

Copyright © 1972 by the Harvard Business School Publishing Corporation. All rights reserved; Figures 2.5, 2.6 from 'Breakpoint: how to stay in the game', *Financial Times Mastering Management*, Part 17 (Strebel, P. 1996) 1st March 1996, © The Financial Times Limited. All Rights Reserved; Figure 2.7 from A causal model of organizational performance and change, *Journal of Management*, Vol 18(3), pp.523–45 (Burke, W.W. and Litwin, G.H. 1992), Copyright © 1992, © SAGE Publications. Reprinted by Permission of SAGE Publications, Inc.; Figure 3.3 from *Creative Organization Theory: A Resource Book* London: Sage (Morgan, G. 1989) p.66, Copyright © 1989 by Sage. Reprinted by permission of Sage Publications, Inc.; Figure 3.7 from The Effective Organization: Forces and Forms, *Sloan Management Review*, Winter 1991, 32 (part 2) p.55 (Mintzberg, H. 1991), Copyright © 1991 by Massachusetts Institute of Technology. All rights reserved. Distributed by Tribune Media Services; Figure 4.2 from Measuring Organizational Cultures: a qualitative and quantitative study across twenty cases, *Administrative Science Quarterly*, Vol 35, p. 291 (Hofstede, G., Neuijen, B., Ohayv, D.D. and Sanders, G. 1990), Copyright © 1990, © SAGE Publications. Reprinted by Permission of SAGE Publications, Inc.; Figure 4.3 from *Managing Cultures: Making Strategic Relationships Work*, Chichester: Wiley (Hall, W. 1995) p.58, reprinted by permission of John Wiley and Sons Ltd; Figure 4.4 adapted from A Competing Values Framework for Analysing Presentational Communication in Management Contexts, *Journal of Business Communication*, Vol 28(3), pp.213–32 (Quinn, R.E. 1991), Copyright © 1991, © SAGE Publications. Reprinted by Permission of SAGE Publications, Inc.; Figure 4.5 from *Managing Change Across Corporate Cultures*, Chichester: Capstone Publishing (Trompenaars, F. and Prud'homme, P. 2004), reprinted by permission of John Wiley & Sons Ltd on behalf of Capstone Publishing Ltd; Figure 4.6 adapted from *Cultures and Organizations*, Maidenhead: McGraw-Hill (Hofstede, G. 1991) Copyright © Geert Hofstede; Figure 4.9 adapted from Matching Corporate Culture and Business Strategy, *Organizational Dynamics*, Vol 10(1), p.36 (Schwartz, H. and Davis, S.M. 1981), Copyright (1981), with permission from Elsevier; Figure 4.10 adapted from Matching Corporate Strategy and Business Strategy, *Organizational Dynamics*, Summer, p.41 (Schwartz, H. and Davis, S.M. 1981), Copyright (1981), with permission from Elsevier; Figure 4.11 adapted from Matching Corporate Strategy and Business Strategy, *Organizational Dynamics*, Summer, p.44 (Schwartz, H. and Davis, S.M. 1981), Copyright (1981), with permission from Elsevier; Figure 6.5 after *Beyond Rational Management: Mastering the Paradoxes and Competing Demands of High Performance*, San Francisco: Jossey-Bass (Quinn, R.E. 1988) p. 48; Figure 6.6 from From transactional to transformational leadership: learning to share the vision, *Organizational Dynamics*, Vol 18(3), p. 22 (Bass, B.M. 1990), Copyright (1990), with permission from Elsevier; Figure 6.7 from Authentic Leadership: The key to Building Trust, *People Management*, August, pp. 46 (Beddoes-Jones, F. 2012); Figure 6.8 from Transformational and Coercive Strategies for Planned Organizational Change: beyond the OD model, *Organization Studies*, Vol 9(3), pp. 317–334 (Dunphy, D. and Stace, D. 1988), Copyright © 1988, © SAGE Publications. Reprinted by Permission of SAGE Publications, Ltd; Figure 6.10 from Strebel, P. (1996) 'Choosing the Right Change Path', *Mastering Management*,

Part 14, Financial Times, pp. 5–7, © The Financial Times Limited. All Rights Reserved.; Figure 6.12 from Creating Readiness for Oragnizational Change, *Human Relations*, Vol 46(6), pp. 681–703 (Armenakis, A., Harris, S.G. and Mossholder, K.W. 1993), Copyright © 1993, © SAGE Publications. Reprinted by Permission of SAGE Publications, Ltd; Figure 8.2 from *Doing Action Research in Your Own Organization*, 4th ed., London: Sage (Coghlan, D. and Brannick, T. 2014), Copyright © 2014, © SAGE Publications. Reprinted by Permission of SAGE Publications, Ltd; Figure 8.7 from Mabey, C. and Pugh, D. (1995) Block 4, Section 6, Planning and Managing Change', Course P679, Milton Keynes: Open University Press.; Figure 9.2 from *Working Futures 2012-2022: Introduction and Commentary* Briefing Paper, UK Commission for Employment and Skills (Wilson, R., Beaven, R., May-Gillings, M., Hay, G. and Stevens, J. 2014) p.11; Figure 9.5 from Creative Hot Spots: A Network Analysis of German Michelin-Starred Chefs, *Creativity and Innovation Management*, Vol 23(1), pp.3-14 (Aubke, F. 2014), © 2013 John Wiley & Sons Ltd; Figure 9.6 from Organizational Change Capacity in Public Services: the case of the World Health Organization, *Journal of Change Management*, Vol 8(1), pp.57–72 (Klarner, P., Probst, G. and Soparnot, R. 2008).

Tables

Table 1.1 from *Working Futures 2012-2022: Introduction and Commentary* Briefing Paper, UK Commission for Employment and Skills (Wilson, R., Beaven, R., May-Gillings, M., Hay, G. and Stevens, J. 2014) p.66; Table 2.2 from Complexity Theory and Strategic Change: an Empirically Informed Critique, *British Journal of Management*, Vol 16 (2), pp.149–66 (Houchin, K. and MacLean, D. 2005), Copyright © 2005, John Wiley and Sons; Table 4.1 adapted from Hofstede, G. (1993) 'Cultural Constraints in Management Theories', Academy of Management Executive, February, p. 91. Copyright © Geert Hofstede.; Table 4.2 after Laurent, A. (1983) 'The Cultural Diversity of Western Conceptions of Management', International Studies of Management and Organization, XIII (1–2), pp. 75–96, Reproduced by permission of Taylor & Francis LLC (http://www.tandfonline.com); Tables 4.3, 4.4 adapted from Koopman et al. (1999) 'National Culture and Leadership Profiles in Europe: some results from the GLOBE study', European Journal of Work and Organizational Psychology, 8(4), pp. 503–520. Copyright © 1999 Routledge, reprinted by permission of Taylor & Francis Ltd (http://www.tandfonline.com); Tables 5.1, 5.2 from *The Female FTSE Board Report 2015*, Cranfield University (Vinnicombe, S., Dolder, E., Sealey, E., Pryce P. and Turner, C. 2015) p.35; Table 5.3 from *Leadership and the management of conflict at work. Survey Report.* London: Chartered Institute of Personnel and Development (CIPD 2008), with the permission of Chartered Institute of Personnel and Development, London (www.cipd.co.uk); Table 5.4 from Understanding Power: bringing about strategic change, *British Journal of Management*, Vol 7 (special issue), pp.S3–S16 (Hardy, C. 1996); Table 6.1 adapted from A Force for Change: How Leadership Differs from Management by John P. Kotter. Copyright © 1990 by John P. Kotter Inc. All rights reserved, with the permission of The Free Press, a Division of Simon & Schuster, Inc.; Table 6.2 after *Beyond*

Rational Management: Mastering the Paradoxes and Competing Demands of High Performance, 1st ed., San Francisco: Jossey-Bass (Quinn, R.E. 1988) p. 48, Republished with permission of John Wiley and Sons Ltd; permission conveyed through Copyright Clearance Center, Inc.; Table 9.1 from Organizational Discourse and New Organization Development Processes, *British Journal of Management*, 19, Special Issue, p.S8 (Marshak, R.J. and Grant, D. 2008), reproduced with permission.

Text

Example 2.2 from The Strategic Management of Corporate Change, *Human Relations*, Vol 46(8), pp.905–20 (Dunphy, D. and Stace, D. 1993), Copyright © 1993, © SAGE Publications. Reprinted by Permission of SAGE Publications, Ltd; Example 2.13 from *Change Management: Guide to Effective Implementation* 2nd ed., London: Sage (Paton, R.A. and McCalman, J. 2000), Copyright © 2000, © SAGE Publications. Reprinted by Permission of SAGE Publications, Ltd; Example 3.3 from Organigraphs: drawing how companies really work, *Harvard Business Review*, Sep/Oct Issue, pp.87–94 (Mintzberg, H. and van der Heyden, L. 1999); Example 3.5 from www.unilever.com, Reproduced with kind permission of Unilever PLC and group companies; Example 3.14 from *Organizations: A Guide to Problems and Practice*, London: Paul Chapman (Child, J. 1988), Copyright © 1988, © SAGE Publications. Reprinted by Permission of SAGE Publications, Ltd; Example 5.10 from Toward Multi-dimensional Values in Teaching: the example of conflict behaviors, *Academy of Management Review*, Vol 12, p.487 (Thomas, K.W. 1977), Copyright © 1977, Academy of Management, Copyright © 1977, Academy of Management; Example 6.5 from From transactional to transformational leadership: learning to share the vision, *Organizational Dynamics*, Vol 18(3), p. 22 (Bass, B.M. 1990), Copyright © 1969, with permission from Elsevier; Example 6.8 from Assessing Leadership: A View from the Dark Side, *International Journal of Selection and Assessment*, Vol. 9(1-2), pp.40-51 (Hogan, R. and Hogan, J. 2001), Copyright © 2003, John Wiley and Sons, Reproduced with permission of Blackwell Publishing; Example 6.11 from Decoding Resistance to Change, *Harvard Business Review*, March/April, pp.99–103 (Ford, J.D. and Ford, L.W. 2009); Example 9.2 from Case Study - On the Rise and Online: Female Consumers in Asia (Going Global - The Economist).

Part One

THE CONTEXT AND MEANING OF CHANGE

The rhetoric of business continues to tell us that the pace of change is accelerating and that anticipating and responding to change are essential for organizational survival. Indeed, it is easy to find examples of organizations, small and large, that have ceased to exist because events overtook them. Poor leadership and slow reactions to competitors are typical management problems linked to change failures.

Part One of this book explores the events that encourage and stimulate organizations to attempt change, large and small, as well as the political background against which attempts to bring about organizational change are played out. Chapter 1 begins by considering what we mean by 'organization' and how organizational life is influenced by many factors, particularly those originating outside the organization. Organizational activities are shown to be the outcomes of historical developments as well as the results of the day-to-day vagaries of political, economic, technological and socio-cultural influences. Chapter 2 investigates the nature of change in more detail.

Chapter 1

Organizations and their changing environments

In this chapter, organizations are defined as systems made up of formal aspects of management and operations which are heavily overlaid by informal aspects of life in organizations deriving from relations between people. Organizational systems are conceptualized as operating in three types of environment – temporal, external and internal – that interact with each other to create the 'triggers' of change.

Learning objectives

By the end of this chapter you will be able to:

- describe the general characteristics of organizations;

- identify triggers for change in a range of organizations;

- discuss the concept of organizations as systems operating in multi-dimensional environments and the implications for understanding the causes of organizational change;

- analyze the level of turbulence in organizational environments.

A view of organizations

At a simple level we can think of organizations as the physical spaces that we work in and interact with. 'Who do you work for?' is a common question when we meet people and our replies give a name and place to the organization that pays our wages or salaries. We might identify strongly with it; or maybe not. Tony Watson (2006) summarized definitions of organizations and noted that a common factor is the idea that organizations have goals which act as a glue holding together the various systems used to produce things. He also points out that although we may speak of 'organizational' goals, the goals are really those devised and promulgated by top managers. They are very personal and might not be shared by everyone. Organizing and managerial action are then assumed to follow the goals.

So organizations can be seen as people interacting in some kind of structured or organized way to achieve some defined purpose or goal. However, the interactions of people, as members of an organization, need managing to give shape and direction to their activities. This implies some structuring of their activities which in turn requires a set of organizational roles (see Illustration 1.1). In addition, the activities of individual organizational members and their interactions with one another imply processes through which work gets done in order to achieve

Illustration 1.1

What are organizations?

Richard Daft, a leading thinker on organizations, defines an organization as a social entity that has goals and purpose, that has deliberately designed structures to control and monitor the activities of members, and operates within and is linked to an external environment (Daft, 2013).

Although organizations are real in their consequences, both for their participants and for their environments, they are essentially abstractions. Rational views of organizations see goals; future-oriented actions towards goals; actions shaped by structure, culture and human resource management practices; hierarchies in which action is cascaded so that smaller actions contribute to something bigger; roles that are created to control and manage action and there will be an awful lot of rules. And of course organizations attempt to change their practices as they acquire new information.

Rules can be formal, for example the factory starts at 07.30; professional, for example deriving from professional training and practice; legal, that is things governed by the law; standards, for example rules set by a governing or accrediting body; and informal, for example dress codes. Organizations have a life cycle and, even though their members change, some last for hundreds of years. Organizations will often contrive to shape how they are perceived in their sector to create a distinctive personality and reputation. Images and symbols are used to perpetuate the image. Boundaries between organizations may be very diffuse as collaboration is used more and more as a way of surviving. Organizations may overlap with professional institutions; consider for instance the overlap between healthcare and the medical profession. Institutions have a big influence on what people are prepared to do and on how they behave (Clegg, Kornberger and Pitsis, 2008).

Rationality gives those in power a sense of control such that they are bewildered when others do not follow them. But one person's rationality is another person's irrationality – which leads us nicely into understanding more about change.

the organization's purposes or goals. Thus we have organizations as entities and organization as ways of organizing. Above all, there is the requirement for decision taking about the processes (the means) by which the goals (the ends) are achieved. Organizations also exist in relation to a network of other things: competitors, investors, institutions and trade unions, for instance. While there are boundaries between these various entities, the boundaries can be clear and rigid, for example between competitors, or porous, for example between a supplier and a manufacturer.

This view of organizations draws on the concept of an organization as a system of interacting subsystems and components set within wider systems and environments that provide inputs to the system and receive its outputs. This is represented in Figure 1.1, which identifies the main elements of most organizations and their functioning. These are grouped into two main subsystems – the formal and informal. Thus elements of the formal subsystem include the organization's strategy, whether this is devised by a single person, as might happen in a small owner–manager company, or by a board of directors and top management group. Other components include the organization's goals and the means of achieving them through the production of goods or services. Management, as the formal decision making and control element, is of course present in all organizations.

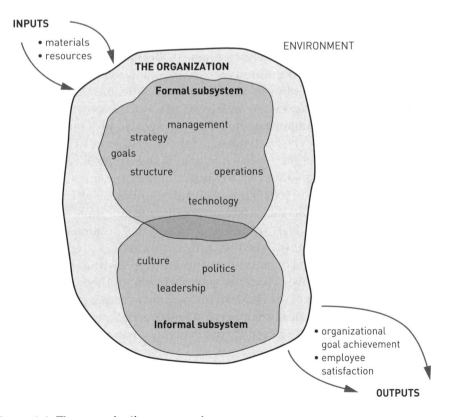

Figure 1.1 The organization as a system

It is clear from any examination of complex systems like organizations that some kind of structuring of activities is required and the concept of organizational structure is central to that of organizational systems. However, over 40 years ago, Child (1973) drew attention to the role of other, much more intangible elements of organizational life such as the political behaviour of organizational members. Nadler and Tushman (1988) included the informal organization (patterns of communication, power and influence, values and norms) in their systems model of organizational behaviour, and Stacey (2007) writes of 'legitimate themes' to describe the conversations that people are comfortable having in open discussions and 'shadow themes' to describe conversations that people cannot have openly and that they would only have with a small number of trusted colleagues. Thus the idea of the 'informal subsystem' encapsulates the more hidden elements of organizational culture and politics and the rather less hidden element of leadership – including those who are led.

These relatively stable subsystems and elements of organizational functioning interact with each other in some kind of transformation process. This means taking inputs such as materials, capital and knowledge and transforming them into product or service outputs. However, while the outputs can be thought of as the primary reason for the organization's existence, other outputs that are particularly relevant to the informal subsystem are employee commitment and satisfaction, given their potential to affect employee behaviour and thus organizational outcomes (Vermeeren, Kuipers and Steijn, 2014).

However, the concept of organizational systems as open systems has not gone without criticism. Silverman (1970) challenged the idea of organizations as systems since the notion rests on an assumption that defining an organization's goals is uncontentious and that, within the organization, there is consensus as to what its goals are. Based on Silverman's ideas, a contrasting view of organizations as being composed of individuals and groups with multiple different interests – who construe their actions in many different ways – came to the fore. Known as the 'social action' approach to understanding organizations, this became recognized as an alternative view to the idea of organizations as systems.

Stacey's (2007) ideas of organizations as *complex* systems emphasize the notion of unpredictability by emphasizing the multitude of interactions in and between the individual (psychological), social, organizational and environmental domains. He also stresses the difficulties or, as he sees them, impossibilities, of trying to understand organizations and the people within them from the point of view of an objective outsider as some open systems theorists have done. Having said this, the concept of organizational systems as *open* systems is an important one; organizations transform inputs into outputs and the strategies employed are influenced by both historical and contemporary environmental demands, opportunities and constraints.

The next section traces some historical trends which have influenced organizational strategies and processes through time. This tracing of history acts as a prelude to a consideration of the more immediate environment of organizations today and as they might present themselves in the future.

The historical context for change

During the agricultural age which prevailed in Europe until the early 1700s (Goodman, 1995) wealth was created in the context of a society based on agriculture that was influenced mainly by local markets for both produce and labour, punctuated by uncontrollable factors such as bad weather, conflict and epidemics. During this time the cycle of activities required to maintain life was predictable even if for most people life was little more than at subsistence level.

The agricultural era was followed by the Industrial Revolution and the industrial age, beginning in the late 1700s, which drove industrial output in the UK and later in America well into the twentieth century. It was characterized by a series of inventions and innovations that reduced the number of people needed to work the land and, through the factory system, provided the means of mass production. To a large extent demand and supply were predictable, enabling companies to structure their organizations along what Burns and Stalker (1966) described as mechanistic lines – as systems of strict hierarchical structures and lines of control.

This situation prevailed into the late twentieth century and of course still exists in some organizations. Demand came largely from domestic markets, organizations struggled to meet consumer demand and the most disturbing environmental influence on organizations of this era was the demand for products which outstripped supply. Henry Ford's remark that 'Any customer can have a car painted any colour so long as it is black' summed up the supply-led state of the markets. Ford did not have to worry about customers' colour preferences; he could sell everything his factories produced.

Figure 1.2 characterizes organizations of this period as 'task oriented', with effort being put into increasing production through more effective and efficient production processes. The push during this period for ever-increasing efficiency of

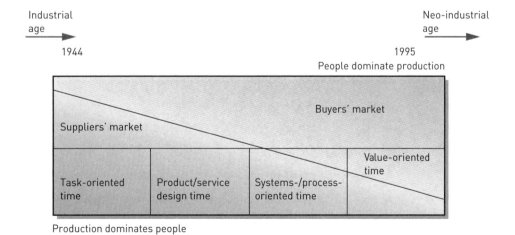

Figure 1.2 Market factors impacting on operations of Western organizations
Source: Goodman, M. (1995) *Creative Management*, Hemel Hempstead: Prentice Hall, p. 38.

production supported the continuing application of the earlier ideas of Scientific Management (King and Lawley, 2013; Mullins, 2013) allied to Fordism that was derived from Henry Ford's ideas of assembly-line production (see Wood, 1989). This was a period mainly of command and control, of bureaucratic structures and the belief that there was 'one best way' of organizing work for efficient production. As time passed, however, this favourable period for organizations began to end as consumers became more discriminating in the goods and services they wanted and as technological progress brought about increased productivity to the point where supply overtook demand. A consequence of this was that organizations began increasingly to develop and access new markets for their outputs.

Towards the end of the twentieth century, organizations faced increasing competition from developing countries. In the West, this forced the decline and near elimination of some high-labour-cost manufacturing sectors (like shipbuilding, textiles and clothing) and a shift from manufacturing to services such as banking, insurance, healthcare and education. In the neo-industrial age of the advanced economies the emphasis has moved towards adding value to goods and services in contrast with the task-oriented, products-/services-oriented and systems-oriented times of the past. The impact of the information age, which began around 1970, is captured by Jones, Palmer, Osterweil and Whitehead (1996):

> ... the pace and scale of the change demanded of organizations and those who work within them are enormous. Global competition and the advent of the information age, where knowledge is the key resource, have thrown the world of work into disarray. Just as we had to shed the processes, skills and systems of the agricultural era to meet the demands of the industrial era, so we are now having to shed ways of working honed for the industrial era to take advantage of the opportunities offered by the information age ... Organizations are attempting to recreate themselves and move from the traditional structure to a dynamic new model where people can contribute their creativity, energy and foresight in return for being nurtured, developed and enthused.

Activity 1.1

Consider how you would describe an organization that you know well in terms of its wealth-creating capacity. For instance:

- *Which business sectors does it operate in?*

- *Does the organization operate at a local, regional, national or international level?*

- *In what ways does the organization need creativity and innovation to survive?*

- *What is the mix of employees – unskilled, skilled, professional?*

- *How well does it attract and keep high-performing employees?*

- *How much autonomy do employees have over the work they choose to do and how they do it?*

- *How much is decision taking devolved to the lowest level possible or kept in the hands of top management?*

An uncertain future

Your responses to Activity 1.1 may show an organization operating in a fairly predictable environment with a sense of security about the future. More likely, other responses may suggest a more turbulent environment characterized by uncertainty about markets, fluctuating demand for its products, the ability to attract and retain good employees, whether employment will increase or decrease, and new and existing legal requirements. Most commentators on organizations agree that business conditions continue to be increasingly complex and more uncertain as the pace of change quickens and the future becomes more unpredictable (Dawson, 2003; Furnham, 2000; Nadler and Tushman, 1999). One of the best-known management thinkers, the late Peter Drucker, writing in 1988, maintained that future organizations would be almost wholly information-based and that they would resemble more a symphony orchestra than the command and control, managed structures prevalent in the past (see Illustration 1.2).

Illustration 1.2

Organizations as symphony orchestras

Writing about the way that information technology is transforming business enterprises and how they would look today, Drucker observed:

> A large symphony orchestra is even more instructive, since for some works there may be a few hundred musicians on stage playing together. According to organization theory then, there should be several group vice president conductors and perhaps a half-dozen division VP conductors. But that's not how it works. There is only the conductor-CEO – and every one of the musicians plays directly to that person

without an intermediary. And each is a high-grade specialist, indeed an artist.

(Drucker, 1988, p. 48)

A study of a conductorless orchestra (think about that for a moment) emphasized creativity by all musicians and the relationship between trust and control – specifically trust in the competence of others and trust in their goodwill (Khodyakov, 2007). The orchestra metaphor is useful to help us imagine how work organizations could function, if only …

With this vision of how organizations would change Drucker predicted the demise of middle management and the rise of organizations staffed almost exclusively with high-grade, specialist staff. Middle management was a victim of the downsizing so popular in the past 30 years (McCann, Morris and Hassard, 2008; Thomas and Dunkerley, 1999), yet the culling did not reach Druckerian proportions. However, for the United Kingdom, the projected growth in the numbers of professionals and knowledge-based workers and the decrease in numbers of lower-skilled workers is supported by economic forecasts (see Table 1.1). In a generation, the UK has gone from having a workforce where higher qualifications were rare to one where higher qualifications are common and where far fewer people have no qualifications.

While the percentages shown in Table 1.1 may not appear particularly gripping at first sight, it is important to appreciate that, given the size of the UK workforce, large numbers of people will be affected by these changes. We will continue

Table 1.1 Percentage share of UK employment, 2002–2022

	2002	2012	2017	2022
Managers and senior officials	9.0	10.3	10.9	11.5
Professional occupations	16.7	19.6	21.2	22.0
Associate professional and technical	12.4	13.1	13.6	14.1
Administrative and clerical	14.0	11.8	10.7	9.7
Skilled trades	12.5	11.0	10.2	9.5
Personal services	7.6	9.0	9.8	10.4
Sales and customer service	8.6	8.4	8.0	7.8
Machine and transport operators	7.2	6.2	5.7	5.3
Elementary occupations	12.0	10.5	9.8	9.7

Source: Wilson, R., Beaven, R., Max-Gillings, M., Hay, G., and Stevens, J. (2014), *Working Futures 2012–2022*, Institute for Employment Research, University of Warwick.

to see significantly more people in managerial and professional jobs and in personal services. In contrast, we see falls in administrative and skilled jobs along with machine operators and people doing elementary work. The UK Office for National Statistics publication *Employee growth by region and industry (2012-2013)* suggests that some of these trends have already occurred with significant rises in three industry groups: the accommodation and food industry; the information and communications industry; and the professional and scientific and technical industry groups. These two sets of statistics indicate some of the challenges, both nationally and global, that employers are currently facing as well as those they have yet to face in the future.

Activity 1.2

Linking to Illustration 1.2, if you work in an organization, think about the people you work with. What are your impressions of your trust in their goodwill and their competence? What might your colleagues think of you in this regard? What do your impressions of trust mean for the likelihood of successful change in the organization?

What seems uncontestable is that both public and private sectors continue to face fast-moving change even if the exact nature of the changes needed is not always clear. In the next section we look in more detail at the environmental forces that disturb organizational life and analyze the factors that trigger organizational change.

Environmental triggers of change

A single major event in recent history was the near meltdown of the banking and financial structures in Western developed economies which, although a few had predicted it, hit us with speed and surprise. Lehman Brothers, the fourth largest investment bank in the US, went into what was then the world's biggest bankruptcy. *The Times* (2008) considered the collapse to have been avoidable and blamed it on an aggressive chief executive who was quick to talk yet slow to listen, backed up by weak board members. Other organizational pillars of the financial community fell or were baled-out. Confidence fell and fear spread among the business community.

The investments that we thought were in safe hands in prudently managed institutions quickly turned out to be anything but. Investments and pension fund values plummeted and the UK and US governments were forced into fast and decisive action – pumping billions into their financial systems to recapitalize the banks, keep them afloat and save themselves. Queues of people waiting to take their money out of high street banks would surely have completely undermined confidence in the economy and possibly led to the downfall of governments. The financial crisis brought the dangers of unfettered profit maximization to the forefront with the public and the government. Capitalism came close to imploding. It was not until the end of 2014 that businesses in the United States and the United Kingdom began to revive with gross domestic product increasing. However, recovery in the European Union was slower and patchy. Political uncertainty, with changes of governments, added to this.

Alongside these macro-economic events, change is also triggered by events that touch the lives of individuals. Individual cases of child or patient abuse, whistle-blowing to expose bad practices, greed or cover-up also lead to calls for changes to procedures and practices in healthcare, education and business organizations.

We see from these examples that change is triggered by large and momentous events and also by events touching a single person that are so unacceptable that something has to be done – or at least appear to be done. In the latter case, it is as if people tolerate what they know are unacceptable situations, idly waiting for the critical incident that will act as a change trigger. Yet while we are all used to hearing calls for change, Burnes (2005, p. 73) observes that while change is all around us, examples of successful change are 'elusive'. Because it is so often a mantra of politicians and managers, change has attracted much theory development in an effort to explain how successful change works. Indeed, if there was a prize for the most theorized yet least effective management practice, organizational change would surely be a candidate!

Figure 1.1 depicts an organization as a system receiving inputs from its environment and releasing outputs back into it. The view of organizations existing as systems of interrelated elements operating in multi-dimensional environments has a number of supporters. Peter Checkland's (1972) work, for instance, is well known for the pioneering development of the soft systems model – an approach designed specifically for analyzing and designing change in what Checkland terms 'human activity systems', most frequently organizational systems. Stacey (2007) uses systems concepts in his discussion of organizations and change. However, before reading any further in this chapter, please have a go at Activity 1.3.

Activity 1.3

For an organization that you know well, what are the main reasons why it has attempted to make changes to products, services, systems and/or structure?

Who is actually set to benefit most from the changes that are being attempted?

When you completed Activity 1.3, did you list anything that falls under any of the following headings?

● changing customer requirements and changing demand for products/services;
● regulatory changes;
● trade union activity;
● actions by competitors;
● business performance (falling incomes or revenues);
● economic climate;
● advances in technology that affect production systems or products;
● production costs (materials, labour);
● the growth of e-commerce and use of the Internet;
● competition from other countries.

Brooks (2011, p. 3) regards the business environment as 'a general concept which embraces the totality of external environmental forces which may influence any aspect of organizational activity'. It is worth noting that while some environmental changes are objective, even measurable, it is the ways that people interpret events that determine how an organization responds (Mason, 2007). Thus the extent to which the environment is real is a social construction of reality. Similar organizations in the same sector while battling with the same forces may construct the significance of events quite differently. These different constructions arise from the following:

● How the characteristics and experiences of people filter information from the environment.
● How organizational cultures influence the ways that managers and others have for interpreting events.
● How organizational politics interpret signals from the environment.
● How the organization has developed in the past and what has worked and not worked.
● How the business sector as a whole interprets the information.

An organization's environment also includes broader influences such as the internationalization of trade, the prevailing political ideology, attitudes to trade unions, changes from public to private ownership or vice versa, demographic changes and changes in family structure. This chapter now considers the environment in more detail and draws attention to the way changes in the organizational environment can trigger consequent changes in the ways an organization and its constituent parts operate.

Analyzing the environment

A common way of grouping different environmental factors examines political, economic, social and technological factors (PEST). Legal and ecological factors can be considered as well (PESTLE); however, these are frequently categorized as political and economic. Figure 1.3 illustrates the PEST factors that, at some time or another, impact upon an organization's formal and informal subsystems and their components as well as the product/service it offers and the markets it serves.

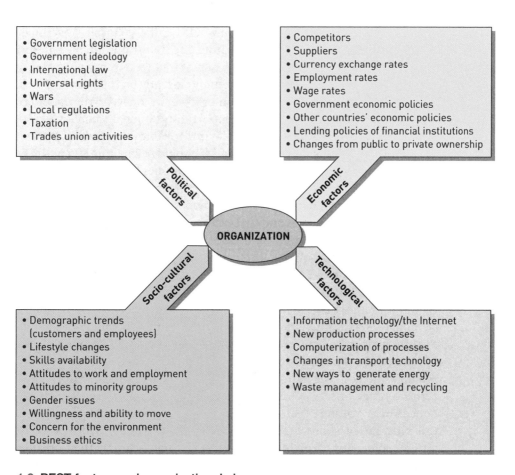

Figure 1.3 PEST factors and organizational change

Political triggers

A plethora of national and international bodies, elected and unelected, influence organizational life to a greater or lesser degree. Consequently, not only do changes in the political environment influence organizations directly, they also interact with changes in the economic environment. Examples include the government-inspired privatization of previously publicly owned institutions such as the UK programme of privatizing utilities and railways, and/or the cooperation of different governments to stimulate trade.

Perhaps the most important aim for governments is to improve economic prosperity. They also act as lawmakers, passing legislation that requires employers to make changes. Consider how working practices have changed in response to legislation addressing discrimination, equal pay and flexible hours, for instance.

The general election in the UK in 1979 was arguably a turning point for management and is a good example of how political decisions influence organizations. The 1970s were characterized by poor industrial relations, ongoing strikes, stoppages and disputes. Union influence on the government and on employers and employees was significant. The conservative government led by Prime Minister Thatcher introduced legislation to curb union powers and assert managers' right to manage. Business had to stand in the face of market forces or it would be allowed to fall. Government intervention through subsidies to prop up fundamentally unprofitable enterprises was no longer an option. The Labour government that was swept to power in 1997 did little to change the prevailing government philosophy on this issue.

The collapse and break-up of the former Soviet Union led to the opening of fledgling market economies and thus to opportunity. Some former Soviet bloc countries are now in the European Union – unthinkable 30 years ago. Spurred on by the political belief that certain public assets would be far more efficiently managed in the private sector, the privatization programmes begun under Prime Minister Thatcher forced huge changes in the sectors affected. Competition was introduced into telecommunications, gas, electricity and water supply and other sectors. Managers faced new challenges and had to learn quickly if their organizations were to survive. Job security changed, as did the working patterns and routines of staff.

Thatcherism and policies from subsequent Labour governments forced big changes upon public-sector organizations; changes which have been emulated elsewhere (see Illustration 1.3). Governments are also major employers and Illustration 1.3 summarizes changes to public service management in recent years. The New Public Management described in the illustration provides both a context and a reason for many change initiatives in the public sector in Europe and elsewhere.

Frameworks for inspection and audit have flourished and ways were found to evaluate and rank the performance of public organizations. Performance targets across a range of services and league tables of hospitals, local authorities and police forces, among others, put organizations into the spotlight. If nothing else this must raise the pressure on managers to act. Seeing public-sector managers on TV apologizing, explaining or justifying some action by their organization is now commonplace. The media is very quick to seize even a minor failure of policy and put managers under intense scrutiny.

Illustration 1.3

New Public Management

New Public Management (NPM) is a term introduced about 1990 to represent new ways of political thinking about how public services should be managed. NPM originated in English-speaking countries but spread to many others. It stressed the role and importance of management in improving public service delivery. It was, and is, overtly managerial in its focus on the efficient production of services and its opposition to systems of self-governance by service providers.

NPM is thought to have originated in the idea that management practices that are successful in the private sector could and should be transferred to and implemented in the public sector. Politically motivated, NPM was an attempt to force two opposing operating systems and cultures together. Characteristics of NPM include:

- introducing competition or at least the principles of competition to public services;
- contracting out some services to private-sector providers;
- introducing targets and explicit performance measures to public organizations and to individual employees;
- depoliticizing service delivery (separating politics from delivery);
- restructuring and separating purchasers from providers;
- budget cuts.

Several observers now feel that public management has moved on from NPM but the legacy of NPM has doubtless had an impact on the ways that services are provided. The outcomes of NPM are mixed; for every successful outcome there is a failure (Pollitt and Dan, 2011) and a range of contextual factors helps to explain the outcomes of public management reforms.

Sources: Levy, R. (2010), 'New Public Management: end of an era?' *Public Policy and Administration*, 25(2), pp. 234–40.
Gruening, G. (2001), 'Origins and theoretical basis of New Public Management', *International Public Management Journal*, 4, pp. 1–25.
Pollitt, C. and Dan, S. (2011), *The Impacts of the New Public Management in Europe: A Meta-Analysis*, 14 December, COCOPS, European Union.

The UK government acted decisively in the winter of 2008 to save the country's financial systems and similar actions were taken by other world leaders. Whereas 35 years ago new attitudes ushered in deregulation of financial systems it does look as if deregulation went too far and allowed too many 'toxic' products that brought the sector to the brink. As governments took a stake in their leading banks there was an expectation that some things would change, for instance restrictions on lending and risk-taking associated with stronger links between performance and employee (particularly at the top) reward.

The financial crisis of 2008 changed many things, especially in Western parts of the world. The period of relative prosperity before 2008 changed, with countries experiencing long periods of economic recessions. These heralded an era of austerity across Europe, and in particular in countries in the south, which led to a reduction in business activity, higher unemployment and increasing national debt. New political parties of the left have emerged with different agendas for how their countries were governed and how to stimulate economic activity and growth. The year 2014 saw the government of Greece taken over by a radical party of the left with policies directly opposed to those of its predecessor.

As we look ahead towards the 2020s, it is clear that the political scene, and its effects on organizations, public, private and voluntary, are uncertain and, to some extent unpredictable, particularly in the east with the increase in efforts by some countries as well as non-governmental radical groupings to take over parts of others. Activity 1.4 asks you to reflect on some of these things.

Activity 1.4

Look again at Figure 1.3 and your answer to Activity 1.3.

What do your conclusions tell you about the interconnections between the various aspects of the PEST environment?

Can you make any interconnections between events and decisions made outside your country that will affect organizations in the country you live and work in?

Economic triggers

Activity 1.4 may show that some factors can be categorized in more than one way. This is normal and simply illustrates the fact that aspects of the organizational environment are interrelated and operate in complex ways to trigger change within organizations. However, because organizations operate in the main to make profits or, in the case of public organizations, to operate within budgets, some of their more serious concerns are with triggers for change in the economic environment. This includes a concern for competitors and other issues, such as exchange rates, corporation tax, wage rates and skills availability which determine their ability to compete.

Political and economic environments are closely related since political decisions shape economic outcomes and economic changes influence political decisions. In general, governments in developed countries aim to keep four key economic indicators in balance (Cook, 2011):

- economic growth;
- a healthy balance of payments;
- low inflation;
- low unemployment.

After a long period of stability in the UK and coincident with a new era of austerity linked to the government's deficit reduction programme, national output began to fall as the long-lasting recession arrived in 2008. A casualty of recession is confidence. Both public and private organizations become less confident about the future; people start to worry about job security and their ability to provide for their dependents. Attitudes change too – what seemed a good idea yesterday is not so appropriate today. Priorities change, projects are shelved and structures change as organizations regroup and reposition in their competitive environment.

Structural changes in Western economies have coincided with an increase in knowledge-intensive jobs and fewer low-skill jobs (see Table 1.1) together with more flexible career patterns. Whereas having several jobs within a single lifetime career was normal, a response to contemporary market conditions for many is to have several jobs in several careers in a working lifetime. There has also been a shift in attitudes away from the paternal employer having the responsibility to look after employees and offer job security towards employees being much more responsible for their own development and for ensuring their own employability. At the root of this are changes to the psychological contract between employer and employee – the sets of mutual expectations that each party has of the other (Rousseau, 2001, 2004; van der Smissen, Schalk and Freese, 2013). Illustration 1.4 is an example of this.

Illustration 1.4

Zero-hours Britain

Number who rely on jobs with no guaranteed shifts leaps to 700,000

The UK business secretary has admitted that some organizations exploit the system of employing people on zero-hours contracts. In 2014, the Office of National Statistics (ONS) reported that an estimated 697,000 people were employed on zero-hours contracts compared with 586,000 in 2013 – a rise of 19 per cent in one year. Because workers often have more than one job, the figures showing the number of contracts offering no minimum hours rose from 1.4 million in 2013 to 1.8 million in the first 9 months of 2014, a 28 per cent increase.

Interestingly, it is not small employers offering these, but some of the largest including fast-food providers and pubs. The ONS said more than half of businesses in the hotel and catering sectors used these contracts, with universities and colleges being large-scale users. Many of these workers are women.

These types of contracts are justified by the employers' industry body as they create thousands of new jobs giving the UK a high employment rate and lower unemployment than many other countries. By contrast, MPs from the Labour government speak of 'Victorian practices' and workers suffering from 'a rising tide of insecurity'.

Source: The Guardian, Thursday 26 February, 2015

Socio-cultural triggers

All the socio-cultural factors listed in Figure 1.3 influence the way organizations are set up, run and managed as well as their capacity to attract people to work within them. Examples of how changes in the socio-cultural environment influence attitudes to work and trigger changes include:

- expectations for continuous increases in the standard of living (recently challenged by austerity in some countries);
- demographic changes such as the age composition of the workforce and the mobility of labour;
- changes in family structures and the roles of men and women which influence preferences for working hours and provision of child care;

- heightened awareness of equality and intolerance of unfair and unethical practices;
- heightened awareness of and sensitivity to cultural and religious differences.

Business practices in long-established organizations have an historical pedigree and in light of socio-cultural changes need to be reviewed to ensure they do not contain any practices that could be seen as discriminatory. Recruitment, selection and promotion policies are particularly vulnerable. Organization cultures can tolerate, even promote, sexist or racist banter and where this happens managers have to act to eliminate it. For example, the Metropolitan Police have received steady criticism for being 'institutionally racist'; criticisms which seem slow to go away despite apparent efforts by senior officers to change the operating culture.

Geert Hofstede (2005) pioneered a better understanding of how national cultures differ, which we discuss in Chapter 4, and his framework and others like it suggest that different cultural groups have different approaches to organizing. This influences the social and power relationships between employees and thus the ways that organizations are structured as well as preferences for teamwork or individualism. A key implication is that what an organization does successfully in one country will probably not work so well if it is simply attempted elsewhere without at least some sensitivity being shown to cultural differences. Managers need to take care, when negotiating overseas contracts or working on projects in other countries, to study the business conventions and ways of operating before they go.

Changing population demographics influence the availability of skills and they influence markets. Healthcare providers are of course at the sharp end of demographics. Life expectancy continues to rise and increases demand for services while new treatments stemming from technological progress can be beyond their budgets. This puts pressure on government health spending which is influenced by the state of the economy. Media interest in patients denied treatment forces healthcare providers to justify their rationing decisions. With new treatments becoming ever more costly, unless governments simply inject more money into healthcare, major changes will be needed to the decision processes and policies that govern who receives potentially life-saving or life-prolonging treatment. The behaviour and work practices in many different healthcare systems (e.g. state-provided free, insurance-based, voluntary, available on condition of payment) will approach patients (their customers?) in varying ways according to what the norms of the systems are and what patients can expect from them.

Activity 1.5

Take the list you made when doing Activity 1.3 and categorize each factor according to whether you consider it to stem from political, economic, technological or socio-cultural forces.

Are there any factors that do not easily fit into these categories?

Technological triggers

Examples of technology triggering change are many and varied and often have a long-run effect on the shape of society and organizations. Investment in technology is seen as a driver of productivity at the level of the organization and, by aggregating organizational output, a driver at national level. It drives productivity and change by replacing labour but at the same time it creates new and different jobs requiring new skills, which in turn has implications for educational organizations who can offer training for such jobs. It enables new products to be marketed – good examples are communication technologies and biotechnology. Consider for a moment the business opportunities created by the Internet and social media in the past 10 years.

In terms of technology use, organizations can be seen in two ways. Most just adopt and use technology to help in the production and delivery of goods and services. However, some exist through the creation of technology itself – consider Microsoft, pharmaceutical manufacturers, telecoms companies and those who are searching for new ways to combat global warming such as alternative technologies for generating energy. Their business is technology-driven and they invest heavily in research and development in order to remain competitive.

Illustration 1.5

Spooks in the office?

The ease with which organizations can monitor how their employees use email and the Internet raises questions. Surveillance of employees is easy, and, in the UK at least, organizations perhaps take a lead from a government that is routinely arguing why access to emails, mobile telephone records and Internet searches will make us all safer. Yet organizations need to be upfront about the surveillance they are doing. They should give reasons for monitoring how employees use email and the Internet and clarify the extent to which they do it. If employees are disciplined over Internet use they would have a strong defence if their employer had not followed above-board procedures and made them clear. Human rights and data protection legislation lurk in the background.

Source: Smith, C. (2006) 'At Work with Big Brother', *Financial Times*, 11 December, p. 13.

The technologies that organizations use affect how they choose to structure for optimum efficiency. They affect the knowledge and skills that employers want and which employees need and lead to retraining and career change. Information and communication technology (ICT) enables teleworking which contributes to efficiency and influences work–life balance. It also shrinks time and space, enabling employees to communicate in new ways, for example as members of virtual teams. It allows employers to carry out surveillance on employee activity, their use of emails and the Internet, thus raising questions about privacy and human rights (see Illustration 1.5). In some sectors, ICT enables employers to monitor how employees spend their time, for example by measuring how long it takes them to complete jobs and compare those times with standard job times. Where actual times exceed standard times, then management will intervene to advise, train and ultimately discipline the employee.

ICT has also influenced the relationships between citizen and state. Our shopping trips, car journeys and Internet usage (among other things) are monitored. Advances in human biology are raising questions about the ethics of medical research, for example on human embryos, and seem likely to have a huge impact on health spending.

What is clear is that there are multiple rationales for the way in which organizations react or interact with triggers for change deriving from the PEST environment and perhaps constraints deriving from their own histories and the influences of their temporal environments. External and internal politics play a part in decisions to change. While rational decision making may seem attractive, and many persuade themselves that they are completely rational, personal circumstances, attitudes and emotions influence the way change is attempted. In addition, not only do triggers for change come from outside, forces for change originate inside organizations – and these also need a response.

Internal triggers and big ideas

So far we have presented change triggers as events that happen outside the organization but at this point we need to introduce another trigger – the power of big ideas. To make this point we draw on what is arguably one of the most powerful ideas ever to occur to a human mind – Darwin's thoughts on natural selection (Dawkins, 2008). For the best part of 2,000 years Christian society had an easy answer to questions about why the earth exists and why it contains such a diversity of species – God created it all. The Koran also tells us how the earth was created, and all religions have a creation story.

Following his travels around the world and his studies of finches and iguanas, English naturalist Charles Darwin wondered why God had created so many different types of the same bird or animal. It occurred to Darwin that life forms were not fixed; they evolved to adapt to their environments. Some finches had narrow, fine beaks to tease out tiny seeds; others had large, strong beaks to crack open bigger seeds. Darwin's theories of evolution were a first step in replacing one set of powerful ideas with another and this really is what change is about. But big ideas need big evidence. Even so, Darwin could not explain how species evolved – the fossil record, DNA and genetic modification were not understood for another 100 years or so. Nevertheless, despite much resistance at the time and since, Darwin's ideas have endured.

In giving this example we do not mean to deny Creationists their beliefs. Perhaps God did create the universe and then allowed things to evolve. The point of the example is to show how a new idea can mean that it is no longer necessary to adhere to established explanations of things. Big ideas don't have to have all the answers if they can stimulate changes to the way we think and the research that we do.

Activity 1.6

Hopefully provoked by this example – what do you think are the five most powerful ideas to occur to the human mind? How did they change society?

As far as work goes, can you identify a particularly big idea that has led to change?

Returning to more mundane matters, the following are indicative of internal triggers for change (Huczynski and Buchanan, 2013; Johnson, Scholes and Whittington, 2014; Paton and McCalman, 2000):

- a new chief executive or other senior manager;
- falling organizational performance;
- a new vision and mission statement;
- high employee turnover, low employee morale;
- recognition or de-recognition of a union;
- relocation and/or redesign of a factory or office layout;
- the adoption of new technology;
- takeover, divestment, or merger and acquisition;
- labour shortages or surpluses.

It is difficult to separate completely internal from external triggers for change since decisions that appear on the surface as internal may be responses to some external event or in some way fit with the organization's strategy which is aimed at responding to external forces. This argument is taken up in more detail in Chapter 3. Meanwhile, as the next section shows, there are other ways of categorizing organizational environments that are more focused on organizations and change.

The future of work

We have seen that specific events occurring in an external environment, and other events internal to an organization, can trigger change. Environmental forces also act together to create a totality of pressures that stimulate change. One interesting angle on this is to consider how the nature of work is changing and what that could mean for organizations in the near future. A survey by the Chartered Management Institute (2014) reported the following trends that will affect business organizations:

- Technology is transforming how organizations function. By 2020, each person will have six different devices that will be connected to the Internet. As a result people skills will become more vital to organizations.
- Managers will need to be able to lead teams consisting of workers who work flexibly, independently and in a broad range of geographical locations. Workplace structures will become wider, flatter and less hierarchical.
- Managers will have tools for analyzing staff emails and social media accounts in order to gauge staff engagement and manage performance.
- Diversity will become even more of a business imperative. Nearly one billion women are likely to enter the global workforce over the next decade. By 2020, women are expected to take up 56 per cent of the next increase in jobs in the UK.
- The proportion of black, Asian and other ethnic minorities in the UK population will rise to 20 per cent by 2051.
- Many of the young people joining companies today will live to 100 years and they will be working until they are about 85.

● Managers need to develop a business culture that makes ethics, corporate social responsibility and sustainability an integral art of the company's business model.
● Future leaders need to be agile, authentic, sustainable and talented.

This list is only an example of some of the things that will affect the future of organizations and how they will need to change and adapt to them. Chapter 9 discusses these and other issues for the future in more detail.

Activity 1.7

Think about the future trends in Illustration 1.5.

What sorts of changes will organizations have to confront if they are to respond to them?

What managerial attitudes would need to change?

Organizational responses to change

Thus far the discussion suggests that organizations operate in at least three types of environment. The first consists of the historical developments bringing changes over time. These range from those activities that are mainly sector-focused to those which rely more on knowledge and human capital – what Handy (1994) calls 'focused intelligence', that is the ability to acquire and apply knowledge and know-how. These can be categorized as the *temporal environment*. This is an environment that influences organizations in at least two ways. The first is in a general way, through the cycles of industry-based innovation, which move organizations through a major series of developments such as shown in Figure 1.2. The second, more specific way, is through the life cycle of the organization itself. This includes its particular history built up from its founder days through periods of expansion and decline, all of which are instrumental in helping to explain an organization's idiosyncrasies of strategy and structure, culture, politics and leadership style.

The second type of environment is the *PEST framework* and the third is the organization's *internal environment* which, to some extent, consists of those organizational changes that are the first-line responses to changes in the external and temporal environments. Figure 1.4 is a stylized depiction of the concept of organizations as systems operating in multi-dimensional environments, with all that this means for organizations and change. However, this way of conceptualizing the organizational environment to some extent misses its dynamic nature and the degree of *strength* of the winds of change.

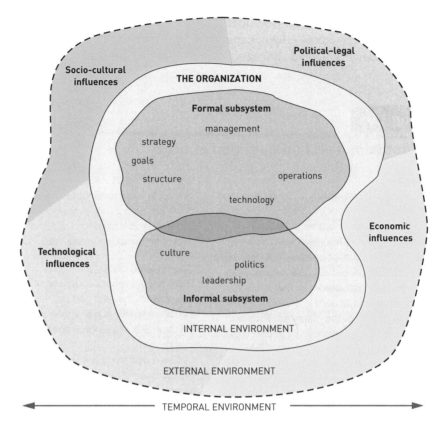

Figure 1.4 The organizational system in multi-dimensional environments

Environmental turbulence

The dynamics of an organization's environment can also be assessed in terms of the degree of environmental turbulence. Ansoff and McDonnell (1990) argue that a firm's performance is optimized when its aggressiveness and responsiveness match its environment, and they propose five levels of environmental turbulence:

- *Level 1: Predictable.* A repetitive environment characterized by stability of markets; where the challenges repeat themselves; change is slower than the organization's ability to respond; the future is expected to be the same as the past.
- *Level 2: Forecastable by extrapolation.* Complexity increases but managers can still extrapolate from the past and forecast the future with confidence.
- *Level 3: Predictable threats and opportunities.* Complexity increases further when the organization's ability to respond becomes more problematic; however, the future can still be predicted with some degree of confidence.
- *Level 4: Partially predictable opportunities.* Turbulence increases with the addition of global and socio-political changes; the future is only partly predictable.
- *Level 5: Unpredictable surprises.* Turbulence increases further with unexpected events and situations occurring more quickly than the organization can respond.

These levels can be compared to three different kinds of change situation proposed by Stacey (1996), namely: closed change, contained change and open-ended change which are described in Illustration 1.6.

Illustration 1.6

Closed, contained and open-ended change

Closed change

When we look back at the history of an organization there are some sequences of events that we can clearly recount in a manner commanding the widespread agreement of the members involved. We are able to say what happened, why it happened and what the consequences are. We are also able to explain in a widely accepted way that such a sequence of events and actions will continue to affect the future course of the business. Thus we have a closed-change situation.

Closed change would normally apply to the continuing operation of an existing business. For example, consider a business that supplies music to the teenage market. Managers in that business are able to say with some precision how the number of customers in that market has changed over the past and furthermore how it will change for the next 15 years or so. Those customers already exist. Managers can establish fairly clear-cut relationships between the number of customers and the number of CDs they have bought and will buy.

Contained change

Other sequences of events and actions flowing from the past are less clear-cut. Here we find that we are able to say only what probably happened, why it probably happened and what its probable consequences were. The impact of such a sequence of events upon the future course of the business has similarly to be qualified by probability statements.

For example, the music supplier will find it harder to explain why particular bands sold better than others. That supplier will find it somewhat difficult to forecast what kinds of music will sell better in the future; but market research, lifestyle studies and statistical projections will enable reasonably helpful forecasts for at least the short term.

Open-ended change

There are yet other sequences of events and actions arising from the past and continuing to impact on the future where explanations do not command anything like widespread acceptance by those involved.

The music company may have decided in the past to diversify into film by acquiring another company already in that business. That acquisition may then become unprofitable and the managers involved could well subscribe to conflicting explanations of why this is so. Some may claim that the market for film is too competitive. Others may say that diversification was a wrong move because it meant operating in a different market with which they were not familiar. Others may say that it is due to a temporary decline in demand and that the market will pick up in the future. Others may ascribe it to poor management of the acquisition, or to a failure to integrate it properly into the business, or to a clash of cultures between the two businesses. What that team of managers does next to deal with low profitability obviously depends upon the explanation of past failure they subscribe to.

Source: Based on Stacey, R.D. (1996), *Strategic Management and Organisational Dynamics* (2nd edn), London: Pitman, pp. 23–24.

Both Ansoff and McDonnell's levels of environmental turbulence and Stacey's closed, contained and open-ended kinds of change situation can also be related to Stacey's concepts of 'close to certainty' and 'far from certainty' (1996, p. 26). Thus, close to certainty describes a situation where organizational members face closed and contained change or, in Ansoff and McDonnell's terms, when the environment resembles Levels 1 to 3. As the degree of environmental turbulence moves from Level 4 to Level 5 or, in Stacey's terms, to a situation of open-ended change, organizations can be said to be far from certainty. These changing situations have significant implications for the actions of managers as they attempt to choose appropriate strategies to deal with them.

Activity 1.8 asks you to carry out an environmental assessment of an organization. It is a challenging activity and you will almost certainly say you need further information. However, organizations always exist in situations of imperfect knowledge and managers have to do their best in the circumstances. A start may be made by (simply?) identifying whether the forces for change are strong, moderate or weak. Strong forces cause a substantial decline or a substantial improvement in performance. Moderate forces have only minor impacts on performance, while weak forces are difficult to identify and ascertain the impact of.

Activity 1.8

Think about two or three organizations with which you are familiar. Carry out an environmental assessment for each organization. To help you with this, consider:

- *the PEST factors and the organizations' internal environments;*

- *how past historical developments (either in societal or organizational terms) have influenced the organizations' strategies and operations.*

Using Ansoff and McDonnell's (1990) framework, make a judgement about the level of environmental turbulence prevailing for each organization.

Match these levels to Stacey's (1996) types of change situations.

Identify the similarities and differences in the three organizational environments.

What lessons can you draw about the probability of each organization responding to future environmental triggers for change?

The strength of the forces for change can be related to the degree of turbulence in the environment: the stronger the force the more probable it is that the environment is moving to Ansoff and McDonnell's (1990) Level 5. What this implies is that the ability to plan and manage change becomes ever more difficult as the forces and levels of turbulence increase. This is related to, but complicated further by, the different types of change that can be experienced by organizations.

 ## Conclusions

Organizations operate in multiple environments (temporal, internal and external). The key task for organizations, and those who work in them, is to work with them and try to manage them – to constantly adapt and evolve the organization to match its operating environment. Indeed, the metaphor of evolution is quite powerful in imagining organizational change; it is not the strongest that survive, but those that adapt best to the conditions that they are faced with. The Nokia case (see p. 27) shows that organizations have to move quickly or risk falling behind the market to a point where catching up becomes very hard if not impossible. The purpose and focus of efforts to respond to environmental shifts, to stay ahead of a market, or to make up lost ground are essentially what managing organizational change is all about. This means understanding more fully how the formal aspects of organizational life respond to pressures from the internal, external and temporal environments – that is how change is leveraged through strategy, structure and operational processes. In addition, it means understanding the more informal processes such as power, politics, conflict, culture and leadership.

However, all environmental scanning tools are limited in some way. It is difficult to identify all the determinants of change; sometimes they are impacting on an organization without it even noticing. Furthermore, the information gathered is subjective and filtered by different people who reach different conclusions about the right ways to react. Albright (2004) argues, however, that if managed effectively and applied progressively a continuous process of identifying, collecting and translating progressive information about external influences will benefit strategic decision making towards establishing a preparatory stance to environmental factors.

Having set the environmental scene in this chapter, Chapter 2 looks in more detail at the impact of the forces for change upon organizations, with a more detailed examination of the nature of change itself.

Discussion questions and assignments

1 To what extent do you think the open systems concept is helpful in understanding how organizational change might happen?

2 Give examples of environmental forces for change that are likely to significantly affect the way organizations operate over the next 10 years. Justify your choices.

3 How realistic do you think it is to categorize types of change within an organization? What might be the advantages and disadvantages of doing this?

4 Carry out an environmental scan of an organization you know well. The following steps should help:

   (a) Using the PEST framework, the results for one of the organizations chosen for Activity 1.8 and the suggestions in Figure 1.3, list those factors you consider could affect the future performance of the organization and/or the way it operates. Concentrate on those factors external to the organization.

   (b) Indicate on your list where there are linkages between the various factors. Using a mind map may help.

   (c) Identify those factors that are critically important to the organization. Consider where they fit in the PEST framework. Are they also linked to the general movement of organizations into value-oriented time?

(d) Finally, list the critically important factors and rank them according to the volatility of the external environment. Consider whether this volatility provides opportunities or threats to the organization and its future performance.

Through carrying out this process you may have realized how much you know about the organization's environment but also how much you do not know! The outcome of this activity may be, therefore, not only an increased understanding of the environmental forces facing the organization, but also a realization that environmental scanning requires continuous vigilance and information analysis that must be used to help predict necessary changes within the organization itself.

Case example ●●●

Strategic change at Nokia

Based in Finland, Nokia transformed from being a diverse conglomerate into a world-leading mobile phone producer in the 1990s. Since then, the company has experienced very tough operating conditions in the face of competition from Samsung and products like the Apple iPhone. Substantial layoffs and plant closures took place across the world as Nokia missed out on consumers who were turning to smartphones. By concentrating on mobile phones, Nokia also faced intense competition from large volume producers in China with lower cost structures.

A new CEO was appointed from Microsoft in 2010 and he quickly sent a memo to all employees. The memo, rich in metaphor, became known as the 'burning platform' memo and basically said that Nokia had missed out on some big consumer trends and was now years behind the market and, while that was happening, top managers in Nokia thought they were doing the right thing and making good decisions.

The new CEO accused Nokia of lacking accountability and leadership, of not collaborating enough internally and not innovating fast enough. He likened the situation that the company faced with being on a burning oil platform, the implication being that Nokia could stay where it is and perish in the flames, or jump into icy waters and have a chance of survival. Despite the new CEO's 'call to arms', market share, revenues, profits and share price continued to fall. In 2013, Microsoft purchased Nokia's mobile phone business and the CEO moved to Microsoft as part of the deal.

If Nokia continues to lose share in the market then the Finnish economy will suffer further. The company had helped put Finland on the map as a technological leader and employer of a lot of people.

Sources: Brown-Humes, C. and Budden, R. (2004), 'Not so mobile: Will Nokia now get the message of changing consumer tastes, new technology and stronger rivals?' *Financial Times*, 7 May 2004.
'Nokia: From "burning platform" to a slimmer management model', available at www.ft.com. Accessed 1 June 2014.

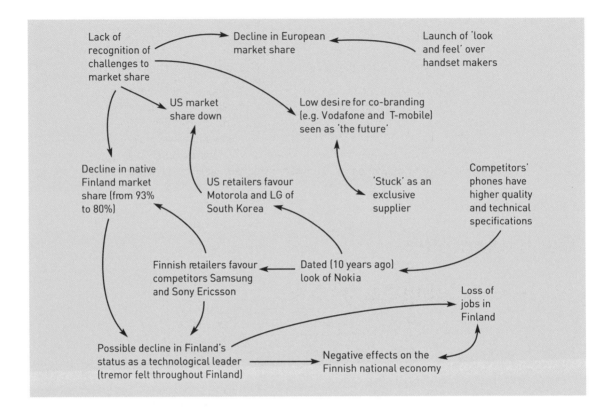

Case exercise: Analyzing the causes of change

Situations of change such as that outlined at Nokia, above, draw attention to the complexity of the change environment. However, we can do more than simply identify the various triggers for change. Analyzing the relationships between them – their systemic nature – is even more important. The multiple-cause diagram in the case example is an attempt to do this.

Multiple-cause diagrams have the power to capture the complex dynamics of change situations. They help bring about a deeper understanding of how changes in one variable can have far-reaching effects in other parts of the situation. They act, therefore, not only as a descriptive model, but also as an analytical tool for understanding and managing change.

1   Using further information from the Internet, write a brief account of how different elements of the temporal and competitive environments interact to influence the situation at Nokia.

2   Consider how you could use multiple-cause diagrams to 'picture' the multiple and interacting causes that bring pressure for change where you work, or in an organization that you know well.

●●●● Indicative resources

Brooks, I., Weatherston, J. and Wilkinson, G. (2011), *The International Business Environment: Challenges and changes*, Harlow: Pearson Education. This text gives a detailed exploration of the business environment.

The Commission on the Future of Management and Leadership (2014) *Management 2020: Leadership to Unlock Long Term Growth*, Chartered Management Institute (CMI), July. This is a future-looking report to give a context for the discussions in the remainder of the book.

Useful websites

www.guardian.co.uk Useful for current affairs articles relating to IT, politics and business.

www.ft.com Useful for business updates on a worldwide level.

www.statistics.gov.uk Useful for information relating to current UK and some European comparisons.

www.managers.org.uk The website of the Chartered Management Institute which contains summaries of research reports on a range of management issues.

References

Albright, K. (2004), 'Environmental scanning: radar for success', *The Information Management Journal*, May/June, pp. 38–45.

Ansoff, I. H. and McDonnell, E.J. (1990), *Implanting Strategic Management*, Englewood Cliffs, NJ: Prentice Hall.

Brooks, I. (2011) 'The international business environment', in Brooks, I., Weatherston, J. and Wilkinson, G. (eds), *The International Business Environment: Challenges and Changes'*, Harlow: Pearson Education, pp. 1–31.

Brown-Humes, C. and Budden, R. (2004), 'Not so mobile: will Nokia now get the message of changing consumer tastes, new technology and stronger rivals', *Financial Times*, 7 May 2004.

Burnes, B. (2005), 'Complexity theories of organizational change', *International Journal of Management Reviews*, 7(2), pp. 73–90.

Burns, T. and Stalker, G.M. (1966), *The Management of Innovation*, London: Tavistock.

Checkland, P.B. (1972), 'Towards a system-based methodology for real-world problem solving', *Journal of Systems Engineering*, 3(2).

Child, J. (1973), 'Organization: a choice for man', in Child, J. (ed.) *Man and Organization*, London: Allen & Unwin.

Clegg, S., Kornberger, M., and Pitsis, T. (2008), *Managing and Organizations*, London: SAGE.

Cook, M. (2011), 'The international economic environment', in Brooks, I., Weatherston, J. and Wilkinson, G. (eds), *The International Business Environment: Challenges and Changes*, Harlow: Pearson Education, pp. 71–119.

Daft, R.L. (2013), *Organization Theory and Design* (11th edn), St. Paul, MN: West Publishing.

Dawkins, R. (2008), 'The Genius of Charles Darwin', broadcast on Channel 4, 4 August 2008.

Dawson, P. (2003), *Reshaping Change: A Processual Perspective*, London: Routledge.

Drucker, P.F. (1988), 'The coming of the new organization', *Harvard Business Review*, January/February, pp. 45–53.

Furnham, A. (2000), 'Work in 2020: prognostications about the world of work 20 years into the millennium', *Journal of Managerial Psychology*, 15 (3), pp. 242–54.

Goodman, M. (1995), *Creative Management*, Hemel Hempstead: Prentice Hall.

Gruening, G. (2001), 'Origins and theoretical basis of New Public Management', *International Public Management Journal*, 4, pp. 1–25.

Handy, C. (1994), *The Empty Raincoat*, London: Hutchinson.

Hofstede, G.H. (2005), *Cultures and Organizations: Software of the Mind* (2nd edn), London, McGraw-Hill.

Huczynski, A.A. and Buchanan, D. (2013), *Organizational Behaviour* (8th edn), Harlow: FT Prentice Hall.

Johnson, G., Scholes, K. and Whittington, R. (2014), *Exploring Corporate Strategy: Text and cases* (10th edn), Harlow: FT Prentice Hall.

Jones, P., Palmer, J., Osterweil, C. and Whitehead, D. (1996), *Delivering Exceptional Performance: Aligning the Potential of Organisations, Teams and Individuals*, London: Pitman.

Khodyakov, D.M. (2007), 'The complexity of trust–control relationships in creative organizations: insights from a qualitative analysis of a conductorless orchestra', *Social Forces*, 86 (1), pp. 1–22.

King, D. and Lawley, S. (2013), *Organizational Behaviour*. Oxford: Oxford University Press.

Levy, R. (2010), 'New Public Management: end of an era?' *Public Policy and Administration*, 25(2), pp. 234–40.

McCann, L., Morris, J. and Hassard, J. (2008), 'Normalised intensity: the new labour process of middle management', *Journal of Management Studies*, 45(2), pp. 343–71.

Mason, R. (2007), 'The external environment's effect on management and strategy: a complexity theory approach', *Management Decision*, 45(1), pp. 10–28.

Mullins, L. (2013), *Management and Organizational Behaviour* (10th edn), Harlow: Pearson Education.

Nadler, D.A. and Tushman, M.L. (1999), 'The organization of the future: strategic imperatives and core competencies for the 21st century', *Organizational Dynamics*, 28(1), pp. 71–80.

Office for National Statistics (ONS) *Employee Growth by Region and Industry 2013*, released 25 September 2014.

Paton, R.A. and McCalman, J. (2000), *Change Management: Guide to Effective Implementation* (2nd edn), London: PCP.

Pollitt, C. and Dan, S. (2011), *The Impacts of the New Public Management in Europe: A Meta-Analysis*, 14 December, COCOPS, European Union.

Rousseau, D. (2001), 'Schema, promise and mutuality: the building blocks of the psychological contract', *Journal of Organizational and Occupational Psychology*, 74, pp. 511–41.

Rousseau, D. (2004), 'Psychological contracts in the workplace: understanding the ties that motivate', *Academy of Management Executive*, 18(1), pp. 120–27.

Silverman, D. (1970), *The Theory of Organisations*, London: Heinemann Educational.

Smith, C. (2006), 'At work with Big Brother', *Financial Times*, 11 December, p. 13.

Stacey, R.D. (1996), *Strategic Management and Organisational Dynamics* (2nd edn), London: Pitman.

Stacey, R.D. (2007), *Strategic Management and Organisational Dynamics. The challenge of complexity* (5th edn), Harlow: FT Prentice Hall.

The Times (2008), 'After the Lehman Disaster', 6 September, p. 2.

Thomas, R. and Dunkerley, D. (1999), 'Careering downwards? Middle managers' experiences in the downsized organization', *British Journal of Management*, 10(2), pp. 157–69.

Van der Smissen, Schalk, R., and Freese, C. (2013), 'Organizational change and the psychological contract: How change influences the perceived fulfillment of obligations', *Journal of Organizational Change Management*, 26(6), pp. 1071–90.

Vermeeren, B., Kuipers, B, and Steijn, B. (2014), 'Does leadership style make a difference? Linking HRM, job satisfaction and organizational performance', *Review of Public Personnel Administration*, 34(2), pp. 174–95.

Watson, T.J. (2006), *Organizing and Managing Work* (2nd edn), Harlow: FT Prentice Hall.

Wilson, R., Beaven, R., Max-Gillings, M., Hay, G., and Stevens, J. (2014), *Working Futures 2012–2022*, Institute for Employment Research, University of Warwick.

Wood, S. (1989), 'The Transformation of Work?' in Wood, S. (ed.) *The Transformation of Work*, London: Unwin Hyman, Chapter 1.

Chapter 2

The nature of organizational change

This chapter introduces the different ways of conceptualizing the types of change that organizations encounter. A basic distinction is made between *convergent* change and *radical* change which is characterized by transformations of strategy, mission and values as well as structures and systems. We also discuss *planned* change and *emergent* change and summarize complexity theory which challenges the viability of planned change. Breakpoints that trigger change are considered along with types of problems that managers can face. The chapter ends by looking at how research into change has itself changed.

Learning objectives

By the end of this chapter, you will be able to:

- describe and discuss the multi-dimensional nature of organizational change;

- analyze change situations in terms of the different types of change experienced;

- explain limitations to the everyday approach to managing change arising from cultural, political and leadership influences;

- critically evaluate the theoretical perspectives relating to the types of change that organizations experience.

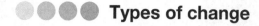

Types of change

The former British prime minister Benjamin Disraeli (1804–81) observed that 'change is inevitable in a progressive country. Change is constant'. His remark is often reported as 'the only constant is change'. Many of us accept this as a truism, yet it is important for organizations to strike a balance between both the forces for stability and the forces for change. Where the right balance lies, however, will vary from situation to situation and is up to people at work to figure out. Change is also far from homogeneous – it comes in many forms.

A starting point for considering the nature of organizational change is Grundy's (1993) three 'varieties of change' as shown in Figure 2.1. The first, 'smooth incremental change', is change that evolves slowly in a systematic and predictable way. This type of change is reminiscent of developed economies from the 1950s to early 1970s, but it became less common by the 1990s. The vertical axis in Figure 2.1 represents the *rate* of change, not the *amount* of change. Thus, smooth incremental change, at whatever level, happens at a constant rate.

The second variety, 'bumpy incremental change', is characterized by periods of relative tranquillity punctuated by acceleration in the pace of change. The bumps can be likened to 'the movement of continental land masses where the "fault" enables periodic readjustment to occur without cataclysmic effect' (Grundy, 1993, p. 24). Triggers for this type of change are from both the environment and internal initiatives such as the periodic reorganizations that organizations go through to improve efficiency. One way of categorizing smooth and bumpy incremental change is to see them as change that is associated more with the *means* by which organizations achieve their goals rather than as a change in the goals themselves.

Grundy's third type is 'discontinuous change' which he defines as 'change which is marked by rapid shifts in strategy, structure or culture, or in all three' (p. 26). Examples include the privatization of previously publicly owned utilities such as water supply and electricity generation and distribution, and the discovery

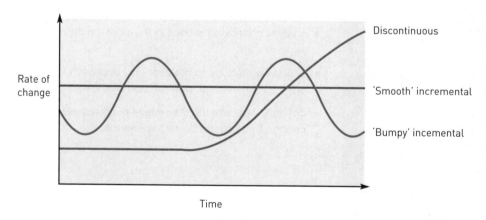

Figure 2.1 Grundy's major types of change
Source: Grundy, T. (1993), *Implementing Strategic Change*, London: Kogan Page, p. 25.

of new business opportunities arising from technological innovation. Health scares rendering some food products temporarily unsaleable can have cataclysmic effects throughout an industry, as can a sudden lack of confidence in a financial institution. Thus discontinuous change can be likened to change in response to sudden and unpredictable high levels of environmental turbulence.

The pace and scope of change

Grundy's three types of change make intuitive sense but they are somewhat simplistic. While this also appears to be the case with Balogun and Hope Hailey's (2008) identification of change 'paths', they go further by suggesting four types of change mapped on two dimensions: scope (incremental or big-bang), and scale (realignment or transformation) (see Figure 2.2).

On the basis of numerous studies and case histories, Tushman, Newman and Romanelli (1988, p. 707) proposed a model of organizational life that consists of 'periods of incremental change, or convergence, punctuated by discontinuous changes'. They suggest there are two types of converging change: fine-tuning and incremental adaptation. Both these types of change have the common aim of maintaining the fit between organizational strategy, structure and processes. However, whereas fine-tuning is aimed at doing better what is already done well, incremental adaptation involves small changes in response to minor shifts in the environment.

Both fine-tuning and incremental adjustments to environmental shifts allow organizations to perform better and optimize the consistencies between strategy, structure, people and processes. Yet Tushman *et al.* (1988) show how, as organizations grow and become more successful and develop internal forces for stability, these same forces eventually produce resistance to hold back further change. Thus, at times of major disruption and turbulence in an organization's environment, incremental adjustment will not bring about the major changes in strategy, structure, people and processes that might be required. When that happens, most

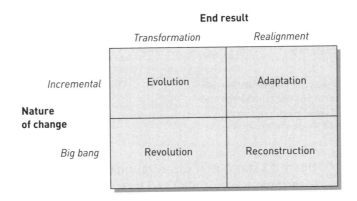

Figure 2.2 Balogun and Hope Hailey's types of change

Source: Balogun, J. and Hope Hailey, V.H. (2008), *Exploring Strategic Change* (3rd edn), Harlow: FT Prentice Hall.

organizations will need to undergo discontinuous or frame-breaking change if they are to survive. Thus, in the lifetime of most organizations, periods of relative tranquillity will be punctuated with (probably shorter) periods of frame-breaking change (see Illustration 2.1).

Illustration 2.1

Frame-breaking change

The need for discontinuous change springs from one or more of the following:

- *Industry discontinuities* – sharp changes that shift the basis of competition. These include: deregulation, privatization, technologies that replace (substitute) products or processes, the emergence of industry standards or dominant designs, major economic changes, legal shifts (e.g. patent protection, trade/regulator barriers).
- *Product life cycle shifts* – over the life cycle of a product different competitive strategies are required. International competition may aggravate these shifts.
- *Internal company dynamics* – as organizations grow beyond the organization built around the founding entrepreneur they give way to more bureaucratic management and revised organization structures.

The scope of frame-breaking change includes discontinuous change throughout the organization. Frame-breaking change is usually implemented rapidly. It is revolutionary, not incremental, and usually involves the following features:

- *reformed mission and core values* – to fit and support new strategies;
- *altered power and status* – reflecting shifts in the power and status that different groups have in the new era;
- *reorganization* – new strategy requires a modification in structure, systems and procedures, change of organization form;

- *revised interaction patterns* – new procedures, work flows, communication networks, decision-making patterns;
- *new executives* – usually from outside the organization, they have no loyalty to the 'old ways'; a small number of symbolic people changes signals a new order.

Frame-breaking change is revolutionary in that the shifts reshape the nature of the organization. It requires discontinuous and concurrent shifts in strategy, structure, people and processes. Reasons for the rapid, simultaneous implementation of frame-breaking change include:

- *to create synergy* – from new people in new roles and new departments;
- *to overcome pockets of resistance* – which are more likely to develop if change is implemented slowly;
- *to leverage a pent-up need for change* – when old constraints are relaxed or swept away change can become fashionable;
- *to control risk and uncertainty* – the longer the implementation period, the greater the period of uncertainty and instability; the quicker it is over, the sooner stability returns.

Source: Based on Tushman, M.L., Newman, W.H. and Romanelli, E. (1988), 'Convergence and upheaval: managing the unsteady pace of organizational evolution', in Tushman, M.L. and Moore, W.L. (eds), *Readings in the Management of Innovation*, pp. 705–17, New York: Ballinger.

Figure 2.3 shows how organizational change can be mapped in terms of its pace (continuous or episodic) and its scope (convergent or radical) (Plowman *et al.*, 2007). Each of the four categories of change differs on the following dimensions:

- the driver of change, namely instability or inertia;
- the form of the change, namely adaptation or replacement;

SCOPE

	Convergent	Radical
Continuous	**1** *Driver*: minor system instability *Form*: small adaptations within an existing framework *Nature*: emergent and local as people improvise and learn *Feedback*: positive, encouraging deviations and adaptations *Connections*: loose coupling which helps local conditions from amplifying	**4** *Driver*: major system instability *Form*: frame-bending adaptations *Nature*: emergent and system-wide as adaptations accumulate into patterns *Feedback*: positive and negative feedback which pulls in two directions *Connections*: tight coupling which enables local adaptations to amplify into radical change
Episodic	**2** *Driver*: minor inertia *Form*: minor replacement within an existing frame *Nature*: intended and local *Feedback*: negative, highlighting the need for minor replacement *Connections*: loose coupling which requires local minor replacements	**3** *Driver*: major inertia *Form*: dramatic frame-bending replacement *Nature*: intended and system-wide *Feedback*: negative, highlighting need for major replacement *Connections*: tight coupling which requires system-wide radical replacement

PACE

Figure 2.3 Plowman's four types of change

Source: Plowman *et al*. (2007), 'Radical change accidentally: the emergence and amplification of small change', *Academy of Management Journal*, 50(3), pp. 515–43.

- the nature of the change, namely emergent or intended;
- types of feedback: negative feedback discourages deviations from the organization's current position whereas positive feedback encourages deviation;
- types of connections in the system which are loose or tight.

The four quadrants portray four types of change:

1 *Continuous and convergent* change which happens slowly and which is channelled into improving systems and practices. Change happens within an organizational template; the template itself is not altered.
2 *Episodic and convergent* change occurs more quickly and perhaps as a result of a specific shock or crisis. Negative feedback pushes minor changes and keeps the template in shape.
3 *Episodic and radical* change happens quickly in response to a major shock or crisis. The template is altered through, for instance, a new top management team or new strategy.
4 *Continuous and radical* change arises out of an accumulation of small changes that gather momentum and lead to a new template being formed. If successful the new template becomes established and is reinforced by new rules, values and norms.

A good example of attempted radical or frame-breaking change is provided by the public-sector reforms that have taken place in many countries (see Chapter 1, Illustration 1.3 on New Public Management). In short, the reforms have tried to move public services away from administration and compliance towards much more proactive strategic management. This requires injecting more competition and business-like behaviour into public management and as such requires organizations and employees to jettison old values and work with new ones. The amount of success that occurs, however, depends upon how the radical changes are attempted (Jones, 2002; Van der Voet, Groeneveld and Kuipers, 2014).

Fine-tuning to corporate transformation

Grundy (1993) does not claim any particular status for his typology of change, conceding that it is not empirically based. The typology proposed by Tushman *et al.* (1988) is based on more research which is also the case with that put forward by Australian academics Dunphy and Stace (1993), which is discussed further in Chapter 6. The four types are shown in Illustration 2.2. Dunphy and Stace's scale types 1 and 2 are typical of Grundy's concept of smooth incremental change, while their scale types 3 and 4 are reminiscent of Grundy's bumpy incremental and discontinuous types of change respectively. The benefit of this model is in the detailed descriptions of each scale type and its testing with the executives, managers and supervisors of 13 Australian service-sector organizations. Organizations operating scale 1- and 2-type changes were in the minority in their small sample.

Illustration 2.2

Defining the scale of change

Scale type 1: Fine-tuning
Here, organizational change is an ongoing process characterized by fine-tuning of the 'fit' or match between the organization's strategy, structure, people and processes. Such effort typically occurs at departmental/divisional levels and deals with one or more of the following:

- refining policies, methods and procedures;
- creating specialist units and linking mechanisms to raise output and better focus on quality and cost;
- developing personnel better suited to the present strategy (improved training and development; tailoring reward systems to match strategic priorities);
- creating/improving individual and group commitment to the company mission and one's own department;
- promoting confidence in the accepted norms, beliefs and myths;

- clarifying established roles and authority and the mechanisms for allocating resources.

Scale type 2: Incremental adjustment
Here, organizational change is characterized by incremental adjustments to a changing environment. Such change involves distinct modifications (but not radical change) to corporate business strategies, structures and management processes, for example:

- expanding sales territory;
- shifting the emphasis among products and services;
- improved production processes;
- articulating a modified mission statement to employees;
- adjustments to organizational structures within or across divisional boundaries to achieve better links in product/service delivery.

Scale type 3: Modular transformation

Here, organizational change is characterized by major realignment of one or more departments/ divisions where radical change is focused rather than on the organization as a whole, for example:

- major restructuring of particular departments/ divisions;
- changes in key executives and managerial appointments;
- work and productivity studies resulting in significantly reduced or increased workforce numbers;
- reformed departmental/divisional goals;
- introduction of significantly new process technologies affecting key departments or divisions.

Scale type 4: Corporate transformation

Here, organizational change is corporation-wide, characterized by radical shifts in business strategy and revolutionary changes throughout the whole organization involving the following features:

- reformed organizational mission and core values;
- altered power and status affecting the distribution of power in the organization;
- reorganization – major changes in structures, systems and procedures across the organization;
- revised interaction patterns – new procedures, work flows, communication networks and decision-making patterns across the organization;
- new executives in key managerial positions appointed from outside the organization.

Source: Dunphy, D. and Stace, D. (1993), 'The strategic management of corporate change', *Human Relations*, 46(8), pp. 905–20.

However plausible Illustration 2.2 appears, care must be taken with schema like this based on a small sample of 13 organizations from one sector only. Nevertheless, this typology is similar to others (Plowman *et al.*, 2007; Tushman *et al.*, 1988). It is fairly clear that they found the same two types of change that are grouped by Tushman *et al.* under the concept of converging change. Both used identical names: 'fine-tuning' and 'incremental adjustment'. Where Dunphy and Stace go further is in splitting what Tushman *et al.* termed 'frame-*breaking*' change into two types: 'modular transformation' and 'corporate transformation'. This is a useful development in detailing more clearly the different levels at which frame-breaking change can take place. It still recognizes the implications of these types of change for goals and purposes, but identifies the fact that these may have different meanings at the departmental/divisional level than at the corporate/ organizational level.

Activity 2.1

Look again at Dunphy and Stace's types of change in Illustration 2.2. Position an organization with which you are familiar on the following scale.

Fine-tuning   Incremental adjustment   Modular transformation   Corporate transformation

$\longleftrightarrow$

How well does the type of change now being experienced by your organization fit the environment in which it is currently operating and that is likely to prevail in the foreseeable future?

Illustration 2.3

Explaining types of change

Some new terms have been introduced in this chapter and for convenience they are summarized below.

Convergent – this is fine-tuning of an existing configuration. The organizational configuration or template is not changed.

Planned – deliberate actions designed to move an organization or part of one from one state to another and having discrete beginning and end points. Change is seen as something that managers can control.

Evolutionary – as its name suggests, this is slow adaptation of existing systems or structures. Also termed continuous change. Although small in nature, changes are not trivial and are cumulative. They can trigger radical change.

Revolutionary – fast-paced and affecting all or most of an organization at the same time. Typically a planned move from one strategy and/or structure to another. It incorporates the idea of episodic change which is intentional but is infrequent, not continuous.

Radical – breaking away from a position such that a very different position is reached. Organizations or parts of them can be seen as being transformed from one template or blueprint to another. Also known as frame-bending or frame-breaking.

Emergent – if the organization is seen as an evolving system then change arises out of experimentation and adaptation. Change is seen as something that managers create the right climate for.

Planned and emergent change

Fine-tuning and incremental change are present in most organizations and, while they can be planned, are frequently associated with change as it *emerges* out of ongoing operations. The idea of emergent change has been linked with the concept of organizations as open systems (Wilson, 1992). Kast and Rosenzweig (1970), Checkland (1972) and McAleer (1982), among others, have produced detailed discussions of the concept of organizational systems. Briefly, these include the idea that organizations are striving to maintain a state of equilibrium where the forces for change are balanced by the forces for stability. Therefore, organizations viewed as systems will always strive to restore equilibrium whenever they are disturbed. According to this view, the organizational system is constantly sensing its environment in order to continuously adjust to maintain its purpose and optimum state.

Illustration 2.4

Holy breakfasts! Accidental radical change

Churchgoers at a US city church were discussing new things to do. The group decided to offer hot breakfasts on Sunday mornings to homeless people. This idea was quickly implemented and soon volunteers were providing over 200 breakfasts. Within a few months a volunteer who was a doctor began to see people who wanted to discuss health

questions. Shortly after, full-scale medical, dental and eye clinics were in place. Within a few years and with the support of grants the Church was running a day centre to help thousands of homeless people. Legal and job search support services were added.

Homeless people began to attend church services and this led to changes in dress codes and in the style of music – quite a shock to a church that had always attracted worshippers from the wealthiest corners of society. The Church's mission was changing and this brought conflict with the local business community for whom the influx of homeless people into the district was unwelcome. These radical changes were not planned – a 'cycle of continuous radical change' had emerged.

Plowman *et al.* argue that existing theories of episodic or continuous change do not explain how small changes escalate and become radical. Whereas radical change is usually seen as occurring in episodes, i.e. with beginning and end, the case of the Church appears to show continuous radical change. No leadership crisis or financial crisis arose to trigger these changes – just an idea to serve hot breakfasts.

Source: Based on Plowman *et al.* (2007), 'Radical change accidentally: the emergence and amplification of small change', *Academy of Management Journal*, 50(3), pp. 515–43.

In an ideal situation, we might think that organizational sensing of the environment would be so effective because enough small incremental change would happen and make frame-breaking change unnecessary. If organizations responded continuously to the need for change, they would have no need for the periodic upheavals that become inevitable. In other words, through their continuous assessment of the environments, change should emerge almost 'naturally'.

However, managers and other employees can become so comfortable with what they do and what they believe is right and important that they become impervious to warning signs of impending or actual danger from the environment. According to Tushman *et al.* (1988), this is the effect of what they term the 'double-edged sword' of converging periods of change. Thus, the habits, patterns of behaviour, ways of finding out the best way to do things and the values that have become important and which have built up during periods of converging change contribute significantly to the success of the organization. However, the organizational history (ways of doing things) built up during this period can also be counterproductive in creating organizational inertia and restricting the vigilance and reactions that the business environment requires and may become a source of resistance to the need for more radical forms of change.

Johnson (1988, p. 44) refers to the organization 'paradigm' to describe the core set of beliefs and assumptions that are commonly and widely held by the managers of an organization and which influence how information is interpreted and decisions made (Johnson *et al.*, 2014). The paradigm, which evolves and solidifies over time, includes assumptions about the organizational environment and how it should be interpreted and responded to. It is surrounded and protected by layers of cultural artefacts – symbols, behaviours, myths and rituals which make it legitimate. Paradigms capture and disseminate reality as far as the organization is concerned and are not, therefore, considered problematical.

However, gradually, and perhaps without noticing, the organization's strategy drifts away from what its operating environment is calling for (Harris, Dopsen and Fitzpatrick, 2009). Cast adrift, organizations may struggle to recognize forces for change or, if they are recognized, fail to grasp their significance because of the process whereby information is filtered through the paradigm. It is at these points that frame-breaking or revolutionary change becomes necessary to realign the organization's purposes and operations with environmental imperatives, if it is not already too late.

From the discussion so far, it is clear that the process of strategic drift forces organizations into a more conscious deliberate *planning* of change such as the four-stage processes of exploration, planning, action and integration discussed by Burnes (2004). Planned change describes situations where a change agent (i.e. a person or group that tries to alter human behaviour and/or organizational systems) takes deliberate actions with the aim of moving an organization or part of one from one state to another, e.g. to a new structure, to more commercial behaviour or to altered working patterns. It contrasts with emergent change which is change that arises out of ongoing activities. Of course, things do not always go to plan in planned change and some 'unintended consequences' occur.

Illustration 2.5

Does change lead to more change?

Beck and colleagues (2008) conceptualize change as 'discrete modification of structural organizational elements' (p. 413). Whether planned or emergent, a popular theme in change research is to examine the effects of past change on the likelihood of future change. A core assumption is that experience of change leads to increased chances of further change; change today is more likely to lead to change tomorrow. Beck and colleagues identify three commonly analyzed change events:

- change of markets, e.g. finding new groups of customers and/or new products/services;
- change of organizational leadership;
- changes to rules and routines that comprise the basic structure of organizations.

The theory behind the 'change leads to more change' assumption is that the more an organization changes things the more it learns about how to do it successfully. People increase their competencies at

making changes of a particular type and raise their confidence as well. As competence and confidence rise then the successful recipes will be applied to an increasing range of situations.

The alternative view is that since change is aimed at improving things, if it works there should be less need to change after change has been made. Not all change leads to improvements of course but even unsuccessful change should enable people to modify the way they attempt it again. Beck and colleagues tested these two views and found that when conventional research methods were used the first view was supported. When an improved method was used they found that change led to a deceleration rather than an acceleration of future change. So it seems that we still don't have a clear answer to this question.

Source: Based on Beck *et al.* (2008), 'Momentum or deceleration? Theoretical and methodological reflections on the analysis of organizational change', *Academy of Management Journal*, 51(3), pp. 413–35.

However, the distinction between emergent and planned change is not clear-cut. Wilson (1992) criticizes the idea that change can be planned logically and systematically. He argues that planned change is a management concept which relies heavily on a single view of the way change ought to be done. This view assumes that the environment is known and, therefore, that a logical process of environmental analysis can be harnessed in the service of planning any change. Wilson says this view emphasizes the role of human agency, that is, that executives and managers are able to invoke the changes they feel are necessary and that this process is not problematic. His argument is that this view does not take account of the context in which change must take place, for instance, the cultural and political components that influence most, if not all, implementations of any planned change.

Jian (2007) provides an interesting account of what happened during one planned change episode and in particular to the unexpected outcomes that were seen as shown in Illustration 2.6.

Illustration 2.6

Unintended consequences of planned change

Unintended consequences are those things that would not have happened if an actor (e.g. a manager) had acted differently and are not what the actor had intended (Jian, 2007, p. 6). The scene for this illustration is a US insurance company. As a result of some acquisitions the (new) top management team engaged consultants to tell it that it needed to cut costs and restructure. And so a plan was hatched.

Top management explained why change was needed and how important it was to keep the company's stock (share) price high. 'If we don't cut costs then we won't be able to generate the new business that we need' – was the general thrust of the message from the top. The basic message precluded consideration of other change paths and in doing so positioned top management as a dominant force. Employees were assured that they would be told of important things as soon as top management knew them. Much was made of not communicating anything before the communication was clear. Employees were assured that they would hear first and that this was important to ensure consistency. But top management was only going to communicate something that had been decided – not what things were being decided.

This positioned top management as being privileged to know things and to debate them and to decide on the best way forward. Employees were simply expected to execute their wishes. This background, Jian writes, sowed the seeds

for the unintended consequences. In this case top managers were deciding on new structures and systems but it was up to employees to make sense of them; to figure out what the changes meant to them. To help them do this, employees used a grapevine to communicate the contradictions and stories around them. The picture constructed along the grapevine was one of management secrecy, betrayal as people were losing their jobs and unfairness because of cutbacks or increased prices to a range of employee benefits provided by the company.

Mass meetings of staff and management did little to help things and were occasions where top management reiterated its position without appearing to appreciate employee concerns. Despite the well-intentioned information releases by management, rumours quickly followed them. This widened the trust gap between management and employees. Other unintended outcomes were higher stress and a loss of productivity as employees diverted energy into analyzing their situations rather than winning new business or cutting costs.

The key lesson from this real case is that managers need to appreciate the meaning of change as seen by employees. They need to help employees make sense of change and help translate new ways of doing things into everyday practice.

Source: Based on Jian, G. (2007), 'Unpacking unintended consequences of planned organizational change', *Management Communication Quarterly*, 21(1), pp. 5–28.

Quinn (1980) has also criticized the idea of planned change as something that is deliberately and carefully thought through and then implemented. His research into the decision-making processes of a number of organizations demonstrated that most strategic decisions are made in spite of formal planning systems rather than because of them. Reinforcing this idea, Stacey (2011, p. 154) summarizes the key points made by Quinn as follows:

1 Effective managers do not manage strategically in a piecemeal manner. They have a clear view of what they want to achieve and where they are trying to take the business. The destination is thus intended.
2 But the route to that destination, the strategy itself, is not intended from the start in any comprehensive way. Effective managers know that the environment they have to operate in is uncertain and ambiguous. They therefore sustain flexibility by holding open the method of reaching the goal.
3 The strategy itself then emerges from the interaction between different groupings of people in the organization, different groupings with different amounts of power, different requirements for and access to information, different time spans and parochial interests. These different pressures are orchestrated by senior managers. The top is always reassessing, integrating and organizing.
4 The strategy emerges or evolves in small incremental, opportunistic steps. But such evolution is not piecemeal or haphazard because of the agreed purpose and the role of top management in reassessing what is happening. It is this that provides the logic in the incremental action.
5 The result is an organization that is feeling its way towards a known goal, opportunistically learning as it goes.

Quinn terms this process 'logical incrementalism' in that it is based in a certain logic of thinking but is incremental in its ability to change in the light of new information and the results of ongoing action. Opportunism plays an important part in this process (see Illustration 2.7).

Illustration 2.7

Managing incrementalism in the development of corporate strategies

Start with unspecific general issues of concern. Then spend some time 'mulling over an issue in your mind' until you reach a conclusion that fits the organization's strategy and purpose, and one that you can put to others without being dogmatic about it. In general, you will hear good suggestions on how to develop the idea into something concrete and, having brought in others to help refine it, you can put it forward more formally. You must be ready to deal with objections and other 'gainsayers'. However, if you have thought of these possibilities in advance, you will be able to cope with them and ultimately reach your goal. However, there are, possibly, many steps and 'trip-ups' between the acceptance of your idea and its implementation. As James Quinn (1979), a leading thinker on strategy, said about how

executives manage incrementalism in the development of corporate strategies:

> You know where you want to get to. You would like to get there in six months. But it may take three years, or you may not get there. And when you do get there, you do not know whether it was originally your own idea – or somebody else had reached the same conclusion before you and just got you on board for it. You never know.

A chief executive or a manager lower in the organization would follow the same basic process, but the former could drive it faster than someone lower down in the organization.

Source: Based on Quinn, J.B. (1979) 'Xerox Corporation (B)', copyright case, Hanover, NH: Amos Tuck School of Business Administration, Dartmouth College.

Predictable change

In some respects, change could be viewed as neither wholly emergent nor planned. As cycles of growth and activity are an essential part of survival, so the concept of an organizational life cycle (Greiner, 1972; Kimberley and Miles, 1980; Quinn and Cameron, 1983) has been used to describe the stages organizations go through as they grow and develop. Figure 2.4 illustrates these stages in terms of the size and maturity of organizations.

Greiner maintains that, as organizations mature and grow in size their activities go through five phases, each of which is associated with a different growth period in an organization's life. In addition, as each growth period moves into the next, the organization goes through a shorter-lived crisis period. These are, respectively, the evolution and revolution stages shown in Figure 2.4. Illustration 2.8 is a brief description of a typical life cycle pattern that is complemented by Clarke's (1994) useful categorization of the characteristics and crisis points associated with each phase of growth (see Table 2.1).

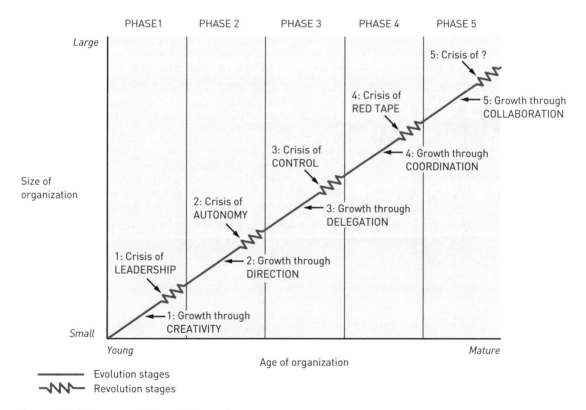

Figure 2.4 The organizational life cycle

Source: Reprinted by permission of *Harvard Business Review*. Greiner, L.E. (1972), 'Evolution and Revolution as Organizations Grow', July–August, p. 41. Copyright © 1972 by the Harvard Business School Publishing Corporation. All rights reserved.

Illustration 2.8

A typical life cycle pattern

1   The entrepreneurial stage

In this first (often entrepreneurial) stage, the primary task is to provide a service or make a product. Survival is the key strategy. Organizational culture is fashioned by the founding entrepreneur. It may be a new organization, a new subsidiary or part of an established, larger organization. Success brings growth and the need to recruit more staff. Staff need managing and the question of future organizational strategy becomes more complex. The alternatives are to limit growth and remain small (but risk competitiveness) or to grow and recruit professional managers.

2   The collective stage

The organization begins to take 'shape'. Departments and functions begin to be defined and the division of labour is the dominant theme. The professional managers recruited tend to be strong leaders who share the same vision as the founders. Further growth brings the need for management control and delegation. The organization has begun to establish its position; internal tasks are allocated along with responsibility and autonomy to carry them out.

3   The formalization stage

Systems of communication and control become more formal. There is a need to differentiate between the tasks of management – to make strategic decisions and to implement policy – and those of lower-level managers, who are expected to carry out and oversee operational decisions. Bureaucratization occurs as systems of coordination and control emerge, including salary structures, reward and incentive schemes, levels in the hierarchy, reporting relationships and formalized areas of discretion and autonomy for lower-level managers. The organization continues to grow, but burdened by the process of bureaucratization the need for the structure to be 'freed up' becomes pressing.

4   The elaboration stage

This is the stage of strategic change. The organization may have reached a plateau in its growth curve and may even show the first stages of decline in performance. Managers used to handling bureaucratic structures and processes usually have to learn new skills to achieve change, such as team work, self-assessment and problem confrontation. This stage may also include the rapid turnover and replacement of senior managers.

Source: Based on Greiner, L.E. (1972), 'Evolution and revolution as organizations grow', *Harvard Business Review*, July–August, 50, pp. 37–46.

Activity 2.2

Consider an organization you know well. Using the descriptions in Illustration 2.8 and Table 2.1, position the organization on the graph in Figure 2.4.

Greiner's model is useful for identifying an organization's situation and providing warnings of the next crisis point it may have to face and helps in the planning of necessary change. It also helps managers and others realize that change is, to some extent, inevitable; organizations must of necessity change as they grow and mature. It therefore helps legitimize the need for change and can be used in discussions aimed at combating resistance to change.

So far in this chapter we have seen several ways of analyzing and describing change and the idea that change can be planned or can emerge out of what people

Table 2.1 Characteristics of Greiner's phases of growth

	Phase 1 *Creativity*	Phase 2 *Direction*	Phase 3 *Delegation*	Phase 4 *Coordination*	Phase 5 *Collaboration*
Structure	• Informal	• Functional • Centralized • Hierarchical • Top down	• Decentralized • Bottom up	• Staff functions • Strategic business units (SBUs) • Decentralized • Units merged into product groups	• Matrix-type structure
Systems	• Immediate response to customer feedback	• Standards • Cost centres • Budget • Salary systems	• Profit centres • Bonuses • Management by exception	• Formal planning procedures • Investment centres • Tight expenditure controls	• Simplified and integrated information systems
Styles/ people	• Individualistic • Creative • Entrepreneurial • Ownership	• Strong directive	• Full delegation of autonomy	• Watchdog	• Team oriented • Interpersonal skills at a premium • Innovative • Educational bias
Strengths	• Fun • Market response	• Efficient	• High management motivation	• More efficient allocation of corporate and local resources	• Greater spontaneity • Flexible and behavioural approach
Crisis point	• Crisis of leadership	• Crisis of autonomy	• Crisis of control	• Crisis of red tape?	?
Weaknesses	• Founder often temperamentally unsuited to managing • Boss overload	• Unsuited to diversity • Cumbersome • Hierarchical • Doesn't grow people	• Top managers lose control as freedom breeds parochial attitudes	• Bureaucratic divisions between line/staff, headquarters/ field, etc.	• Psychological saturation

Source: Clarke, L. (1994), *The Essence of Change*, Hemel Hempstead: Prentice Hall.

do. Another very important spotlight on change, and in particular an antidote to theories of planned change, is provided by complexity theory.

Complexity theory

The concept of 'complexity' and complex systems

Burnes (2005) provides a useful review of complexity theory which is drawn on below. Complexity theory is a set of ideas stemming from the study of natural systems such as weather patterns and animal behaviour and which draws on mathematical principles to help explain how organizations behave. Like natural systems, it sees organizations as highly complex entities where a natural order comes to exist through the process of self-organization where some form of overall order or coordination arises out of the local interactions between the components of an initially disordered system.

The concepts of *complexity* and *complicated* are frequently thought to be identical. However, whilst complicated systems can have very many elements and interactions between them, theoretically, they can all be known. For instance, a computer is a complicated system, but not a complex one; an airplane is a highly complicated vehicle, but given sufficient skilled designers, builders and maintenance staff, all its parts and how they operate can be described and understood. Complicated systems, although often difficult to understand, are ordered systems. By contrast, a complex system, as mentioned above, is disordered in the sense that it is unpredictable.

One of the best known proponents of complexity theory is Stacey, who together with colleagues identified three cornerstones of complexity theory (Stacey *et al.*, 2002; Stacey, 2011):

1 Chaos theory – chaotic systems are characterized by constant transformation analogous to the ways that species evolve. Events in chaotic systems are not proportional to the sum of causes and effects. Small events or perceptions of small events in an environment can lead to large changes in patterns of behaviour. These new structures and patterns are known as dissipative structures.

2 Dissipative structures – these need energy and impetus from outside otherwise they reduce to next to nothing (dissipate). Analogous to natural systems, they can withstand large forces acting on them or undergo radical self-reorganization in response to small events. The new structures adopted are unpredictable but are stable arrangements arising from the constituents of the system.

3 Complex adaptive systems – these are made up of agents each of which conforms to its own principles that shape its behaviour in relation to other agents. If we can understand how the agents (e.g. employees) behave individually, then this will help to understand, but not wholly explain, how the entire system will behave. An illustration of this occurs in the popular TV documentaries of meerkat colonies. The colony (system) functions as a result of different agents including dominant males, females caring for youngsters, juveniles, foraging parties and sentries.

The implications of considering organizations as complex entities, and in particular complex adaptive systems, having the properties listed above, is that any type of change can happen at any time, whether planned or not, with unpredictable results. However, that is not to say that no change can be planned, but, by being aware of the nature of these organizational systems, appropriate types of change can be made, whilst always remaining aware that the unexpected probably will happen. For instance, Burnes (2005, p. 82) advises that managers should learn how to 'promote self-organizing processes and how to use small changes to create large effects' (Burnes, 2005, p. 82). In place of bureaucracy delimiting what can and cannot be done, experimentation needs to be encouraged and mistakes/mishaps have to be accepted as part of the adaptive and more transformative change processes. This of course is not especially new and is reminiscent of the advice given by Peters and Waterman (1982) and Kanter (1989). Burnes, however, proposes three implications of applying complexity theory to organizations:

1 There is a need to move beyond 'narrow employee participation in change' towards much more democracy and equalization of power. This gives employees the scope to act.
2 The extremes of incremental change and large-scale transformation are not realistic and rarely work. Between the two extremes lies a continuous approach based on self-organization to improving products and processes.
3 To fuel the continuous change ideal, self-organization needs the presence of 'order-generating rules'. These rules evolve and are part of the processes of self-organization.

Despite its origins in natural sciences and mathematical principles, as far as understanding organizations goes, complexity theory is a set of ideas that acts as a metaphor for understanding how change happens and how it is sustained (Haynes, 2008; Murray, 2003). The metaphor gives managers new insights into how their organizations work and how they can conceive change, and those who act to effect it, in a new way.

Classic thinking about organizational change assumes that planning processes rely on the ability to join up causes and effects: for example, the assumption that certain actions will lead to certain outcomes. This model underpins the top-down approach to strategy analyses and implementation. Complexity theory, however, holds that change, of whatever type, will occur in systems that are some distance away from the simple equilibrium model. A more realistic description is that organizations exist in non-equilibrium conditions where cause and effect break down (Stacey, 1995). Any organization at a moment in time:

> ... is a result of every detail of its history and what it will become can only be known if one knows every detail of future development, and the only way one can do that is to let the development occur. The future of such a system is open and hence unknowable until it occurs.
>
> (Stacey, 1995, p. 491)

Stacey argues that while managers and leaders can decide what their next action will be and attempt to implement it, they cannot determine the eventual outcomes of those actions in future time. An implication of this, and quite a big one, is that if complexity theory is an accurate portrayal of organizational life and behaviour, then it is difficult to use theory-testing, hypotheses-testing research to identify things that lead to success and then generalize from them. Hence, recipes for organizational change, albeit helpful as starting points, should be looked on with caution. In many circumstances the type of change that occurs, as opposed to that which was planned, can be unpredictable and unexpected.

Complexity theory and the concept of complex adaptive systems have practical applications when considering organizational change. For example, Houchin and Maclean (2005) suggest that complexity theory gives us insights into how organizational patterns of order develop and how organizations learn and adapt. It views organizations as existing in a state of non-equilibrium; a state in which forces of adaptation are acting on the parts of the system, pushing it towards an equilibrium that is rarely, if ever, reached. It rejects the notion that change from one stable state to another can proceed through a series of linear steps.

These authors, in line with others before them, perceive complexity theory as a metaphor giving new understandings into how change happens (p. 72). They give an ethnographic account of change in a newly formed agency, of around 500 employees, made up from several predecessor, conventionally structured and operated, organizations. The new agency had a remit to handle environmental regulation and protection. The managers of the new agency planned for a new structure, culture and processes based on democratic, participatory principles. However, it can be seen from Table 2.2 that after four years of studying the change, there were key differences between what types of change were intended and what actually emerged.

Table 2.2 Emergent order after 4 years

Desired future state of the organization at the start of the 4-year period – the desired equilibrium	Actual future state of the organization at the end of the 4-year period – the new equilibrium
1 Wide spans of control	1 Hierarchical organization
2 Emphasis on employee flexibility	2 Emphasis on traditional professional specialisms
3 Empowered managers, delegation to its lowest point	3 Increasingly restricted managers, increase in bureaucratic procedures
4 Emphasis on value for money	4 Emphasis on cost reduction
5 Strong culture	5 Regional independence
6 Influencer and Regulator	6 Regulator – target-driven

Source: Houchin, K. and Maclean, D (2005) 'Complexity Theory and Strategic Change: an Empirically Informed Critique', *British Journal of Management,* 16 (2), pp. 149–66.

Houchin and Maclean offer a number of explanations as to why this alternative, unplanned equilibrium state came to exist. Apart from the unfamiliarity of the new ideas of how the organization should operate, the authors concluded that, in spite of the excitement of working for a new organization, some individuals' and groups' underlying anxieties about their futures and prospects led to destabilizing actions taken to reduce the effects of the changes. These actions were used by individuals to help them feel in control and as ways of reducing conflict. These in turn led to individuals reducing the amount of interactions with others (e.g. project groups, consultation, training events) which meant that actions designed to lead to new ways were infrequent and ineffective. Houchin and Maclean also propose that the order that developed did not emerge within the organization's legitimate systems, but within a 'shadow system' (see Stacey, 2002): the old network that employees had before the new organization was formed still existed, meaning that employees could, to a point, continue with their established working ways. In sum, the order that emerged in the new organization was largely the same as that which had existed in the organizations from which it was made up.

The concept of a shadow system, which works (sometimes unwittingly) to destabilize the legitimate system and establish a different organizational equilibrium, is crucial to understanding organizational change. This is particularly the case with transformational or frame-breaking change including managements' attempts to change (sometimes all at once) organizational strategies, structures and processes. In addition, if these attempts are based on formal, logical reasoning that neglects the worries and unease felt by those expected to change, the chances of success are slim.

The tipping points of change

Another complexity theory concept that helps us to understand the nature of change is the idea of a tipping point (Boyatzis, 2006). Here, events occur and are contained within a system which lead up to and culminate in a tipping point. Illustration 2.9 is a good example of how unexpected change occurred not just in one organization, but across several organizations which were part of the same industry. This started with some actions that were considered unremarkable at the time, but which then led to a tipping point where a major part of that industry was brought down.

Illustration 2.9

Crossing the line: a tipping point in the hacking scandal

Politicians know that newspapers influence the outcome of elections through the stories they run and by supporting a particular party. In the UK in the 1990s and early twenty-first century a close, incestuous relationship developed between the media and senior politicians. Reporters and senior media figures used information to play one politician against another as a way of getting new stories. Some police officers allowed themselves to be corrupted by people in the media and supplied confidential information which was used to get stories – yet the police showed little interest in

➡

Illustration 2.9 *continued*

investigating claims that officers were accepting payment for information.

A culture had developed such that phone hacking had become widespread and targets included victims of crime, criminals, celebrities and politicians. When a member of the Royal Family was hacked the police were forced into showing more interest in hacking allegations and this was compounded by public disgust when it was revealed that the family of a young murder victim had also been targeted by the hackers. Against this background, the British prime minister appointed, in spite of warnings not to, a former newspaper editor who was tainted with hacking allegations to head up communications as his communications director. This person, along with others, was later convicted of criminal charges related to phone hacking and sent to prison. After years of denial and in the face of public outrage,

the police had gathered large amounts of evidence that staff at the publishing organization, News International, had been involved in hacking. A popular UK 'red top' newspaper, *The News of the World,* was closed down in response to hacking revelations.

This story shows how politicians, the press and the police became far too close, to the point that criminality was being overlooked. The three main parties were in a cosy relationship which lasted for at least several years until someone's behaviour crossed a line and in doing so created a tipping point after which each player had to act to explain and be seen to be correcting their past wrong-doing. Although the repercussions of phone hacking seemed extensive with several prosecutions, only time will reveal whether the tipping point was enough to trigger genuine change in the culture that accepted it for so long.

Another good example of this phenomenon is the recent financial crisis. Several years of 'easy' money, available finance and rising property prices seemed to suit lenders and borrowers alike. Unfortunately, these halcyon days led to unsafe lending in the United States (sub-prime lending) which eventually caused great turbulence as the frailty of heavily interconnected financial systems was exposed. In September 2007 the UK bank Northern Rock tipped almost overnight from being a competitive institution to a complete lame-duck when it asked the Bank of England for assistance. This erosion of confidence led to the first run on a bank (people queuing *en masse* to withdraw their money) in over 100 years. A government loan of £25 billion was needed to sustain the bank and to protect its customers. Other financial institutions were compromised by collapsing share prices. The UK government was forced into immediate action by the events that happened.

Share values in banking and finance crashed, the supply of money for lending fell and the terms and conditions of borrowing were tightened, making home ownership even harder for first-time buyers. The seeds of the UK credit crunch were sown when the generally prudent and careful building societies in the UK converted to banks around 20 years previously. Executives were in the enviable position of receiving bonuses beyond the comprehension of lesser mortals if their organizations met targets and yet significant compensation if they failed to meet them or were sacked. Prudence had gone out of the window and in the language of change the 'butterfly effect' was set in train. This metaphor captures the idea that tiny variations in air pressure caused by the beat of a butterfly's wings in one place can, in theory, set in motion a chain of weather events that lead to a hurricane on the other side of the world.

Illustration 2.10 is a good account of how decisions made at one point in time, with good intentions, can, at another point in time, turn stability into chaos as the possible outcomes of those decisions were not predicted, and may even (except with hindsight) have been unpredictable at the time. Equitable Life were 'prisoners' of environmental forces which arose unexpectedly and which could be managed only with drastic results for its customers and itself.

Illustration 2.10

Equitable Life: creating chaos out of order

A good case of chaos emerging out of order is shown by the Equitable Life Assurance Society. For 200 years Equitable was a 'safe pair of hands' looking after life insurance and pensions typically for society's professionals – doctors, engineers, teachers and managers. However, in the years before 1988 it sold policies to some investors that guaranteed the pay-out of certain benefits. Time passed and interest rates rose and fell. A situation built up in which Equitable did not have enough money to keep paying out to those to whom it had guaranteed returns. Realizing this, Equitable tried to stop paying out the rates it had guaranteed. But people with the guaranteed return policies wanted their money. Legal action was taken, ending up in the House of Lords where the Law Lords ruled that the policies had to be honoured. But where could Equitable find the money to honour its promises? Its answer was to take money from its policyholders who did not have guaranteed return policies and give it to those with guarantees.

The Lords' decision caused Equitable to close to new business – not that anyone in their right mind would have taken out a new policy with them. Most of its policyholders were worried about their investments and many looked to transfer their policies to a secure institution. Equitable's 200-year-old world collapsed and along with it the well-being of thousands of policyholders. Investors who decided to transfer their money out to another investment company

saw the value of their policies reduced by transfer penalties. Even so, many investors cut their losses and transferred to what they hoped would be a safer investment company. The Lords' decision forced Equitable to seek a buyer but with a £1.5 billion gap in its funds it was not an attractive proposition.

The point of this case is to illustrate how ongoing operations which seemed quite acceptable, even very desirable, built up an organizational time-bomb that one day exploded. The events central to this case appear to be traceable to decisions taken by 'top' managers under the influence of environmental forces. That said, if the Law Lords had come to a different decision then perhaps Equitable and thousands of its customers would have avoided so big a crisis. So some environmental 'throw of the dice' was at play. We can also see how warning signs and signals were ignored. Before the turmoil, the Treasury had realized that Equitable would be insolvent if it had to find cash to meet its guarantees (Senior, 2001). Furthermore, the true poor performance of Equitable was an open secret in financial circles, yet it continued to pay out relatively high bonuses (and so top the league tables) in preference to putting aside funds that could be used when markets were less prosperous (Miles, 2000). The Board, in what seems to be a rather pathetic action, thought about suing former executives, financial advisors and auditors.

Activity 2.3

Look back at the section on 'Environmental turbulence' in Chapter 1.

Which (one or more) of the five levels of environmental turbulence do you think fits the situation Equitable Life found itself in?

What type(s) of change was Equitable Life pushed into?

University of Ulster LIBRARY

Having looked at how change is conceptualized and at how it might be possible to predict the next turning or crisis point (through application of the organizational life cycle concept), more needs to be done to develop ways of bringing about the necessary changes from one stage to another. It is useful therefore to have models and techniques for diagnosing the type of change situation prevailing at any one time in order to determine what kind of change approach to take.

Diagnosing change situations

> Those who pretend that the same kind of change medicine can be applied no matter what the context are either naive or charlatans.
>
> (Strebel, 1996b, p. 5)

Standard recipes for managing change are illusory because what works in one setting may not work in another. While some steps are good practice and so are likely to occur in change situations, the uniqueness of each workplace means that the ways that particular practices are implemented must differ.

The ability to diagnose change situations is, therefore, important if organizations are going to have any chance of responding to and managing change successfully. However, diagnosing an organizational situation is far from being an exact science. There are, though, some tools and techniques that can help. For instance, Greiner's model of the organizational life cycle is useful for drawing attention to periods when organizational change is likely to be needed. In addition, techniques such as stakeholder, SWOT and PEST analysis can lead to planned change and can increase awareness of the need for continuous incremental change. Multiple-cause diagrams which help understand the relationships among events leading to outcomes can lead to a better understanding of the interactions between the many different and often simultaneous causes of change.

There are, however, a number of other methods that can be used for anticipating when change is imminent and for deciding an appropriate approach to use for its management and implementation.

Looking for breakpoints

To help organizations focus on environmental scanning for signals that could trigger change, Strebel (1996a) suggested a model of industry behaviour which is linked to an organization's competitive environment (see Figure 2.5). He uses the concept of the 'evolutionary cycle of competitive behaviour' to introduce the idea of 'breakpoints', that is those times when organizations must change their strategies in response to changes in competitor behaviour.

The cycle of competitive behaviour involves two main phases. One is the innovation phase when a new business opportunity is discovered. This triggers a breakpoint to introduce a phase in the evolutionary cycle that causes a *divergence* in competitor behaviour as they attempt to exploit new opportunities with

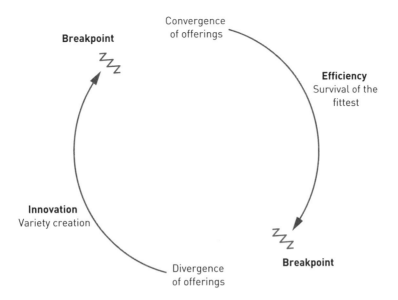

Figure 2.5 Evolutionary cycle of competitive behaviour

Source: From 'Breakpoint: how to stay in the game', *Financial Times Mastering Management*, Part 17 (Strebel, P., 1996) 1st March 1996, © The Financial Times Limited. All Rights Reserved.

innovative new offerings. Strebel (1996a) says this phase corresponds to variety creation in the evolutionary cycle and, with respect to changes in product development, he says:

> Divergent competitive behaviour aimed at enhancing the value of offerings continues until it becomes impossible to differentiate offerings because value innovation has run its course and imitation of the competitors' best features has taken over. As the offerings converge and the returns to value innovation decline, someone sees the advantage of trying to reduce delivered cost. Competitors converge on total quality management, continual improvement, and re-engineering or restructuring of the business system in an attempt to cut costs and maintain market share.
>
> (Strebel, 1996a, p. 13)

This brings about the second of the two phases – *convergence*. During this phase, the least efficient leave the scene and only the fittest survive. This is a phase of cost-cutting and consolidation until the returns from cost reduction decline and people see the advantage of looking for a new business opportunity – bringing a new breakpoint with the cycle starting all over again. In summary the competitive cycle suggests that there are two basic types of breakpoint (Strebel, 1996b):

● Divergent breakpoints associated with sharply increasing variety in the competitive offerings, resulting in more value for the customer.
● Convergent breakpoints associated with sharp improvements in the systems and processes used to deliver the offerings, resulting in lower delivered cost.

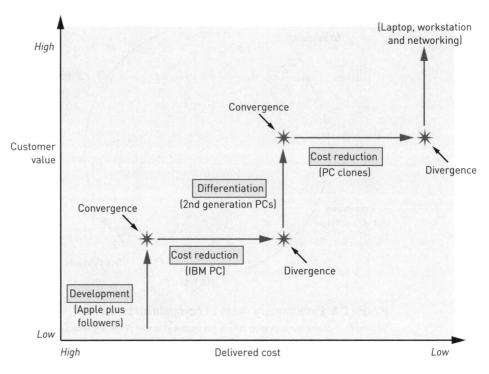

Figure 2.6 Breakpoint evolution of personal computer industry

Source: From 'Breakpoint: how to stay in the game', *Financial Times Mastering Management*, Part 17 (Strebel, P., 1996) 1st March 1996, © The Financial Times Limited. All Rights Reserved.

The vertical axis in Figure 2.6 represents the innovation–variety creation phase of the cycle of competitive behaviour; the horizontal axis represents the efficiency–survival phase. The vertical arrows denote periods of innovation (following divergence breakpoints) while the horizontal arrows denote periods of efficiency-seeking and cost-cutting (following convergence breakpoints). Over time, industries move up the diagonal with increasing customer value and lower delivered cost. Clearly some industries (e.g. those based on commodities) offer less opportunity for innovation and customer-value creation. Others (e.g. clothing and fashion) offer fewer opportunities for cost reduction. They evolve mainly through innovation.

Strebel's model is very useful in explaining the external environment in which organizations operate (Hayes, 2010), as is his advice on how to detect patterns in the environment that indicate a breakpoint might be imminent (see Illustration 2.11).

It is clear there are a number of issues associated with the identification of breakpoints. First, organizations need to have both formal and informal systems tuned in to searching for indicators in the environment. The formal systems will probably include environmental scanning, benchmarking, data collection and interpretation. In addition, the way in which organizations are structured must help to gather and interpret information. Just as important are the more informal

Illustration 2.11

Looking for breakpoints with leading indicators

The timing of breakpoints is impossible to predict because they might be triggered by many different factors and because they require both a latent market and a supplier with the right business system. However, with an understanding of an industry's evolution it is possible to look for patterns indicating that a breakpoint may be imminent. Specifically, the competitive cycle can be used to look for leading indicators of a potential breakpoint.

The tendency of the competitive cycle to oscillate between divergence (variety creation) and convergence (survival of the fittest) provides the framework. Convergence is usually easier to anticipate because it is built on a situation that already exists. Typical indicators are as shown below. When several of these are in place, all that is needed is a player or event to trigger a breakpoint:

- *Competitors*: when convergence is visible in increasingly similar products, service and image (no differentiation).
- *Customers*: when the differentiation between offerings looks increasingly artificial to customers and the segmentation in the market starts breaking down.
- *Distributors*: when the bargaining power in an industry shifts downstream to distributors who play competitors against each other.

- *Suppliers*: when they cannot provide a source of competitive advantage because everyone knows how to use their inputs.

Divergence is more difficult to anticipate because it is based on a new offering that does not yet exist. However, if the following are in place the industry is ready for a new offering that breaks with the past:

- *Customers*: when an increasingly saturated market is accompanied by declining growth rates and restless customers.
- *New entrants*: when restless customers are attracting new entrants.
- *Competitors*: when declining returns may force them to experiment with new offerings or look elsewhere for profits.
- *Suppliers*: when new resources and, especially, new technology are frequently the source of a divergent breakpoint.
- *Distributors*: when they lag behind because they have to adapt to the new offering.

Source: Strebel, P. (1996a), 'Breakpoint: how to stay in the game', *Mastering Management*, Part 17, *Financial Times*.

aspects of organizations, such as open attitudes on the part of managers and personnel, a degree of cooperation rather than destructive competition between divisions and departments, and a culture supportive of innovation and change (see the chapters in Part Two of the book).

Although it is not a model to identify causes of change, the Burke–Litwin model usefully draws together the array of variables that come into play when a change is triggered (Burke and Litwin, 1992). The model shown in Figure 2.7 contains 12 interrelated factors or variables and shows the interconnections between the operating environment at the top and individual and organizational performance at the bottom.

As an open systems model, change could be initiated anywhere. However, a classic case would be that some environmental event influences leadership behaviour which in turn affects management practices which affect the working climate which affects human motivation and through motivation affects performance.

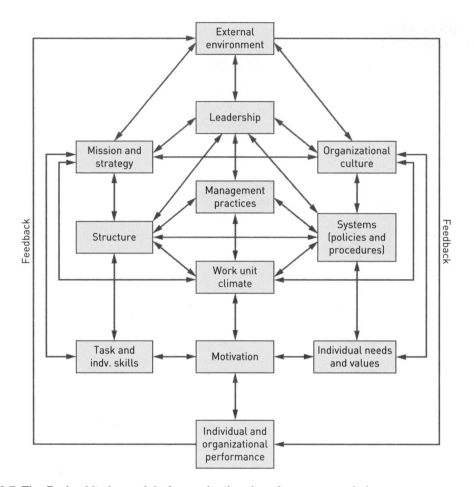

Figure 2.7 The Burke–Litwin model of organizational performance and change

Source: Burke, W.W. and Litwin, G.H. (1992), 'A causal model of organizational performance and change', *Journal of Management*. 18(3), pp. 523–45.

Environmental triggers may also force a re-think of mission and strategy which affects the culture of the organization which influences individual values, motivation and performance.

The model highlights how things are interconnected and illustrates the 'ripple effect', that is how a change in one factor or variable extends throughout the organization. It gives clues about where managers could intervene to initiate change and the knock-on effects. Not all variables in the model have the same weight (impact). For example, incremental, low-level change would involve variables in the lower part of the figure only and have little, if any, impact at the top level. Transformation and radical change are more likely, although not always, to begin at the top and would impact at the lower level.

The discussion so far has, to a large extent, concentrated on diagnosing change by scanning the organization's competitive environment. Another way of diagnosing change characterizes organizational problems (and therefore the need for change) in terms of their complexity, variability, people involvement and how much consensus there is on what constitutes the problem and what might bring a solution.

Hard (difficult) and soft (messy) problems

The discussion so far shows how situations forcing change vary in complexity and seriousness. A minor event in some part of an organization's internal environment can bring about (usually) small-scale change. By contrast, disturbances from the external environment will have a much more wide-ranging impact on an organization's strategy, structure and processes.

Sometimes, however, the signals that managers get are not clearly categorized as breakpoints; neither can they always be separated easily into issues concerned with competitors, customers, suppliers and distributors. These signals are frequently confused and diffuse and it is not easy to see clearly just what type of situation prevails – the only thing managers perceive are 'problems'. These problems may vary in complexity and seriousness, ranging from minor upsets to major catastrophes, from temporary hitches to gnawing 'tangles'. Paton and McCalman (2000) use the terms 'hard' and 'soft' to describe, respectively, these two types of problems. Another way of seeing situations is as difficulties and messes, the latter term based on Ackoff's (1993) article titled 'The art and science of mess management'. Puzzles are relatively easy since they are well-defined problems that have specific solutions (Ackoff, 1974).

Illustration 2.12 demonstrates some differences between difficulties and messes and shows how difficulties are simply more limited sorts of problems, where possible solutions are conceivable. Messes are much larger and much more taxing for those who want some kind of change to 'solve' the problem. However, they are not just bigger than difficulties, they are qualitatively different.

Illustration 2.12

Difficulties and messes

Difficulties are bounded in that they:

- tend to be smaller-scale and are less serious in their implications;
- can be considered in relative isolation from their organizational context;
- have clear priorities as to what might need to be done;
- generally have quantifiable objectives and performance indicators;
- have a systems/technical orientation;
- generally involve few people;
- have facts that are known and which can contribute to the solution;

- have agreement by the people involved on what constitutes the problem;
- tend to have solutions of which the type at least is known;
- have known timescales;
- are 'bounded' in that they can be considered separately from the wider organizational context and have minimal interactions with the environment.

Messes are unbounded in that they:

- tend to be larger-scale and have serious and worrying implications for all concerned;

Illustration 2.12 *continued*

- are an interrelated complex of problems that cannot be separated from their context;
- have many people of different persuasions and attitudes involved in the problem;
- have subjective and at best semi-quantifiable objectives;
- have an absence of knowledge of factors and uncertainty as to what needs to be known;

- have little agreement on what constitutes the problem, let alone what might be possible solutions;
- have usually been around for some time and will not be solved quickly, if at all: bringing about an improvement may be all that can be hoped for;
- have fuzzy timescales;
- are 'unbounded' in that they spread throughout the organization and, sometimes, beyond.

In distinguishing between these two types of problem, Stacey (2002) uses the terms 'close to certainty'/'far from certainty' juxtaposed with the terms 'close to agreement'/'far from agreement'. Put simply, difficulties can be conceived as close to certainty in finding solutions that generally will have the agreement of most concerned. Messes are problems that are far from certainty in how they can even be conceived let alone 'solved' and where there is little agreement among those involved with any changes.

With messes it can be hard to know where to begin a change. Reforming public services or dealing with climate change are examples of messes that face governments. It is a challenge for leaders of change to realize which of the above they are dealing with. Engineers might think they are dealing with a temporary hitch when they really have a difficulty, which, although complex, can be dealt with and 'solved' by splitting the problem into separate parts. Executives might think they face a difficulty when they are really facing a mess, which requires a more holistic approach and might take many months or years to 'solve'. (Ison, 2010; Mansfield, 2010). There are similarities here with the idea that in change situations there are differences between complicated systems and complex systems (Sammut-Bonnici and Wensley, 2002). Complicated systems can be highly detailed but the details can be known and problems associated with these can usually be solved using logical rational reasoning; for instance in the construction of a Boeing 747 or working out the best timetables for workers on production lines to achieve the most output.

By comparison, complex systems have a great many elements and people, and are heterogeneous in terms of people, knowledge and information, all of which are interconnected. A common problem in change management is that managers are trained to solve complicated systems using logic and linear, sequential thinking much more than they are trained to resolve complex systems of parallel dilemmas and which have no definitive solution (Higgs and Rowland, 2005).

The introduction of new working practices is an example of a messy problem. For instance, not everyone will agree there is a problem and a need for new working practices and there will be even less agreement about the best solutions. Some will interpret this action as a hidden agenda such as a desire to reduce the workforce or an attempt to split up certain work groups. Others may view this optimistically in terms of getting extra experience and perhaps new responsibilities. Management is likely to think it a 'good thing' while trade unions will want to know the implications for their members. What is more, if the changes have implications for pay and status, the potential losers will see the world very differently from the potential winners.

Activity 2.4

1 *Using the descriptions in Illustration 2.12, identify three 'difficulties' you have faced at work or in similar situations elsewhere.*
2 *Identify two or three 'messes' you have faced or been involved in.*
3 *Using Illustration 2.12, list the ways in which the difficulties differ from the messes. What might this tell you about ways of dealing with them?*

The change spectrum

Asking a number of questions about a change situation may help to identify whether it is characterized by hard or soft complexity and whether it is more of a difficulty or more of a mess. Using the terms 'hard' and 'soft' to distinguish these two types of problem, Paton and McCalman (2000) have devised what they call the 'TROPICS' test to help locate a change situation on a continuum from hard to soft. Illustration 2.13 presents the TROPICS factors as dimensions on which a change situation can be positioned, according to whether it is further towards the hard or soft end of each factor.

The TROPICS test, as with any analysis of problems according to the lists in Illustration 2.13, can only be a guide to the nature of the problem. What is important is to have undertaken exercises like these to better understand the type of change situation faced, in order to guide the design, planning and implementation of any change. This is because problem solving and managing subsequent changes are not simply intellectual problems. As situations move away from being difficulties and towards a mess, they encompass issues which have emotional and social dimensions requiring different kinds of approaches to resolve them. Simplistically, these approaches can be categorized as hard and soft and there are a number of models of change that, in broad terms, attach to these different approaches. These are considered further and in much more detail in Part Three, when the issues of 'doing' change are addressed.

Illustration 2.13

The TROPICS factors

Hard		Soft
Timescales clearly defined/ short to medium term		Timescales ill-defined/ medium to long term
Resources needed for the change clearly identified		Resources needed for the change uncertain
Objectives clearly stated and could be quantified		Change objectives subjective and ambiguous
Perceptions of the problem and its possible solution shared by all		No consensus on what constitutes the problem/conflicts of interest
Interest in the problem is limited and defined		Interest in the problem is widespread and ill-defined
Control is maintained by the managing group		Control is shared with people outside the managing group
Source of the problem originates from within the organization		The source of the problem originates from outside the organization

Activity 2.5

Take each example you thought of in Activity 2.3 and apply the TROPICS test to it. To do this, put a cross on each line according to whether your example is nearer to one end or the other of the factor. When you have done this for all factors for each example, make a judgement as to whether your example is, overall, a hard or soft problem/change situation.

Did the TROPICS test confirm or refute your judgement of what is a difficulty and what is a mess in terms of your answer to Activity 2.3?

How change has changed

As we near the end of this chapter it is useful to summarize how change has itself changed over the past 50 or 60 years of management research and this is summarized in Table 2.3. Key differences found in traditional and contemporary discourses are a move away from managerialist approaches to leading episodes of change caused by environmental and competitive triggers towards a state in which change is more of a 'taken-for-granted' aspect of organizational life in climates of continuous improvement in contrast to problem solving. This does not suggest that this is the way organizations have changed necessarily – anecdotally many traditional approaches have been used. The differences in the table reflect changes in the way change is discussed in the management research literature (Oswick *et al.*, 2005).

As time advances, theories of change get more convoluted and, arguably, less valid (Schwarz and Huber, 2008). Indeed, a general trajectory of change theory is to explain in ever increasing detail why there are few, if any, generalizations. Granted, we know the processes by which change happens and the content of change (i.e. what changes) but the conditions for successful, large-scale change are unique to each situation. They are the accumulation of every moment in the organization's past and are the outcome of unfathomably complex networks, relationships and interactions between employees and stakeholders with an interest in the organization.

Table 2.3 The changing nature of change

Comparator	Traditional discourse	Contemporary discourse
Temporality	Episodes of change with discrete beginning and end points	A philosophy that continuous organizational change is necessary to cope with the environment
Ethos	Fixing problems, focusing on negative events	Recognizing that things working well can be improved, improving already positive situations
Inputs	Analysis of data, 'running the numbers'	Constructive ongoing dialogues about what's working
Targets	Tangible features of the workplace, systems, structures	In addition to traditional targets the less tangible areas of organizations such as reputation and image
Drivers	Top and middle management	Involvement of people at all levels
Narratives	Managerialist, top-down, recipes for change	Debating what works, more focus on rhetoric of change in the particular organizational setting

Source: Based on Oswick *et al.* (2005), 'Looking forwards: discursive directions in organizational change', *Journal of Change Management*, 18(4), pp. 383–90.

There are parallels between the questions 'why can some organizations manage big change successfully?' and 'why are some organizations much more successful than others in the same sector?' Both questions can be answered through the complex arrays of relationships that exist between employees and others.

As we saw in Chapter 1, change sometimes arises not because of discrete events but from new ideas, new ways of thinking. Change theory could be said to be calling for such an infusion of new ideas right now.

Conclusions

Organizational change can be categorized in three dimensions: pace, scope or content, and planned–emergent. As the typologies reviewed here show, not only are there different types of change, change also appears differently at different levels of an organization. Planned change can lead to unintended outcomes that can lead to escalating positive or negative events. Change also occurs as an unintended outcome of decisions elsewhere. Complexity theory questions whether planned change is possible. Of course managers can plan, but to what extent are the changes that happen actually connected to their plans? There is still doubt around the question of whether change today makes change tomorrow more or less likely – more research is needed in this area. Strebel's model of change at the industry level is useful in looking to the wider environment for triggers for change. This model, together with the TROPICS test, can be used to analyze situations where change is considered desirable in order to understand which approach might be adopted in order to make it happen.

Chapter 1 examined the different environments in which struggles for organizational survival take place. Table 2.4 summarizes the similarities between the theories and research discussed in Part One which sets the scene for the more detailed discussion of change in Part Two.

Table 2.4 Environmental conditions and types of change

Environmental forces for change		Types of change				
Ansoff and McDonnell (1990)	Strebel (1996a)	Tushman et al. (1988)	Dunphy and Stace (1993)	Balogun and Hope Hailey (2008)	Grundy (1993)	Stacey (1991)
Predictable	Weak	Converging (fine-tuning)	Fine-tuning	Adaptation	Smooth incremental	Closed
Forecastable by extrapolation	Moderate	Converging (incremental)	Incremental adjustment	Evolution		Contained
Predictable threats and opportunities			Modular transformation	Reconstruction	Bumpy incremental	
Partially predictable opportunities	Strong		Corporate transformation	Revolution		
Unpredictable surprises		Discontinuous or frame-breaking			Discontinuous	Open ended

Discussion questions and assignments

1 Discuss the proposition that: 'All change can be categorized as either incremental or radical.' Use examples from your own experience to support your argument.

2 To what extent are Dunphy and Stace's four types of change helpful in working with 'real-life' examples of change? Illustrate your answer with examples from organizations you know well.

3 Discuss Quinn's (1979) contention that change occurs through a process of 'logical incrementalism'. Give examples to support your argument.

4 To what extent do organizational messes get treated as if they were difficulties? What are the organizational consequences of this? Does it matter how change situations are classified?

5 To what extent do you think the environmental scanning tools are effective in diagnosing the environment for organizations? Are there situations when they might not be effective?

Case example ●●●

Professional service firms

Professional service firms occur in sectors like architecture, law and accounting. These sectors are characterized by extensive and long traditions of professional practice, highly regulated professional training and examination, and a professional partnership (PP) style of organization. The PP model means that the firm can operate quite differently to a typical limited company. Professional service firms may have many partners in the business and there are tax advantages that normal limited companies do not have. On the other hand, each partner is liable for any wrong-doing by other partners and the liabilities of the firm – so their personal risk is much higher.

Firms of accountants, lawyers, and doctors among other professional groups tend to be similar because they conform to a sectoral archetype of what a professional firm should look like. Their structures and methods of organizing are similar because they want to conform to the social expectations that exist in their sectors. These expectations push for structural and organizational conformity as a way of legitimizing the firm in its sector. Without legitimacy, a firm would struggle to be seen as a serious operator.

However, competitive and institutional pressures in the various sectors have caused professional service firms to re-think their business model. The main pressures at sector level were increasing competition and the need to be much more efficient. Partners in the firms began thinking about the merits of changing the organizational form away from a partnership to a managed professional business (MPB) which typically has a more hierarchical governance structure, more centralized decision making, more separation of management from professional tasks and tighter management control.

Across the various professional sectors, however, research has shown that some firms in a sector have made the transition from PP to MPB, whereas others have not. This is intriguing because, since external conditions affect firms in a sector in the same way, different outcomes from attempts to change look like they have explanations lying inside the firm.

Three PP firms providing legal services were studied (Lawrence, Malhotra and Morris, 2012) and the triggers for change in the firms included: a profit crisis; the retirement of a senior partner; a merger between two partnerships; under-performance; high-profile partners leaving for jobs in other partnerships and taking their teams with them; demands for new types of professional service following regulatory change; and high profitability which increased commitment to stronger management control.

Key changes at the three law firms over a 10-year period included:

Law firm 1 – Some roles were abolished and an executive committee was turned from being decision making to advisory. Divisional structures were introduced along with a principle of divisional autonomy. The service portfolio was refocused around two market sectors and the creation of a new third business division. Different reporting systems were introduced as were formal procedures for HR practices such as hiring and promoting.

Law firm 2 – A new management team was formed and made up equally of partners from two merged firms. The central management team was expanded and appointed/replaced heads of particular law practice groups. At first the portfolio was expanded to reflect the two firms that merged but this was later refocused into two major practice areas. System changes included HR and billing. Financial systems identified partner performance and led to counselling and the managed exit of poor performers. Over several years there was continuing resistance to the changes by some groups.

Law firm 3 – Strengthened central management and adoption of the vocabulary used by corporate clients (e.g. to talk of the board of directors, shareholders). Refocusing on core law practice areas and reduction of other areas. New appointments were made from outside alongside promotions at senior level. A new firm-wide strategic planning and monitoring system was introduced. Specialists were hired to manage HR and marketing. Stronger people management such as processes to measure partner performance were introduced.

Case exercise

Using the various models given in this chapter, how would you classify the attempt to change from a professional partnership to a managed business?

Given that competitive and institutional forms are the same in each sector, why have some firms made a successful transition and others not?

Indicative resources

Balogun, J. and Hope Hailey, V. (2008), *Exploring Strategic Change* (3rd edn), Harlow: Financial Times Prentice Hall. This book focuses on the change process itself and is a good text for considering change at the strategic level.

Useful websites

www.ft.com *The Financial Times* website has a useful search facility to find examples of organizations that are responding to change.

https://www.youtube.com/watch?v=eakKfY5aHmY This video clip, whilst perfectly illustrating a flock of birds on the move, also illustrates the concept of 'self-organization' discussed in the chapter.

https://www.futurelearn.com/courses/complexity-and-uncertainty-2/todo/1542 This website is from a programme of free courses (generally produced by universities). The name of the course referenced here is 'Decision Making in a Complex and Uncertain World'.

●●●● References

Ackoff, R.L. (1974), *Redesigning the Future: A Systems Approach to Societal Problems*, New York/London: J. Wiley & Sons.

Ackoff, R.L. (1993), 'The art and science of mess management', in Mabey, C. and Mayon-White, B. (eds) *Managing Change* (2nd edn), London: PCP.

Ansoff, I.H. and McDonnell, E.J. (1990), *Implanting Strategic Management*, Englewood Cliffs, NJ: Prentice-Hall.

Balogun, J. and Hope Hailey, V. (2008), *Exploring Strategic Change* (3rd edn), Harlow: Financial Times Prentice Hall.

Beck, N.,Bruders, J. and Woywode, M. (2008), 'Momentum or Deceleration? Theoretical and methodological reflections on the analysis of organizational change', *Academy of Management Journal*, 51(3), pp. 413–35.

Boyatzis, R. (2006), 'An overview of intentional change from a complexity perspective', *Journal of Management Development*, 25(7), pp. 607–23.

Burke, W.W. and Litwin, G.H. (1992), 'A causal model of organizational performance and change', *Journal of Management,* 18(3), pp. 523–45.

Burnes, B. (2004), *Managing Change: A Strategic Approach to Organisational Dynamics* (4th edn), Harlow: Financial Times Prentice Hall.

Burnes, B. (2005), 'Complexity theories and organizational change', *International Journal of Management Reviews*, 7, pp. 273–90.

Checkland, P.B. (1972), 'Towards a systems based methodology for real world problem solving', *Journal of Systems Engineering*, 3(2), pp. 87–116.

Clarke, L. (1994), *The Essence of Change*, Hemel Hempstead: Prentice Hall.

Dunphy, D. and Stace, D. (1993), 'The strategic management of corporate change', *Human Relations*, 46(8), pp. 905–20.

Future Learn (2015), *Decision Making in a Complex and Uncertain World,* University of Groningen, the Netherlands, accessed through the website: https://www.futurelearn.com/courses/complexity-and-uncertainty-2/todo/1542

Greiner, L.E. (1972), 'Evolution and revolution as organizations grow', *Harvard Business Review,* July–August, 50, pp. 37–46.

Grundy, T. (1993), *Managing Strategic Change*, London: Kogan Page.

Harris, M., Dopson, S. and Fitzpatrick, R. (2009), 'Strategic drift in international non-governmental development organizations – putting strategy in the background of organizational change', *Public Administration and Development*, 29(5), pp. 415–28.

Hayes, J. (2010), *The Theory and Practice of Change Management* (3rd edn), Basingstoke: Palgrave.

Haynes, P. (2008), 'Complexity theory and evaluation in public management', *Public Management Review*, 10(3), pp. 401–19.

Higgs, M. and Rowland, D. (2005), 'All changes great and small: exploring approaches to change and its leadership', *Journal of Change Management,* 5(2), pp. 121–51.

Houchin, K. and Maclean, D. (2005), 'Complexity theory and strategic change: an empirically informed critique', *British Journal of Management*, 16 (2), pp. 149–66.

Ison, R. (2010), *Systems Practice: How to Act in a Climate Change World*. London: Springer.

Jian, G. (2007), 'Unpacking unintended consequences of planned organizational change', *Management Communication Quarterly*, 21(1), pp. 5–28.

Johnson, G. (1988), 'Processes of managing strategic change', *Management Research News*, 11 4/5, pp. 43–6. This article can also be found in Mabey, C. and Mayon-White, B. (eds) *Managing Change* (2nd edn), London: PCP.

Johnson, G., Whittington, R., Scholes, K., Angwin, D., and Regner, P. (2014), *Exploring Strategy* (10th edn), Harlow: Pearson.

Jones, R. (2002), 'Leading change in local government: the tension between evolutionary and frame-breaking reform in NSW', *Australian Journal of Public Administration*, 61(3), pp. 38–53.

Kanter, R.M. (1989), *When Giants Learn to Dance: Mastering the Challenges of Strategy, Management and Careers in the 1990s*, Unwin: London.

Kast, F.E. and Rosenzweig, J.E. (1970), *Organization and Management: A systems approach,* New York: McGraw-Hill.

Kimberley, J.R. and Miles, R.H. (1980), *The Organizational Life-cycle*, San Francisco, CA: Jossey-Bass.

Mansfield, J. (2010), T*he Nature of Change or the Law of Unintended Consequences,* World Scientific.

McAleer, W.E. (1982), 'Systems: a concept for business and management', *Journal of Applied Systems Analysis*, 9, pp. 99–129.

Miles, R. (2000), 'High bonuses masked high performance', *The Times*, Money Section, 16 December, p. 5.

Murray, P. (2003), 'So what's new about complexity?', S*ystems Research and Behavioural Science*, 20(5), pp. 409–17.

Lawrence, T.B., Malhotra, N. and Morris, T. (2012), 'Episodic and systemic power in the transformation of professional service firms', *Journal of Management Studie*s, 49(1), pp. 102–43.

Oswick, C., Grant, D., Michelson, G. and Wailes, N. (2005), 'Looking forwards: discussive directions in organizational change', *Journal of Change Management*, 18(4), pp. 383–90.

Paton, R.A. and McCalman, J. (2000), *Change Management: Guide to Effective Implementation* (2nd edn), London: Sage.

Peters, T.J. and Waterman, R.H. (1982), *In Search of Excellence: Lessons from America's Best Run Companies*, Harper and Row: London.

Plowman, D.A., Baker, L.T., Beck, T.E., Kulkani, M., Solansky, S.T. and Travis, D.V. (2007), 'Radical change accidentally: the emergence and amplification of small change', *Academy of Management Journal*, 50(3), pp. 515–43.

Quinn, J.B. (1979) 'Xerox Corporation (B)', copyright case, Hanover, NH: Amos Tuck School of Business Administration, Dartmouth College.

Quinn, J.B. (1980), 'Managing strategic change', *Sloan Management Review*, Summer, pp. 3–20.

Quinn, R.E. and Cameron, K. (1983), 'Organizational life cycles and shifting criteria of effectiveness: some preliminary evidence', *Management Science*, 29(1), pp. 33–51.

Sammut-Bonnici, T. and Wensley, R. (2002), 'Darwinism, probability and complexity: market-based organizational transformation and change explained through the theories of evolution', *International Journal of Management Reviews*, 4(3), pp. 291–315.

Schwarz, G.M. and Huber, G.P. (2008), 'Challenging organizational change research', *British Journal of Management,* 19, special issue, S1–S6.

Senior, A. (2001), 'Equitable may sue advisors and FSA', *The Times*, Money Section, 20 October, p. 12.

Stacey, R. (1995), 'The science of complexity: an alternative perspective for strategic change processes', *Strategic Management Journal*, 16(6), pp. 477–95.

Stacey R.D., (2002), *Strategic Management and Organisational Dynamics: The Challenge of Complexity* (3rd edn), Harlow: Prentice Hall.

Stacey, R. (2011), *Strategic Management and Organisational Dynamics: The Challenge of Complexity* (6th edn), Harlow: Financial Times Prentice Hall.

Stacey, R., Griffin, D. and Shaw, P. (2002), *Complexity and Management: Fad or Radical Challenges to Systems Thinking*, London: Routledge.

Strebel, P. (1996a), 'Breakpoint: how to stay in the game', *Mastering Management*, Part 17, *Financial Times*.

Strebel, P. (1996b), 'Choosing the right path', *Mastering Management*, Part 14, *Financial Times*, 16 October.

Tushman, M.L., Newman, W.H. and Romanelli, E. (1988), 'Convergence and upheaval: managing the unsteady pace of organizational evolution', in Tushman, M.L. and Moore, W.L. (eds), *Readings in the Management of Innovation*, New York: Ballinger.

Van der Voet, J., Groeneveld, S. and Kuipers, B. (2014), 'Talking the talking or walking the walk? The leadership of planned and emergent change in a public organization', *Journal of Change Management*, 14(2), pp. 171–91.

Wilson, D.C. (1992), *A Strategy of Change*, New York: Routledge.

Part Two

CHANGING ORGANIZATIONS

The idea of organizations as systems operating in a wider environment was developed in Part One. The strategy an organization pursues and the way in which it is structured form part of the response to environmental forces and have a big influence upon the capacity to respond to and initiate change.

Strategy and structure can be thought of as the more formal, overt aspects of how organizations function. As important, however, are the more informal, covert aspects of organizational life such as organizational culture (set in the context of national culture), organizational politics, as well as the way the organization is led.

Part Two investigates these aspects of organizational life in terms of their relations with the external environment and the opportunities and constraints for change. The four chapters in Part Two reflect this focus and prepare the ground for the more practically oriented material on the designing and implementing of change in Part Three.

Chapter 3 considers how organizations structure their activities, while Chapters 4 and 5 concentrate on culture and politics and their significance for the success of change processes. Chapter 6 discusses leadership and its impact on change.

Chapter 3

Organizational design, structure and change

This chapter introduces the characteristics of different organizational designs and structures. Advantages and disadvantages of each are given in relation to organizational performance and the ability of organizations to introduce and implement change. Network and virtual organizational forms are examined in the context of best-fitting contemporary business environments. Factors influencing designs and structure are introduced along with explanations of structural inertia and why structural change is not easy to implement.

Learning objectives

At the end of this chapter you will be able to:

● define what is meant by organizational design and structure;

● explain the organizational forms that are commonly found;

● discuss the relationship between strategy and structure;

● evaluate the contingency relationships between organizational structure, size, technology and the external environment;

● assess the extent to which different structures can cope with and adapt to a variety of change processes.

The meaning of organization structure

Social systems usually group people in different ways to get work done. In order to achieve goals and objectives, organizations need ways of dividing work up and allocating it to their members. The allocation of responsibilities, the grouping of workers' activities and their coordination and control are basic elements of structure.

At a simple level, structure is something managers design and put in place to enable efficient production and delivery of the organization's outputs. It 'describes the way an organization is configured into work groups and the reporting and authority relationships that connect individuals and groups together' (Swailes, 2008, p. 191).

Organization structure and design are not the same and the difference is worth noting. Design refers to the way a structure might be drawn on an organization chart. Organizational designs are 'managerialist responses' to the contingencies thrown up by the environment and the main framework for understanding organizational design is called contingency theory (Clegg, Kornberger and Pitsis, 2008, p. 528). Large organizations, for instance, typically organize around centralized decision making; here the contingency (size) is shaping the response (centralization). Design shows the formal reporting relationships and areas of responsibility drawn to impress the organization's various stakeholders. Yet if you have worked in an organization you will know that very often employees ignore the formal design to get things done – they use the actual operating structure, not the formal design. So we can see structure as the incarnation of a design with 'patterned regularity' being a dominant feature of structure (Willamott, 1981, p. 470).

Keeping the design/structure distinction in mind is also important since the real working structure of an organization can be seen as something that is socially constructed (Bate, Khan and Pyle, 2000). Changes to design can have no impact on the social structures that are overlaying them and through which things actually get done. 'Empty restructuring' is the phrase used by Paul Bate (1995) to describe what happens when managers change designs but disregard the overlaying social interactions. Social structures can be seen as informal structures that are not designed by management but are the outcome of friendship and interest groupings as well as groups that serve political purposes (see Chapters 4 and 5), not always related to the organization's goals.

The dimensions of structure

Organization structure can vary in many ways but a classic study identified the following six primary dimensions (Pugh, Hickson, Hinings and Turner, 1969):

1 *Specialization*: the extent to which there are different specialist roles and how they are distributed.

2 *Standardization*: the extent to which an organization uses regularly occurring procedures that are supported by bureaucratic procedures of invariable rules and processes.

3 *Formalization*: the extent to which written rules, procedures, instructions and communications are set out for employees.

4 *Centralization*: the extent to which authority to make decisions lies with the apex (top) of the organization. Decentralization refers to attempts to push decision making down to lower levels in the hierarchy.

5 *Configuration*: the shape and pattern of authority relationships; how many layers there are and the number of people who typically report to a supervisor.

6 *Traditionalism*: how many procedures are 'understood' in contrast to being written; how commonly accepted is the notion of 'the way things are done around this organization'.

Derek Pugh and his colleagues established four underlying dimensions:

1 *Structuring of activities*: the extent to which there is formal regulation of employee behaviour through the processes of specialization, standardization and formalization.

2 *Concentration of authority*: the extent to which decision making is centralized at the top of the organization.

3 *Line control of workflow*: the extent to which control of the work is exercised directly by line management rather than through more impersonal procedures.

4 *The support component*: the relative size of the administrative and other non-workflow personnel performing activities auxiliary to the main workflow.

Support for these dimensions was provided by Child (1988) who added:

- the way sections, departments and divisions are grouped together;
- systems for communication, the integration of effort and participation;
- systems for motivating employees such as performance appraisal and reward.

It is clear from this that structure is a multidimensional concept such that organizations can be structured in many different ways according to where they fit on the dimensions above. Every organization has a unique structural 'fingerprint'. Despite this it is possible to discern similar ways of designing organizations and to identify some general patterns. There is also evidence to show that some types of structures are a better fit with environments than others and we discuss this later. First it is necessary to understand the broad types of structures used.

Structural types

Bureaucratic structure

One of the best-known ways of structuring is the bureaucratic form (King and Lawley, 2013). Three ideas that are central to the concept of bureaucracy are: the idea of rational legal authority; the idea of 'office' and the idea of 'impersonal order' (from Henderson and Parsons' translation of Weber (1947) found in Pugh, 1990).

These ideas are based on:

- a continuous organization of official functions bound by rules;
- a specified sphere of competence, i.e. differentiation of function;
- the organization of offices (i.e. positions) follows the principle of hierarchy;
- the separation of members of the administrative staff from ownership of production or administration;
- no appropriation by the incumbent of their official position;
- administrative acts, decisions and rules are formulated and recorded in writing, even in cases where discussion is the rule or is essential.

Illustration 3.1 summarizes the characteristics of the pure form of bureaucratic structure.

Illustration 3.1

Bureaucracy

Weber specified several characteristics of his ideal organization structure of which the main four are:

1. Specialization and division of labour. Work is finely divided between well-defined and highly specialized jobs or roles.
2. Hierarchical arrangement of positions. Roles are hierarchically arranged with a single chain of command from the top of the organization to the bottom.
3. A system of impersonal rules. The incumbents of roles (or positions) carry out their duties impersonally in accordance with clearly defined rules.
4. Impersonal relationships. Coordination of activities relies heavily on the use of rules, procedures and written records and on the

decision of the lowest common superior to the people concerned.

Other characteristics of a bureaucracy identified by Weber are: the selection of officials solely on the basis of technical qualifications; appointment, not election; remuneration by fixed salaries with a right to pensions; only under certain conditions can the employing authority terminate an employment; the employee can leave at any time and a system of promotion according to seniority or achievement or both.

Source: Based on Weber, M. (1947), *The Theory of Social and Economic Organisation*, Free Press, translated and edited by Henderson, A.M. and Parsons, T. in Pugh, D. (1990) *Organization Theory. Selected readings*, Penguin. (German original published in 1924).

The bureaucratic form is an enduring approach to structuring that is still found in most, if not all, large public-sector organizations. For instance, McHugh and Bennett's (1999, p. 81) account of an attempt to bring about change in a large public-sector agency describes organizations like it in the following way:

> A rigid bureaucratic maze typified structural formation within many such organizations with the majority of members having narrowly defined and highly specialized jobs, and being protected from making decisions through their constant deference to authority and reference to their rule books.

The difficulties expressed by McHugh and Bennett regarding the problems of changing such a structure are consistent with Weber who was convinced of the case for the bureaucratic form. For instance, he says (Pugh, 1990, p. 12):

It would be sheer illusion to think for a moment that continuous administrative work can be carried out in any field except by the means of officials working in offices ... For bureaucratic administration is, other things being equal, always, from a formal, technical point of view, the most rational type. For the needs of mass administration today, it is completely indispensable.

Illustration 3.2 is a brief description of a construction company called the Beautiful Buildings Company. The organization chart illustrates its current bureaucratic structure. The company is used later in this chapter to illustrate other types of organizational structures that try to overcome problems of bureaucracy.

Illustration 3.2

The Beautiful Buildings Company

The Beautiful Buildings Company designs and builds a variety of different buildings. It is known for its imaginative designs and the construction of a range of factory and other industrial buildings and prides itself on having won contracts to build a new civic hall in one of the world's leading cities. Just over 12 months ago it took over a smaller building company specializing in home building for middle- to higher-income families. It would like to develop further into the area of commercial office buildings.

During the past 20 years the company has grown from operating solely in the UK to securing contracts in Australia and North America, and it has footholds in a number of mainland European countries.

The BB Company is headed by Gillian Lambeth, the daughter of the previous owner. There are a number of directors reporting to Gillian who are each in charge of one of the company's main functions. Marcus Davidson, the Marketing Director, has been the person most involved in promoting the company's activities outside the UK.

Currently the company is structured on typical bureaucratic lines as illustrated in the simplified chart shown below.

Activity 3.1

- *Obtain an official organization chart for an organization that you know well. To what extent would you regard the organization's structure as indicative of a bureaucratic structure and indicative of how work actually gets done?*

- *To what extent does the organization of work conform to Weber's bureaucratic principles?*

- *For organizations structured as bureaucracies, what barriers might exist to structural change?*

Of particular interest are the differences between individual perceptions of organization structures and the formal design chart and the stories told by senior management. Jackson and Carter (2000), for instance, offer a strong argument for the view that structure is not, in the case of organizations, something *concrete* and *objective*, but essentially *abstract*. Adopting what they term 'a post-structuralism' approach to explaining structure, they maintain (in contradiction to Weber) that there is no obvious and *natural* way of ordering the management of organizational activities. What is more, they maintain that what one person perceives or experiences as (say) an authoritarian, oppressive structure, another person perceives as democratic and fair.

Weber would have supported the second of these two views as his bureaucracies were intended to portray neutrality and fairness in the way people were treated. However, the term *bureaucracy* has, more recently, taken on negative connotations of undesirable and burdensome rules and regulations, and an overwhelming feeling of control.

Flatter structures

In a search for better responsiveness to markets, and sometimes to reduce operating costs by removing layers of management, some organizations have tried to 'flatten' their core design. In flatter structures, widening the span of control (the number of people reporting to a supervisor) reduces the number of levels in the structure, while retaining the same number of staff. One rule of thumb is that the more similar jobs are at any one level (job standardization), the more people a manager can coordinate and control. Managing many people doing very different kinds of jobs requires more managerial attention which limits the effective span of control. Another general rule is that the more decision making is decentralized and therefore reducing the burden on each manager, the broader the span of control can be. Other factors that affect the span of control are the physical location or geographical spread of subordinates, the abilities of subordinate staff and the ability and personal qualities of the manager concerned (Mullins, 2013).

With regard to the number of levels in the structure of the organization (the 'scalar chain' or 'chain of command'), Drucker (1999) suggests that these should be as few as possible. Too many levels bring difficulties in understanding and communicating objectives both up and down the hierarchy. In a study of over 300 US companies Rajan and Wulf (2006) found that the number of managers between the CEO and the lowest managers with profit-centre responsibility fell by over 25 per cent between 1986 and 1998. Possible explanations include:

- *Increased competition* – each managerial layer takes time to make decisions and faster decision making is needed as competition intensifies. Hence, removing layers should accelerate decision making. Tougher competition may also be raising the complexity of the decisions that are needed. Flatter hierarchies seem more conducive to greater creativity by decision makers compared to a ladder of micromanagers.
- *Better corporate governance* – this may have contributed to the elimination of layers of management.
- *Information technology* – if this increases the capacity of middle and junior managers to make decisions then the effective span of control can increase.

Rajan and Wulf conclude that while CEOs are more directly connected 'deeper down' the organization and across more business units (akin to centralization) there is a trend to push decision-making authority downwards (akin to decentralization). This is an interesting finding that suggests that centralization and decentralization are not reciprocally related and that they can coexist.

Illustration 3.3

Organigraphs

Uncomfortable with the classic portrayals of structure using organization charts, Henry Mintzberg and colleague Ludo van der Heyden use 'organigraphs' to show how organizations really function.

Organigraphs contain two basic components: sets and chains. Sets are machines or groups of people that rarely interact with each other. For example, teachers of physics and sociology in a university rarely interact even though they are supported by the same infrastructure. Chains are systems for converting inputs into outputs such as assembly lines; something is processed and passed on to the next link in the chain.

In addition, there are hubs and webs. Hubs are where 'people, things and information' move and they can be buildings, machines or people. Webs show how points in an organization communicate with each other.

Unlike charts, organigraphs show the multiple relationships between components of organizations. There is no single correct organigraph – it is just a matter of how a particular manager sees how the organization works. There is no one way of symbolizing the four components either – they can be drawn in many ways. Herein lies a criticism of the idea: if they can be anything, then what analytical value do they have? But that is perhaps missing the point that organigraphs are ways of visualizing how things work as a prelude to imagining change.

Source: Mintzberg, H. and van der Heyden, L. (1999), 'Organi-graphs: drawing how companies really work', *Harvard Business Review*, Sep/Oct, pp. 87–94.

Horizontal differentiation – the departmentalization of work

The decision on which way to departmentalize frequently relies on the characteristics of the work to be done, the size of the organization, the physical locations of activities and the need to maintain a balance between high-level strategic decision making and lower-level operational imperatives. Power struggles also play a part. Some organizations design around functional areas, others departmentalize by product, customer or geographical region. Each method of structuring has its advantages and disadvantages.

Multifunctional structures

Multifunctional structures are a common structural form particularly in the stages of an organization's development when the early entrepreneurial phase gives way to a more settled phase of sustained growth (see Figure 2.4 in Chapter 2). Large corporations of the early twentieth century were mostly structured on these lines due to the emphasis in early management theories on specialization, span of control, relationships, authority and responsibility (Cummings and Worley, 2009). Common functional specialisms are purchasing, production, marketing, purchasing and finance.

Functional structures serve organizations well as they move from Greiner's (1972) 'growth by creativity' stage in a company's development to the 'growth by direction' stage (see Figure 2.4 in Chapter 2). However, as they grow and diversify in customer and product markets they pass through what Greiner calls a 'crisis of autonomy'. This is characterized by demands for greater autonomy on the part of middle managers who frequently possess greater knowledge about markets and operations than top management. As different product groups can experience different market conditions, organizing around products rather than functions can be more efficient. Illustration 3.4 lists advantages and disadvantages of functional structures together with the factors that provide the forces for moving towards them.

Illustration 3.4

Advantages and disadvantages of functional structures

Advantages

Departmentalization by function has advantages in its logical mirroring of the basic functions of business. Each function has its high-level representative to guard its interests. Tight control is possible at the top. It encourages the development of specialist skills and expertise and provides a career structure within the function. Training can be organized along specialist lines. In organizations where technical skill gives competitive advantage, the functional structure can enhance this.

Disadvantages

As organizations grow and diversify or locate in geographically distributed places, coordination of activities across functions can become more

difficult. Functionalism sometimes encourages narrow thinking which works against innovation which requires cooperation across functions. Important market intelligence can be overlooked. Functional structures limit the opportunity for the development of general managers.

Contingency factors

These are based on the factors suggested by Cummings and Worley (2009):

- stable and certain environment;
- small to medium size;
- routine technology, interdependence with functions;
- goals of efficiency and technical quality.

Multidivisional structures

It is easy to imagine the problems that the Beautiful Buildings (BB) Company might have with a multifunctional structure. Its current and hoped-for activities cross at least four product areas (public buildings, industrial buildings, houses/homes and commercial accommodation). Each of these product areas is governed by different sets of customer expectations, research and design problems, and building regulations. Each is prey to different environmental influences. Departmentalizing by product might then be a sensible move for BB. Figure 3.1 shows how it could look if designed around its markets.

Multidivisional structures are built around outputs rather than inputs. They overcome the dangers of poor coordination and responsiveness and allow faster responses to market conditions. This was the reason for Unilever's restructuring, which began in 2004 as they clearly saw advantages in restructuring around product markets (see Illustration 3.5).

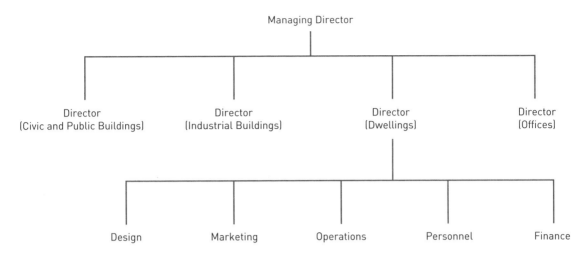

Figure 3.1 The BB Company – departmentalization by product

Departmentalization by product or service has advantages of maximizing the use of employees' skills and specialized market knowledge. There is more opportunity for innovative ideas for new or modified products to flourish. Product differentiation facilitates the use of specialized capital. Product divisions can be made profit-centres in their own right, thus making them responsible for budgets and sales. Differentiation by product makes it easier to concentrate on different classes of customer, particularly when different products coincide with different customer groupings. Where a product division has its own set of business functions these

Illustration 3.5

Structural transformation at Unilever

Unilever, a leading supplier of fast-moving consumer goods known for global brands such as Birds Eye, Flora, Cif, Marmite, Hellmann's and Ben & Jerry's, restructured in response to competition and performance results. Unilever has about 200,000 employees in nearly 100 countries.

Unilever combined three operating companies to create a new and more efficient structure to concentrate on product sales specific to the individual countries in which it operates. The reasoning was to simplify management to enable faster local decision making and improve agility in the marketplace. A 'one Unilever' programme created single operating companies in each country together with outsourcing of support functions such as IT, human resources and finance. Senior management numbers fell by about 40 per cent. Each operating company is better suited to match its product portfolio to the country it operates in. The rationale for the structural changes was:

● single point responsibility;
● faster decision making;
● clear accountability for delivery;
● leadership close to customer and consumer;
● balance between market focus and scale.

But structural change was ongoing and in late 2006 the Foods group further restructured into six Centres of Excellence in Europe. This meant reorganizing 1,160 people in 60 locations into 29 food research and development locations with a loss of about 240 jobs.

Illustration 3.5 *continued*

Old management structure

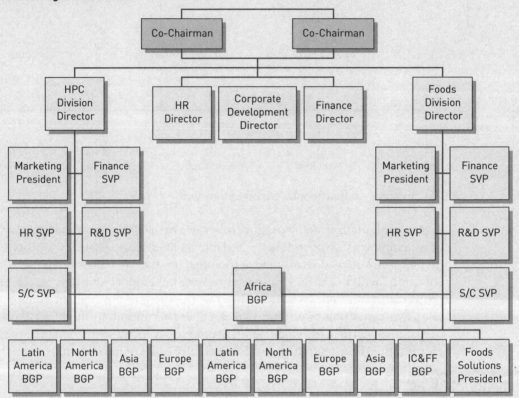

New management structure

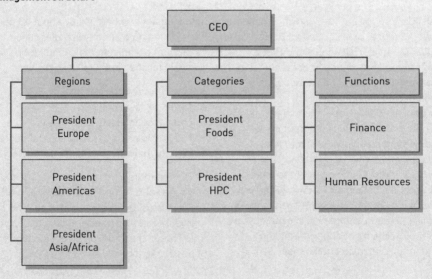

Source: www.unilever.com

can be coordinated towards the product markets. Lastly, this type of structure offers good opportunities for the training of general managers.

Disadvantages are that there can be overlap of functions from one product division to another, that is, duplication of central service and other support activities. Overall administration costs tend to be higher than in pure functional structures. Where business functions are not wholly devolved, product-based divisions are 'top sliced' to provide resources for more centralized functions. This can be felt by product line managers as burdensome overheads, which detract from their overall profits. Top management may have more difficulty in controlling what happens at the product divisional level. Coordinating policy and practice across product areas can be complex.

Matrix organization

The essence of a matrix design is that a typical vertical hierarchy is overlaid with a horizontal structure commonly designed around big projects. Employees find that they report to different people for different areas of responsibility. Figure 3.2 shows a hypothetical matrix structure for an advertising agency. In this case, the heads of marketing, finance, personnel, and research and development form the vertical lines of reporting while the different customer bases represent the divisions that operate horizontally across the structure.

Faced with shortening product life cycles Texas Instruments realized that its traditional functional hierarchy would not cope with the need to reduce time to market and introduced a 'balanced matrix' structure in one of its divisions. A key

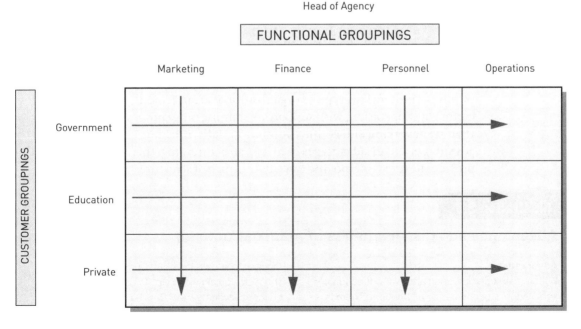

Figure 3.2 Matrix structure for an advertising agency

finding from the restructuring was that initially performance can fall but improved later on (Bernasco *et al.*, 1999).

Drawing on Davis and Lawrence's (1977) work, Bartol and Martin (1994) maintain that organizations which ultimately adopt a matrix structure usually go through four identifiable stages:

Stage 1 is a *traditional structure*, usually a functional structure, which follows the unity-of-command principle.

Stage 2 is a *temporary overlay*, in which managerial integrator positions are created to take charge of particular projects (e.g. project managers), oversee product launches (e.g. product managers), or handle some other issue of finite duration that involves co-ordination across functional departments. These managers often lead or work with temporary interdepartmental teams created to address the issue.

Stage 3 is a *permanent overlay* in which the managerial integrators operate on a permanent basis (e.g. a brand manager coordinates issues related to a brand on an ongoing basis), often through permanent interdepartmental teams.

Stage 4 is a *mature matrix*, in which matrix bosses have equal power.
                                                        (Bartol and Martin, 1994, pp. 321–2)

Cummings and Worley (2009) suggest that matrix structures are appropriate under three important conditions. First, there needs to be pressure from the external environment for a dual focus, such as university lecturers focusing on teaching quality and capturing research grants. Second, a matrix structure is of benefit when an organization must process a large amount of information. This is particularly useful when organizations operate in an environment of unpredictability or need to produce information quickly. Finally, there must be pressures for sharing resources which matrices support.

Matrix structures rely heavily on teamwork with managers needing high-level people management skills. The focus is on solving problems through team action. In a mature matrix structure, team members are managed simultaneously by two different managers – one is their functional line manager and the other the team or project leader. This type of organizational arrangement, therefore, requires a culture of cooperation, with supporting training programmes to help staff develop their teamworking and conflict-resolution skills. Illustration 3.6 summarizes the advantages and disadvantages of matrix structures, together with the factors that provide the forces for moving towards this type of structure.

Illustration 3.6

Advantages and disadvantages of matrix structures

Advantages

With a matrix design, specialized and functional knowledge is connected to all projects. There is increased flexibility in being able to form and re-form cross-functional teams. These teams can monitor their own localized business environments and move quickly to adapt to changes in them. Matrices facilitate mechanisms for dealing with multiple sources of power. By allocating functional staff to one or more projects on a permanent or semi-permanent basis, loyalties to the projects are built. Matrix structures allow for flexible use of human resources and the efficient use of support systems.

Disadvantages

Matrix structures are complex and can be administratively expensive. They can be difficult to introduce. There can be confusion over who is ultimately responsible for staff and project outcomes, particularly if things go wrong. The dual arrangement and need for enhanced communications between the 'arms' of the matrix can increase the potential for conflict, particularly between the functional and project managers. Unhelpful power struggles and conflict can arise. Staff may have to juggle their time between different projects or divisions and project managers may make competing and inconsistent demands on staff who work across more than one team.

Matrix structures work well when:
- a dual focus on unique product demands and technical specialization is crucial;
- there is pressure for high information-processing capacity;
- there is pressure for shared resources (e.g. resources are scarce).

Source: Adapted by Cummings, T. and Worley, C. (2009), *Organization Development and Change* (9th edn), Mason, OH: Thomson South-Western, from McCann, J. and Galbraith, J.R. (1981), 'Interdepartmental Relations' in Nystrom, P.C. and Starbuck, W.H. (eds) *Handbook of Organizational Design: Remodelling organizations and their environment*, vol. 2, New York: Oxford University Press.

Activity 3.2

Matrix-type organizations occur frequently in construction, aerospace, marketing and management consulting firms in which professionals work together on a project (Koontz, 2010). Using your general knowledge, attempt to design a matrix structure for the way the Beautiful Buildings Company, as a whole, might operate.

New organizational forms

The main point about new organizational forms is that they are an attempt to go beyond the classic bureaucratic models. Figure 3.3 illustrates the transition from bureaucracy to what Morgan (1989) calls the 'project organization' and the 'loosely coupled organic network'.

According to Morgan (1989), the project organization carries out most of its activities through project teams. Functional departments exist but only to play a supporting role. The main work of the organization is done wholly through teams that rely for their success on being 'dynamic, innovative, powerful and exciting' and to which senior management tries to give free rein within the strategic direction of the organization:

The organization is much more like a network of interaction than a bureaucratic structure. The teams are powerful, exciting, and dynamic entities. Co-ordination is informal. There is frequent cross-fertilization of ideas, and a regular exchange of information, especially between team leaders and the senior management group. Much effort is devoted to creating shared appreciations and understandings of the nature and

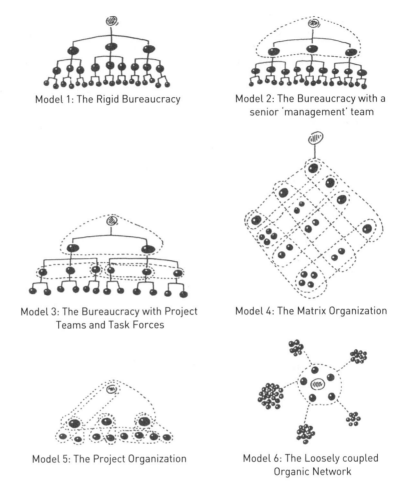

Model 1: The Rigid Bureaucracy

Model 2: The Bureaucracy with a senior 'management' team

Model 3: The Bureaucracy with Project Teams and Task Forces

Model 4: The Matrix Organization

Model 5: The Project Organization

Model 6: The Loosely coupled Organic Network

Figure 3.3 From bureaucracies to matrix, project and network organizations

Source: Reprinted by permission of Sage Publications, Inc. Morgan, G. (1989) *Creative Organization Theory. A Resource Book*, London: Sage, p. 66. Copyright © 1989 by Sage.

identity of the organization and its mission, but always within a context that encourages a learning-oriented approach. The organization is constantly trying to find and create the new initiatives, ideas, systems, and processes that will contribute to its success.

(Morgan, 1989, p. 67)

The project organization has overlapping characteristics with what Mintzberg (1983, p. 262) calls the 'Adhocracy'. The adhocracy, as its name suggests, is an *ad hoc* group of people (mainly professionals) who are brought together for a single purpose associated with a particular project. The team is usually short-lived and once the project is complete the team will disband – for example a group of professionals coming together to make a film. Adhocracies are characterized by having few formal rules and regulations or standardized routines. The shape of the organization is flat, but with horizontal differentiation generally high because adhocracies are staffed mainly by professionals, each with their own specialism.

The project organization usually employs its own staff. The adhocracy may also do this but may additionally have staff who work on a contract basis in contrast with Morgan's (1989) description of the loosely coupled organic network. In terms of a continuum of organizational forms, this type of network organization might be seen as furthest from the rigid bureaucracy. The loosely coupled organic network describes a form of structure that, rather than employing large numbers of people directly, operates in a subcontracting mode. The small number of permanent staff set the strategic direction and provide the necessary operational support to sustain the network. However, while project teams and adhocracies have limited lives, the loosely coupled network can be a permanent structure. Figure 3.4 depicts three types of network: internal, vertical and dynamic, whilst Illustration 3.7 sets out the advantages and disadvantages of network organizations.

Illustration 3.7

Advantages and disadvantages of network organizations

Advantages

They enable flexible and adaptive responses to fast-moving environments and have the potential to create 'the best of the best' organization to focus resources on customers and markets. Due to the fast pace and flexible nature each organization can leverage its distinctive competence. This structure can expand rapidly if needed. In addition, they can produce synergistic results.

Disadvantages

Managing lateral relations across autonomous organizations is difficult. It is also difficult motivating members to give up some of their autonomy to join the network. There are also issues relating to sustaining membership, and benefits can be problematic. Networks may give partners access to knowledge and technology that one partner may want to keep confidential.

Network structures

- work well when operating environments are complex and uncertain;
- fit organizations of all sizes;
- fit situations where organizational specialization and innovation are critical;
- operate well in worldwide operations.

Source: Cummings, T. and Worley, C. (2009), *Organization Development and Change* (9th edn), Mason, OH: Thomson South-Western.

Internal networks

According to Snow *et al.* (1992, p. 11), the internal network 'typically arises to capture entrepreneurial and market benefits without having the company engage in much outsourcing'. Internal networks are typical of situations where an organization owns most or all of the assets associated with its business. However, it has usually created 'businesses within the business' that, although still owned by the organization as a whole, operate independently in terms of the discipline of the market. The argument is that if they are subject to market forces they will constantly seek to improve performance. A typical example

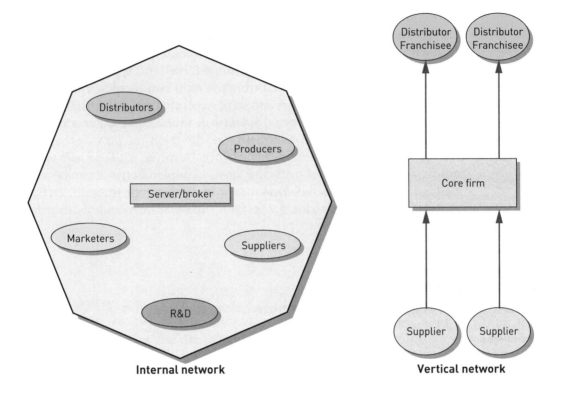

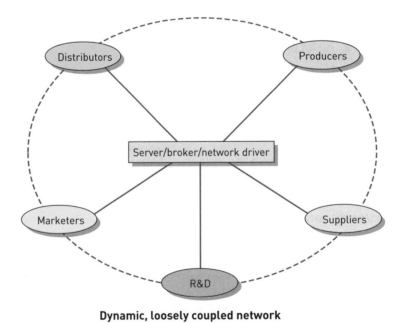

Figure 3.4 Common types of network

would be a training and development unit that, on the one hand, 'sells' its services to its parent organization and, on the other, seeks to sell its services outside. The internal network is similar to Morgan's (1989) description of a project organization.

Vertical networks

The vertical network (Hinterhuber and Levin, 1994) is typical of the situation where the assets are owned by several firms but are dedicated to a particular business. This is similar to what Snow *et al.* (1992, p. 13) call a 'stable' network that consists of 'a set of vendors ... nestled around a large "core" firm, either providing inputs to the firm or distributing its outputs'. Thus the core organization spreads asset ownership and risk across a number of other independent organizations and gains the benefits of dependability of supply and/or distribution. Toyota could be perceived as the core firm within a stable network of subcontractors, many of which had plants within the production complex surrounding Toyota in Toyota City (Clegg, 1990, referring to Cusamano, 1985).

Dynamic, loosely coupled networks

For Snow *et al.* (1992, p. 14), the dynamic network organization is the one that has 'pushed the network form to the apparent limit of its capabilities'. This form operates with a lead firm (sometimes called the 'server', 'broker' or 'network driver') that identifies and assembles assets which are owned by other companies. The lead firm may, itself, provide a core skill such as manufacturing or design. However, in some cases the lead firm may merely act as broker. The dynamic network is probably the form nearest to Morgan's loosely coupled organic network.

Illustration 3.8 describes TFW Images, a communications and image design organization where the lead firm provides the core skill of design and 'brokers' other activities such as photography and illustration, printing, translation and marketing.

However, whether dynamic networks operate in a partial or pure broker capacity, they are unlikely to function effectively without good and effective communications between their component parts. This is what is likely to distinguish dynamic or loosely coupled organic networks from the more 'in-house' internal and stable networks. For instance, TFW Images could not operate without fast and effective information technology links to the other organizations. Telecommunications links enable TFW Images' design team to send its output anywhere to be modified, marketed, printed or manufactured. Except for its relatively permanent status, the company might be likened to what some are now calling the 'virtual organization', particularly given its link-up with Omni-Graphics.

Illustration 3.8

TFW Images

TFW Images was formed in 1989 by two former employees of IBM who became the managing director and creative director of the new company and were very soon joined by a sales director. The main business of TFW Images is communications in its widest sense. Examples of its activities are designing corporate brochures such as annual reports as well as advertising material, designing and organizing conferences and all the material that goes with them, creating company logos and other symbols of corporate identity.

TFW Images' main client was IBM. In fact, the rise of the company coincided with the large-scale changes IBM went through as it refocused its efforts away from large-scale business computing markets towards personal computers. As technology began to displace jobs, TFW Images was able to take advantage of the willingness of companies such as IBM to outsource some of their design requirements.

In a volatile market one reason for the company's success is its ability to maintain a flexible structure that could be tailored to the demands of the market. Essentially, TFW Images is an organization that 'brokers' services from other organizations to bring its products to the market. Rather than employing printers, photographers, illustrators, market researchers and additional writers and designers directly, it closely associates with other companies and independent consultants who offer these services. Telecommunications facilitate the transfer of the part-finished products from one sector of the network to another.

Most recently, TFW Images has joined in partnership with Omni-Graphics, a well-established design company operating in publishing and arts. Given the equality of skills and size of the two organizations, the benefits of the partnership come from their complementary activities (TFW Images is business oriented while Omni-Graphics is arts oriented) and the financial advantages that will flow from this. The management of the two partner organizations will remain separate and both will keep their own names. Thus, to clients nothing will have changed. Yet, conceptually and financially, a new overarching organization has been 'virtually' created.

(This is a real example in which the names of the companies have been changed.)

The virtual organization

Virtual organizations use information and communication technology to link people, assets and ideas to create and distribute things without having to rely on conventional organizational boundaries and locations. They have been defined as 'a geographically distributed organization whose members are bound by a long-term common interest or goal, and who communicate and coordinate their work through information technology' (Ahuja and Carley, 1998, p. 742). Because of their dependence on information technology, the people in them seldom meet (Burkhard and Horan, 2006). Illustration 3.9 summarizes the key attributes of the virtual organization.

It seems clear from Illustration 3.9 that network (particularly dynamic network) and virtual organizations are suited to organizational environments that are themselves dynamic. The emphasis in these forms of organization is on horizontal rather than vertical structuring and the concept of partnership rather than command and control. However, organizations structured on these principles have implications for employment and the reward expectations of employees, whether full-time, part-time, contract or in other kinds of relationships with the organization. Network and virtual organizations are only able to offer stable, secure employment to a few. The idea of the ultra-flexible firm is attractive for the owners and core staff,

Illustration 3.9

Characteristics of the virtual organization

- Informal communication is high because of a general lack of rules, procedures and reporting relationships. Formal communication is less because there is less formal hierarchy in the organization.
- Communication networks: extensive informal communication reveals patterns of communication.
- Groups exist, dispersed and connected by electronic communications,

but the group members do not meet much if at all.
- They are non-hierarchical and decentralized (in theory at least).
- Virtual organizations are less permanent than alternative structures and can break apart when their objectives are met.

Source: Ahuja, M. and Carley, K. (1998), 'Network structure in virtual organizations', *Organization Science*, 10(6), pp. 741–57.

but can bring a sense of 'being used' to those who are employed on a short-term contract basis, particularly if these people are employed in temporary, perhaps part-time, less skilled, lower-paid jobs. Lack of commitment may not be restricted to the lower paid. More highly paid consultants and contractors will give service as long as it suits them, but may leave as soon as something more attractive comes along.

The main issue for organizations is not whether one form of structure is any better than another. It is whether the structure currently adopted is one that is able to facilitate the achievement of the organization's purpose and respond to the need for organizational change in the prevailing environmental circumstances.

Illustration 3.10

Post-bureaucratic organization

A post-bureaucratic model of organizations assumes 'shifting intra and extra-organizational boundaries, recourse to a contingent labour force, teamwork and consensual decision making' (Briand and Bellemare, 2006, p. 65) but there are serious questions about the extent to which organizations like this actually exist and whether employees are more emancipated.

Briand and Bellemare (2006) review an attempt by a Canadian public scientific research centre to adopt a post-bureaucratic structure. Staff numbers reduced by about 25 per cent, divisions were merged, management levels were reduced and performance indicators introduced. Government funding reduced for the centre. Sound familiar? In theory the reforms were an attempt to go post-bureaucratic, for instance:

- placing much greater focus on servicing consumers not on itself;
- focusing on results above processes;
- linking funding more closely to performance.

Reforms were far-reaching but led to 'disorder and insecurity' (p. 72). A problem that arose was a clash of values. Post-bureaucratic models are rooted in private-sector values (efficiency, teamwork, innovation) and these conflicted with stronger concerns for ethical and democratic values. They found that the new organization, as experienced by employees, intensified surveillance and produced a new structure of domination. The case raises doubts whether anything approaching a post-bureaucratic form was achieved in this instance.

Structuration theory, actor-networks and institutional theory

Structuration theory

So far, we have emphasized the tangible side of design and structure. However, structuration theory offers an alternative view of organizational structure as structuration theorists regard structure, not so much as 'patterned regularity' but, as something that emerges from 'the routine behaviour of people, (which in turn) influences those behaviours' (Cunliffe, 2008, p. 37).

Organizations have structure, within which the departments and divisions are used to arrange and contain distinct, but sometimes overlapping, activities. It is in these structures that people (whom Giddens terms 'actors') do their work. Structuration theory, developed by Giddens (1984, 1991), focuses on the reciprocal nature of interactions between structures and the actors within them. Organizational structures allow us to do some things but not others; they give certain freedoms but also lay down boundaries within which these freedoms are exercised.

As well as departmental and divisional structures, structure can be seen in the rules and operating procedures that have to be followed; job descriptions are an example. These procedures influence what we do and how we do things. Consider what you would do differently at work if you were liberated from the constraints of your organization's structure. However, by abiding by the rules and following procedures, we enforce, reinforce and perpetuate them.

Hence there is a relationship between actions and structure. Giddens (1991, p. 204) explains structuration theory as offering a way of understanding how actors create the social systems in which they work while simultaneously being creations of them. We create structures and then become dependent upon them.

Consequently, actors have to be knowledgeable in relation to the social systems in which they act. They need to know how the systems function and what will be the consequences of the actions that they contemplate or enact. Supplementing this general awareness of actions and outcomes is a need to be thoughtful and reflective about oneself. Reflection helps actors to monitor what they are doing and to change and adjust future actions. By virtue of their knowledge and reflection actors are free agents to decide whether they will contribute, or not, to events. Knowledge and reflection give at least limited power to intervene and try to influence what is going on.

According to structuration theory, structures exist only in the sense that actors/agents continue to reinforce them. In a bureaucratic organization it is only by routine referral of decisions to, say, a Director of This and That, that that part of the structure functions. If actors ignore the director, then that part of the structure would not exist, except in the flesh. So structures only exist in so far as we continue to reinforce them. They do not exist in and by themselves.

Giddens (2001, p. 668) argues that although we are constrained by aspects of society the same aspects 'do not determine what we do'. Drivers can choose to drink and drive albeit at greater risk of accident and punishment. We are not simply unquestioning followers of society's norms and values – people do make choices. Social structures and individual actions are therefore linked and are in a constant state of renewal. There are democratic political processes for electing leaders of nations that have evolved over centuries. The leaders influence government actions and the actions of government agents such as local authorities and the police. If all voters refused to vote, the political structure would have to change.

Sometimes at work you might have thought that 'the structure gets in the way' or 'the structure won't let this good idea happen'. However if we see structures not as a fixed thing that organizations are built upon but as a dynamic thing, a set of rules and procedures that can be changed, then new views open up. Of course, from a practical point of view it may be very sensible to conclude that 'the structure will get in the way' and move on to something more fruitful. However, from a critical point of view, structuration theory provides a new perspective on structure; seeing it as a social construction and as a collective consciousness.

Structuration and change

What this means for organizational change is that the paths followed and outcomes achieved are influenced by how actors understand the organization and the social settings that they are in. In similar organizations in terms of size and product/market, facing the same or similar business challenges, it is the actors' pattern and depth of understanding that explain why different strategic paths are followed and why different outcomes are reached.

Sarason (1995) also uses the idea of organizational identity to explain why organizations differ. As well as seeing the outcomes of change initiatives being dependent upon how well actors understand their organizations, outcomes are also shaped by a sense of identity. Do actors see their organization as a dynamic risk-taker not afraid to take bold decisions and learn from mistakes or as a nervous and cautious place? Illustration 3.11 shows how organizational identity can both restrain and catalyze change.

Chu and Smithson (2007) give an account of applying structuration theory to an attempt by a major motor manufacturer to implement e-business, claiming that structuration theory was useful:

> ... in understanding the interaction between the e-business initiative (agency) and the organizational structures. It facilitated the examination of the heterogeneous systems of meaning, power relations and norms of the different stakeholder groups. The interaction of agency and structure was easy to apply ... It also helped us to understand the complex structures that guide, facilitate and contain peoples' working lives while the notion of duality shows how these structures are themselves constructed, maintained and sometimes changed by the people concerned.
>
> (Chu and Smithson, 2007, p. 386)

By duality, they mean that 'structure is both the medium and the outcome of human interaction' (p. 372).

Illustration 3.11

Changing organizational identity

One of us worked for an organization that provided technical and management consulting to manufacturing and retail supply chains. For about 70 years it provided services to organizations only in high-labour-cost countries largely in northern Europe and North America. For decades this strong organizational identity impacted upon all discussions and decisions and shaped strategic direction. The company would never do business with low-labour-cost producers even though business would have been easy.

Slowly, however, as new manufacturing capacity in southern Europe and Asia came on stream in the 1980s and became an undeniable threat to European and North American companies, new business opportunities emerged and the organizational identity began to transform. Suddenly it was OK to talk about working with low-cost producers and this led to what, for the organization, was a transformational strategic change. For decades, strategic actions reinforced the same organizational identity but then new actions began to signal a new identity.

Giddens introduced the concept of structuration to explain how social structure is made and re-made. Structure and action are intertwined since the constant repetition of action strengthens the constraining structure. Giddens called this the duality of structure: 'all social action presumes the existence of structure. But at the same time structure presumes action because "structure" depends on the regularities of human behaviour' (2001, p. 669). Structuration theory explains therefore how the constant repetition of behaviour perpetuates structures whether they be good, bad or indifferent. It is only through behavioural change that old structures and the constraints that go with them are dismantled and re-made.

Actor-Network Theory (ANT)

The actor-network concept (Latour, 2005) recognizes that actors build networks involving other actors which can be human or non-human (individuals, groups or animals). Non-human actors could be management systems in place before a change is attempted (Langstrand and Elg, 2012) or a species around which human actors are manoeuvring. For instance, conservationists dedicated to the reintroduction of the Red Kite in England would see the bird as an actor in the network. Actor-networks can also be seen operating on a global level. The decision to invade and occupy Iraq involved political networks of institutions and key individuals such as presidents and prime ministers, anti-war groups, arms manufacturers and construction companies, among others. Gao (2005) applied ANT to analyze change in China's telecommunications market. The market was defined as a non-human actor and the public, the state and the operators made up three groups of human actors. Stanforth (2007) applied ANT to help understand the causes of e-government success or failure.

Actors create networks and thus themselves – but these networks are undergoing constant transformation and renewal. At a point in time we can imagine a social entity to be made up of interconnecting networks but 'there is no social order. There are only endless attempts at ordering through the formation and stabilization of networks' (Stanforth, 2007, p. 39). Think of the past few months in your life. Perhaps you have made new friends and contacts who sympathize with what you are trying to achieve. In or out of work, they may open up some of the resources that you need. Perhaps there are one or two actors that you have given up on and who, if you get your way, will not feature in your network much longer.

Van der Duim and van Marwijk (2006) use ANT to explain innovation in the sense that innovation means new 'patterns of coordination between people and organizations, technologies and environmental phenomena' (p. 450). In the case of an organization, for example one trying to implement a new project, ANT helps to explain how the social order is built. It involves the idea of 'translation' which involves explaining things in ways that persuade actors to fit with what a network is trying to achieve. Conservationists would try to persuade farmers to adopt particular land management practices that will raise breeding populations of birds and animals. Objections and queries by farmers, perhaps about economics, might be met by rationalizations of species decline and the non-financial value of biodiversity. Successful translation involves four stages:

1 *Problematization*: here the project is 'sold' to actors as a way of tackling their problems if they sign up to it.
2 *Interessement*: this is about translating/projecting the rationale for and the concerns that go with a project onto others involved and then stabilizing a network.
3 *Enrolment*: if interessement occurs then the behaviour of those involved is geared to achieving the outcomes desired by the enrolling actors.
4 *Mobilization*: if enrolment is successful then a new network will exist that works towards outcomes and solutions that fit the initial rationale for project set-up.

One of the features of recent and contemporary business and public management is the growth of networks in getting things done. For example, public spending constraints, the sheer size and complexity of projects, the specialist knowledge needed and the risks involved have led to much more collaboration between organizations in a sector and/or a region. ANT explains how and why the networks that are initiated are more or less successful. It describes how ways of ordering at time 1 and which are not capable of delivering are altered, so that they are viable at time 2. If the four stages of translation are achieved the outcome is known as a *collectif*. Something that could not be achieved before is achievable through the collectif.

ANT was also used to study change in a US telecommunications company (Sarker, Sarker and Sidorova, 2006). Examining the failure of change, they observed that while leadership, vision and communication were put forward as key ingredients of change success, top management needed to '(re)define the interests of human and non-human elements in the organization consistent with those of the initiative' (p. 81). It is not just about top management sharing a vision but about making connections between the interests of multiple actors and the global mission held by leadership. It is also about persuading others that their interests are best served by connecting up to the global vision.

Dent (2003) explored ANT in relation to a UK hospital threatened with closure. For instance, a hospital contains networks of professional groups of clinicians, managers and administrators and it is networked with external organizations under the National Health Service umbrella. For long periods these networks can be fairly stable, albeit showing minor reconfiguration as interests evolve. Periodically, something happens to disturb the relative peace such as new legislation or new government directives and targets, with subsequent disturbance to the roles of professionals and their relationships to managers, noting of course that many professionals are also managers. Dent found that interessement, the coming together of agents into a network, involves 'persuasion, intrigue, calculation and rhetoric' (Miller, 1992) and that these tools were used in the processes of actors reconfiguring to help their network resist the disturbances. Using ANT, Dent was able to 'delineate more clearly the complex configuration of relationships within which a hospital is embedded. In particular, it facilitated the exploration of the changing professional–management relations' (p. 123).

'Translation' helps to understand how the different interests of the several actors become aligned into a socio-technical arrangement. Even non-human actors are seen to have interests, e.g. the interests of skylarks are appropriated into the interests of human actors in a conservation scheme. Collectively, the interests of other actors are appropriated and translated into the interests of each actor. When interests are internalized by the several actors then an actor-network exists.

Figure 3.5 shows actors in a speed reduction initiative in a particular locality. Double-headed arrows represent alignment of interests of the three initiating actors. This diagram is a simple model to which could be added national government, which has road safety targets, as well as self-styled road safety groups. The model shows drivers as being a target of the actor-network and uninvolved in interest sharing. Of course, one could represent drivers' interests but for simplicity they are not shown.

The socio-political context includes pressure put upon police and local government to reduce accidents and injuries and the general efforts to raise awareness of the dangers of excessive speed. There may be localized pressures, such as the presence of schools or an accident 'black spot'. An additional interest affecting drivers is the punitive regime, that is, what happens to them if they are convicted of speeding. In time, the socio-political contexts change and the interests of the actors change. If drivers' attitudes to speeding changed such that ignoring speed limits became much less common then the need for an actor-network would diminish. If the penalties in the form of fines for speeding were substantially reduced or increased this would impact upon the interests of law enforcement actors.

Actor-network theorists regard structure 'as the process of organizing' people, technology, knowledge and other things into a stable network (Cunliffe, 2008, p. 49). Illustration 3.12 provides an example of just one form of structure.

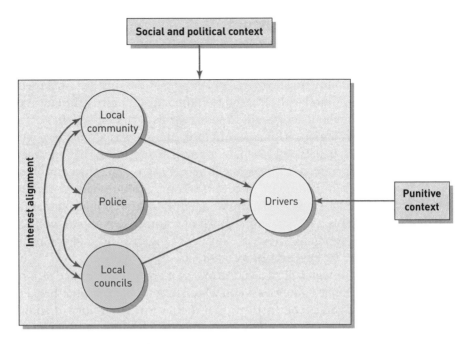

Figure 3.5 Actor Network

Illustration 3.12

Plane Stupid

Protest groups are a feature of our times and in December 2008 one group made the headlines for 'invading' Stansted Airport near London. Stansted is a busy regional airport, so much so that there are plans to build another runway, much to the consternation of the locals. Protesters are often well educated and/or middle-class people of all ages and associate with a group called Plane Stupid.

What is of interest here is the way the group organizes. It is said to be based on the 'rhizome concept' developed by Deleuze and Guatteri as a non-hierarchical way of connecting people to share ideas. Taking the name from the type of plant, the rhizome connects any point in the group to all other points. It is not built around units but around dimensions. It does not have a beginning or end, rather it has a middle from which it keeps growing.

Unlike classic organizational structures which have lines and positions, the rhizome has only lines of connection. Anyone who has dug a root of potatoes will know what the rhizome looks like – there are lots of potatoes all connected to each other and to the original seed potato from which everything grew. The rhizome organization uses horizontal connections and communications, unlike the vertical, horizontal and hierarchical communications found in typical structures that resemble family trees.

Whatever we think of their tactics of disruption, for protest groups this way of organizing seems effective and for students of organization structure quite interesting.

Source: Deleuze, G. and Guattari, F. (1980), *A Thousand Plateaus: Capitalism and schizophrenia*, translated by B. Massum, 2004; Gourlay, G. and Montague, B. (2008), 'Meet the plane stoppers', *Sunday Times*, 14 December, p. 18.

Institutional Theory

The earlier part of this chapter dealt with structures as if they are a rational choice; things that are shaped by internal drives for improvement and by best fit with environmental pressures and opportunities. Institutional theory, which has much in common with structuration theory, emphasizes the cultural influences on decisions about design and structure (Amis and Aissaoui, 2013). The people who decide what organizations should look like are 'suspended in a web of values, norms, rules, beliefs and taken for granted assumptions that are at least partially of their own making' (Barley and Tobert, 1997, p. 93). The combination of these things gives the culture of the organization its unique identity and the culture influences decisions about structure which may be sub-optimal. Rather than seeing organizations as 'rational actors', albeit operating in a complex world, institutional theory 'views organizations as captives of the institutional environment in which they exist' (Tolbert and Zucker, 1983, p. 22).

Through culture, institutions work within a bounded rationality which restricts the range of responses and which raises the likelihood that certain types of behaviour will occur. Institutional theory is not a theory of change but it is a way of explaining the similarities of arrangements that are often found in a sector and can explain why things do not change. Before going further though it is necessary to distinguish between an organization and an institution. Barley and Tobert (1997, p. 94) describe institutions as 'socially constructed templates for action, generated and maintained through ongoing interactions' and herein lies the similarity to structuration. They go on to define institutions as 'shared rules and typifications that identify categories of social actors and their appropriate activities or relationships' (p. 96).

Business organizations can be thought of as existing and operating in institutional fields; each field having a particular set of assumptions and practices. Organizations in the same sector are influenced by the same field and this explains why they structure and operate in very similar ways. Institutions are created out of action but, once created they tend to restrict actions within them. Hence we find institutions inside organizations and the structures that are found in organizations reflect those institutions. A good analogy is with speech and grammar. The sentence 'The dog ran after the cat' has a particular meaning. If 'cat' and 'dog' are transposed the sentence has a different meaning. Grammar brings structure to speech and institutions bring structure and meaning to organizations. Another analogy is to the idea of scripts, such that people are playing to scripts in their day-to-day behaviour. For example, we defer to the same people for decisions even though we know they will give us the same scripted answer – perhaps something like, 'It's a good idea but don't bother pushing it because Jim in Marketing doesn't like it'.

Johnson, Smith and Codling (2000, p. 573) define scripts as 'the cognitive schema informing behaviour and routines appropriate in particular contexts'. They applied institutional theory to privatization; the deinstitutionalization of public-sector templates and the institutionalization of private-sector templates. To enact change, the scripts used by actors have to change. New scripts develop through experiences as people move from a familiar set of routines to experimentation with another. Barley and Tobert (1997) also saw scripts as more than cognitive schema considering them as behavioural regularities, that is, something that can be observed. They suggest that the accreditation processes used by universities are examples of scripts in action as elaborated on in Illustration 3.13.

Illustration 3.13

University accreditation: Institutionalization in practice

Universities are very sensitive to league tables and in particular to their position in them. The tables rank universities on a combination of factors like staff/student ratios, research income and the percentage of staff with doctorates. Let's face it, when we know how we are being measured we tend to divert attention into bettering our performance on those measures. One of the accolades that business schools seek is accreditation by bodies such as the Association of MBAs (AMBA) and the European Quality Improvement System (EQUIS). A common accreditation strategy is as follows:

The school applies for accreditation having checked itself against broad criteria set by the accrediting body.

If the application is accepted, the school writes a set of self-assessment documents (SADs) detailing and reflecting on its performance in relation to accreditation criteria. Changes to operating methods are likely to better align with the criteria.

A small panel of senior academics drawn from top business schools is despatched to the school who entertain them for several days during which the panel meets and questions a range of groups representing the school's activities (research, teaching, consulting and so on).

The panel writes a report including recommendations and conditions for accreditation that is considered by the board of the accrediting body.

The actors are playing out a script. As well as scripts operating at a grand level we can also see scripts at individual level and influencing individual participation in the accreditation visits. The school, if it is smart, will be briefing groups of employees before they have meetings with the panel and debriefing them afterwards so that issues can be passed on to the next group. Those in charge bang on with exhortations such as, 'We can be really proud of X so make sure you tell them about it but make sure they never get to know about Y'.

We are not suggesting that the outcomes can be taken for granted or that the processes are not useful; far from it. Useful recommendations and ideas for change usually come out of these processes, and accreditation, if achieved, is a valuable thing. Yet the scripts used lead to similar outcomes and push schools to look and behave in similar ways. The scripts used in these events lead to a bounded and institutionalized level of performance improvement.

Institutional theory explains how the principles of organizing are accepted and perpetuated and how conformity to norms leads to particular outcomes. Survival of the main protagonists (typically top managers) and conformance to norms explain actions more so than rational responses in the search for better performance. For example, institutional theory provides a good theoretical explanation for the recent financial crisis. Ashby, Peters and Devlin (2013, p. 2681) found that:

Structural features of financial institutions (for example compensation arrangements) hindered individual reflexivity and critical evaluation and reinforced the natural tendency of individuals to pursue their own self-interest by making extreme risks seem both acceptable and deniable. At the industry level, the observation that building strong collective beliefs of invulnerability was widespread supports this finding.

These beliefs were reinforced by optimistic economic forecasts and weak interventions by regulators. Ashby and colleagues argue that introducing more regulation and capping banker bonuses, for example, will not change the underlying problematic attitudes to risk in the financial sector; deeper cultural change geared around better risk management procedures is called for.

Institutional theory is useful to explain why things exist as they do, and stay as they are, but is less informative about how change to institutions occurs (Kondra and Hinings, 1998). One of the reasons for this is the idea of *isomorphism* which refers to the tendency of organizations in the same field to adopt the same or similar structures and ways of thinking and doing, which lead to isomorphism of performance. Indeed, performance standards can themselves become institutionalized. Three reasons for this can be put forward (Kondra and Hinings, 1998):

1 People who think they can see ways of improving things do not bother to pursue their ideas because compliance with norms is much easier.

2 Mimetic behaviour occurs (that is, when organizations copy each other's behaviour) and is perhaps more likely to persist when performance measures are not well defined as is the case with the public-sector organizations. Day, Armenakis, Field and Norris (2012) use mimetic behaviour to explain why a university simply copied downsizing tactics being used elsewhere and by taking such an uncritical approach to what it was doing created big problems for itself.

3 Mimetic behaviour can also occur because of risk aversion. A dominant coalition (such as a management team) can argue that not implementing what might be a performance-enhancing action in the short term is an efficient strategy in the long term when the risks of the actions are considered. If the coalition can be confident of return X in the future, why seek greater than X when there is a risk that the actual returns could be less than X?

Greenwood and Hinings (1996) go further, however, in showing how institutional theory connects to a theory of change. They propose three characteristics of neo-institutional theory (neo-institutional theory includes developments to the original theory).

Institutional context – organizations embed institutions even though these institutions have little or no impact on performance. The professional partnership form of organizing stems from the philosophy that professionals in a business venture should be jointly liable for their professional decisions. Accountants and lawyers, for instance, typically organize as partnerships. Clearly it is an effective way of organizing, otherwise they would not keep doing it, but this is an institutional feature rather than a rational analysis of the most efficient way to organize.

Templates – pressures from institutions push organizations in the same sector to adopt the same or similar forms and designs, that is, templates for organizing, shaped by underpinning ideas and values. These arise from mimetic behaviour and lead to isomorphism in the sector. Hence institutional theorists focus more on what they term populations of organizations in a particular field, seeing them as networked and interconnected and subject to the institutional pressures in the field. Universities illustrate the point well. There are about 100 universities in the UK which serve different segments of the market, but there are, arguably, more similarities between them than there are differences in the way they respond to the institutionalization of higher education.

Resistance to change – templates for organizing cover not just designs and forms but also ways of thinking and thus inertia. Institutional theory therefore emphasizes the stability of arrangements and while accepting that change occurs it sees change as 'reproduction and reinforcement of existing models of thought and organization' (p. 1027). It explains convergent and incremental change much more than radical change which is far more problematic. Greenwood and Hinings (1996) point out the reciprocal nature of the relations between an organization and the field it is in. A university, for instance, does what the field expects of it and behaves in ways that are acceptable to the field. Behaviours manifest as policies on a wide range of issues affecting staff and students (policies that would look very similar if put side by side), similar products delivered to students in similar ways, similar ways of allocating work to employees and similar ways of measuring performance.

To help explain the pace and scope of change two additional concepts are used: tight coupling and sectoral permeability (Greenwood and Hinings, 1996). Tight coupling occurs when a sector exerts a high level of influence and control over the structural templates that organizations in the sector use. Professional practices and public organizations are subject to high levels of regulation and expectations and are examples of tight coupling. Any new organization entering the field would be subject to such pressures to comply and conform. Contrast this with a new private business venture – let's say to design and manufacture fashion accessories. So long as it complies with the law no one is concerned about how it is organized or about how it organizes. Similarly, in new sectors that form around a technological breakthrough the institutional pressures will be less well developed so we could expect change to be less impeded by inertia.

Sectoral permeability describes how much a sector is insulated from others. A sector with low permeability experiences a low influx of people from other sectors so the transfer of ideas is within the sector, not across sectors. Where permeability is higher and people come into the sector from other sectors we would expect higher import of ideas and thus higher rates of radical change. Examples of where institutional theory has been used include analyzing change in an accounting and financial system (Tsamenyi, Cullen and Gonzalez, 2006), law firms (Sherer and Lee, 2002) and professional associations (Greenwood, Suddaby and Hinings, 2002).

Activity 3.3

Think of a small part of an organization that you know well and try to identify where the routine actions of people are creating structure and structural relationships.

Then consider why these situations exist, for example individual management styles, dominating personalities and organizational politics.

How amenable are these structures to change?

Activity 3.4

If you work in an organization, consider the institutional field that it operates within. Identify aspects of organizational design and structure that exist because of conformity to the field and not because in themselves they add value.

Influences on structure

Choosing how to structure is not straightforward and choices are closely linked to many factors as Figure 3.6 shows. As identified earlier, one of the most important links is the relationship between strategy and structure – as an organization changes its strategy to respond to environmental triggers, so should its structure change to maintain the strategy–structure relationship. However, apart from technological advances outside the organization, which may force changes in production methods or in the way that services are delivered, the organization's own use of technology, particularly information technology, will affect the way in which it is structured. The earlier discussion shows also how organizational structure is likely to change as organizational size increases.

Less tangible are the roles that organizational culture and politics play on structure one way or another. That is why in Figure 3.6 these two factors are shown as mediating variables rather than as direct influences. There is nothing set, however, in the way all these variables should be regarded. Figure 3.6 is offered as a helpful descriptive device for summarizing the factors that influence organizational forms rather than as a tried and tested model of how they work in practice. Even so, there is a body of literature that helps us understand which organizational structure is most appropriate to which set of circumstances. Before moving to this, it is worth pausing to think why 'good' or appropriate organizational structure is so important to the efficient and effective operation of organizations.

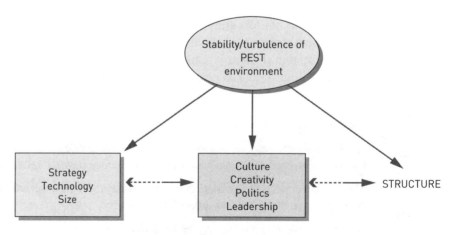

Figure 3.6 The determinants of organizational structure

The consequences of deficient organizational structures

The consequences of a deficient organizational structure are shown in Illustration 3.14. What is interesting about this list is that some of the main 'dysfunctions' listed (e.g. motivation and morale) could be regarded as having little to do with structure. Yet, as the other points make clear, structural deficiencies could very well be major contributing causes.

Illustration 3.14

Consequences of deficient organizational structures

There are a number of problems that so often mark the struggling organization and which even at the best of times are potential dangers. John Child suggests the following dangers that structural deficiencies exacerbate:

1 Motivation and morale may be depressed because:
   (a) Decisions appear to be inconsistent and arbitrary in the absence of standardized rules.
   (b) People perceive that they have little responsibility, opportunity for achievement and recognition of their worth because there is insufficient delegation of decision making. This may be connected with narrow spans of control.
   (c) There is a lack of clarity as to what is expected of people and how their performance is assessed – perhaps due to inadequate job definition.
   (d) People are subject to competing pressures from different parts of the organization due to absence of clearly defined priorities, decision rules or work programmes.
   (e) People are overloaded because their support systems are not adequate. Supervisors, for instance, have to leave the job to chase up materials and equipment as there is no adequate system for communicating what people need.

2 Decision making may be delayed and lacking in quality because:
   (a) Necessary information is not transmitted on time – perhaps due to an over-extended hierarchy.

   (b) Decision makers are too segmented into separate units and inadequately coordinated.
   (c) Decision makers are overloaded due to insufficient delegation on their part.
   (d) There are no adequate procedures for evaluating the results of similar decisions made in the past.

3 There may be conflict and a lack of coordination because:
   (a) There are conflicting goals that have not been structured into a single set of objectives and priorities. People are acting at cross-purposes. They may, for example, be put under pressure to follow departmental priorities at the expense of product or project goals.
   (b) People are working out of step with each other because they are not brought together into teams or because liaison mechanisms are poor.
   (c) The people who actually carry out operational work and who are in touch with changing contingencies are excluded from participating in work planning – a breakdown between planning and operations.

4 An organization may not respond innovatively to changing circumstances because:
   (a) It has not established specialized jobs concerned with forecasting and scanning the environment.
   (b) There is a failure to ensure that innovation and planning of change are mainstream activities backed up by top management through appropriate procedures to provide them with adequate priority, programming and resources.

Illustration 3.14 *continued*

(c) There is inadequate coordination between the people responsible for identifying changing market needs and the people who could provide solutions.

5 Costs may be rising rapidly, particularly in administration, because:

(a) The organization has a tall hierarchy with a high ratio of managers to workers.

(b) There is an excess of procedure and paperwork distracting people's attention away from productive work and requiring additional staff personnel to administer.

(c) Some or all of the other organization problems are present.

Source: Child, J. (1988), *Organizations: A Guide to Problems and Practice*, London: Paul Chapman.

Activity 3.5

1 *Considering an organization that you know well, to what extent do any of the five consequences of structural deficiencies listed in Illustration 3.14 apply to it?*

2 *If you think that some of these deficiencies are present, what does this imply for the way the organization is structured? What changes for the better could be made?*

Strategy–structure fit

For the purpose of this discussion the definition of strategy given by Johnson, Scholes and Whittington (2014, pp. 3–4) is used: 'strategy is the long-term direction of an organization'. There are two advantages of this definition:

1 It can include both deliberate, logical strategy and more incremental, emergent patterns of strategy, as well as allow for both deliberate and unplanned actions and outcomes.

2 It can include both strategies that emphasize difference and competition, and those that recognize the roles of cooperation and even imitation.

Strategies can exist at three levels: corporate level, business level and operational level (Johnson *et al.*, p. 7). In order to function effectively, an organization's structure should be in tune with its strategy. Changes in organizational strategy are nearly always linked to changes in its structure.

Chandler's strategy–structure thesis

Chandler (1962) found that the owner-managed companies that were predominant during the 1800s usually started with a single product line and a structure where the owner–manager took all major decisions and monitored the activities of employees. This type of organization has an 'agency' structure, given that key subordinates act as agents of the owner–manager to ensure their wishes (Miles and Snow, 1984b).

As companies grew they became more complex and were more likely to employ professional managers who began the process of dividing the organization into different functional areas. The appearance of the functional organization (around 1900) enabled growth to occur, particularly through acquiring suppliers, to ensure guaranteed inputs, and through market penetration. As strategies led to restructuring, Chandler concluded that structure follows strategy.

The 'structure follows strategy' dictum is widely accepted and the reason why different structures associated with different strategies was simply economic efficiency. Amburgey and Dacin (1994) show that although there is a strategy–structure relationship it is not a simple, one-way path; strategy has a stronger influence on structure than structure has on strategy.

Mintzberg's forces and forms

Mintzberg (1991) offers the concepts of forces and forms that can be loosely translated as strategy and structure. Figure 3.7 illustrates the seven forces, each of which is associated with a particular form. The seven forces which drive the organization are:

- The force for *direction*, which can be likened to having a 'strategic vision'. This gives a sense of where the organization must go as an integrated entity.
- The force for *efficiency*, which balances the costs and benefits – the lower the ratio of costs to benefits, the higher the efficiency. The force for efficiency tends to encourage standardization and formalization, focusing on rationalization and restructuring for economy.
- The force for *proficiency*, that is for carrying out tasks with high levels of knowledge and skills.
- The force for *concentration*, which means the opportunity for particular units to concentrate their efforts on serving particular markets. This is necessary in organizations that are diversified in structure.
- The force for *innovation*, which encourages the search for new products or services or for different ways of delivering them. The force for innovation encourages adaptation and learning.
- The forces for *cooperation* and *competition* are the forces Mintzberg calls 'catalytic'. Cooperation describes the pulling together of ideology, that is, the culture of norms, beliefs and values that 'knit a disparate set of people into a harmonious, cooperative entity' (Mintzberg, 1991, p. 55). Competition describes the pulling apart of politics in the sense of politics as the non-legitimate, technically non-sanctioned organizational behaviour. Mintzberg uses the term 'configuration' to describe the form an organization is driven towards by the system of forces (see Illustration 3.15).

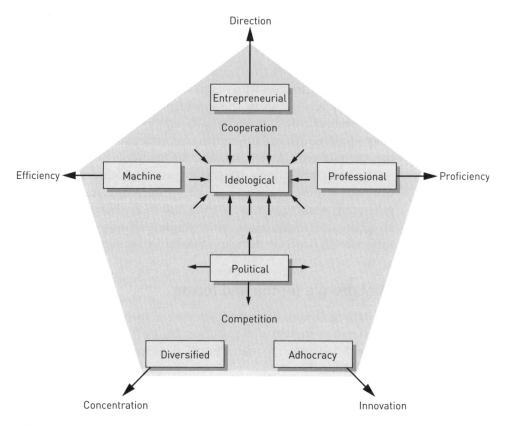

Figure 3.7 A system of forces and forms in organizations

Source: The Effective Organization: Forces and Forms, *Sloan Management Review*, Winter 1991, 32 (part 2) p. 55. (Mintzberg, H. 1991), Copyright © 1991 by Massachusetts Institute of Technology. All rights reserved. Distributed by Tribune Media Services.

Illustration 3.15

Mintzberg's organizational forms

- **Entrepreneurial form** – tends to be low in formalization and standardization, but high in centralization with authority located in a single person.
- **Machine form** – high formalization and standardization, centralized authority vested in rules and regulations, functional departments.
- **Professional form** – high in complexity and formalization, but low in centralization; allows the employment of trained specialist staff for the core work of the organization.
- **Adhocracy form** – very low in standardization and formalization, little hierarchy, much use of temporary project teams.

- **Diversified form** – a combination of functions and products, with products dominating; they can be of matrix form or organized as divisions on the basis of products/markets.

These five forms are based on Mintzberg (1979, 1983). His 1991 paper, on which much of this section is based, adds the *ideological* and *political* forms, giving as examples the Israeli kibbutz and a conflictual regulatory agency respectively. However, these two forms are uncommon.

The *entrepreneurial* form tends to dominate when the forces for direction are paramount. This tends to be in start-up and turnaround situations and in small, owner-managed organizations. The *machine* form tends to appear when the forces for efficiency become paramount, for instance in situations of mass production and mass service organizations. Hospitals, accounting practices and engineering consultancies illustrate the *professional* form of organization that results from the force for proficiency. The drive here is for perfecting existing skills and knowledge rather than inventing new ones. This is different from the force for innovation that pushes organizations into an *adhocracy* form, which is characterized by independent project teams with fluid structures. Finally, the *diversified* form arises as a result of the force for an organization to concentrate on more than one distinct product or market. Each division will have a different structure and enjoy considerable autonomy from the small central headquarters.

Mintzberg calls the fit between the forces and forms that organizations take 'configuration'. 'My basic point about configuration is simple: when the form fits, the organization may be well advised to wear it, at least for a time' (Mintzberg, 1991, p. 58). This argument supports the proposition that organizational structure should align with organizational strategy. The implications of this are that, as an organization's strategy changes, so must its structure if tensions, contradictions and, eventually, crises are not to ensue. However, strategy is not the only factor upon which structure is contingent.

Other influences on structure

Size

The classic study by Pugh *et al.* (1969) found that size (measured by the number of employees) was positively correlated to overall role specialization and formalization of procedures. Child (1988), from his studies of the effects of size on organizational performance, found that large organizations performed better when bureaucratically structured and vice versa for small organizations.

However, in current times, organizations could be considered large even though they do not directly employ very many people. For instance, organizations with self-governing profit-centres consisting of businesses in their own right (but supplying only the main organization), could be considered large, even though they do not employ, directly, all the individuals concerned. Therefore, the relationship of organizational size and structure is tenuous.

Technology

All organizations use technology of some sort to convert inputs into outputs and the choice of technology (e.g. small batch, large batch and mass production) has a big influence on organizational structure and particular forms of organizing (e.g. role specialization and formalization of work) are best suited to particular systems of production (Woodward, 1965). By contrast with Woodward, who concentrated on production technologies, Perrow (1967) defined technology more generally and suggested that technology could be viewed as a combination of two variables: 'task variability' and 'problem analyzability'. Thus a task that is highly routine would be low in task variability and vice versa. In other words, variability refers to the number of exceptional or unpredictable cases which have to be dealt with. Problem analyzability refers to the extent to which problems are clearly defined and can be solved by using recognized routines and procedures, that is whether a task is clearly defined or whether it is ambiguous in terms of the task itself or how it might be completed. Where task completion requires innovative thinking, it is likely to be low on problem analyzability.

Perrow used these two dimensions to construct a two-by-two matrix that provided a continuum of technology ranging from the routine to the non-routine as shown in Figure 3.8. The cells in the matrix represent four types of technology: routine, engineering, craft and non-routine.

Like Woodward, Perrow argued that each type of technology would produce the best organizational performance if linked to an appropriate structure. Consequently, the technologies described in cell 1 are most likely to fit well with mechanistic structures. Cell 2 technologies require mechanistic structures but with aspects of organic organizational forms. Cell 4 technologies link most closely to much 'looser' organic structures (perhaps of the matrix, project or network type) while cell 3 technologies require mainly organic structures with aspects of mechanistic bureaucracies.

Research in this area is very difficult to undertake because it needs to take place over long time periods. However, in their research on Italian manufacturers, Colombo and Delmastro (2002) found that advanced manufacturing technologies as well as new human resource management practices favour organizational change.

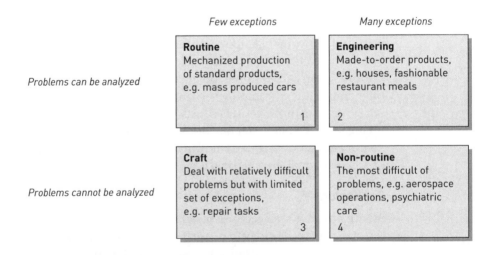

Figure 3.8 Perrow's technology classification

Source: Based on summaries by Robbins, S.P. (2003) *Organizational Behavior* (10th edn), Englewood Cliffs, NJ: Prentice Hall and Mullins, L. (2005) *Management and Organizational Behaviour* (7th edn), Harlow: Financial Times Prentice Hall.

Information technology

Information and communication technology gives managers the ability to push information closer to the point where it is used and to increase responsibility on employees to use it effectively. Information, communications and technology (ICT) has had the following impacts on structure (Mukherji, 2002):

- Supporting decentralization by enabling communication and control from a distance, and assisting matrix and network structures.
- Increasing the routinization of some jobs.
- Reducing hierarchy.
- Creating much closer links across supply chains.
- Making the boundaries between divisions in an organization and even between organizations fuzzier and less relevant.
- Revolutionizing how small businesses can operate, e.g. by Internet businesses.

Robbins (2003) talks of 'boundaryless' organizations where both internal and external boundaries are eliminated. He refers to Lucas's (1996) use of the term 'the T-form (or technology-based) organization'. The removal of internal vertical boundaries flattens the hierarchy with status and rank minimized. This type of organization uses cross-hierarchical teams, which are used to coordinating their own work. The removal of external barriers against suppliers has been mentioned already. With regard to customers, the increasing use of what Hollinger (2000) refers to as 'e-tailing' makes the buying of goods from a wide range of producers and retailers much easier for those linked up to the Internet.

The breaking down of organizational barriers extends also to the home/work boundary. Lyons (2000, p. 60) says:

> For many people, the division between work and life is becoming blurred ... people now live and work in the post-farm, post-factory setting. They travel, they work at home. They even work while they travel – in hotels, planes, cyber cafés, and at 'touch down spaces'.

This division is becoming blurred mainly because of the ability of workers to maintain contact with their offices and organizations through the use of email, tablets and mobile phones, which can also be used to send and accept emails and other telecommunications. Cooper (2000, p. 32) remarks: 'The future of employment seems to lie either in small and medium-sized businesses or in outsourced and portfolio working for virtual organizations.'

Illustration 3.16

ICT and retail banking

One of the most vivid examples of how technology impacts on structural change at sector and organization level is found in retail banking (Consoli, 2005). The main breakthroughs were:

1965   Automated bank statements are produced

1966   The first credit card in the UK

1967   Database management systems automate money transfer

1970s   Microprocessors enable branches to become fully automated

Illustration 3.16 *continued*

1970s	Automatic teller machines spread ('holes in the wall')
1982	Microchips in cards enable direct debiting
1990s	Internet banking enables services from anywhere

In conjunction with changes to the ways retail banking is regulated, technology has reshaped the speed and convenience of transactions. It has also increased consumers' exposure to fraud and for investors their ability to get money out relies upon the operating system working. Given recent events in financial markets it is easy to imagine a bank shutting down its e-banking systems in order to keep your money in times of emergency! Consoli (2005, p. 472) argues that technological change 'triggers the emergence and/or demise of activities, competences, processes and services at the firm

level. At industry level the pace of change is driven by the amount of interaction between organizations, suppliers, consumers and regulators.'

He found that the disappearance of competition between branches had led to the decline of the vertically integrated structures that had been commonplace. In their place there was much more need to coordinate a bigger range of services, some of which were outsourced. ICT was at the root of 'radical transformation' by incumbent organizations and enabled the entry of new organizations which reshaped the boundaries and structure of the industry.

In light of the credit crisis of 2008 we might wonder how much these structural changes enabled the creation of very high-risk (toxic) products that, coupled with a failure of corporate social responsibility, created the conditions for the crisis in the first place.

The influence of the external environment on structure

Environmental stability and turbulence

One of the best-known studies on the effects of the environment on organizational structure (Burns and Stalker, 1961) concluded that organizations had different structures depending on whether they operated in stable environments that changed little over time or in dynamic, changeable environments. Two main structural types were found: mechanistic structures that were more suited to stable unchanging environments; and organic structures which were more suited to the unpredictable, more dynamic environments.

Mechanistic structures conform to Morgan's models 1 and 2, shown in Figure 3.3 (bureaucracies and bureaucracies with a senior management team) and Mintzberg's 'machine' form of organization (see Illustration 3.14). Organic structures resemble Morgan's models 4, 5 and 6 and Mintzberg's 'adhocracy' and 'diversified' forms of organization.

Key characteristics of organic forms are the harnessing of knowledge and experience upon tasks rather than specialized task definitions, emphasis on communication across the organization (not just up and down) and fast changes to how tasks are defined. While the organic form is generally thought best for large organizations in complex environments, Sine *et al.* (2006) argue that the theory breaks down with new ventures in turbulent environments. They found that new ventures, which are by nature very flexible, can lack the benefits of structure such as role clarity and higher efficiency. New ventures with more role clarity and specialization in the founding management teams outperformed others.

Waldersee, Griffiths and Lai (2003), in a study of major changes in Australian organizations, found that mechanistic organizations could implement technological and structural change successfully but were not so good at implementing social change, e.g. attitudinal, behavioural and cultural. Organic organizations were good at technical, structural and social change.

Robbins (2003) also addresses the issue of environments specific to different parts of organizations. He suggests that environments can be characterized in terms of three key dimensions. The first is the *capacity* of the environment, which refers to the degree to which it can support growth. The second is the degree of *stability* in the environment; stable environments are low in volatility whereas unstable environments are characterized by a high degree of unpredictable change. The third is environmental *complexity*, that is the degree of homogeneity or heterogeneity among environmental elements. Given this three-dimensional definition of environment, Robbins concludes that the scarcer the capacity and the greater the degree of instability and complexity, the more organic a structure should be; the more abundant, stable and simple the environment, the more mechanistic a structure should be.

Socio-cultural influences

The discussion so far has concentrated on macro influences on organizational structure: size, technology and environment. Increasing size pushes organizations towards increasingly bureaucratic structures, which remain an efficient way to organize large-scale activities. By the same token, the desire of employees for more flexible ways of organizing their home/leisure/work relationships, coupled with the opportunities for self-employment and/or virtual forms of working, may force organizational structures into newer forms.

Regardless of the size of organizations and type of technology used, more flexible working patterns and ways of structuring the work appear to be increasing. An interesting issue, however, is whether this trend is a result of initiatives taken by employers for the sole benefit of business or in response to the changing expectations of the labour force. For instance, Cooper (2000, p. 32) says:

> The future of employment seems to lie either in small and medium-sized businesses or in outsourced and portfolio working for virtual organizations. Since the industrial revolution, managerial and professional workers have not experienced high levels of job insecurity, so will people be able to cope with permanent job insecurity without the security of organizational structure?

In contrast, Bevan (2000, p. 20) reporting on work/life balance found that employees who have benefited from more flexible work arrangements imply few difficulties as they choose arrangements to suit their particular home and life circumstances. The benefits to employers and businesses seem to outweigh the disadvantages.

It is difficult to know whether most people who work on production lines and supermarket checkouts would prefer to do something else. Work serves many purposes besides being a source of income. According to Robbins (2003), however:

> While more people today are undoubtedly turned off by overly specialized jobs than were their parents and grandparents, it would be naïve to ignore the reality that there is still a segment of the workforce that prefers the routine and repetitiveness of highly specialized jobs.

Not everyone is suited to working in highly organic or loosely structured networks, let alone working in virtual organizations.

People choose organizations as much as organizations choose people. Those working in organizations are more likely to remain in organizations whose structures, with their particular degrees of centralization, formalization, specialization and traditionalism, suit their individual and group preferences and needs. Designing organizational structures that satisfy the needs of those working in and associated with them is not straightforward. Indeed, designing organizational structures for change, while at the same time ensuring that the needs of the market and of employees are met, is as much an art as a science.

Organizational structure and change

There is no one best way to design organizational structures or any particular form that will guarantee successful performance. Depending on factors such as strategy, size, technology used, the degree of predictability of the environment and the expectations and lifestyle of employees, an organization could well be successful and respond to the need for change whether it was structured along bureaucratic, mechanistic lines or as one of the newer network forms.

Care must be taken, however, not to assume that these contingency relationships are straightforward and that, provided the 'formula' is learned and applied, success will result. Robbins (1993, p. 528), drawing on the work of Child (1972) and Pugh (1973), states that: 'Strategy, size, technology and environment – even when combined – can at best explain only fifty per cent of the variability in structure.' In addition, the idea that there is a one-way causal relationship between an organization's environment and its structure is questionable.

Illustration 3.17

Beyond hierarchy?

Oxman and Smith (2003) argue that structure is increasingly irrelevant to how work is done. They observe that the regularity of restructuring is testimony to how ineffective it is:

- Information technology cuts across the old boundaries.
- Performance management is often shaped by more than one party, i.e. it is not the old style of boss on subordinate – performance on projects cuts across this.
- Layoffs contribute to alienation of employees to an 'organization' and reduced relevance of what the 'organization' is.

- Networking in the managerial and professional classes supplements whatever the old structure is contributing and networking fills roles once taken by the organization.
- Knowledge management, storing and sharing of organizational learning and knowledge saps some of the power from traditional hierarchies in which it could be stored.
- Cross-unit cooperation is important to ensure that the best brains are attached to a project.

While organizations are influenced by their environments, some are able to exert some control over them – for example, oil producers by cutting or increasing production. The political environment can be influenced by lobbying, customers influenced through advertising and people's expectations of employment influenced by the way organizations design jobs. Organizations in monopoly markets are well placed to influence their environments. In times of high unemployment, the introduction of technology that significantly changes working practices will be easier because the bargaining power of employees is low.

If organizations are able, to some extent, to manipulate their environments to suit their strategies and structures, this will enable them to preserve existing structures and operational arrangements. The pressure to do this is evident from Mullins' (2005, p. 648) statement that: 'Developing organizations cannot, without difficulty, change their formal structure at too frequent an interval. There must be a significant change in contingency factors before an organization will respond.' This implies a considerable time lag between situational change and changes in structure. Therefore, even if changes in strategy, size, technology and environmental factors do build forces for changes in organizational structure, there are other factors that may accelerate or, more likely, impede this process.

Therefore, successful structural change is difficult to achieve without some sort of unintended adverse consequences. One context in which structure is routinely debated is in the provision of public services: for example, the possible ways in which healthcare and local government could be structured for optimum efficiency. Despite this clearly defined terrain, there is little information on whether the purported benefits of structural change ever arrive and whether any benefits outweigh the costs and disruption to services (Andrews and Boyne, 2012). In their study of local authorities, Andrews and Boyne (2012) found that impending structural change introduced levels of uncertainty such that the performance of the authorities deteriorated before new structures were implemented.

One of these factors is associated with the concept of 'strategic choice' (Child, 1972) and draws attention to the power of senior managers to choose which criteria they will use in assessing what organizational changes should take place. Managers who may lose power and/or position are unlikely to choose those alternatives that, from a logical–rational point of view, maximize the organization's interest. Robbins (1993, p. 528) summarizes this view of structure as the 'power–control' explanation of organizational structure, that is: 'an organization's structure is the result of a power struggle by internal constituencies who are seeking to further their interests'. Thus, given the discretion available to management, rather than changes in organizational structure being logically planned and implemented, what results will be a structure that 'emerges' to satisfy not only the imperatives of the internal and external environments, but the personalities and power needs of dominant stakeholders.

Structural inertia and population ecology

As we have emphasized, organizations scan their environments and change their designs accordingly. Usually this is incremental adjustment affecting only a small part of the business and part of being a good manager is the ability to adapt structures smoothly to bring about desired effects and avoid unintended outcomes that have adverse impacts on operations. Substantial changes to organizational designs and structures are much less frequently attempted.

From this perspective organizations are *adapting* to their environments using a form of 'social Darwinism' (Hannan and Freeman, 1979, p. 930). In what has become a classic paper in its field, Michael Hannan and John Freeman suggested, however, that not all of the variation that we can observe in the way organizations are structured can be explained by adaptation. They introduced the idea that there exists in organizations pressures and processes that bring about a level of structural inertia as Illustration 3.18 shows. Adaptive flexibility decreases with increasing inertia such that when inertia is high the organization is more likely to fall victim to the forces of natural selection – that is, cease operating. Internal forces creating inertia include:

- Past investment (sunk costs) in plant, technology and people that is not easily switched into other tasks (see Colombo and Delmastro, 2002).
- Decision makers having to work with incomplete information about environments (bounded rationality). Because people have incomplete information, they cannot be sure that decisions will bring about the desired changes – so unless the situation is drastic people stay with the structure they know and wait until new information is obtained.
- Structural change which means disturbance to the 'political equilibria' that exist at any point in time. In a structure existing at time 1, people receive a particular set of benefits that accrue from their past investments in the organization (e.g. time spent working hard to get promoted). At time 1, benefits are distributed in a particular way across the employees. If, at a later time, structural change happens, then that distribution of benefits (e.g. prestige, influence, income) will also change and so individuals are likely to influence (and if necessary resist) change to protect or enhance the benefits they are receiving. Resistance can be big enough to put off future reorganization.
- Organizational history leads to ways of operating that become embedded. Organizations survive because they have sets of successful routines that are used to solve problems and which automatically come into play following particular signals from the environment. By their embedded nature, these routines are very difficult to modify and act to lock an organization into a particular structure.

External forces include:

- The barriers to exiting one industry and entering another such as regulation, capital investment and market knowledge.
- The costs of acquiring specialist knowledge about unfamiliar markets.
- Organizations acquire a certain public legitimacy from their past actions which can act as an asset. Attempts to move into new areas can be compromised by lack of legitimacy in those areas. Failing shoe factories do not change into hospitals; fundamental structural change of this magnitude simply does not happen.

● A successful adaptive strategy for one organization may not lead to successful adaptation by another – there is no general strategy that organizations can
follow.

Inertia theory suggests that because older organizations have more stable and
standardized routines they will have higher inertia. Likewise, as size increases,
so does predictability and inflexibility and thus inertia. Hence both age and size
should increase resistance to change (Kelly and Amburgey, 1991). Organizational
complexity is also assumed to raise inertia and hence increase the duration of reorganization and the risk of failure. Complexity in this context is not the number of
departments but the links between them. If a unit can reorganize without affecting others then complexity is low. If changes in one unit require responses in other
units, which in turn require further changes in the initiating unit, then complexity is high (Hannan and Freeman, 1984).

To better understand the links between organizations and environments
Hannan and Freeman borrowed ideas from biology and in particular ideas about
how populations of species survive. Although it is true that every organization has
a distinctive structure (in terms of rules, processes and activities) groups of organizations share a 'blueprint' that allows them to be considered similar enough to
consider them as a species. Although there are many owls, for instance, each type
of owl is a separate species adapted to survive in a particular environment. Organizations with similar blueprints are similar in terms of their vulnerability to the
environment and constitute a population of organizations in the same sense that
there is a population of tawny owls.

Although broad structural types are found (multifunctional, for instance) from
looking at exactly how organizations function, it is clear that organizations with
the same general structure are uniquely different. In the same way as we can ask
why there are so many different plants and animals we can ask why there are so
many types of organizations (blueprints). In answer to this:

> In each distinguishable environmental configuration one finds, in equilibrium, only
> that organizational form optimally adapted to the demands of the environment.
>
> (Hannan and Freeman, 1979, p. 939)

Forms that are not optimally adapted are 'selected out' of business. Yet we can see
that organizations have to adapt and this calls for a certain level of slack in the
structure. Slack can be seen as resources that are not committed and which can be
used – some might call it waste or inefficient use of resources.

While adaptation explains to some extent whether organizations survive or
not, it is not the only explanation. Hannan and Freeman (1979) argued that selection rather than adaptation is important. Structural inertia impedes adaptation
such that organizations drift away from their environment and are replaced by
others that are better equipped to survive. A powerful fact in favour of this argument is that lists of the top 100 or top 500 companies in a country change over
time. What proportion of the organizations in business 50 years ago is still trading? How many companies in the top 100 list of 1980, 2000 and 2010 are still in
business? There are no exact answers to these questions but it is likely that the

Illustration 3.18

Resisting arrest?

The first decade of the twenty-first century saw new forms of terrorism and in 2008 three men were convicted in the UK of offences relating to planning to bring down aircraft with 'liquid' bombs. Yet according to a former senior police officer, the structure of policing in the UK could impede the fight against terrorism (Hayman, 2008).

Policing in England and Wales is still substantially organized around counties which are themselves largely administrative districts dating from medieval times. While adequate for local policing, coordination across county forces could get in the way of a long and at times fast-moving surveillance operation where targets are moving around. Communication systems do not always line up and 'the lines of command and control become stretched'. Local resources may not be sufficient to provide what a particular operation needs.

Plans to reduce the 43 police forces and create fewer but larger forces each with a more strategic capability struggle to gain favour. Hayman implies that this is due to an inability to resolve 'competing interests' in policing and to placate egos. Presumably these are the egos of senior officers who could see their forces disappear in mergers and perhaps see their posts eliminated. Structural change in policing and the creation of a national counter-terrorist force appear to be compromised by structural inertia and police politics.

Source: Based on Hayman, A (2008), 'Police politics are stalling our war on terror', *The Times*, 10 September, p. 28.

attrition rate is quite high. Failure is common. Selection rather than adaptation is a strong argument here. Inertia also explains why it seems many organizations need to experience a 'survival-threatening crisis' before they embark on meaningful change processes (Schaefer, 1998).

Conclusions

We have seen that design is not the same as structure, which has a stronger social action perspective. Design change is influenced by strategy, size, production technology, ICT and environment. Different organizational forms have been described. Defective designs and structures have serious consequences for organizational performance. Redesigning an organization's structure has to be carefully planned with change taking place as current business performance has to be sustained. This implies a mixture of incremental and transformational change.

Chapter 1 showed how organizations are, to some extent, a product of their history. In addition, organizations have existing structures, workforces (who are used to working in them), existing cultures, current businesses to sustain and, in many cases, trade unions to satisfy. Given this context, it is interesting to see how organizations have managed to adapt their formalized structures and developed matrix and virtual organizations layered over their existing structures to ensure responsiveness in fast-moving operating environments.

Small businesses with less than 200 people make up the majority of organizations worldwide and the traditional approaches to structure will need adapting to fit. Managers need to be vigilant about changes in the environment and respond to them but if restructuring is to make a difference it has to change what people do – not just how they are grouped and who they report to. Without an alteration in behaviour, changes to design do not have much impact on the 'real' structure. People push their own interests and networks of aligned interests are continually forming and dissolving.

The next chapter extends this discussion by exploring the links between culture and change.

Discussion questions and assignments

1 Consider the following statement:

Starting from scratch underplays the fact that significant redesign has to be planned and implemented in a real-life context that won't go away. Hospitals' re-engineering projects run into the problems of physician power. Government projects are often stifled by a context where people can't see the need for fundamental change. In manufacturing and service organizations, plans to implement a new way of doing business are often undermined by the thinking and mindsets of the old way. These realities have to be actively managed and changed if new initiatives are to succeed.

(Morgan, 1994)

To what extent do these or similar issues apply to your own organization or one you know well? What issues arise and how can they be managed?

2 In spite of the talk about network and virtual organizations, most organizations conform to more traditional structure types. Why is this?

Case example ●●●

Suits you Sir....

UK retailer Marks & Spencer has over 1000 stores in Britain and Europe. Its financial performance is basically sound but city analysts see it as declining. Recent performance is disappointing despite a series of efforts to revitalize it. Several top management teams have tried but with only partial success. After another round of disappointing results, bookmakers took bets on when the new(ish) chief executive would be replaced.

This is a company in which a great strength may have become a problematic weakness. For a long time M&S was, and in many respects still is, a High Street stalwart; dependable, reliable and offering good value. At its peak performance in the 1990s it became one of the most profitable retailers in the world and one of UK's largest listed companies. Following this peak position there was a battle for control of the company and several changes of personnel at the top.   ➡

The biggest challenge has been to have a clothing range that appeals to a young audience while not putting off the loyal older customers. Other, more general, challenges are how to deal with the increasing number of customers who shop on the Internet, and stiffening competition from Waitrose for its food lines and John Lewis, a more diversified department store chain. Food sales have held up well, but the biggest problem was customers turning away from clothing and general merchandise. New appointments were made to oversee strategy and purchasing in the problem areas.

Off the record, company directors were reported as saying that the once highly successful business model of combining food and clothing is now broken. On top of that, the international stores are not performing particularly well along with the Internet arm of the business. In mitigation, the depressed state of the UK economy since 2008 needs to be taken into account; several retail chains have closed down completely.

Question

1 Consider the complexity of making changes in a company of this size and structure. What might the company be risking in trying to raise financial performance?

FT Source: Based on 'Are you being served?' *The Sunday Times*, 13th January 2013, Business Section, p.6.

Indicative resources

Daft, R.L. (2010), *Organization Theory and Design* (11th edn), South-Western, Cengage Learning. A comprehensive text on design and structuring.

Huczynksi, A.A. and Buchanan, D. (2013), *Organizational Behaviour* (8th edn), FT Prentice Hall. This book has a good coverage of structure and design in Chapters 14 to 16.

Watson, T. (2006), *Organising and Managing Work* (2nd edn), Harlow: Pearson Education. The aim of this text is to provide a resource for understanding present-day work activities and how they are managed. Chapter 7 relating to structure and culture is particularly relevant.

Useful websites

www.istheory.yorku.ca/structurationtheory.htm

www.lancs.ac.uk/fass/centres/css/ant/antres.htm

References

Ahuja, M.K. and Carley, K.M. (1998), 'Network structure in virtual organizations', *Organization Science*, 10(6), pp. 741–57.

Amburgey, T.L. and Dacin, T. (1994), 'As the left foot follows the right? The dynamics of strategic and structural change', *Academy of Management Journal*, 37(6), pp. 1427–52.

Amis, J.M. and Aissaoui, R. (2013), 'Readiness for change: an institutional perspective', *Journal of Change Management*, 13(1), pp. 69–95.

Andrews, R. and Boyne, G. (2012), 'Structural change and public service performance: the impact of the reorganization process in English local government', *Public Administration*, 90(2), pp. 297–312.

Ashby, S., Peters, L.D. and Devlin, J. (2013), 'When an irresistible force meets an immovable object: the interplay of agency and structure in the UK financial crisis', *Journal of Business Research, 67*, pp. 2671–83.

Barley, S.R. and Tobert, P.S. (1997), 'Institutionalization and structuration: studying the links between action and institution', *Organization Studies*, 18, (1), pp. 93–117.

Bartol, K.M. and Martin, D.C. (1994), *Management* (2nd edn), Maidenhead: McGraw-Hill.

Bate, P. (1995), *Strategies for Cultural Change*, Oxford: Butterworth-Heinemann.

Bate, P., Khan, R. and Pyle, A.J. (2000), 'Culturally sensitive restructuring: an action research-based approach to organization development and design', *Public Administration Quarterly*, 23(4), pp. 445–70.

Bernasco, W., Weerd-Nederhof, P.C., Tillema, H. and Boer, H. (1999), 'Balanced matrix structure and new product development processes at Texas Instruments', *R&D Management*, 29(2), pp. 121–31.

Bevan, S. (2000), 'Flexible designs on domestic harmony', *Financial Times*, 5 October, p. 5.

Briand, L. and Bellemare, G. (2006), 'A structurationist analysis of post-bureaucracy in modernity and late modernity', *Journal of Organizational Change Management*, 19(1), pp. 65–79.

Burkhard, R.J. and Horan, T.J. (2006), 'The virtual organization: evidence of academic structuration in business programs and implications for information science', *Communications of AIS*, 17, Article 11, pp. 2–48.

Burns, T. and Stalker, G. M. (1961), *The Management of Innovation*, London: Tavistock.

Chandler, A. D. (1962), *Strategy and Structure: Chapters in the History of the Industrial Enterprise*, Cambridge, MA: MIT Press.

Child, J. (1972), 'Organization structure, environment and performance: the role of strategic choice', *Sociology*, January, pp. 1–22.

Child, J. (1988), *Organizations: A Guide to Problems and Practice* (2nd edn), London: Paul Chapman.

Chu, C. and Smithson, S. (2007), 'E-business and organizational change: a structurational approach', *Information Systems Journal*, 17, pp. 369–89.

Clegg, S.R. (1990), *Modern Organizations: Organization Studies in the Postmodern World*, London: Sage.

Clegg, S., Kornberger, M. and Pitsis, T. (2008), *Managing and Organizations: An Introduction to Theory and Practice* (2nd edn), London: Sage.

Colombo, M., and Delmastro, M. (2002), 'The determinants of organizational change and structural inertia: technological and organizational factors', *Journal of Economics and Marketing Strategy*, 11(4), pp. 595–635.

Consoli, D. (2005), 'The dynamics of technological change in the UK retail banking services: an evolutionary perspective', *Research Policy*, 34, pp. 461–80.

Cooper, C. (2000), 'Rolling with it', *People Management*, 28 September, pp. 32–4.

Cummings, T. and Worley, C. (2009), *Organization Development and Change* (9th edn), Mason OH: Cengage Learning.

Cunliffe, A.L. (2008), *Organization Theory*, London: Sage.

Cusamano, M. (1985), *The Japanese Automobile Industry: Technology and management at Nissan and Toyota*, Cambridge, MA: Harvard Industry Press.

Davis, S.M. and Lawrence, P.R. (1977), *Matrix*, Reading, MA: Addison-Wesley.

Day, K.M., Armenakis, A., Field, H.S. and Norris, D.R. (2012), 'Other organizations are doing it, why shouldn't we? A look at downsizing and organizational identity through an institutional theory lens', *Journal of Change Management*, 12(2), pp. 165–88.

Deleuze, G. and Guattari, F. (1980), *A Thousand Plateaus: Capitalism and Schizophrenia*, trans. B. Massum, 2004, London: Continuum.

Dent, M. (2003), 'Managing doctors and saving a hospital: rhetoric and actor networks', *Organization*, 10(1), pp. 107–26.

Drucker, P.F. (1999), *The Practice of Management*, Oxford: Butterworth Heinemann.

Gao, P. (2005), 'Using actor-network theory to analyse strategy formulation', *Information Systems Journal*, 15, pp. 255–75.

Giddens, A. (1984), *The Constitution of Society*, University of California Press: Berkeley.

Giddens, A. (1991), *Modernity and Self-Identity*, Cambridge: Polity Press.

Giddens, A. (2001), *Sociology* (4th edn), Cambridge: Polity Press.

Gourlay, G. and Montague, B. (2008), 'Meet the plane stoppers', *Sunday Times*, 14 December, p. 18.

Greenwood, R. and Hinings, C.R. (1996), 'Understanding radical organizational change: bringing together the old and new institutionalism', *Academy of Management Journal*, 21(4), pp. 1022–54.

Greenwood, R., Suddaby, R. and Hinings, C.R. (2002), 'Theorising change: the role of professional associations in the transformation of institutionalised fields', *Academy of Management Journal*, 45(1), pp. 58–80.

Greiner, L. (1972), 'Evolution and revolution as organizations grow', *Harvard Business Review*, July–August, pp. 37–46.

Hannan, M.T. and Freeman, J. (1979), 'The population ecology of organizations', *American Journal of Sociology*, 82(5), pp. 929–64.

Hannan, M.T. and Freeman, J. (1984), 'Structural inertia and organizational change', *American Sociological Review*, 49, April, pp. 149–64.

Hayman, A. (2008), 'Police politics are stalling our war on terror', *The Times*, 10 September, p. 28.

Hinterhuber, H.H. and Levin, B.M. (1994), 'Strategic networks: the organization of the future', *Long Range Planning*, 27(3), pp. 43–53.

Hollinger, P. (2000), 'Festive internet rush may surprise retailers', *Financial Times*, 30 October, p. 6.

Jackson, N. and Carter, P. (2000), *Rethinking Organisational Behaviour*, Harlow: Financial Times Prentice Hall: Pearson Education.

Johnson, G., Whittington, R. Scholes, K., Angwin, D. and Regner, P. (2014), *Exploring Corporate Strategy* (10th edn), Harlow: Pearson Education.

Johnson, G., Smith, S. and Codling, B. (2000), 'Microprocesses of institutional change in the context of privatisation', *Academy of Management Review*, 25(3), pp. 572–80.

Kelly, D. and Amburgey, T. (1991), 'Organizational inertia and momentum: a dynamic model of strategic change', *Academy of Management Journal*, 34(3), pp. 591–612.

King and Lawley (2013), *Organizational Behaviour*, Oxford: Oxford University Press.

Kondra, A.Z. and Hinings, C.R. (1998), 'Organizational diversity and change in institutional theory', *Organization Studies*, 19(5), pp. 743–67.

Koontz, H. (2010), *Essentials of Management: An International Perspective* (8th edn), Tata McGraw-Hill Education.

Langstrand, J. and Elg, M. (2012), 'Non-human resistance in changes towards lean', *Journal of Organizational Change Management*, 25(6), pp. 853–66.

Latour, B. (2005), *Reassembling the Social: An Introduction to Actor-network Theory*, Oxford: Oxford University Press.

Lucas, H.C., Jr (1996), *The T-Form Organization: Using Technology to Design Organizations for the 21st Century*, San Francisco, CA: Jossey-Bass.

Lyons, L. (2000), 'Management is dead', *People Management*, 26 October, pp. 60–4.

McCann, J. and Galbraith, J.R. (1981), 'Interdepartmental Relations' in Nystrom, P.C. and Starbuck, W.H. (eds), *Handbook of Organizational Design: Remodelling Organizations and Their Environment*, vol. 2, New York: Oxford University Press.

McHugh, M. and Bennett, H. (1999), 'Introducing teamwork within a bureaucratic maze', *The Leadership and Organization Development Journal*, 20(2), pp. 81–93.

Miles, R.E. and Snow, C.C. (1984a), 'Designing strategic human resource systems', *Organisational Dynamics*, 13(8), pp. 36–52.

Miller, P. (1992), 'Accounting and objectivity: the invention of calculating selves and calculable spaces', *Annals of Scholarship*, 9, pp. 61–86.

Mintzberg, H. (1979), *The Structuring of Organizations*, Englewood Cliffs, NJ: Prentice-Hall.

Mintzberg, H. (1983), *Structure in Fives: Designing Effective Organizations*, Englewood Cliffs, NJ: Prentice-Hall.

Mintzberg, H. (1991), 'The effective organization forces and forms', *Sloan Management Review*, Winter, 32(2), pp. 54–67.

Mintzberg, H. and van der Heyden, L. (1999), Organigraphs: drawing how companies really work, *Harvard Business Review*, Sep/Oct, pp. 87–94.

Morgan, G. (1989), *Creative Organization Theory: A Resource Book*, London: Sage.

Morgan, G. (1994), 'Quantum leaps ... step by step', *The Globe and Mail* (Canada's national newspaper), 28 June. Also available at http://www.imaginiz.com/ leaps.html.

Mukherji, A. (2002), 'The evolution of information systems: their impact on organizations and structures', *Management Decision*, 40(5), pp. 497–507.

Mullins, L. (2005), *Management and Organizational Behaviour* (7th edn), Harlow: Financial Times Prentice Hall.

Mullins, L. (2013), *Management and Organizational Behaviour* (10th edn), Harlow: Pearson Education Ltd.

Nystrom, P.C. and Starbuck, W.H. (eds) (1981), *Handbook of Organizational Design: Remodelling Organizations and Their Environment*, vol. 2, New York: Oxford University Press.

Oxman, J.A. and Smith, B.D. (2003), 'The limits of structural change', *MIT Sloan Management Review*, 45(1), pp. 77–83.

Perrow, C. (1967), *Organizational Analysis: A Sociological View*, London: Tavistock.

Pugh, D.S. (1973), 'The measurement of organisation structures: does context determine form?' *Organisational Dynamics*, Spring, pp. 19–34.

Pugh, D. (1990) *Organization Theory: Selected Readings*, Harmondsworth: Penguin.

Pugh, D.S., Hickson, D.J., Hinings, C.R. and Turner, C. (1969), 'Dimensions of Organization Structure', *Administrative Science Quarterly*, 17, pp. 163–76.

Rajan, R.G. and Wulf, J. (2006), 'The flattening firm: evidence from panel data on the changing nature of corporate hierarchies', *Review of Economics and Statistics*, 88(4), pp. 759–73.

Robbins, S.P. (1993), *Organizational Behavior*, Englewood Cliffs, NJ: Prentice-Hall.

Robbins, S.P. (2003), *Organizational Behavior* (10th edn), Englewood Cliffs, NJ: Prentice Hall.

Sarason, Y. (1995), 'A model of organizational transformation: the incorporation of organizational identity in a structuration theory framework', *Academy of Management Proceedings*, pp. 47–51.

Sarker, S., Sarker, S. and Sidorova, A. (2006), 'Understanding business process change failure: an actor-network perspective', *Journal of Management Information Systems*, 23(1), pp. 51–86.

Schaefer, S. (1998), 'Influence costs, structural inertia, and organizational change', *Journal of Economics & Management Strategy*, 7(2), pp. 237–63.

Sherer, P.D. and Lee, K. (2002), 'Institutional change in large law firms: a resource dependency and institutional perspective', *Academy of Management Journal*, 45(1), pp. 102–19.

Sine, W.D., Mitsuhashi, H. and Kirsch, D.A. (2006), 'Revisiting Burns and Stalker: formal structure and new venture performance in emerging economic sectors', *Academy of Management Journal*, 49(1), pp. 121–32.

Snow, C.C., Miles, R.E. and Coleman, H.J., Jr (1992), 'Managing 21st century network organizations', *Organizational Dynamics*, Winter, pp. 5–19.

Stanforth, C. (2007), 'Using actor-network theory to analyse e-government implementation in developing countries', *Information Technologies and International Development*, 3(3), pp. 35–60.

Swailes, S. (2008), *Organizational Structure*, in Brooks, I., *Organizational Behaviour* (4th edn) pp. 189–231, London: FT Prentice Hall.

Tsamenyi, M., Cullen, J. and González, J. (2006), 'Changes in accounting and financial information system in a Spanish electricity company: a new institutional theory analysis', *Management Accounting Research*, 17(4), pp. 409–32.

Tolbert, P.S. and Zucker, L.G. (1983), 'Institutional sources of change in the formal structure of organizations: the diffusion of Civil Service reform, 1880–1935', *Administrative Science Quarterly*, 28, pp. 22–39.

Van der Duim, R. and van Marwijk, R. (2006), 'The Implementation of an environmental system for Dutch tour operators: an actor-network perspective', *Journal of Sustainable Tourism*, 14(5), pp. 449–72.

Waldersee, R., Griffiths, A. and Lai, J. (2003), 'Predicting organizational change success: matching organization types, change types and capabilities', *Journal of Applied Management and Entrepreneurship*, (8)1, pp. 66–81.

Weber, M. (1947), *The Theory of Social and Economic Organization*, Free Press, trans. and ed. by Henderson, A.M. and Parsons, T., in Pugh, D.S. (1990), *Organization Theory: Selected Readings*, Harmondsworth: Penguin. (German original published in 1924.)

Willamott, H. (1981), 'The structuring of organizational structure: a note', *Administrative Science Quarterly*, 26, pp. 470–4.

Woodward, J. (1965), *Industrial Organization: Theory and Practice*, London: Oxford University Press.

Chapter 4

Culture and change

This chapter explores the concept of culture as it influences organizational life and organizational change processes. The meaning of culture at organizational and national levels is discussed and different models and typologies are compared. Ways of diagnosing and describing culture are discussed together with the links between organizational culture and change and difficulties of changing organizational culture.

Learning objectives

By the end of this chapter you will be able to:

- recognize the importance of culture and its role in relation to organizations and change;

- explain the meaning of culture;

- compare and contrast different cultural models and typologies;

- identify the origins of organizational culture;

- examine how cultural differences impact upon organizational change.

The informal organization

Organizations are made up of formal, tangible components such as structure, systems, technology, goals and financial resources. These formal organizational features are, in the main, susceptible to the process of *planned* change. However, as Chapter 2 showed, organizational life is not as neat and tidy as this implies. This was captured by French and Bell (1990, 1999) who used the 'iceberg' metaphor to represent the formal and informal organization (see Figure 4.1). The iceberg metaphor depicts two contrasting aspects of organizational life. The visible part, above water, contains the formal and easily seen aspects of organizations. The invisible part contains the more covert aspects of organizational life including the values, beliefs and attitudes held by management and employees, the emergent informal groupings that occur, the norms of behaviour which are rarely talked about but which influence how things are done and the politics of organizational life that drive decisions and actions.

The iceberg metaphor points to the overt and covert aspects of organizations and emphasizes that the informal systems, as well as being largely hidden, are the greater and perhaps the most troublesome part of the organization. French and Bell (1990, p. 18) considered that: 'Traditionally, this hidden domain either is not examined at all or is only partially examined.' However, recognition that the informal organization exists and that it has a powerful influence on organizational activity is reason enough to examine how it impacts upon the extent to which organizations can deal with change.

Culture, politics and power represent much of what is included in the informal organization. Furthermore, they play a crucial role in helping or hindering the

Figure 4.1 The organizational iceberg

process of change, as Morgan (1989) observes: 'The culture and politics of many organizations constrain the degree of change and transformation in which they can successfully engage, even though such change may be highly desirable for meeting the challenges and demands of the wider environment.' Regardless of how well change might be planned in terms of the more formal organizational characteristics, it is the hidden and informal aspects of organizational life that will ultimately help or hinder an organization's success.

The meaning of culture

Kroeber and Kluckhohn (1952, p. 181) examined over 100 definitions of culture and offered this summary definition:

> Culture consists in patterned ways of thinking, feeling and reacting, acquired and transmitted mainly by symbols, constituting the distinctive achievements of human groups, including their embodiment in artifacts; the essential core of culture consists of traditional (i.e. historically derived and selected) ideas and especially their attached values.

Another much quoted definition by Hofstede (1981, p. 24) is that:

> Culture is the collective programming of the human mind that distinguishes the members of one human group from those of another. Culture in this sense is a system of collectively held values.

These definitions refer to culture at national and societal level but they have much in common with the way we think about organizational cultures:

> The culture of the factory is its customary and traditional way of thinking and of doing things, which is shared to a greater or lesser degree by all its members, and which new members must learn, and at least partially accept, in order to be accepted into service in the firm. Culture in this sense covers a wide range of behaviour: the methods of production; job skills and technical knowledge; attitudes towards discipline and punishment; the customs and habits of managerial behaviour; the objectives of the concern; its way of doing business; the methods of payment; the values placed on different types of work; beliefs in democratic living and joint consultation; and the less conscious conventions and taboos.
>
> (Jaques, 1952, p. 251)

Culture is:

> A set of understandings or meanings shared by a group of people. The meanings are largely tacit among members, are clearly relevant to the particular group, and are distinctive to the group. Meanings are passed on to new group members.
>
> (Louis, 1980)

> Culture is 'how things are done around here'. It is what is typical of the organization, the habits, the prevailing attitudes, the grown-up pattern of accepted and expected behaviour.
>
> (Drennan, 1992, p. 3)

Drennan's definition is short and to the point. In pointing out that culture is about how things are done in a particular setting, it draws attention to how things are not done and to ideas and behaviour that would not be welcome or acceptable. The connections between culture and what is possible in a particular culture are, therefore, becoming clearer.

These definitions imply that culture can be described and that it delineates and differentiates one human grouping from another; possibly even different groups within the same organization. Culture has cognitive (to do with thinking), affective (to do with feeling) and behavioural characteristics. However, this does not mean that different cultures are easily identified and, on the whole, this is not so. Schein (1992, p. 6) sums this up by referring to organizational culture as:

> The deeper level of basic assumptions and beliefs that are shared by members of an organization, that operate unconsciously and define in a basic 'taken for granted' fashion an organization's view of its self and its environment.

By its nature, culture is deep-seated and, therefore, is likely to be resistant to change. On the other hand, Bate (1996, p. 28) argues that: 'Culture can be changed, in fact it is changing all the time'. The issue is the degree of change to which culture can be subjected over the short and long term and the process for changing it. Much depends on the perspective adopted and the type of change proposed. Three perspectives can be identified: that culture *can* be managed; that culture *may* be manipulated; and that culture *cannot* be consciously changed (Ogbonna and Harris, 1998). Most of the research on culture change deals with managing and manipulating culture. The third perspective, if true, presents problems for change agents who will perhaps need some external and perhaps unpredictable forces to make change happen. The recent collapse in financial systems may help to catalyze change in the reward/risk culture that characterized banks, for instance. This chapter, therefore, concentrates on issues associated with the first two perspectives on the assumption that much of what is said would apply if culture change occurs spontaneously rather than as a result of a more planned process.

Advice on how to *achieve* culture change is plentiful (for examples, see Bate, 1996; Carnall, 2007; Hartmann and Khademian, 2010; Ogbonna and Harris, 1998; Sims, 2000). There is general agreement that there is a need to:

1 Assess the current situation.
2 Have a good idea of what the aimed-for situation looks like.
3 Work out the 'what' and 'how' of moving the organization, or part of it, away from its current culture to what is perceived to be a more desirable one.
4 Intervene to bring about cultural change.
5 Monitor outcomes and adjust as needed.

The five steps above are all very logical/rational but, as we will see, very difficult to do.

 ## The ingredients of culture

At the most basic level we can list some characteristics of culture and descriptions of culture can be framed in terms of these characteristics. For instance, Brown (1995, p. 8) lists the following:

- artefacts;
- language in the form of jokes, metaphors, stories, myths and legends;
- behaviour patterns in the form of rites, rituals, ceremonies and celebrations;
- norms of behaviour;
- heroes (past and present employees who do great things);
- symbols and symbolic action;
- beliefs, values and attitudes;
- ethical codes;
- basic assumptions about what is important;
- history.

Robbins and Judge (2013) (see Illustration 4.1) give seven characteristics of culture. Have a look at these and then attempt Activity 4.1.

Illustration 4.1

The characteristics of organizational culture

1 **Innovation and risk taking**. The extent to which employees are encouraged to be innovative and take risks.
2 **Attention to detail**. The degree to which employees are expected to exhibit precision, analysis and attention to detail.
3 **Outcome orientation**. The degree to which management focuses on results or outcomes rather than on the techniques and processes used to achieve those outcomes.
4 **People orientation**. The degree to which management decisions take into consideration the effect of outcomes on people within the organization.

5 **Team orientation**. The degree to which work activities are organized around groups rather than individuals.
6 **Aggression**. The degree to which people are aggressive and competitive rather than easy-going.
7 **Stability**. The degree to which organizational activities emphasize maintaining the *status quo* in contrast to growth.

Source: Robbins, S.P. and Judge, T.A. (2013), *Organizational Behaviour* (15th edn), New Jersey: Pearson Education, pp. 512–13.

The seven characteristics of organizational culture are useful but do not tell us how they may be related or ordered. Figure 4.2 illustrates ideas about 'levels' of culture and that culture manifests itself at the deepest level through people's values and at the shallowest level in terms of the things that symbolize those values.

Activity 4.1 Appraising your own organization

The scales below relate to the organizational culture characteristics listed in Illustration 4.1. Indicate on each scale how you rate your own organization (or one you know). If possible, ask others who know the organization to do the same. You could find some different views of the culture emerging.

Organizational culture characteristics

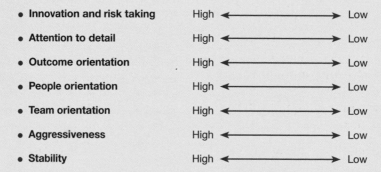

- **Innovation and risk taking**   High ←———————→ Low
- **Attention to detail**   High ←———————→ Low
- **Outcome orientation**   High ←———————→ Low
- **People orientation**   High ←———————→ Low
- **Team orientation**   High ←———————→ Low
- **Aggressiveness**   High ←———————→ Low
- **Stability**   High ←———————→ Low

Analyze how your views and your colleagues' views differ. Consider why their views differ to yours.

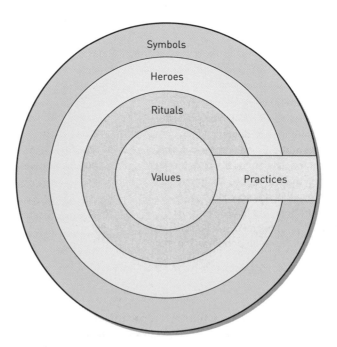

Figure 4.2 Different levels of culture

Source: Hofstede, G., Neuijen, B., Ohayv, D.D. and Sanders, G. (1990) 'Measuring organizational cultures: a qualitative and quantitative study across twenty cases', *Administrative Science Quarterly*, 35, p. 291.

Objectivist and interpretive views of culture

Schein (2004) suggests three levels that are from the shallowest to the deepest: the *artefacts* level (the visible organizational structures and processes such as language, environment, rituals, ceremonies, myths and stories); the *espoused values* level (the organization's strategies, goals, philosophies); and the *basic underlying assumptions* level (the unconscious, taken-for-granted beliefs, perceptions, thoughts and feelings that are the ultimate source of values and actions). Thus the rituals, heroes and symbols in Figure 4.2 equate with Schein's artefacts level. However, the values level is, apparently, split into two levels by Schein, who distinguishes between the beliefs, values and attitudes associated with the espoused values level and the deeper level of basic assumptions. Dyer's (1985) four-level model proposes *artefacts, perspectives, values* and *tacit assumptions*.

The characteristics in Illustration 4.1 are amenable to being *used* to describe culture in practical terms. However, the levels model can be used in similar fashion. In this case, the process requires interpretation of signs and symbols, as well as language used, to assess the prevailing values and underlying assumptions about how the organization operates.

Objectivist and interpretive views of culture

List and levels models show how the concept of culture can be imagined and described. Alvesson (1993), Bate (1996) and Brown (1995) all draw attention to the distinction between two classifications of culture. The first, of which the list in Illustration 4.1 might be considered an example, treats culture as a critical variable that partly explains why organizations differ in the ways that they operate. This is an objectivist or functional view of culture (Alvesson, 1993). Alternatively, culture can be defined as a set of behavioural and/or cognitive characteristics (Brown, 1995) such that culture sits alongside structure, technology and the environment (for instance) as one of the variables that influence organizational life and performance. In summary, this view of culture implies that organizations *have* cultures (see Brooks and Bate, 1994) and further implies that changing cultures is not that difficult if certain procedures are followed.

A second view interprets the meaning of culture as a metaphor for the concept of organization itself. Pacanowsky and O'Donnell-Trujillo (1982, p. 126) for instance, remarked that: 'Organizational culture is not just another piece of the puzzle. From our point of view, a culture is not something an organization *has*; a culture is something an organization *is*' [authors' emphasis]. Gareth Morgan (2006) used the metaphor 'organizations as cultures' in a range of metaphors that present different images of organization:

> Shared meaning, shared understanding and shared sense making are all different ways of describing culture. In talking about culture we are really talking about a process of reality construction that allows people to see and understand particular events, actions, objects, utterances, or situations in distinctive ways. These patterns of understanding also provide a basis for making one's own behaviour sensible and meaningful.

(Morgan, 2006, p. 134)

Morgan maintains that members of organizations are creating the organization itself. In essence this means that organizations are *socially* constructed realities and that, rather than being defined by their structures, rules and regulations, they are constructed as much in the heads and minds of their members and are strongly related to members' self-concepts and identity. This view of culture implies that, if an organization's culture is to be understood, it is necessary to look at the routine aspects of everyday life as well as at the more obvious and more public signs, symbols and ceremonies, which are more frequently associated with organizational leaders. It also implies a requirement to examine how culture is created and sustained. This means recognizing that culture is part of a much bigger historical pattern, and therefore that 'more often it is a *recurrence* rather than just an occurrence' (see Bate, 1996, p. 29). A model of organizational culture which brings together the idea of culture as congruent with everything that happens in an organization is the cultural web described in Illustration 4.2 (Johnson, Whittington, Scholes, Angwin and Regner, 2014).

The cultural web

It can be seen from Illustrations 4.2 and 4.3 that the cultural web is all-encompassing in the organizational elements that it includes. Johnson *et al.* (2008) draw attention to the influence of prevailing organizational paradigms (i.e. the beliefs and assumptions of the people making up the organization) in any attempt to bring about strategic change. They do not go as far as Morgan in equating culture fully with organization, but neither do they completely objectify culture as separate from other aspects of organizational life.

The cultural web is a useful tool that can be applied as a way of revealing organizational cultures. In contrast, Morgan's suggestion that organizations *are* cultures discusses (among other things) differences in national cultures, including the way these have formed through historical processes. The notion of culture as a metaphor for organization also recognizes that sub-cultures can coexist in the same organization. This is reinforced by Alvesson (1993), who recommends combining perspectives at three levels:

- the organization as a culture (unitary and unique);
- the organization as a meeting place for great cultures (which includes national ethnic and class cultures);
- local perspectives on organizational sub-cultures.

Illustration 4.4 is an account where organizational cultures and sub-cultures (influenced perhaps by national cultures) clashed to the detriment of both companies.

Illustration 4.2

The cultural web

Johnson *et al*. (2008) explain the different elements of the cultural web as follows:

- The *routine* ways that members of the organization behave towards each other and that link different parts of the organization make up 'the way we do things around here', which at their best lubricate the working of the organization and may provide a distinctive and beneficial organizational competency. However, they can also represent a taken-for-granted approach to how things should happen that is extremely difficult to change and highly protective of core assumptions (and people) in the paradigm.

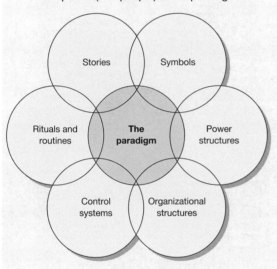

- The *rituals* of organizational life, such as training programmes, promotion and appraisal procedures, point to what is important in the organization and reinforce 'the way we do things around here'. They signal what is important and valued.
- The *stories* told by members of the organization to each other, to new recruits and to outsiders embed the history in the present and flag up important events and personalities, as well as mavericks who 'deviate from the norm'.
- The more *symbolic* aspects of organizations, such as logos, office furnishings, titles, status differentials and the type of language and terminology commonly used become a shorthand representation of the nature of the organization.
- The *control systems*, what gets measured and the reward systems emphasize what it is important to monitor in the organization and to focus attention on.
- *Power structures*: the most powerful managerial groupings in the organization are likely to be the ones most associated with core assumptions and beliefs about what is important.
- The *formal organizational structure* or the more informal ways in which the organizations work are likely to reflect power structures and, again, to delineate important relationships and emphasize what is important in the organization.

Source: Based on Johnson, G., Scholes, K. and Whittington, R. (2008), *Exploring Corporate Strategy: Texts and cases* (8th edn), Harlow: Pearson Education.

Illustration 4.3

A cultural web of Paper Unlimited, a large UK-based paper distributor

Stories
- Son of the founder (recently deceased) and his influence on the company policies and practices – a people-oriented company
- Frequent need to expand paper stacking space as example of continuing success

Symbols
- New building and warehouses
- Swimming pool and leisure facilities for employees and families
- IIP award
- Quality award
- Award for excellence in the use of IT

Rituals and routines
- Walk-about management – always available to employees
- Management can be interrupted
- Lots of talking
- Yearly employee/family outing

Paradigm
Dedicated to the philosophy laid down by the recently deceased original owner's son, who ran the company for over 40 years. This implies being:
- A people-oriented organization also dedicated to high task performance
- Provider of long-term employment
- Aware of success while also aware of the need continuously to analyze the environment to detect new markets
- Committed to incremental rather than radical changes

Power structures
- Long-serving managers and workforce
- Can 'work your way up'
- Positions based on expertise in the business rather than on qualifications
- Paternalistic style of management
- Emphasis on continuity
- Relaxed attitudes
- Cooperation at head office, competition between the branches where selling occurs

Controls
- IT controls most operations
- Error measurement
- Help given to improve

Organization structure
- Hierarchical at head office – bureaucracy with a human face
- Teamworking in the branches with team-based rewards
- Profit-related pay
- Responsibilities clearly defined

Activity 4.2 *Creating a cultural web for your organization*

Illustration 4.3 shows the cultural web for an organization involved in paper production. Using this as a guide, construct a cultural web for an organization you know well.

If you wanted to initiate strategic change in the company that you have described, what features of the culture present the biggest barriers to change and how would you go about changing them?

Illustration 4.4

Daimler and Chrysler: cultural differences in a merger

The auto industry has a long history of mergers and acquisitions. One high-profile merger took place in 1998 between German company Daimler-Benz (best known for Mercedes perhaps) and US car producer Chrysler. At the time Daimler wanted to expand into new markets and develop new products. As the company stood, however, executives felt that this would not be achieved through Mercedes alone and that a link with another auto producer was needed. Chrysler, although the most profitable vehicle producer at the time, was aware of overcapacity in the industry and executives felt that there had to be a shake-out of manufacturers. To compete, Chrysler felt it needed a partner. After full due diligence investigations focusing on the assets and financial structures of the two organizations a decision to merge was made.

During negotiations by the merger teams some socio-cultural issues emerged. Daimler was never going to be seen as the junior partner but was happy with the idea of 'a merger of equals'. Would the merged organization be German or American? There was no way that Daimler could end up as American so it was agreed that the new company would be German. A new name, DaimlerChrysler, was agreed reflecting the strength of the German position.

When the two companies were being integrated further, socio-cultural issues came out. Rewards for the top American executives were much higher than their counterparts in Germany. Daimler employees flew first-class because this fitted the company's market position. Only the top Chrysler executives flew first-class and reconciling travel policies took six months to resolve. Working patterns differed. For instance,

there were differences in dress codes, informal versus formal behaviour in business meetings, the ways decisions were made and the hours worked. Financial reporting in the US was geared to quarterly reporting unlike the annual cycle seen in Germany.

Another problem was the culture surrounding the two brands. One was a luxury brand built around superior engineering and the other much more associated with a brash American image and 'blue collar' purchasers. The two companies 'didn't just make cars differently; they lived in different worlds' (Badrtalei and Bates, p. 310).

The upshot of this was that the merger quickly began to falter. Financial performance collapsed and in 2001 the company announced big job losses and closure of plants to turn around a loss-making situation. Chrysler had benefited from Mercedes, e.g. through the use of shared production systems and components, but benefits to Daimler were harder to find. In 2007 Daimler sold 80 per cent of its stake in Chrysler for $7.4 billion – far less than it had invested in the venture.

Mergers and acquisitions only make sense if they create more than the partners were already achieving when separate. On this measure, this particular partnership was a failure. Analyzing the causes of failure in a case like this could rely on economic, market and technical explanations and they cannot be overlooked. However, it does seem that cultural clashes were inevitable in this case and that they were not sufficiently accounted for in pre-merger analysis.

Source: Based on Badrtalei, J. and Bates, D.L. (2007) 'Effect of organizational cultures on mergers and acquisitions: the case of DaimlerChrysler', *International Journal of Management*, 24(2), pp. 303–17.

The cultural compass

Hall (1995) offers a model that appears to accommodate the three levels of culture proposed by Alvesson (1993). The compass model of culture and its associated culture typologies have been developed through an apparent interest in cultural differences in 'partnerships', by which she means inter-company relationships typically in the form of alliances, mergers or acquisitions and which are based on two components of behaviour. The first of these is *assertiveness*, which is the degree to which a company's behaviour is seen by others as being forceful or directive:

Companies which behave in high assertive ways are seen to be decisive, quick and firm. There is little hesitation in their action. If they introduce a new product or enter a new market they do so with full force ... Low assertive companies behave in more slow and steady ways. They are careful to consider what they do before they take firm action. They introduce a new product or enter a new market step by step, keeping their options open. Unlike the one-track mind of the high assertive company, the low assertive company has a 'multi-track mind'.

(Hall, 1995, p. 52)

The second behavioural component of culture in this model is *responsiveness*, which is the extent to which an organization's behaviour is seen by others as being emotionally expressed. Thus:

> Companies which behave in high responsive ways are seen to be employee friendly, relaxed or spontaneous. These companies give the impression that they compete on feelings more than on facts. In industry gatherings, high responsive companies tend to be very 'likeable'. They seem more open than other companies. Low responsive companies behave in more reserved or closed ways. They are not so much liked as 'respected'. They tend to be more rigid, their employees serious. Low responsive companies compete more on facts than on feelings.

(Hall, 1995, pp. 54–5)

Behaviours that indicate high assertiveness include being individualistic, pushy, controlling and fast-moving. Behaviours that indicate high responsiveness include being sensitive, compromising, trusting and loyal. Hall maintains that the four different combinations of the two behavioural components (high or low assertiveness and responsiveness) result in four different cultural styles. Figure 4.3

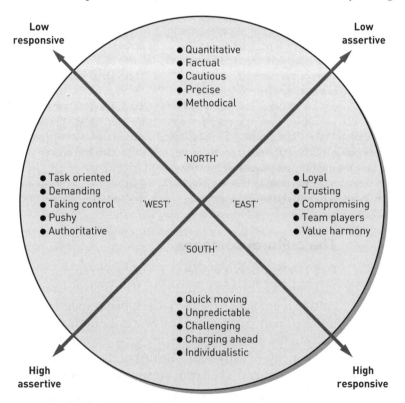

Figure 4.3 The compass model: characteristics of each style

Source: Reprinted by permission of John Wiley and Sons Ltd. Hall, W. (1995) *Managing Cultures: Making Strategic Relationships Work*, Chichester: Wiley, p. 58.

illustrates the compass model, so-called because each of the four styles is labelled as one of the four points of the compass. The various characteristics of high–low responsiveness versus assertiveness are shown in each quadrant.

Competing values framework

Quinn and Rohrbaugh (1983) proposed a competing values model as a way of understanding variations in organizational effectiveness. The model represents a framework or cognitive map used by people when they describe organizations and it has since been adapted to interpret culture (Cameron and Quinn, 2005; Kwan and Walker, 2004; Howard, 1998; Igo and Skitmore, 2005). The framework is a familiar 2×2 matrix in which the vertical axis represents flexibility and change versus stability and control. The horizontal axis represents an internal, person-centred focus versus an external, organization-centred focus. Each of the four quadrants represents one of four models or cultures as shown in Figure 4.4.

The human relations model embodies flexibility and a focus on people. Morale, cohesion, team spirit and training and development are valued with the end focus being on well-being and personal development. The open systems model embodies flexibility with an external focus. It is about being adaptable, looking for growth and acquiring resources, with the focus being more on the organization than the people in it. The rational system model embodies an external focus and control. Managers will emphasize planning, goals, target setting and monitoring in the pursuit of efficiency and productivity. The internal

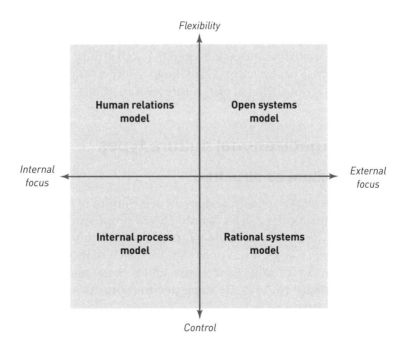

Figure 4.4 Competing values framework

Source: Adapted from Quinn, R.E. (1991) 'A competing values framework for analysing presentational communication in management contexts', *Journal of Business Communication*, 28(3), pp. 213–32.

process model embodies a people focus with control. Information management and communication are valued in the pursuit of stability and control (Quinn and Rohrbaugh, 1983).

The diagonals connect models that are in stark contrast to each other, e.g. human relations and rational systems. The four cultures illustrate the ongoing conflicts, i.e. the competing values, of life in organizations. The competing values framework does not suggest that organizations fit into one of the four types nor does it suggest that one model is better than another. What it emphasizes is that these tensions coexist. Managers seek growth but there are forces for stability. They seek high productivity but also want high levels of cooperation between employees. Although any attempt to reduce the undeniable complexity and uniqueness of culture to models like this oversimplifies, they are useful in cutting through the myriad views of culture.

Activity 4.3 *Competing values?*

Thirty years have passed since the competing values framework was introduced. Perhaps management has changed since then. To what extent do you think that the four values are in competition? For instance, can organizations focus both on their employees and on the organization? Can they have flexible approaches to work with an overlay of managerial control and centralization?

So far we have seen several attempts to objectify and describe, even measure, culture. This is useful in helping us understand cultures even if they do not capture the rich description achieved through ethnographic studies in single organizations. Consequently, it is useful to consider other typologies that allow a relatively easy comparison of one culture with another.

Organizational culture types

Culture as structure

These views of culture draw on descriptions of different structural forms for their expression. Charles Handy (1993) proposed four types using the Greek gods for inspiration. Handy refers to organizational culture as atmosphere, ways of doing things, levels of energy and levels of individual freedom – or collectively, the 'sets of values and norms and beliefs – reflected in different structures and systems' (p. 180). He suggested four organizational culture types as shown in Illustration 4.5.

Illustration 4.5

A structural view of organizational culture

The power culture

Power cultures are those in which a single person or group dominates. Handy refers to this culture as a *web* in the sense that a spider in the middle of its web senses and is connected to all movement elsewhere in the web. Decision making is centralized. This type of culture is seen as essentially political since decisions are taken on the basis of influence rather than through a logical rational process. Power is held by the centre by virtue of personal charisma or the control of resources. Family businesses, small entrepreneurial companies and, historically at least, trade unions are likely to have this type of culture. The strength of the culture depends on the strength of the centre and the willingness of other organizational members to defer to the power source. Handy likens this culture to the Greek god Zeus who ruled by whim and impulse, by thunderbolt and shower of gold from Mount Olympus.

The role culture

Handy likens role cultures to a *Greek temple*. The patron god here is Apollo, the god of reason, the argument being that role cultures work by logic and rationality. The pillars of the temple are strong in their own right and activity is controlled more by rules and regulations than by personal directive from the top. The base of the temple is seen as coordinating activity rather than overtly controlling it. Emphasis is on defined roles and occupants are expected to fulfil these roles but not overstep them. Role cultures flourish in stable situations and are the least conducive to change.

The task culture

The task culture is represented by a *net*. The dominant concept in a task culture is project work associated with matrix-type structures. Handy pushes the Greek mythology association somewhat here in suggesting Athena, whose emphasis was on getting the job done. The task culture, therefore, is not particularly concerned with personal power or hierarchy, but with marshalling the required resources to complete work efficiently and effectively. People are connected via networks. Decision making is devolved to the project groups to enhance flexibility of working method and speed the outcomes. The task culture is said to flourish where creativity and innovation are needed particularly in organizations concerned with research and development, marketing, advertising and new ventures.

The person culture

According to Handy, this culture is unusual as it exists only to service the needs of the participating members. It does not have an overarching objective as is found in more conventionally structured organizations. Examples of person cultures are barristers' chambers, doctors' centres and small consultancy firms. Person cultures have minimal structures and can be likened to a cluster or galaxy of individual stars. Handy proposes Dionysus as its patron deity – the god of the self-oriented individual.

Source: Based on Handy, C. (1993), *Understanding Organizations*, London: Penguin, pp. 183–91.

Activity 4.4

Consider your own organization in terms of Handy's four cultural types. Which description best matches the culture as you see it?

Culture, strategy and environment

Deal and Kennedy (1982) also proposed four generic cultures: the tough-guy, macho culture; the work-hard/play-hard culture; the bet-your-company culture and the process culture. Their model takes more account of the organization's competitive environment (see Illustration 4.6).

Illustration 4.6

Deal and Kennedy's typology

The tough-guy, macho culture

People in macho cultures regularly take high risks and receive rapid feedback on what they do. Examples cited are police departments, publishing, sports and entertainment. In tough-guy cultures the stakes are high and there is a focus on speed rather than endurance. Staff tend to be young and financial rewards come early, but failure is punished harshly. Burnout, internal competition and conflict are normal. This means tantrums are tolerated and people try to out-do each other. However, while tough-guy cultures can be highly successful in high-risk, quick-return environments they are less suited to long-term investments. Being unable to benefit from cooperative activity, these organizations tend to have a high turnover of staff and thus often fail to develop a strong and cohesive culture.

The work-hard/play-hard culture

This culture exists where there is low risk but quick feedback on actions such as sales organizations that incorporate hard work and fun. Persistence, keeping at it and working to recognized procedures are typical of work-hard/play-hard cultures. The risks are small because an individual sale is unlikely to severely damage the salesperson. In addition production systems are built to withstand temporary hitches. However, being selling oriented, all employees gain quick feedback on their performance. Heroes in these organizations are the super-salespeople who turn in volume sales. Contests, conventions and other means of encouraging intense selling are used. Yet the culture emphasizes the team because it is the team that makes the difference, not the achievements of single individuals. However, although work/play cultures can achieve high sales, this can be at the expense of quality.

Bet-your-company culture

These cultures are typical of organizations where the risks are high and the feedback on actions and decisions takes a long time. Bet-your-company organizations are those that invest heavily in projects which take years to come to fruition. Examples include aircraft manufacturers and oil companies. In contrast to tough-guy cultures, people in bet-your-company cultures bet the company rather than themselves. Consequently there is a sense of deliberateness that manifests itself in ritualized business meetings. All decisions are carefully thought through. Decision making tends to be top down, reflecting the hierarchical nature of the organization. The survivors in these organizations respect authority and technical competence and have the stamina to endure long-term ambiguity with limited feedback. They will act cooperatively, and have proved themselves over a number of years – immaturity is not tolerated. Bet-your-company cultures lead to high-quality inventions and major scientific breakthroughs, but their slow response times make them vulnerable to short-term economic fluctuations. However, these companies may be those that the economy needs most.

The process culture

This culture is typical of organizations where there is low risk and slow feedback on actions and decisions. Examples (at the time of the research 30 years ago) were banks, insurance companies, public and government organizations and regulated industries. (Banks, as we have discovered to our cost, were deregulated.) Working with little feedback, employees have no sense of their own effectiveness or otherwise.

Consequently they tend to concentrate on the means by which things are done rather than what should be done. Values tend to focus on technical perfection, working out the risks and getting the process right. Protecting one's back is what most employees do, so the people who prosper are those who are orderly and punctual and who attend to detail. The ability to weather political storms and changes becomes a desirable trait. In process cultures there is considerable emphasis on job titles and status and the signs that symbolize them, such as style of office furniture. Position power is desired. Staying with the organization is valued through long-service awards. Process cultures are effective when dealing with a stable and predictable environment, but find it difficult to react quickly to changing circumstances.

Deal and Kennedy's typology dates from the 1980s and while the cultural types may still be relevant, it is questionable in light of political and regulatory changes whether the examples of each type given are still valid. Deal and Kennedy (2000, p. 169) agreed that previous assumptions needed revising. For instance, banks (as examples of process cultures) have evolved more into sales-type organizations but do not, perhaps, yet fit the work-hard/play-hard culture suggested for sales-ori-ented companies. Figure 4.5 shows Trompenaars and Prud'homme's (2004, p. 67) depiction of these four types with more up-to-date examples of each culture. Even this recent update raises questions about the placement of banks in the pro-cess-culture category. Given their more recent behaviour, a 'bet-your-company' category would seem more fitting.

In contrast to previous emphases on links between culture and the inter-nal and external environment, Scholz (1987) brought these together, using

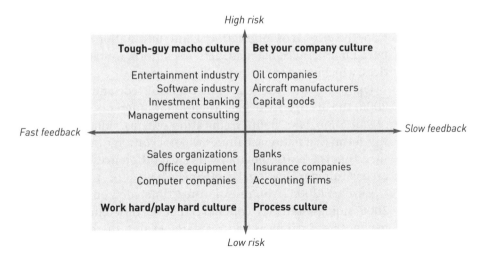

Figure 4.5 Deal and Kennedy model for corporate culture

Source: Reprinted by permission of John Wiley & Sons Ltd on behalf of Capstone Publishing Ltd. Trompenaars, F. and Prud'homme, P. (2004) *Managing Change Across Corporate Cultures*, Chichester: Capstone Publishing.

three dimensions. The external-induced dimension of organizational culture draws Deal and Kennedy's four culture types. The internal-induced dimension identifies three culture types (production, bureaucratic and professional) that derive from organizational structure characteristics. The evolution-induced dimension goes beyond earlier models in its relationship to the strategic orientation of the organization and its environment. From these, five culture types are identified:

1 *Stable,* with a time orientation towards the past and an aversion to risk.
2 *Reactive,* with a time orientation towards the present and an acceptance of 'minimum' risk.
3 *Anticipating,* also oriented towards the present but more accepting of 'familiar' risks.
4 *Exploring,* with a time orientation towards the present and the future and an acceptance of increasing risk.
5 *Creative,* looking forward to the future and accepting risk as normal.

Thus far we have seen how culture is expressed and have noted the influences of dominant personalities, professional norms and market economics, among others, on shaping organizational culture. Organizational history also plays a part. Another important overlay comes from national cultural differences.

The influence of national culture

The literature on cultural similarities and differences between nations contains a long-standing question in the form of the convergence–divergence debate. In summary, those who support the convergence view argue that the forces of industrialization and globalization as well as increasing organization size will push organizations, whatever their location, towards particular configurations with respect to strategy, structure and human resource management practices. In addition, the growth of international and multinational organizations increases the need for 'international managers' to conform to standardized management practices, whichever part of the world they are in.

Opposing this view (e.g. Hofstede, Hofstede and Minkov, 2010; Javidan *et al.,* 2006) the divergence debate argues that differences in language, religion, social organization, laws, politics, education systems, values and attitudes will, of necessity, mean that national cultures will not converge but continue to remain distinct such that there will inevitably be local differences in the organization cultures even within multinational companies.

Gerhart (2008) who re-examined Hofstede's and the GLOBE (Javidan *et al.,* 2006) studies' statistics, concludes that the differences between national cultures may not be as strong as had been argued and, therefore, they do not necessarily constrain organizational cultures. On the other hand he also says that his findings do not mean that national cultural differences are unimportant and in some circumstances might or might not influence organizational cultures. He concludes: 'Therefore, organizations may have more discretion in choosing whether to localize or standardize organizational culture and related management practices (either to the forces of industrialization or nation cultures) than is suggested by conventional wisdom' (p. 255).

Illustration 4.7

Driving change at Ford

In an interview for the *Harvard Business Review* (1999) Jacques Nasser, Chief Executive Officer of Ford Motor Company, spoke of his attempt to bring about radical change in the company 'mindset' of everyone working there. According to the interview account, Nasser asked his employees in 200 countries 'to think and act as if they own the company'. 'To adopt, in other words, the capital markets' view of Ford – to look at the company in its entirety, as shareholders do.' Nasser says that this is 'a radically different mentality for Ford'. This mentality (or culture as it might be termed in the context of this discussion) is very different from the one that has, apparently, prevailed for much of the time since the company was formed over 100 years ago – one Nasser describes as: 'A collection of fiercely independent fiefdoms united under the flag of their functional or regional expertise'. Each division in this 'collection' appears to have its own organizational sub-culture for which, as Nasser comments, there were 'legitimate historical reasons'.

Elaborating on this he says: 'Think about Ford's history in three chunks: from its founding in 1905 to the early 1920s, the late 1920s through to the 1950s, and the 1960s through the 1980s.' The first period was one of 'colonization' and the opening of assembly plants (which were smaller versions of the original company in Detroit) in other countries, but with very little competition from other automotive companies. The second period was one of 'intense nationalism' with large automotive companies growing up in the United Kingdom, France, Germany, Australia, all making their own vehicles and exporting them to others – but in their own regions. The third period saw the rise of regionalism and the emergence of the European Union and the North American Free Trade Association (NAFTA). It was this period that saw the entrenchment of the regional and functional fiefdoms.

Nasser comments that, given the prevailing environment at that time, this arrangement worked very well: squeezing 'every last ounce of efficiency out of the regional model'. However, he goes on to say that this model does not work any more in the current environment of increasing globalization of capital, communications, economic policy, trade policy, human resources, marketing, advertising, brands – and so on. Consequently there is a perceived need to 'reinvent' Ford as a global organization with a single focus on consumers and shareholder value.

Nasser talks of striving for some kind of DNA that drives how Ford does things everywhere. This includes a global mindset, an intuitive knowledge of customers and a strong belief in leaders as teachers. However, this does not mean that the same products are produced and sold everywhere. What it does mean is that, although Ford cars have many common systems that bring scale efficiencies, they can also be tailored to individual local markets. What is more, although Ford would like to see common reward systems for staff wherever they work, Nasser recognizes that different cultures have different attitudes to pay and rewards, for instance about the balance between fixed and variable rewards. What is also clear is that different tax laws require different attitudes to employment, stock purchase and so on.

Having said all this, it is clear that Nasser was looking for a significant cultural shift. The article describes, in some detail, the approach taken to help this to happen – an approach based on a multi-faceted teaching initiative, led by senior and middle managers and aimed, eventually, at all Ford employees wherever they are located. Nasser said: 'The Ford you see today has no resemblance to the Ford of five years ago. If you dissected us and inspected every blood vessel, we're different; our DNA has changed. I don't think we'll go back.'

Source: Based on Nasser, J. and Wetlaufer, S. (1999), 'Driving Change: an interview with Ford Motor Company's Jacques Nasser', *Harvard Business Review*, March–April, pp. 76–88.

The diversity of national cultures

Illustration 4.8 summarizes a widely referenced framework that describes the cultural orientation of societies in terms of six basic dimensions.

Illustration 4.8

Six different cultural orientations of societies

1 *People's qualities as individuals in terms of whether people are seen as basically good or basically bad*. Societies that consider people good tend to trust people, while those that consider people bad tend to start from a premise of mistrust and suspicion.

2 *People's relationship to their world*. Some societies believe they can dominate their environment while others believe the environment and themselves to be inseparable and, therefore, that they must live in harmony with it.

3 *People's personal relationships in terms of individualism or collectivism*. Some societies encourage individualism and the notion of being self-supporting with achievement being based on individual worth, while others are more group-oriented, where people define themselves as members of clans or communities (which might be the work organization) and consider the group's welfare to be more important than the individual.

4 *An orientation to either doing or being*. Societies that are doing- and action-oriented stress accomplishments which are measurable by standards believed to be external to the individual; societies oriented to being are more passive, believing that work should be enjoyed and they should live more for the moment.

5 *People's orientation to time*. Some societies are past-oriented, believing that current plans and actions should fit with the customs and traditions of the past, while future-oriented societies justify innovation and change in terms of future pay-offs, believing radical change to be desirable as well as acceptable.

6 *People's use of space*. Societies differ on such matters as offices in relation to status, the designation of public space compared to private space, the separation of managers from subordinates.

Source: Kluckhohn, F. and Strodtbeck, F.L. (1961), *Variations in Value Orientations*, Evanston, IL: Row Peterson.

Regarding the good–bad dimension or trust–mistrust dimension, the way one group of people regards another will differ according to whether they start with the assumption that people are trustworthy or that all people will cheat if given the opportunity. This translates, for instance, into whether information is freely available, the extent of surveillance and how one group's actions are interpreted by another.

Adler (1997) describes the strong individualistic tendencies of Americans as evidenced in their use of assertive language and their recruitment and promotion practices based on criteria relating to individual knowledge and skills. This contrasts with more group-oriented societies such as Japan, China, Indonesia and Malaysia that put more stress on assignments, responsibilities and reporting relationships in collective terms. People in collective societies are more likely to gain employment through personal contacts who can vouch for their trustworthiness and ability to work with others. Favouring family friends when making decisions is not seen as unusual but it would be less acceptable in more individualistic societies. Adler points out that different time orientations impact significantly on attitudes to timekeeping and punctuality and influence the length of time someone might be given to show their worth in a job and the focus on short-term or long-term results.

The concept of geographically identifiable, culturally differentiated regions based on national boundaries is supported by substantial evidence (Hofstede, 2001; Hofstede, Hofstede and Minkov, 2010). This research initially found four dimensions on which cultures could be described and a fifth dimension was added based on further studies that incorporated Chinese and Confucian values (Minkov and Hofstede, 2010). The five dimensions are described in Illustration 4.9.

Illustration 4.9

Hofstede's dimensions of national culture

Power distance

Power distance refers to how a society deals with the fact that people are unequal, for instance in physical and intellectual abilities. Some societies let these inequalities grow over time into inequalities in power and wealth whereas others try to play down inequalities. In high power distance societies, inequalities of power and wealth are accepted not only by the leaders but also by those at the bottom of the power hierarchy, with corresponding large differences in status and salaries. In low power distance societies, inequalities among people will tend to be minimized, with subordinates expecting to be consulted by superiors over decisions that affect them, and to be treated more as equals of those with the power. Status differentials vary according to power distance.

Individualism/collectivism

Individualism/collectivism refers to relationships between an individual and their fellow individuals. In an individualistic society, the ties between individuals are very loose. Everybody is expected to look after self-interest and perhaps that of their immediate family. Individuals in these societies have high freedom of action. In collectivist societies the ties between individuals are very tight. The concept of the extended family is important and can reach out to work groups and organizations. Everybody is supposed to look after the interests of their in-group, which will protect them when they are in trouble.

Masculinity/femininity

Masculinity/femininity refers to the degree to which social gender roles are clearly distinct. In high-masculinity societies, the social division between the sexes is maximized, with traditional masculine social values permeating the society. These values include the importance of showing off, of making money and of 'big is beautiful'. In more feminine societies, the dominant values – for both men and women – are those more traditionally associated with the feminine role of nurturing and caring, putting relationships before money, minding the quality of life and 'small is beautiful'.

Uncertainty avoidance

Uncertainty avoidance refers to how a society deals with the fact that time runs only one way – from the past to the future – and that the future is unknown and, therefore, uncertain. Some societies are more comfortable with uncertainty than others. Uncertainty avoidance manifests, for example, in the creation of rules, systems and procedures to cope with events. People in low uncertainty avoidance societies tend to accept each day as it comes and are comfortable with a higher degree of risk taking. Societies demonstrating strong uncertainty avoidance characteristics socialize their people into trying to beat the future. Precision and punctuality are important in a context of fear of ambiguous situations and unfamiliar risks.

Illustration 4.9 *continued*

Long-term/short-term orientation

Different societies look at the past, the present and the future in different ways; some societies give a high priority to maintaining traditions and are cautious about change to the society; others are less connected to the past and are more open to change. Societies with a long-term orientation stand for the fostering of virtues oriented towards future rewards, in particular perseverance and thrift. People living in these societies have a respect for traditions and fulfilling social obligations. 'Saving face' is important. Leisure time is not important. Societies with a short-term orientation look more to the present and the immediate future. There is an emphasis on quick results. People in these societies care more about fixing present and near-future problems than seeking sustainable long-term solutions. Status is not a major issue in relationships. Protection of one's reputation (face) is important and ideas about what is good or bad are firmer (more absolute) than in societies with high long-term orientations.

When countries are mapped in terms of their relative scores on the five dimensions some logical groups and clusters emerge. Scandinavian countries group together around collectivism and consensus. Germany, Austria and Switzerland group together around efficiency. The UK, North America, Australia and New Zealand emphasize individualism and personal achievement. France, Spain, Italy and Japan group together based on bureaucracy and high power distance (Burnes, 2007, p. 206). Table 4.1 shows how a sample of countries score on these five dimensions.

Figure 4.6 illustrates four organizational models that refer to empirically derived relationships between a country's position on the power distance/uncertainty avoidance matrix and models of organizations implicit in the minds of people from the countries concerned. Hofstede uses the metaphors of a

Table 4.1 Culture dimension scores for 10 countries

Country	Power distance	Individualism*	Masculine**	Uncertainty avoidance	Long-term orientation***
China	High	Low	Moderate	Moderate	High
France	High	High	Moderate	High	Low
Germany	Low	High	High	Moderate	Moderate
Hong Kong	High	Low	High	Low	High
Indonesia	High	Low	Moderate	Low	Low
Japan	Moderate	Moderate	High	High	High
Netherlands	Low	High	Low	Moderate	Moderate
Russia	High	Moderate	Low	Low	Low
United States	Low	High	High	Low	Low
West Africa	High	Low	Moderate	Moderate	Low

*A low score implies collectivism. **A low score implies feminine orientation. ***A low score implies short-term orientation.

Source: Adapted with permission from Hofstede, G. (1993), 'Cultural constraints in management theories', *Academy of Management Executive*, February, p. 91. Copyright © Geert Hofstede.

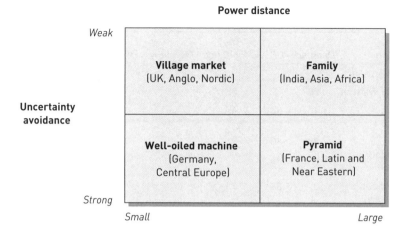

Figure 4.6 Implicit models of organization

Source: Adapted with permission from Hofstede, G. (1991) *Cultures and Organizations*, Maidenhead: McGraw-Hill. Copyright © Geert Hofstede.

village market, a well-oiled machine, a pyramid and a family to describe different approaches to organizing. Thus, people from countries with a 'village market' culture do not have the same need for hierarchy and certainty as those from a pyramid-type culture. These contrast with people from cultures reminiscent of 'well-oiled machines' – such as Germany – where hierarchy is not particularly required because there are established procedures and rules to which everyone works. People who live in countries or regions located in the 'family' quadrant – such as India, West Africa and Malaysia – are said to have an implicit model of organization that resembles a family in which the owner–manager is the omnipotent (father) figure.

It is clear that if these differences between cultural groupings exist and, assuming any convergence between them is slow, there is a good chance that they will influence organizational cultures in correspondingly different ways. The grouping together of countries into the four models depicted in Figure 4.6 is an oversimplification of the complexity of national cultures, let alone differences within countries, but it is helpful in appreciating that differences can and do exist.

However, while there are arguments against attempts to quantify and compare things as complex as national cultures, other research on this topic has supported Hofstede's basic propositions. Laurent (1983) for instance, focused on the views of senior and middle managers in a large number of different organizations, spread across nine European countries and the US. Laurent's hypothesis was that the national origin of managers significantly affects their views of what proper management should be. From his survey across 10 countries, Laurent identified four dimensions, which he labelled: organizations as political systems; organizations as authority systems; organizations as role-formalization systems; and organizations as hierarchical-relationship systems. Table 4.2 summarizes the relative position of

Table 4.2 Cultural differences between countries

Dimension	Denmark	UK	The Netherlands	Germany	Sweden	US	Switzerland	France	Italy	Belgium
Organizations as:										
Political systems	26	32	36	36	42	43	51	62	66	-
Authority systems	46	48	49	34	46	30	32	65	61	61
Role-formalization systems	80	80	67	85	57	66	85	81	84	81
Hierarchical-relationship systems	37	36	33	47	25	28	43	50	66	50

Source: Summarized from Laurent, A. (1983), 'The cultural diversity of Western conceptions of management', *International Studies of Management and Organisation*, XIII (1–2), pp. 75–96.

the 10 countries on each dimension. The results show that France and Italy score highly on all dimensions – meaning that they were politicized, hierarchical, had high degrees of role formalization and believed in the authority of individuals. Denmark and the UK are positioned similarly to each other with low levels of hierarchy and politicization, moderate degrees of belief in individual authority and high levels of role formalization. Sweden had the lowest score in terms of hierarchical relationships with moderate scores on the other three dimensions. Other similarities and differences can be seen from the table.

The GLOBE framework

The Global Leadership and Organization Behaviour Effectiveness (GLOBE) study extended previous work on national cultures (see House *et al.,* 2004). The research reported in this study spanned 62 countries in 10 world regions, taken from a very wide range of organizations and sectors. GLOBE specifically tried to understand how cultural values connected to organizational behaviour.

The study found nine dimensions of national culture as shown in Table 4.3. These show similarities to Hofstede's typology with the main differences, at least linguistically, being the addition of dimensions relating to concern for performance and concern for gender equality. However, there is some debate about the validity of all nine dimensions (e.g. Minkov and Blagoev, 2012) though Hofstede (2006) argues that after allowing for 'data reduction' the nine dimensions are a strong reflection of his earlier work.

To illustrate how different countries were ranked on each dimension some sample data are extracted in Table 4.4.

Based on these rankings, GLOBE data suggest the following for the countries shown (partly tongue in cheek). The Swiss are exercised by achievement, future planning and minimizing uncertainty. The Swedes are exercised by assertiveness and group collectivism. The English seem relatively average although they are

Table 4.3 Dimensions of national culture from the GLOBE study

GLOBE Dimension	Summary	Code
Achievement, performance orientation	Focus on performance improvement and rewarding it	ACH
Future orientation	Focus on short-term or long-term results	FUT
Assertiveness	Focus on dominating others	ASS
Collectivism	Use of groups in society and organizations	COLL1
Gender egalitarianism	Concern for gender equality	GEN
Humane orientation	Desire and concern for fairness and tolerance	HUM
Power distance	The extent to which power is unequally distributed	POW
Family collectivism	The integration of people into the family	COLL2
Uncertainty avoidance	Focus on alleviating unpredictable outcomes, trying to minimize uncertainty	UNC

Source: Adapted from Koopman *et al.* (1999), 'National culture and leadership profiles in Europe: some results from the GLOBE study', *European Journal of Work and Organizational Psychology*, 8(4), pp. 503–20.

Table 4.4 Selected country ranks from the GLOBE study

	ACH	FUT	ASS	COLL1	GEN	HUM	POW	COLL2	UNC
Switzerland	1	2	36	37	53	53	46	56	1
Sweden	48	9	1	1	9	30	50	59	2
England	34	11	32	30	14	48	36	53	13
Italy	55	56	28	56	37	51	20	41	42
Hungary	58	58	54	60	3	58	12	37	60

Source: Adapted from Koopman *et al.* (1999), 'National culture and leadership profiles in Europe: some results from the GLOBE study', *European Journal of Work and Organizational Psychology*, 8(4), pp. 503–20.

relatively short term in their outlook. The Italians seem relaxed about most things but do like a bit of power distance. Hungarians seem most of all to be concerned with gender equality. Koopman *et al.* (1999) concluded that European countries do fit in 'culture clusters' and cautioned against the idea of a European culture. Culture clusters are explained by differences in language roots (e.g. Germanic versus Latin), geographic proximity, post-war Soviet expansion, religion (e.g. Protestant versus Catholic) and political/economic systems, among other things.

Some of the cultural dimensions found in studies of this type correlate with national prosperity (or poverty) which poses an important question of whether some dimensions are proxies for levels of economic development rather than true cultural differences.

Based on interviews with human resource directors in 40 large European companies, Calori and De Woot (1994) suggested the clusters of management systems shown in Figure 4.7, and Illustration 4.10 summarizes their descriptions of Anglo-Saxon, Latin and Northern European (using the German model as an example) groupings.

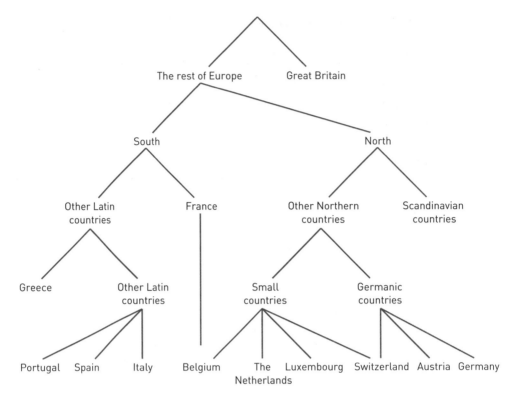

Figure 4.7 Clustering of management systems in Europe

Source: Calori, R. and De Woot, P. (1994) *A European Management Model Beyond Diversity*, Hemel Hempstead: Prentice Hall, p. 20.

Illustration 4.10

Differences between the United Kingdom, Southern Europe and Northern Europe

The United Kingdom, an exception in Europe

Management in the United Kingdom has more in common with the United States than the rest of Europe. It has:

- a short-term orientation (more than continental Europe);
- a shareholder orientation (compared to the rest of Europe which has more of a stakeholder orientation);
- an orientation towards trading and finance (the importance of the stock market was more developed than in continental Europe);
- a higher turnover of managers;
- a greater liberalism towards foreigners (e.g. the Japanese);
- more freedom for top management in relation to employees and government;
- more direct and pragmatic relationships between people;
- more variable remuneration.

However, different from the United States, it additionally has:

- adversarial relationships with labour*;
- the tradition of the manager as a 'gifted amateur' (as opposed to the professionalism of US managers);
- the influence of class differences in organizations.

The Latin way of doing business

Southern Europe (including France) differs from the rest of Europe in that it has:

- more state intervention;
- more protectionism;

- more hierarchy in the firm;
- more intuitive management;
- more family business (especially in Italy);
- more reliance on an elite (especially in France).

The German model

Characteristic of Germany, Austria and, to some extent, Switzerland and the Benelux countries, the German model is based on three cultural and structural characteristics:

- strong links between banks and industry;
- a balance between a sense of national collectivity and the *Länder* (regional) system;
- a system of training and development of managers.

It has the following five components:

- the system of co-determination with workers' representatives present on the board;

- the loyalty of managers (and employees in general) who spend their career in a single firm, which then gives priority to in-house training;
- the collective orientation of the workforce, which includes dedication to the company, team spirit and a sense of discipline;
- the long-term orientation that appears in planning, in the seriousness and stability of supplier–client relationships and in the priority of industrial goals over short-term financial objectives;
- the reliability and stability of shareholders, influenced by a strong involvement of banks in industry.

*Since the late 1980s employee relations in the UK have been generally good and this description probably reflects the high levels of unrest seen in the 1970s and early 1980s.

Source: Based on Calori, R. and De Woot, P. (1994), *A European Management Model Beyond Diversity*, Hemel Hempstead: Prentice Hall, pp. 22–29.

Activity 4.5

Compare and contrast Calori and De Woot's country groupings and characteristics (see Figure 4.7) with the same countries' positions on Laurent's cultural dimensions (see Table 4.2) and the models presented in Figure 4.6. To what extent do any of these characterizations agree with your own experience, either through business or tourism?

World Values Survey

In addition to the research and models already discussed, the World Values Survey is another attempt to understand national cultures and how they are changing. Inglehart and Baker (2000) offer some revealing findings about the convergence–divergence debate from their longitudinal analysis of 65 societies. They found evidence for both 'massive cultural change and the persistence of distinctive cultural traditions' (p. 19). They found that economic development promotes a shift away from traditional values to less religious values such that if economic development continues then institutionalized religious systems will decline. Consider the fall in religious observance in Protestant industrialized Europe, for example.

Societies that enter a post-industrialist era see a departure from absolute norms. However, the historic cultural roots, e.g. Protestantism, Islam or Confucianism, persist in shaping societies. So, rather than converge, societies are changing but moving in parallel 'shaped by their cultural heritage' (p. 49). Inglehart and Baker also caution against seeing cultural change as 'Americanization'. In contrast, they found that the Nordic countries (Denmark, Finland, Norway, Sweden) best illustrate the culture that others are moving towards.

National culture and organizational culture

Activity 4.5 shows how difficult it is to fit national culture into categories, yet it would be hard to argue that differences of this type do not exist. In addition, the evidence points to close relationships between national culture and organizational culture. For instance, Furnham and Gunter (1993) provide examples of organizations in Australia, Israel and Denmark (low scores on power distance) having common organizational structures. Their structures incorporated low centralization of decision making and flatter pyramids of control, reminiscent of Handy's task culture. These structures contrasted with those in countries such as the Philippines, Mexico and India, which scored highly on power distance. Here, organizations were typified by strict hierarchical structures and centralized decision making, reminiscent of Handy's role culture.

National cultures overlay principles, practices and assumptions that affect management practices such as selection, development and reward and as such influence interpersonal relationships and individual performance. Indeed, one of the GLOBE dimensions relates to a performance orientation in national culture. However, variations between organizational cultures in the same country (within-country variations) are more influential than national cultural differences (Gerhart and Fang, 2005; Gerhart, 2008). Put another way, in a cross-border merger the two organizational cultures have more bearing on outcomes that the two national cultures. In a study of international alliances, differences in professional cultures had the most disruptive effect on outcomes followed by organizational culture which was more disruptive than differences in national cultures (Sirmon and Lane, 2004). Professional cultures exist in groups of people in similar occupations and develop through education, training, the ways knowledge is generated and the ways competence is demonstrated – consider differences in engineering, literature and accounting for instance. In a study of organizations in the US, Brazil and India, Nelson and Gopalan (2003) found clusters of organizations with cultures matching the national culture (isomorphism) and clusters that rejected national values (rejective). This led them to suggest that debates about *either* convergence or divergence are unhelpful and that it would be better to talk about how forces for convergence interact with forces for divergence in the local setting.

Activity 4.6

Look again at Figure 4.6 which positions four models of organization on Hofstede's power distance and uncertainty avoidance dimensions. Consider Deal and Kennedy's four culture types described in Illustration 4.6 and consider how far each can be related to one or more of Hofstede's organizational models. What conclusions can you derive from this?

Both Adler (1991) and Hofstede (1994) draw attention to the way that organizational theory, as it relates to factors such as motivation, decision making and leadership, is culturally determined. Because most management and organizational theory derives from research in Western universities, particularly the US, caution is advised before extending it uncritically elsewhere. For instance, cultures that value participative styles of leadership and decision making may not be welcomed in societies that see consultation by leaders as a weakness and where workers would be embarrassed if consulted by their managers.

Organizational culture and change

Wilson and Rosenfeld (1990, p. 237) say: 'The pervasive nature of organizational culture cannot be stressed too much.' We contend that this is to a large extent true and, particularly so, with respect to organizational change. However, as discussed previously, organizational cultures come in many forms, and therefore are likely to have varied influences on efforts to bring about change. These are depicted in Figure 4.8.

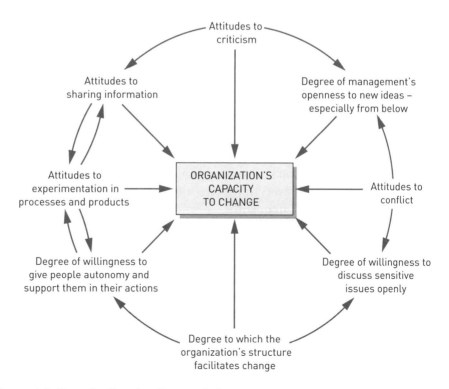

Figure 4.8 Organizational culture and change

Cultures in defence against, or in support of change

An examination of the elements in Figure 4.8 will give some idea of how each one could obstruct or support change. One element of organizational design that is particularly relevant to the ease with which change comes about is that of an organization's structure. Indeed, some of the typologies of organizational culture, discussed earlier in the chapter, are closely related to types of organizational structure. Burns and Stalker's (1961) classic research is a good example of the merger of the concepts of structure and culture as is seen in their argument that organic types of organization are much more likely to be able to respond to the need for change than mechanistic forms. However, this is not to say that mechanistic-type organizations *defend* against change but they are less open to it. They are, however, unlikely to support, without serious trauma, the frame-breaking, transformational or revolutionary types of change discussed in Chapter 2. Structural characteristics as well as attitudes, beliefs and values are more likely to act as barriers.

Kanter (1983) describes two extremes of organizational culture that differ, not only in structural characteristics, but also in the underlying attitudes and beliefs of the people working in them. The first she calls a 'segmentalist' culture and the other an 'integrative' culture (see Illustration 4.11).

In addition, she offers the following 10 'rules for stifling innovation':

1 Regard any new idea from below with suspicion – because it is new, and because it is from below.
2 Insist that people who need your approval to act first go through several other levels of management to get their signatures.
3 Ask departments or individuals to challenge and criticize each other's proposals. (That saves you the task of deciding; you just pick the survivor.)
4 Express your criticisms freely and withhold your praise. (That keeps people on their toes.) Let them know they can be fired at any time.
5 Treat identification of problems as signs of failure, to discourage people from letting you know when something in their area isn't working.
6 Control everything carefully. Make sure people count anything that can be counted, frequently.
7 Make decisions to reorganize or change policies in secret, and spring them on people unexpectedly. (That also keeps people on their toes.)
8 Make sure that requests for information are fully justified and make sure that it is not given out to managers freely. (You don't want data to fall into the wrong hands.)
9 Assign to lower-level managers, in the name of delegation and participation, responsibility for figuring out how to cut back, lay off, move people around or otherwise implement threatening decisions you have made. And get them to do it quickly.
10 And above all, never forget that you, the 'higher-ups', already know everything important about this business.

Illustration 4.11

Segmentalist and integrative cultures

Segmentalist cultures:

- compartmentalize actions, events and problems;
- see problems as narrowly as possible;
- have segmented structures with large numbers of departments walled off from one another;
- assume problems can be solved by carving them up into pieces that are then assigned to specialists who work in isolation;
- divide resources up among the many departments;
- avoid experimentation;
- avoid conflict and confrontation;
- have weak coordinating mechanisms;
- stress precedent and procedures.

Integrative cultures:

- are willing to move beyond received wisdom;
- combine ideas from unconnected sources;
- see problems as wholes, related to larger wholes;
- challenge established practices;
- operate at the edge of competencies;
- measure themselves by looking to visions of the future rather than by referring to the standards of the past;
- create mechanisms for exchange of information and new ideas;
- recognize and even encourage differences, but then be prepared to cooperate;
- are outward looking;
- look for novel solutions to problems.

Source: Based on Kanter, R.M. (1983), *The Change Masters*, London: Routledge,

Organizational learning and types of change

Argyris (1964) pointed to the difference between two kinds of learning. *Single-loop learning* is indicative of a situation where an objective or goal is defined and a person works out the most favoured way of reaching the goal. In single-loop learning, while many different possibilities for achieving personal or organizational goals might be considered, the goal itself is not questioned. Single-loop learning is also referred to as individual learning, that is, learning which an individual achieves but that seldom disseminates into the organization in any coherent way.

In contrast, with *double-loop learning* questions are asked not only about the *means* by which goals can be achieved, but about the *ends*, that is, the goals themselves. Johnson (1990) refers to this type of learning as *organizational relearning*, which he says is a 'process in which that which is taken for granted and which is the basis of strategic direction – the paradigm – is re-formulated' (p. 189). Given that the organizational paradigm lies at the heart of the cultural web, this implies change throughout the organization in all aspects of its behaviour.

Individual or single-loop learning is most likely to be the dominant form to occur in a segmentalist or defensive culture. The characteristics of this type of culture act significantly against the sharing of information and openness that are required for organizational learning to take place. Therefore, while it could be sufficient for the types of change, which Dunphy and Stace (1993) define as 'fine-tuning' and 'incremental adjustment', it will be unable to cope with the kind of radical thinking required to bring about change in the organization's direction – strategic change. In addition, the inability of an organization to operate double-loop learning contributes to the process of 'strategic drift' (Johnson *et al.*, 2014) which can lead to change being forced upon organizations.

People can learn but can an organization learn over and above what its people learn? Organizations can of course store knowledge in databases and systems that capture past learning. Furthermore, an organization's culture does capture and express accumulated learning – recall the blunter definitions of culture as 'the way we do things around here' and the way cultures perpetuate stories and recipes. The idea of organizational memory was explored by van der Bent *et al.* (1999) in a Dutch electronics firm. They identified four 'memory carriers': culture, structure, systems and procedures. By following a major change programme in the firm over several years they concluded:

1 Change managers must become intimate with the memory carriers at the start of a change intervention. Organizational memory while a force for stability is also a barrier to change. Which carriers can impede the change?
2 Memory carriers are not isolated; rather they are interconnected. Efforts to change one carrier must appreciate how they will touch upon others. Both the carriers and their relationships need attention.
3 Not all carriers lead to organizational learning. Memories led to learning where the changes were more complex and hard to achieve. Use of memories operated at a deep level and influenced change issues that employees felt were important to the organization. Remembering was more likely in relation to important organizational issues.
4 Outcomes of change are influenced by the spirit in which they are pursued as much as the intended changes *per se*. Organizational memory is part of that spirit.

Cultural change to effect organizational change

Culture is, by definition, a dominant influence on organizational life. It follows then that in order to bring about significant organizational change it may be necessary to change an organizational culture, which means changing many if not all, elements of Johnson *et al.*'s (2014) cultural web. It is clear that cultures *do* change, but generally, over longer time periods than is hoped for or assumed. What is less clear is *how* a culture can be changed.

Assessing cultural risk

Schwartz and Davis (1981) thought culture could be changed and devised a way of measuring culture in terms of descriptions of the way management tasks are typically handled in company-wide, boss–subordinate, peer and interdepartmental relationships as a way of assessing the degree of cultural compatibility with any proposed strategic change. Figure 4.9 is an example of their corporate culture matrix designed to carry out the first part of this process. It has been completed for the UK-based division of a company in the computer services industry.

At this stage we ask readers to carry out Activity 4.7 as this gives a way of making judgements about how an organization's culture fits with any required

Tasks	Relationships				
	Companywide	Boss-subordinate	Peer	Inter-department	Summary of culture in relation to tasks
Innovating	Innovation if part of the mission	Bosses open to suggestions	Teamwork	Teamwork	Encourage creativity and innovation
Decision making	Has to fit in with strategy	Input from subordinates encouraged – boss has final word	Collective decisions	Work together to produce an integrated package	Collaborative decision making but boss has the final word; corporate strategy rules
Communicating	Easy, use of email and phone	Friendly	Face to face and open	Easy, use of email and phone	Easy, informal and friendly communications
Organizing	Market focus	Democratic	Professional relationships	Collaborative	Organized on the basis of skills and professional relationships
Monitoring	Shareholder-led organization	Meet short-term profit targets and deadlines	Project management	Project management	Need to meet short-term profit goals
Appraising and rewarding	Encourage performers	Hard work = good rewards	Results important	Results important	Meritocracy
Summary of culture in relation to relationships	Allow freedom to managers as long as they operate within the strategy and meet profit targets; output-oriented	Friendly, rely on each other for success	Highly skilled professionals who help each other out	Work together	Overall performance and profit matter in a culture that welcomes dynamic and performance-related individuals

Figure 4.9 Corporate culture matrix

Source: Matrix adapted from Schwartz, H. and Davis, S.M. (1981) 'Matching corporate strategy and business strategy', *Organizational Dynamics*, Summer, p. 36; example from the author's own experience. Copyright (1981), with permission from Elsevier.

Activity 4.7

For an organization you know well use the basic matrix in Figure 4.9 to do the following:

1 *Write in the cells of the main part of the matrix, words and/or phrases that encapsulate the different relationships (listed horizontally) according to the management of the tasks (listed vertically).*
2 *In the final column on the right, summarize the corporate culture for each task.*
3 *In the bottom row, summarize the corporate culture for each of the relationships.*

What do the summaries tell you about this organization's overall culture?

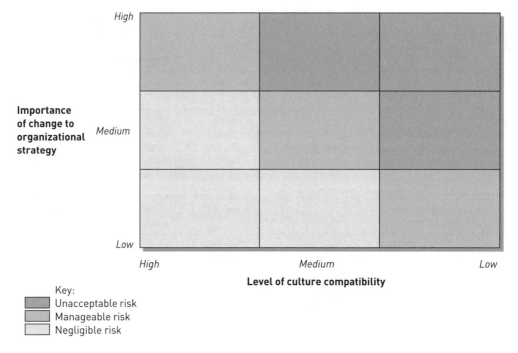

Figure 4.10 **Assessing cultural risk**

Source: Matrix adapted from Schwartz, H. and Davis, S.M. (1981) 'Matching corporate strategy and business strategy', *Organizational Dynamics*, Summer, p. 41. Copyright (1981), with permission from Elsevier.

changes. The framework for this comparative assessment is shown in Figure 4.10 as a matrix that allows elements of the proposed strategy changes to be positioned against their importance to the strategy and the degree to which they are compatible with the culture. For instance, if a change to a matrix structure is needed yet the culture resembles a role culture, the need for a matrix structure would be positioned in the top right cell of the matrix in Figure 4.10 (high importance but low cultural compatibility). Other elements of the changes might be low in level of culture compatibility but if they are of low importance in the overall change strategy they would be positioned towards the lower right-hand part of the matrix.

The relevance of culture change to organizational change

Assessing cultural risk helps management pinpoint where resistance to change could occur because of incompatibility between strategy and culture. This allows managers to make choices regarding whether to:

(a) ignore the culture;
(b) manage around the culture;
(c) try to change the culture to fit the strategy; or
(d) change the strategy to fit the culture, perhaps by reducing performance expectations.

Ignoring the culture

Ignoring culture could be dangerous and seems likely to carry a high risk of future problems such as disruption to operations and lack of progress.

Managing around the culture

The second option – managing around the culture – is a real possibility given that there are, in most cases, more ways than one of achieving desired goals. Figure 4.11 gives an example of how to manage around an organization's culture. This outlines four typical strategies that companies might pursue and suggests 'right' organizational approaches to implement them. The two columns on the right of Figure 4.11 illustrate possible cultural barriers to these 'right' approaches and the alternative approaches that could be used.

Changing the culture

The third option, deliberately changing the culture to fit the desired strategic changes, is a popular form of management intervention (Chatman, 2014; Ogbonna

	Strategy	'Right' approach	Cultural barriers	Alternative approaches
Company A	Diversify product and market	Divisionalize	Centralized power One-person rule Functional focus Hierarchical structure	Use business teams Use explicit strategic planning Change business measures
Company B	Focus marketing on most profitable segments	Fine-tune reward system. Adjust management information system	Diffused power Highly individualized operations	Dedicate full-time personnel to each key market
Company C	Extend technology to new markets	Set up matrix organization	Multiple power centres Functional focus	Use programme coordinators Set up planning committees Get top management more involved
Company D	Withdraw gradually from declining market and maximize cash throw-offs	Focus organization specifically Fine-tune rewards Ensure top management visibility	New-business driven Innovators rewarded State-of-the-art operation	Sell out

Figure 4.11 Managing around company culture

Source: Matrix adapted from Schwartz, H. and Davis, S.M. (1981) 'Matching corporate strategy and business strategy', *Organizational Dynamics*, Summer, p. 44. Copyright (1981), with permission from Elsevier.

and Harris, 2002). However, as much of the literature cautions, this can be an extremely difficult and lengthy process, particularly if culture is strong (Scholz, 1987; Furnham and Gunter, 1993; Wankhede and Brinkman, 2014).

Structural changes have seen an increase in the employment of professional and knowledge workers and for some workers an erosion of security of employment and predictable career paths. Two problems arise from this. The first is that knowledge workers are less likely to be open to cultural manipulation because of their professional and technical backgrounds and allegiances. Second, where there are histories of downsizing or delayering in an organization, some cynicism about the purposes and consequences of change seems inevitable, at least in the short term. As such, 'employees in general may be less receptive to evangelical calls for shared cultural values' (Hope and Hendry, 1995, p. 62).

Beer, Eisenstat and Spector's (1993) view that trying to change attitudes and values directly is futile is still relevant; particularly their comment that the way to bring about organizational change is first to change behaviour as behavioural change will then help to change attitudes and values. Thus Beer *et al.* argue for changing the organizational context (people's roles, responsibilities and the relationships between them) first, in an effort to change behaviour and attitudes. This view of change rests on the assumption that changing organizational structures, systems and role relationships, which comprise, in the main, the formal aspects of organizational life, will bring about desired cultural changes incorporating organizational members' attitudes and beliefs. Many (arguably uncritical) models of planned change subscribe to this view such as the 'Six steps to effective change' shown in Illustration 4.12.

Illustration 4.12

Uncritical approaches to culture change

The following six steps relate to transformation of a supply chain (Halm, 2014).

1 Identify a best practice operating model to create a vision of what the new supply chain configuration would look like.
2 Implement a comprehensive governance system for the change project.
3 Aggressively transition to the new organization structure involving new jobs, new job descriptions and new appointments, and rapid action to fill new jobs.
4 Pro-actively manage stakeholders, employee engagement and communications. This involves tailored communications with stakeholder groups, engaging employees as 'change ambassadors'.

5 Define and implement new business processes and allocate personal accountability.
6 Develop employee capabilities and reinvent the culture using teamwork and alignment meetings to enable employees to converse around accelerating project performance.

Although steps like these occur regularly in change recipes, the complexity of some steps, e.g. 'reinvent the culture', are highly complex and usually need much more than teamwork and meetings if they are to be successful.

Source: Based on Halm, D. (2014), 'The 30% solution', *OD Practitioner*, 46(1), pp. 42–8.

Supporters of the 'culture can'/'cannot be changed' camps can both find support in the literature. Methods of attempting culture change call upon education and persuasion or, in some cases, coercion, to help bring about changes in attitudes (Anthony, 1994) and storytelling to communicate values, norms and ideology (Dolan and Bao, 2012). Other tactics involve changing human resource management practices (Barratt-Pugh, Bahn and Gakere, 2013) which can involve reshaping selection, promotion, reward and redundancy policies to 'refresh' the composition of the workforce by attracting and retaining people with the beliefs, values and attitudes that are associated with the desired culture.

Illustration 4.13 portrays an example of a large organization that was able to manage around its culture for a number of years and during that time still succeeded in growing and developing in the global market. However, to achieve longer-term success, the organization decided to create a strategy that would ultimately attempt to change the culture.

Illustration 4.13

Cultural change at the BBC

Now over 90 years old, Auntie Beeb (the BBC) is a strong yet vulnerable institution. Funded out of compulsory TV licence fees it enjoys a guaranteed income, yet following an explosion of new satellite TV channels the BBC is exposed. After all, when viewers can choose the satellite packages they want, why should UK residents be forced to pay the BBC an annual licence fee just to own a television?

By the 1990s the belief in the supremacy of market forces in the UK had extended to include the creation of quasi or internal markets in some public organizations. In the BBC this was attempted by separating the people who commissioned programmes (the purchasers) from those who produced them (the providers). This change was aimed at transforming the organization away from a highly bureaucratic outfit ill-suited to change into a market-driven organization better placed to respond and compete. According to an account written by BBC insiders, the first phase of the BBC's change programme dealt with restructuring and faster decision making (Grossman and Smith, 2002). The second phase aimed at changing the culture. Top management decided upon four priorities:

- clarifying purpose and vision;
- changing culture by altering how employees behaved;

- developing leadership to reflect and articulate a new culture;
- shifting internal and external perceptions of the Corporation.

The new vision emphasized being 'the most creative organization in the world'. Quite a challenge! Communication was a big part of the cultural change programme and this included listening to how employees felt about the organization. Employees said they were concerned about lack of leadership, feeling undervalued, lack of rewards for creativity and a risk-averse culture. Constructive criticism was encouraged. Staff expressing concerns and ideas were asked to put forward solutions and take ownership of them. Change had to be positive and all staff had a responsibility to play their part. Key principles were: 'just do it', make workspaces better for all, live the values of the BBC, understand what leadership is and demonstrate it, value people, inspire creativity everywhere and stay in touch with viewers and listeners.

This summary account is not untypical of management-led change. Indeed, if a management group decides to try and change organizational culture then these are the sort of things that are usually attempted. But did it work? Harris and Wegg-Prosser (2007) offer a revealing account of

Illustration 4.13 *continued*

change in the BBC from 1991 to 2002 and are rather doubtful.

Staff attitude surveys showed improvements but were these merely reflecting employees' feel-good ratings while they thought someone was showing interest in them? The sight of a chief executive brandishing a 'Cut the crap – make it happen' card would probably be welcome in many workplaces and may well have enthused staff to think and act differently. But how sustainable was it? In short, several years later the producer-choice initiative had not brought about the behavioural and cultural changes intended according to Harris and Wegg-Prosser (2007). The crap-cutting chief executive left in 2004. The strong bureaucracy that prevailed had evolved and absorbed the narratives of strategic change and the new mechanisms within it. The point of this illustration is that major initiatives run over several years can struggle. Rather than being a story of decisive organizational changes the BBC story can be seen as 'surges of managerial control' overlaying periods of creative autonomy (Harris and Wegg-Prosser, 2007, p. 299).

 ## Conclusions

The concept of culture is complex given its application to societies, organizations and groups, all of which interact one with another. Efforts to describe national culture typically produce a set of bipolar dimensions on which cultures vary. Different studies have produced similar schema. Managers working across international borders need to appreciate cultural differences and in particular the implications for the way work is organized and the behavioural expectations of employees.

Organizations can be seen *as* cultures rather than as *having* them. Every culture is unique yet many typologies have been produced in efforts to describe and classify their common features and the main types found. Within an organization, different sub-cultures can exist that reflect different histories, personalities and professional norms. When people join an organization they learn how to act according to expectations and norms even though outside the organization they may behave differently. Selection processes often look for cultural fit in prospective employees and can be used to support large-scale employee turnover. Given that organic and integrative organizational cultures are said to support change and, given the increasing requirement for creativity and innovation in organizations, it seems reasonable for many organizations to attempt to change their cultures in these directions. However, attempts to change culture are frequently problematic. Consequently, if attempting to change culture is too risky then ways of managing around the culture or even changing the strategy to take account of the culture are needed.

Discussion questions and assignments

1 Drawing on your experience, consider how realistic it is for managers to try and change organizational culture.

2 To what extent does an organization's structure influence its culture and its capacity to work with change?

3 Review the evidence for and against the notion that national cultures are converging.

4 Drawing on typologies of culture, prepare a presentation to demonstrate how cultural types relate to different types of organizational change.

5 How could organizations that are moving towards a merger or acquisition begin to carry out a cultural audit? In particular, how could they assess the compatibility of their respective cultures to identify possible problem areas that could impede integration?

6 To what extent can an organization culture change yet still retain the majority of employees?

Case example ●●●

The Civil Service

Governments come and go, each promising to deliver change and reforms to improve the economy and society. But government policy and strategy are filtered through and buffered by the civil service and it looks as if long-running attempts to reform the British Civil Service have met with little success. A recent report into the way the Civil Service works found it relied too much on 'generalist amateurs', distrusted outsiders (including people in government), was overly tolerant of poor management and is an organization where promotion is linked to tenure and conformity rather than innovation. Similar conclusions were made in a previous review in 1967 – so it seems the criticisms have been around for quite a time! Other criticisms levelled at the Civil Service are that it is too big, over-staffed, that sickness absence is high, and that it is a 'wet blanket' that smothers ideas.

The Civil Service recruits some of the smartest graduates available and has rigorous selection processes – so we can safely assume that its employees are quite capable of understanding what government ministers want to do. However, working in Whitehall is characterized by conformism to rules and procedures rather than risk taking; conformity

gets rewarded and is what gets people promoted. Several recent high-profile projects have been delayed and/or have seen cost over-run. The culture is one of caution and of giving advice to ministers (arguably good characteristics) but it is also characterized as being weak, particularly when it comes to making changes to itself.

One of the tensions of course is that most ministers are often in post for a short time only, perhaps only a few months, whereas the nation has to be administered for the long run. Arguably, it is in the public interest to have a cautious civil service to intervene between short-lived ministers, many of whom, despite their new ideas, have little experience of anything outside politics and public relations.

The situation has been described as a power struggle fought at the highest level between senior career civil servants and government ministers. Another observer concluded that people just have different views and there are vested interests that get in the way of making changes. A former UK prime minister remarked that the 'traditional skill set of the Civil Service' is not what is required to drive through the changes needed; at least the changes needed by government.

➡

Case exercise

1 Assuming that the claims made about the Civil Service are fair, why do you think that the Service has been able to resist cultural change over such a long period?

2 Why do you think that successive governments have been unable to introduce cultural change in the Civil Service?

Source: Based on 'Subtle and courteous, this is a power struggle at the highest level', *The Times*, 14th January 2013, pp. 8–9

Indicative resources

Cameron, K.S. and Quinn, R.E. (2011), *Diagnosing and Changing Organizational Cultures: Based on the Competing Values Framework* (3rd edn), San Francisco, CA: Jossey-Bass.

Hofstede, G.H. (2010), *Cultures and Organizations: Software of the Mind* (3rd edn), London: McGraw-Hill. This book is an essential read for any student or manager interested in work relating to culture, both at national and organizational level.

Schein, H.E. (2004), *Organizational Culture and Leadership* (3rd edn), San Francisco, CA: Jossey-Bass. This book covers national and organizational culture in depth and contains useful case examples.

Trompenaars, F. and Prud'homme, P. (2004), *Managing Change Across Corporate Cultures,* Chichester: Capstone Publishing. This book focuses on culture at company, national and international levels. It offers theoretical perspectives relating to corporate culture, and includes case studies and research conducted by the authors.

Useful websites

http://www.geert-hofstede.com This site explains dimensions of national culture and explains how different countries compare.

https://www.youtube.com/watch?v=Rd0kf3wd120 'What is organizational culture? Why culture matters to your organization'.

https://www.youtube.com/watch?v=EcHpgsTg458 'Corporate culture Apple example'. An interesting insight into a specific organization culture.

https://www.youtube.com/watch?v=j518qByx2Ng 'Two different approaches to cultural change'. This video describes 'top-down' and 'middle-out' approaches.

References

Adler, N.J. (1991), *International Dimensions of Organizational Behavior* (2nd edn), Belmont, CA: Wadsworth Publishing Company.

Adler, N.J. (1997), *International Dimensions of Organizational Behavior* (3rd edn), Cincinnati, OH: South Western College Publishing, ITP.

Alvesson, M. (1993), *Cultural Perspectives on Organizations*, Cambridge: Cambridge University Press.

Anthony, P. (1994), *Managing Culture*, Milton Keynes: Open University Press.

Argyris, C. (1964), *Integrating the Individual and the Organization*, New York: Wiley.

Badrtalei, J. and Bates, D.L. (2007), 'Effect of organizational cultures on mergers and acquisitions: the case of DaimlerChrysler', *International Journal of Management*, 24(2), pp. 303–17.

Barratt-Pugh, L., Bahn, S. and Gakere, E. (2013), 'Managers as change agents: implications for human resource managers engaging with culture change', *Journal of Organizational Change Management*, 26(4), pp. 748–64.

Bate, S.P. (1996), 'Towards a strategic framework for changing corporate culture', *Strategic Change*, 5, pp. 27–42.

Beer, M., Eisenstat, R.A. and Spector, B. (1993), 'Why change programs don't produce change', in Mabey, C. and Mayon-White, B. (eds), *Managing Change* (2nd edn), London: PCP.

Brooks, I. and Bate, S.P. (1994), 'The problems of effecting change within the British Civil Service: a cultural perspective', *British Journal of Management*, 5, pp. 177–90.

Brown, A. (1995), *Organisational Culture*, London: Pitman.

Burnes, B. (2007) *Managing Change* (5th edn), Harlow: Financial Times Prentice Hall.

Burns, T. and Stalker, G.M. (1961), *The Management of Innovation*, London: Tavistock.

Calori, R. and De Woot, P. (1994), *A European Management Model Beyond Diversity*, Hemel Hempstead: Prentice Hall.

Cameron, K.S. and Quinn, R.E. (2005), *Diagnosing and Changing Organizational Culture: Based on the Competing Values Framework*, San Francisco, CA: Jossey-Bass.

Carnall, C. (2007), *Managing Change in Organizations* (5th edn), Harlow: Financial Times Prentice Hall.

Chatman, J. (2014), 'Culture change at Genentech: accelerating strategic and financial accomplishments', *California Management Review*, 56(2), pp. 113–29.

Deal, T.E. and Kennedy, A.A. (1982), *Corporate Cultures: The Rites and Rituals of Corporate Life*, Reading, MA: Addison-Wesley.

Deal, T.E. and Kennedy, A.A. (2000), *The New Corporate Cultures*, London: Perseus Books.

Dolan, S.L. and Bao, Y. (2012), 'Sharing the culture: embedding storytelling and ethics in the culture change management process', *Journal of Management and Change*, 29, pp. 10–23.

Drennan, D. (1992), *Transforming Company Culture*, London: McGraw-Hill.

Dunphy, D. and Stace, D. (1993), 'The strategic management of corporate change', *Human Relations*, 46(8), pp. 905–20.

Dyer, W. (1985), 'The cycle of cultural evolution in organizations', in Kilmann, R.H., Saxton, M.J. and Serpa, R. (eds), *Gaining Control of the Corporate Culture*, San Francisco, CA: Jossey-Bass.

French, W.L. and Bell, C.H., Jr (1990), *Organization Development: Behavioral Science Interventions for Organization Improvement* (4th edn), Englewood Cliffs, NJ: Prentice-Hall.

French, W.L. and Bell, C.H., Jr (1999), *Organizational Development* (6th edn), Englewood Cliffs, NJ: Prentice-Hall.

Furnham, A. and Gunter, B. (1993), 'Corporate culture: diagnosis and change', in Cooper, C.L. (ed.) *International Review of Industrial and Organisational Psychology*, Chichester: Wiley.

Gerhart, B. (2008), 'How much does national culture constrain organizational culture?', *Management and Organization Review*, 5(2), pp. 241–59.

Gerhart, B. and Fang, M. (2005), 'National culture and human resource management: assumptions and evidence', *International Journal of Human Resource Management*, 16(6), pp. 971–86.

Grossman, R. and Smith, P. (2002), 'Humanizing cultural change at the BBC', *Strategic Communication Management*, 7(1), pp. 28–32.

Hall, W. (1995), *Managing Cultures: Making Strategic Relationships Work*, Chichester: Wiley.

Halm, D. (2014), 'The 30% solution', *OD Practitioner*, 46(1), pp. 42–8.

Handy, C. (1993), *Understanding Organizations*, Hamondsworth: Penguin.

Harris, M. and Wegg-Prosser, V. (2007), 'Post-bureaucracy and the politics of forgetting: management of change at the BBC 1991–2002', *Journal of Organizational Change Management*, 20(3), pp. 290–303.

Hartmann, J. and Khademian, A. (2010), 'Culture change refined and revitalized: the road show and guides for pragmatic action', *Public Administration Review*, 70(6), pp. 845–56.

Hofstede, G. (1981), 'Culture and organizations', *International Studies of Management and Organizations*, X(4), pp. 15–41.

Hofstede, G. (1993), 'Cultural constraints in management theories', *Academy of Management Executive*, February, pp. 81–94.

Hofstede, G. (1994), 'Management scientists are human', *Management Science*, 40(1), pp. 4–13.

Hofstede, G. (2001), *Culture's Consequences: Comparing Values, Behaviors, Institutions, and Organizations Across Nations*, London: SAGE.

Hofstede, G. (2006), 'What did GLOBE really measure? Researchers' minds versus respondents' minds', *Journal of International Business Studies*, 37, pp. 882–96.

Hofstede, G., Hofstede, G.J. and Minkov, M. (2010), *Cultures and Organizations: Software of the Mind*, Maidenhead: McGraw-Hill.

Hope, V. and Hendry, J. (1995), 'Corporate cultural change: is it relevant for the organisations of the 1990s?', *Human Resource Management Journal*, 5(4), Summer, pp. 61–73.

House, R., Hanges, P.J., Javidan, M. Dorfman, P.W. and Gupta, V. (2004), *Culture, Leadership and Organizations: The GLOBE Study of 62 societies*, Thousand Oaks, CA: Sage.

Howard, L.W. (1998), 'Validating the competing values model as a representation of organizational cultures', *International Journal of Organizational Analysis*, 6(3), pp. 231–50.

Igo, T. and Skitmore, M. (2005), 'Diagnosing the organizational culture of an Australian engineering company using the Competing Values Framework', *Construction Innovation*, 6, pp. 121–39.

Inglehart, R. and Baker, W.E. (2000), 'Modernization, cultural change and the persistence of traditional values', *American Sociological Review*, 65(1), pp. 19–51.

Jaques, E. (1952), *The Changing Culture of a Factory*, New York: Dryden.

Javidan, M., Dorfman, P. W., de Luque, M. S. and House, R. J. (2006), 'In the eye of the beholder: cross cultural lessons in leadership, project GLOBE, *The Academy of Management Perspectives*, 20(1), pp. 67–90.

Johnson, G. (1990), 'Managing strategic action: the role of symbolic action', *British Journal of Management,* 1, pp. 183–200.

Johnson, G., Scholes, K. and Whittington, R. (2008), *Exploring Corporate Strategy: Texts and Cases* (8th edn), Harlow: Pearson Education.

Johnson, G., Whittington, R., Scholes, K., Angwin, D. and Regner, P. (2014), *Exploring Strategy: Texts and Cases* (10th edn), Harlow: Pearson Education.

Kanter, R.M. (1983), *The Change Masters*, London: Routledge.

Kluckhohn, F. and Strodtbeck, F.L. (1961), *Variations in Value Orientations*, Evanston, IL: Row, Peterson.

Koopman, R., den Hartog, D.N. and Konrad, E. (1999), 'National culture and leadership profiles in Europe: some results from the GLOBE study', *European Journal of Work and Organizational Psychology*, 8(4), pp. 503–20.

Kroeber, A.L. and Kluckhohn, F. (1952), *Culture: A Critical Review of Concepts and Definitions*, New York: Vintage Books.

Kwan, P. and Walker, A. (2004), 'Validating the Competing Values Model as a representation of organizational culture through inter-institutional comparisons', *Organizational Analysis*, 12(1), pp. 21–37.

Laurent, A. (1983), 'The cultural diversity of Western conceptions of management', *International Studies of Management and Organisation*, XIII (1–2), pp. 75–96.

Louis, M.R. (1980), 'Organizations as culture-bearing milieux', in Pondy, L.R. *et al.* (eds), *Organizational Symbolism*, Greenwich, CT: JAI.

Minkov, M. and Blagoev, V. (2012), 'What do Project GLOBE's cultural dimensions reflect? An empirical perspective', *Asia Pacific Business Review*, 18(1), pp. 27–43.

Minkov, M. and Hofstede, G. (2010), 'Hofstede's fifth dimension: new evidence from the World Values Survey', *Journal of Cross-Cultural Psychology*, 43(1), pp. 3–14.

Morgan, G. (1989), *Creative Organization Theory: A Resource Book*, London: Sage.

Morgan, G. (2006), *Images of Organizations,* London: Sage.

Nasser, J. and Wetlaufer, S. (1999), 'Driving change: an interview with Jacques Nasser', *Harvard Business Review*, March–April, pp. 76–88.

Nelson, R.E. and Gopalan, S. (2003), 'Do organizational cultures replicate national cultures? Isomorphic, rejective and reciprocal opposition in the corporate values of three countries', *Organization Studies*, 24(7), pp. 1115–51.

Ogbonna, E. and Harris, L.C. (1998), 'Managing organizational culture: compliance or genuine change', *British Journal of Management*, 9, pp. 273–88.

Ogbonna, E. and Harris, L.C. (2002), 'Managing organisational culture: insights from the hospitality industry', *Human Resource Management Journal*, 12(1), pp. 33–51.

Pacanowsky, M.E. and O'Donnell-Trujillo, N. (1982), 'Communication and organizational culture', *The Western Journal of Speech Communication*, 46, Spring, pp. 115–30.

Quinn, R.E. and Rohrbaugh, J. (1983), 'A spatial model of effectiveness criteria: towards a competing values approach to organizational analysis', *Management Science*, 29(3), pp. 363–77.

Robbins, S.P. and Judge, T.A. (2013), *Organizational Behaviour* (15th edn), Englewood Cliffs, NJ: Pearson Education.

Schein, E.H. (1992), *Organizational Culture and Leadership* (2nd edn), San Francisco, CA: Jossey-Bass.

Schein, E.H. (2004), *Organizational Culture and Leadership* (3rd edn), San Francisco, CA: Jossey-Bass.

Scholz, C. (1987), 'Corporate culture and strategy: the problem of strategic fit', *Long Range Planning,* 20(4), pp. 78–87.

Schwartz, H. and Davis, S.M. (1981), 'Matching corporate strategy and business strategy', *Organizational Dynamics*, Summer, pp. 30–48.

Sims, R.R. (2000), 'Changing an organization's culture under new leadership', *Journal of Business Ethics,* 25(1), pp. 65–78.

Sirmon, D.G. and Lane, P.J. (2004), 'A model of cultural differences and international alliance performance', *Journal of International Business Studies*, 35, pp. 306–19.

Schwartz, H. and Davis, S.M. (1981), 'Matching corporate strategy and business strategy', *Organizational Dynamics,* Summer, p. 36; example from the author's own experience. Copyright (1981), with permission from Elsevier.

Trompenaars, F. and Prud'homme, P. (2004), *Managing Change across Corporate Cultures*, Chichester: Capstone Publishing.

Van der Bent, J., Paauwe, J. and Williams, R. (1999), 'Organizational learning: an exploration of organizational memory and its role in organizational change processes', *Journal of Organizational Change Management*, 12(5), pp. 377–404.

Wankhede, P. and Brinkman, J. (2014) 'The negative consequences of culture change: management evidence from a UK NHS ambulance service', *International Journal of Public Service Management*, 27(1), pp. 2–25.

Wilson, D.C. and Rosenfeld, R.H. (1990), *A Strategy of Change: Concepts and Controversies in the Management of Change*, London: Routledge.

Chapter 5

Power, politics and change

Power plays and conflict are part of organizational life and create a backdrop against which change is played out. Indeed, they have a big influence on the outcomes of change initiatives. Their importance is recognized in this chapter through a discussion of the sources of power and the way political action, as an expression of power, is used in the management of change. The concept of powerlessness is discussed, particularly in relation to the position of women and minorities in organizations. The dysfunctional and functional sides of conflict are explored.

Learning objectives

By the end of this chapter, you will be able to:

● explain what is meant by organizational politics;

● distinguish between different sources of power and ways of using power to influence change;

● discuss the links between power, politics and conflict and their effect on change;

● suggest different ways of resolving conflict and the situations they can be applied to.

 Organizational politics

> Politics is the act of preventing people from taking part in affairs which properly concern them.
>
> (Paul Valéry, 1943 – French critic and poet, 1871–1945)

The concepts of politics, power and conflict, particularly in the context of resistance to change, are frequently cast as being among the more undesirable aspects of organizational life. For instance, Robbins and Judge (2013, p. 412) describe power and politics as 'the last dirty words ... People who have power deny it, people who want it try not to look like they are seeking it, and those who are good at getting it are secretive about how they do so.'

Defining power and politics

Huczynski and Buchanan (2013, p. 797) define power as:

> The capacity of individuals to overcome resistance on the part of others, to exert their will, and to produce results consistent with their interests and objectives.

Political behaviour is the practice of power and includes both overt and covert actions by which people use their power to favour their interests. The concept of 'power in action' is echoed by Robbins and Judge (2013, p. 424) who maintain that this happens whenever people get together in groups and where an individual or group seeks to influence the thoughts, attitudes or behaviours of another individual or group. Acting politically is also a part of negotiation as a means to overcoming resistance and of resolving conflict. It can, however, be the cause of conflict in that an individual or group seeks to affect, negatively, another individual or group. However, as Hardy (1994) points out, although power can be used to overcome conflict it can also be used to avert it.

Politics can be divided into 'legitimate' and 'illegitimate' political behaviour, the former being 'normal' everyday politics such as bypassing the chain of command, forming coalitions, obstructing organization policies and so on; the latter being deliberate sabotage, whistle-blowing and groups of employees reporting sick. This view is expressed in the following definition of political behaviour:

> ... political behaviour in organizations consists of those activities that are not required as part of an individual's formal role but that influence, or attempt to influence, the distribution of advantages and disadvantages within the organization.
>
> (Robbins and Judge, 2013 p. 424)

These definitions see political behaviour as an aspect of organizational life which mirrors Morgan's (2006) 'objectivist' view of organization culture, discussed in Chapter 4. Morgan poses organizations as political systems displaying different types of political rule as summarized in Illustration 5.1.

Illustration 5.1

Organizations and modes of political rule

- **Autocracy**. Absolute government where power is held by an individual or small group and supported by control of critical resources, property or ownership rights, tradition, charisma and other claims to personal privilege.
- **Bureaucracy**. Rule exercised through use of the written word, which provides the basis for a rational–legal type of authority or 'rule of law'.
- **Technocracy**. Rule exercised through use of knowledge, expert power and the ability to solve relevant problems.
- **Codetermination**. The form of rule where opposing parties combine in the joint management of mutual interests, as in coalition government or corporatism, each party drawing on a specific power base.

- **Representative democracy**. Rule exercised through the election of officers mandated to act on behalf of the electorate and who hold office for a specified time period or so long as they command the support of the electorate, as in parliamentary government and forms of worker control and shareholder control in industry.
- **Direct democracy**. The system where everyone has an equal right to rule and is involved in all decision making, as in many communal organizations such as cooperatives and kibbutzim. This political principle encourages self-organization as a key mode of organizing.

Source: Morgan, G. (2006), *Images of Organizations*, London: Sage.

In his discussion of different types of political rule, Morgan draws attention to how the suffix *-cracy*, which appears in these terms, is derived from *kratia* – a Greek term meaning power or rule. Thus the word *autocracy* implies the rule of one person; *bureaucracy* is associated with people who sit at bureaux or desks, making and administering rules; a *technocracy* is associated with the power of those with technical knowledge and skills and *democracy* draws on the meaning of the prefix *demo-* from the Greek *demos,* or 'populace', so that, in democratic forms of organization, power rests with the people as a whole or through their representatives. Like culture, politics surrounds us but it is the form that differs. In order to understand the relationship between the politics of organizations and their ability to cope with change we need to understand more about power, conflict and resistance.

 ## Power in organizations

What is power?

Consider these definitions.

> Power influences who gets what, when and how.
>
> (Morgan, 2006, p. 166)

> ... power is the probability that one actor within a social relationship will be in a position to carry out his own will, despite resistance and regardless of the basis on which this probability rests.
>
> (Weber, 1947, p. 47)

> Power is ... the dimension of relationships through which the behaviours, attitudes or opportunities of an actor are affected by another actor, system or technology.
>
> (Lawrence, Namrata and Morris, 2012, p. 105)

> Power is defined as the potential ability to influence behaviour, to change the course of events, to overcome resistance, and to get people to do things that they would otherwise not do.
>
> (Pfeffer, 1993, pp. 204–5)

These definitions emphasize one thing – power means being able to influence the behaviour of others, sometimes in a direction which the person or group would not, otherwise, have chosen. Power is a function of relationships. It is not something a person has regardless of what other people are thinking or doing; it only manifests when one person has something that the other values, such as a manager's ability to recommend someone for promotion. People can take power and people can be bestowed with or imbued with power.

Power also derives from differences between people and groups. Some people have more knowledge, expertise or resources than others do and, if these are scarce and desired, that person or group will have more power than others. This can be referred to as the 'elasticity of power'. In universities, lecturers with good research records usually have more mobility and bargaining power in the job market than those without and are better placed to negotiate favourable outcomes for themselves.

Furthermore, power to some extent is bestowed upon people by others; it is partly in the eye of the beholder. While resources or knowledge can give someone power, so can the belief by A that B can exercise power over them. Handy (1993, p. 125) refers to the 'relativity of power' to describe the situation where one person or group perceives another to have power while a second person or group believes otherwise: 'The group that overawes one person with its prestige and renown looks ludicrous to another.' Handy also notes that power is rarely one-sided. Hitting back or saying no is an option open to those who are seemingly powerless, although doing so may not be in their interest.

In summary, power is about the potential to influence as well as the actual use of influence. It is a function of relationships and differences between people, their beliefs about each other and how much one person has in relation to another.

Sources of power

Five sources of power were identified by French and Raven (1959) and their ideas have had a big influence on organizational research (Blois and Hopkinson, 2013; Frost and Stahelski, 2006; Peiro and Melia, 2003):

1 Positional (legitimate) power – power invested in a person's formal position in a hierarchy, for example, the power to issue a formal performance warning.

This is perhaps the most obvious source of power that we are used to. We give our boss some power simply because they are our boss and they have rights to ask us to do things.

2 Expert power – this derives from a person's skills and knowledge and was recognized by Francis Bacon (1597) in his observation 'knowledge itself is power'. For instance, we credit doctors with expert power when we visit them.

3 Referent power – this is power deriving from charisma, i.e. the ability to attract others to a cause. It is about liking and identifying with another. Referent power can cut across hierarchy – a well-liked person at the bottom of an organization may develop referent power perhaps as a spokesperson in communications with higher management. Conversely, a lack of charisma in a senior manager could diminish their power and influence.

4 Reward power – the ability to give some sort of reward, for example, salary, promotion, time off or access to a resource.

5 Coercive power – the power of forcing someone to do something that they would not want to do. It is negative and based on the use of punishment for non-compliance.

Using French and Raven's ideas, Robbins and Judge (2013) suggest two broad categories of power: formal power and personal power. Formal power relates to the position of the individual within the organization and incorporates coercive, reward, legitimate and information power, all of which are particularly important in times of uncertainty and change. Personal power derives from the 'unique characteristics' of individuals such as their skills and expertise, their personalities and their favoured association with others from whom they gain status and other desirable resources. An alternative list of 14 sources of power as developed by Morgan is shown in Illustration 5.2. (Note Morgan's comment at the end of the list.)

Illustration 5.2

Sources of power in organizations

1 Formal authority.
2 Control of scarce resources.
3 Use of organizational structure, rules and regulations.
4 Control of decision processes.
5 Control of knowledge and information.
6 Control of boundaries.
7 Ability to cope with uncertainty.
8 Control of technology.
9 Interpersonal alliances, networks, and control of 'informal organization'.
10 Control of counter-organizations.
11 Symbolism and the management of meaning.
12 Gender and the management of gender relations.
13 Structural factors that define the stage of action.
14 The power one already has.

The sources of power provide organizational members with a variety of means for enhancing their interests and resolving or perpetuating organizational conflict.

Source: Morgan, G. (2006), *Images of Organizations*, London: Sage, p. 167.

Activity 5.1

1. Can you categorize the sources of power listed in Illustration 5.2 as either 'formal power' or 'personal power' as described by Robbins and Judge above?

2. In relation to French and Raven's sources of power, identify individuals in your own organization whom you consider 'fit' each of the five categories.

3. Repeat the activity above but this time thinking of people outside your organization. They might be in the media, government or entertainment and use one or more sources of power to influence opinions and actions – even your own!

The discussion above is helpful in differentiating one type and source of power from another, given that each manifests itself in varying ways. However, in order to understand the **use** *of power, we need also to consider the concept of* **influence** *as closely related to power.*

Power sources, influence and change

Weber (1947) drew attention to three types of authority (see King and Lawley, 2013). The first derives from tradition, that is, authority legitimized by custom and practice and a belief in the right of certain individuals to rule others. The second is charismatic authority, which is legitimized through the leader's particular qualities being valued and an inspiration to others. The third type of authority Weber called 'rational–legal authority'. This type of authority characterizes the power held by people because of their position in some formal or understood hierarchy that has some independent standing with regard to the rules and procedures sustaining it. The explanations of these types of authority give an idea of how power can be used to influence others to behave in certain ways. Power and influence are not necessarily the same thing, but they are closely linked, as can be seen from Illustration 5.3 which compares the two and the way various forms of power and influence can overlap. For instance, a particular method of influence could be used in conjunction with several sources of power.

Illustration 5.3

Power and influence

The possible sources of individual power that give one person the ability to influence others are as follows:

- *Physical power*: the power of superior force.
- *Resource power*: the possession of valued resources; the control of rewards.

- *Position power*: legitimate power; comes as a result of the role or position held in the organization.
- *Expert power*: vested in someone because of their acknowledged expertise.
- *Personal power*: charisma, popularity; resides in the person and in their personality.
- *Negative power*: illegitimate power; the ability to disrupt or stop things happening.

Methods of influence

Different types of power are used in different ways. Particular methods of influence attach themselves (more or less) to particular types of power:

- *Force*: derived from having physical power; bullying, loss of temper.

- *Rules and procedures*: derived from having position power, backed by resource power; devising rules and procedures to result in particular outcomes.
- *Exchange*: derived from having resource power; bargaining, negotiating, bribing.
- *Persuasion*: derived from having personal power; use of logic, the power of argument, evidence of facts.
- *Ecology*: derived from different power sources; manipulating the physical and psychological environment to achieve certain purposes.
- *Magnetism*: derives from personal and sometimes expert power; inspiring trust, respect; using charm, infectious enthusiasm.

Source: Based on Handy, C. (1993), *Understanding Organizations*, London: Penguin, pp. 126–41.

Position and resource power

Position power is generally considered to be 'legitimate' power, given that it derives from a position of authority inside the organization (Lunenburg, 2012). Position power bestows certain rights on those who have it, for instance the right to order others to do things or to refuse other people's requests. Position power or formal authority is a distinctive source of power in organizations and is distributed asymmetrically – a few people have a lot, most have little and even perceptions of vertical differences influence the power one person believes another person has (Schubert, 2005).

Resource power is frequently associated with position power. It stems from the power associated with being able to distribute or withhold valued rewards. In order to influence others, both 'push' and 'pull' strategies can be used, as Illustration 5.4 shows.

Of interest in the account in Illustration 5.4 is the comment that 'pull strategies can be used from any of the power bases'; for example, a reward may be offered

Activity 5.2

Think about some occasions at work when you have tried to achieve something that you wanted. To what extent were 'push' or 'pull' strategies used?

Were the strategies successful? If so, why do you think they worked?

If any of the strategies were not successful, why was this?

Illustration 5.4

Influencing others through push and pull strategies

'Push' or 'threat' strategies

Push strategies attempt to influence people by imposing or threatening to impose 'costs' on the people or groups concerned if they do not do what is desired. This may be done either by *withdrawing* something that the 'target' of influence values, for example your cooperation and support, or by threatening a sanction if the target does not comply, for example disciplinary action, a poor appraisal, removal of a bonus or perhaps public criticism. The ability to impose such costs will depend largely on a person's *position* and the *resources* that they control.

'Pull' or 'reward' strategies

If push strategies are the 'stick', then pull or reward strategies are the 'carrot'. They reflect content

theories of motivation that emphasize material, social and other extrinsic rewards. Rewards are often used to influence people by a process of *exchange*. Pull strategies may follow from any of the power bases. Resources, such as extra pay or extra staff, may be offered, expertise or information may be traded, increased status may be conferred or access to valuable contacts given. Less obvious, but perhaps more common, are the friendship and favour, approval and inclusion that can be found in a group.

Source: Based on Handy, C. (1993), *Understanding Organizations*, London: Penguin, pp. 126–41.

from those with little power but the power they have is appropriate to the particular circumstances in which it is used.

Invisible power

Control over resources such as budgets or rewards such as promotions are examples of *visible assets* of the power holder but we can also 'see' invisible assets (Paton, 1994). One invisible asset is the power to control information. Handy (1993, p. 129) observed:

> A flow of information often belongs as of right to a 'position' in the organization. If it does not already belong it can often be originated as a necessary input to that position. This can be horizontal information, i.e. information, often of a technical nature, from the same level of the organization; vertical information, from above or from below but potentially trapped in the particular 'position' and to be dispersed with the agreement of the occupant.

The ability to slow down or accelerate the flow of information gives power to people who may not occupy senior positions but who simply act as messengers or copiers of information from one part of the organization to another. Some people in organizations get to hold 'gatekeeper' positions. They are so called because they can open or close access to information thereby including or excluding others from the information. By controlling who is included and excluded in information flows, gatekeepers contribute to sustaining structural situations (Brink and Benschop, 2014).

The idea of gatekeepers goes back to Kurt Lewin writing in the mid-twentieth century about the 'focal points of social changes in communities' (Barzilai-Nahon, 2008, p. 1493). Relative to the gatekeepers, the majority of people that they have control over are 'gated' and Illustration 5.5 shows how the gated are affected by different power sources. Although gatekeepers can be identified in most organizations, they also exist in wider society. Academics who want to publish articles face gatekeepers in the journal reviewers and journal editors who decide whether to publish or not and who have an influence on what the article eventually says.

Illustration 5.5

Types of 'gated'

There are several types of 'gated' with each type shaped by how much of four key attributes they possess: political power; the ability to produce information; relationships with the gatekeeper; and alternatives to get around the gatekeeper's control. These attributes are variable, not fixed, so a person may have more or less of them over time. Furthermore, the attributes are socially constructed rather than objective realities; five classes of gated can be theorized depending on which combination of attributes a person possesses.

Tier 0 – Traditional gated who possess none of the four attributes. They are controlled by the gatekeeper.

Tier 1 – Dormant gated possess one attribute. For example, the 'captive audience' has a relationship with the gatekeeper and thus a communication channel. But any information exchanged conforms to the prevailing agenda and orthodoxy.

Tier 2 – Potential gated possess two attributes. For example, the 'exploited apprentice' has the ability to produce and exchange information with a gatekeeper but has no political power or alternatives.

The gatekeeper uses reciprocity to raise and communicate only 'safe' information.

Tier 3 – Bounded gated possess three attributes. For example, the 'threatening gated' possess political power, alternatives and information but lack the communication channels with the gatekeeper so they cannot open a discourse that could lead to change. The gatekeeper is threatened because this type of gated could develop alliances with other gatekeepers and leverage their attributes.

Tier 4 – Challenging gated possess four attributes. This class of gated has the highest bargaining power. However, having all four attributes does not make them into gatekeepers. To make that transformation they need to have the capability to perform acts of information control and the discretion to exercise gatekeeping behaviour, which may derive from close affiliation with a powerful top manager.

Source: Based on Barzilai-Nahon, K. (2008), 'Toward a theory of network gatekeeping: a framework for exploring information control', *Journal of the American Society for Information Science and Technology*, 59(9), 1493–515.

A second type of invisible asset is that of right of access, for example, to alliances and the informal organization:

The skilled organizational politician systematically builds and cultivates such informal alliances and networks, incorporating whenever possible the help and influence of all those with an important stake in the domain in which he or she is operating.

(Morgan, 2006, p. 181)

The right to organize which stems from position power is another invisible asset. This fits with Morgan's (2006) idea that a source of power is being able to use the organization's structure, rules and regulations to suit one's own purposes. An example is the power to say who gets the best offices or to overlook certain rules according to convenience.

Controlling decisions and covert power

Position power includes the right to make certain decisions and this is frequently visible and unquestioned because of the position. However, issues that are not, strictly speaking, directly concerned with the decision itself can be presented in such a way as to influence the outcome.

This type of power is 'covert' power. 'Here power is exercised through "non-decision making" rather than by means of attempts to influence readily identifiable (and commonly known) decision topics' (Wilson, 1992, p. 54). Invisible or covert power associated with decision making takes many forms. For instance, it may take the form of the power to 'set' the agenda under which something will be discussed, limiting who may or may not take part in the discussion or defining the scope of the discussion – so-called safe agendas where issues important to some groups are not discussed (Hardy, 1994). Some topics and people are deliberately excluded from the decision-making process and exclusion can also happen because participants do not have the knowledge or expertise to take part in any meaningful debate. The role of the 'expert' appears in many guises.

Expert or knowledge power

On some issues we rely on and accept the judgements of people who possess a particular know-how or understanding. Those who have specialist knowledge or expertise in scarce supply have a particular kind of resource power.

> The middle-ranking research chemist who calmly says 'it just can't be done' can stop the marketing director of a chemical firm dead in his or her tracks. If the director is unwise enough to press the point he or she simply invites a lecture on, say, some finer points of polymer chemistry, whereupon – whether he or she pretends to understand and agree, or instead admits to not understanding and refuses to agree – the point is irretrievably lost.

(Paton, 1994, p. 191)

However, expert power is something that one group gives to another group or person. The IT technician who can decide when to fix a computer has, albeit temporarily, power over someone who may be much more senior, as shown in Illustration 5.6.

Illustration 5.6

Controlling decisions with expert power

Consider this recent episode that was written by one of the actors in the performance. One of the managers of a strategic business unit (SBU) of about 150 people wanted to push through changes to the unit's product offering. The stimulus for this was largely due to recommendations made by assessors for external quality schemes that, if awarded, are seen as an important boost to status and which boost the competitive position of the organization.

There are five fairly autonomous product groups in the SBU each with their own staff. What happens in one group does not have much impact on the other areas. The top management of the SBU like to think it is democratic and inclusive and so a 'working group' was formed to look at alternative ways of changing the portfolio before recommending to the top management team (TMT). The working group consisted of a 'director' in the chair and one representative from each of the five areas. Previous 'rationalization' had already hit one of the groups – let's call it Consulting as it provided products and services in that general area. The representative from Consulting was a new member of staff unused to (1) the complexity of product offerings and (2) organizational politics.

After several meetings a proposal emerged which met the working group's initial remit and which would streamline the product offering. The Consulting group was a clear loser in the proposals, seeing a substantial cut in its services if the recommendations were implemented. The chair of the working party said that 'the mood of the meeting' was that the proposals were the best overall for the SBU. Translated, that means that the Consulting group representative's voice was downplayed and the more experienced representatives from other areas all convinced themselves that their interests would be protected. They didn't really care about recommendations that hit areas other than their own.

The working group's proposals were put before a full meeting of the Consulting group at which strong and considered objections were made. Surprisingly, the head of the group did not speak against the objections which raises speculation as to why.

Objections were minuted but to no avail. The TMT, on which the chair of the working group sits, rejected the objections and so accepted the proposals. Further rationalization of the Consulting group's services went ahead.

So what does this tell us? First, that the chair's grasp of the minutiae of the total product offerings (i.e. information) was a source of power used to favour certain points of view and disfavour counter points. Second, that membership of the working party could be (and was) engineered to minimize the arguments against what many believed had been thought out by one or two TMT members in the first place. The working party can be seen simply as an illusion of democracy giving legitimacy to pre-planned intentions and not as a democratic exercise at all.

Third, that filtering of the objections raised by the Consulting group took place. They were downplayed in the final group meeting. When others heard of the proposals and objected, their views were also downplayed as they were being raised outside the formal processes. The minutes of the Consulting group's meeting to discuss the proposals did not convey the intensity of feeling that had arisen over concerns about jobs and careers as well as alternative views of viable changes. Fourth, it shows how one person's knowledge of organizational systems and access to others allows them to manoeuvre for outcomes in their interest.

The case is a microcosm of organizational politics. In the eyes of the TMT the working party chair led a democratic process that came to a clear decision that doubtless reflected upon their abilities. Others see it as a stage-managed political process rooted in self-interest and self-promotion that was rigged from the outset. This is one explanation for the lack of fight and engagement shown by the group head – had she already been 'nobbled'? Resistance was useless.

This case is an account of a real and recent change event and is a reminder of Vera Brittain's quote (1964): 'Politics are usually the executive expression of human immaturity'.

Symbolic power

Symbolic power is widespread in political systems, for instance statues of former leaders, the use of violence by police or surveillance by security forces. Individual managers and politicians use it to hold on to their positions (Bourdieu, 1991). The power that comes from the ability to manipulate symbols comes from the capacity to signal to others the meaning, not of the symbol itself, but of what they stand for. This is implicit in Morgan's (2006) reference to symbolism as the management of meaning. Artefacts can also be seen as possessing three dimensions (Vilnai-Yavetz and Rafaeli, 2006):

- *Symbolic* – what meaning does the artefact carry for the beholder?
- *Aesthetic* – what emotions are aroused by the artefact?
- *Instrumental* – how does the artefact influence performance?

Symbolic power is, therefore, the power to manipulate and use symbols to create organizational environments and the beliefs and understandings of others to suit one's own purposes. Hardy includes the use of language, rituals and myths as examples of symbolic power. The use of phrases such as 'all pulling in the same direction', 'we are a happy team', or 'flatten the opposition' all give their own specific, covert messages about expected behaviour. The use of phrases such as 'we are a happy team' negates the need to say that conflict and disagreement are not expected in this organization. Rituals involving who sits where at meetings and how people greet each other are indications of who holds power in relation to whom. Leaving the chair at the head of the table free symbolizes that the person about to occupy it has a power base. Addressing someone as 'boss' symbolizes their power in relation to others. If you work in an organization then you can probably see how people in powerful positions align with selected others, thus symbolizing the chosen person's favourable standing in relation to them. We can also see how ambitious organizational climbers try to position themselves in relation to bosses in attempts to gain more power for themselves simply by virtue of the associations they are making.

Morgan (2006) uses the term 'theatre' to describe the physical settings, appearances and styles of behaviour that can add to someone's power. He says of those who seek to add to their power in this way: 'Many deserve organizational Oscars for their performances' (p. 184). Examples of the use of theatre are the size and furnishing of offices, the seating of visitors and the often unspoken rules of dress.

Organizational change often requires change to symbols and symbolic actions, for example changing the time spent on things, reinterpreting things that happened in the past or which are happening in the present. However, most employees in large organizations do not interact much with people in senior positions and symbolic action is what most employees see – and maybe it is all they need to see to begin to appreciate why and how management's ideas change (Das, 1988).

Symbols of power are inevitably intertwined with an organization's culture and are frequently an outward expression of it. Any analysis of power in organizations must take account of not only the types of power which are exercised over the content of decisions, but also the types of power that influence attitudes and behaviour, frequently in ways that those influenced are hardly aware of. Activity 5.3 helps to show how symbolic power can be used.

Activity 5.3

This activity will help identify the routines, rituals and symbols prevalent in an organization and who uses them. Think of your own organization or one you are familiar with.

1 *Which routines and rituals are most emphasized? How are they enforced (think of the people and systems behind them)?*
2 *How do the organization's leaders use language to perpetuate their own values and keep power to themselves and their chosen followers? What does this tell you about the topics that can be debated and which topics are out of bounds?*
3 *Who, in the organization, has the most impressive 'trappings' of office (size, furnishings, car, expense account etc.)? What kind of power do they symbolize?*
4 *Give examples of two people who use gamesmanship to get their own way: (a) one who does so aggressively; and (b) one who does so by operating craftily and with a low profile. What are they manipulating in these processes?*

Individual power

In addition to power sources deriving from how an organization is structured and the roles played by people working in them, there is another source of power – that which derives from the personal characteristics of those wielding power (Pfeffer, 1992 in Huczynski and Buchanan, 2013, p. 764). These include:

● energy, endurance and physical stamina;
● ability to focus energy and to avoid wasteful effort;
● sensitivity and an ability to read and understand others;
● flexibility and selecting varied means to achieve goals;
● personal toughness; willingness to engage in conflict and confrontation;
● able to 'play the subordinate' and 'team member' to enlist the support of others.

In a way, power derived from these sources is potentially available to anyone given its non-dependence on position, status or control of knowledge or resources. However, the use of power is unlikely to succeed unless used in conjunction with these other sources. This leads to the issue of those who lack power – in other words the issue of powerlessness.

The politics of powerlessness

If there is one thing that symbols of power are intended to do, it is to make others who do not control these symbols feel their own lack of power. Likewise, many people are relatively powerless because of the way particular organizational factors affect them. In addition, some groups of people appear powerless in relation to the majority groups, who are often, although not always, white males. People with physical disabilities may be excluded from positions of status and decision making because of prejudice or simply a lack of physical access to the spaces and places where the exercise of power takes place.

Gender and powerlessness

The relative power of women in organizations has received a lot of attention (Brescoll, 2011; Nemoto, 2013; Schuh *et al.*, 2014). Morgan (2006) argues that formal organizations typically mirror what, in the West, has been (and to a large extent still is) a patriarchal society. 'Strategic' jobs such as marketing, production or finance are generally done by men and jobs that involve caring, supporting and helping others tend to be done by women. This gender segregation across occupations goes some way to explaining why in spite of 'equal pay for equal work' legislation and much greater parity of women in educational systems, women earn less than men on average, why they occupy a much greater proportion of jobs at the lower levels of organizations and why many women's jobs are part-time and/or temporary. A similar picture is seen on an international scale. In many sectors the higher the ladder, the fewer women are found and the percentage of women in top jobs in big corporations is small (ILO, 2012).

Vinnicombe, Doldor and Turner (2014) in *The Female FTSE Report* showed that 80 per cent of FTSE 250 companies had women on the board but that the percentage of women on boards was only 15.6 per cent. There were eight female chief executives in the FTSE top 250 but some top UK companies still had no women on the board. The FTSE report argued that companies should make concerted efforts to increase the number of women at senior executive level to create a better pipeline for promotion. Illustration 5.7 demonstrates the slow progress made by women entering the higher levels of management.

Illustration 5.7

Women in the boardroom

Looking across Europe there is a north–south divide reflected in the make-up of the boardrooms of big business. In the north, women occupy 38 per cent of board seats in the largest companies in Norway and 28 per cent in Sweden in 2010. Boards in Italy and Portugal, however, remain almost exclusively male. The split is revealed by a survey indicating that across Europe women hold just 11.7 per cent of the directorships in over 300 large companies, up from 8 per cent in 2004. Between the extremes of Norway and Portugal lies the UK where women have 13 per cent per cent of seats, the Netherlands with 15 per cent and France with 12 per cent. However, over the last few years the proportion of women on the board has been rising in most countries.

Greater representation of women in top management in Scandinavia can be explained by a traditional acceptance of feminine values in society (see the discussion of national culture in Chapter 4) coupled with a more radical understanding of gender equality together with professionalization of gender equality work (Wahl and Hook, 2007). Furthermore, Norway tops the list because it introduced quotas to increase women's representation in the boardroom. However, across Europe only a handful of women have become chief executive officers. Although women's representation in Scandinavia has grown steadily in the past few years, outside the region change has been slow.

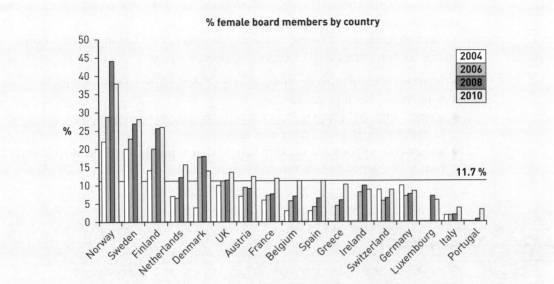

% female board members by country

Source: European PWN Board Women Monitor 2004, 2006, 2008, 2010. © European PWN 2010. Web site www.EuropeanPWN.net

Evidence is building that diverse boards lead to better organizational performance. A study of German listed companies found a U-shaped relationship between women on boards and firms' performances (Joecks, Pull and Vetler, 2013). It was only after about 30 per cent of seats on a board were filled by women that firm performance improved. A survey of Dutch companies found that those with women on boards performed better (Luckerath-Rovers, 2013). On a wider geographical scale, a survey (the seventh) of 13,124 global leaders, undertaken by the Global Leadership Survey (2014/2015) found that companies with a higher percentage of women in leadership roles performed better financially. In addition, they found that females accounted for over a third (33 per cent) of leadership roles in the top 20 per cent of financial performers, compared to the bottom 20 per cent of businesses where 19 per cent of leaders were women.

By contrast, a 5-year study (1998–2002) of women and ethnic minority board members in 641 American firms by the Investor Responsibility Research Centre (IRRC) found no evidence for a link between gender and ethnic diversity of board members and the firms' performance (Carter et al., 2010). A British study of 126 companies in the FTSE 100 Index during the years 2001–2005 also found no link between women board members and performance and even suggested a negative link (Haslam et al., 2010). However, the mean number of women on the boards in any of the years studied was never greater than 1.3 per cent. Consequently, the difficulty in demonstrating whether greater representation of women and ethnic minority people on company boards and in management positions (assuming they have the necessary knowledge and experience) would enhance company performance is that the numbers are currently low, with some boards consisting entirely of white males. It is only when these numbers and proportions rise that firm conclusions can be reached.

Even so, progress is being made, as the reasons for having more women on boards become increasingly recognised. These include:

- men and women bring complementary skills to corporate management;
- women may be more risk averse;
- women who make it to the top are better managers than men because they had to perform much better than men to get there;
- assessors of corporate reputation believe that women contribute distinctively to boards (Brammer, Millington and Pavelin, 2009).

Activity 5.4

Some studies have shown that organizations with women in the boardroom outperform men-only boards. The same reports imply that gender diversity is a causal factor in explaining better performance. If this is true, then how would you explain the causal mechanism? Would an all-women board perform less well than a mixed board?

Countries outside Europe have a much lower percentage of women board members (11.6 per cent overall) compared to Europe (21.2 per cent overall), the key exceptions being Australia (22.6 per cent) and the USA (21.2 per cent) (Vinnicombe *et al.* (2015) in *The Female FTSE Board Report 2015*.

In the UK the number of women in management is rising steadily. Table 5.1 shows the numbers and percentages of women board members for the FTSE 100 and 250 company indexes. From this it can be seen that FTSE 250 companies lag behind the FTSE 100 companies. It is also of note that female *executive* directors form only a small proportion of board members. This is not surprising considering that, as Table 5.2 indicates, in the FTSE 350 companies, female senior executives are present in much lower numbers than men.

Table 5.1 Women on boards of FTSE 100 and FTSE 250 companies

At March 2015	FTSE 100	FTSE 250
Female held directorships	263 (23.5%)	365 (18%)
Female executive directorships	24 (8.6%)	25 (4.6%)
Female non-executive directorships	239 (28.5%)	340 (23%)

Source: Vinnicombe, S., Dolder, E., Sealey, E., Pryce P. and Turner, C. (2015), *The Female FTSE Board Report 2015*, Cranfield University, p. 35.

Table 5.2 FTSE 350 senior executives

Senior Executives	Females	Males	Total
FTSE 100	434 (20.9%)	1,638 (79%)	2,072
FTSE 250	456 (18.5%)	2,008 (81.6%)	2,464

Source: Vinnicombe, S., Dolder, E., Sealey, E., Pryce P. and Turner, C. (2015), *The Female FTSE Board Report 2015*, Cranfield University, p. 35.

In 2015 The Chartered Institute of Personnel and Development (CIPD) reported the results of a survey of 452 UK-based human resources professionals, which found a variety of reasons for having a good representation of female board members. These were:

- female members can bring different perspectives to boardroom discussion/decisions (85 per cent);
- it helps to reflect the wider diversity in society and in the company's client base (79 per cent);
- boards with a good degree of diversity can improve business performance (68 per cent);
- female directors at the top of an organization serve as positive role models (65 per cent);
- boards with a good degree of diversity are more innovative and creative (62 per cent);
- it helps to promote the organization's reputation externally as a diverse employer (56 per cent).

(Note: the percentages in brackets indicate the percentage of respondents who agreed with the statements)

Even though the number of women in management is rising, there is still a difference in pay between the sexes. For example, *The Guardian* newspaper (19 August 2014) reported that: 'More than 40 years after the Equal Pay Act outlawed less favourable pay and conditions in the workplace, the data shows that discrepancies in salaries widen at the higher echelons of management'. Quoting the (CMI) National Management Salary Survey of 2014, it comments: 'Including male and female managers of all ages, women are earning only three-quarters (77 per cent) of men in full-time comparable jobs'.

It is clear from the above that the situation for women board members and managers is improving; however, it is too soon to say that feminization of the workplace will make a difference to the endemic organizational issues of power imbalances and the nature of organizational politics. There are still obstacles to women's advancement at work.

Barriers to change

There are several explanations for why women, on average, do less well than men and, if they have achieved professional status, still do not rise in similar proportions to the higher levels in their profession or to the higher levels of management. They include:

- Perceptions of the social roles that men and women should perform, although social attitudes are changing to lessen these distinctions.
- Placement of women in non-strategic roles from which it is harder to progress to the top and which brings exclusion from networks that are important in underpinning career advancement.
- Child-bearing and child-care, which limit the amount of time available for work given that progress to the top often calls for long working hours; perceptions of the 'visible' commitment of women, i.e. consistently being present at work, can be compromised by this factor.

Structuralist theorists argue that the structure of jobs affects the job holder's ability to exercise power (Ness, 2012). Kanter (1979), for instance, argues that women are typically shepherded into powerless jobs and hence find themselves in positions without much influence. Entry to a succession of powerless jobs perpetuates the situation. In contrast, socialization theory argues that it is learned behaviour, that is the behaviour that girls and young women are socialized into in the family and at school, and that makes them less effective users of power in the workplace (Barbulescu and Bidwell, 2013; Kalantari, 2012). Hence there is a big question around whether the behaviours of men and women at work are a result of their situations or a result of more stable differences between men and women.

In addition, there are fewer women in the workforce generally than men. For instance, in the world region of developed economies and the European Union, the difference in employment rate in 2012 between men and women was 14.7 per cent (ILO, 2012). Consequently, the lack of a 'critical mass' of women in some organizations and/or occupations tends to restrict any power and influence they might have in them.

The use of upward influence tactics helps individuals to advance at work and there may be differences in the ways that men and women use influence (O'Neill, 2004; Smith *et al.*, 2013). Upward influence concerns the ways that people try to influence the attitudes of people above them in their favour. Tactics include:

- *Rationality* – using facts and figures to support arguments and thinking.
- *Coalition* – claiming that lots of other people support you.
- *Ingratiation* – managing the impressions of others and flattering them.
- *Exchange* – using the exchange of benefits to gain favour.
- *Assertiveness* – being forceful in pushing for your way of thinking.
- *Upward appeal* – getting support of higher levels of managers for one's ideas and plans.

Smith and colleagues (2013) found subtle differences in the influence tactics used by men and women. Men were more disposed to using assertive and direct methods whereas women used more ingratiation and collaborative approaches. Women may also be less likely to use self-promotion tactics and rely on their own high performance and commitment (Singh, Kumra and Vinnicombe, 2002).

Another reason put forward for relative lack of power and influence is that the prevailing structures and power balances in organizations, which are predominantly based on a male model of what organization and management is about, conspire indirectly to reduce the power sources of women (Morgan, 2006). Access to power structures in organizations is an important part of the explanation of wage inequalities. In Sweden, women working in power structures populated by men earned less than women in power structures with more women in them (Hultin and Szulkin, 1999, 2003). This was explained through differential access to networks which determine rewards in labour markets. 'Women are less central than men in those networks in which organizational power is located and important decisions on organizational policies are made. Hence women may receive less support for their arguments and their claims' (1999, p. 459). Their research shows that it is not individual discrimination against women that is occurring but attitudes towards typically female jobs and barriers to higher-paid positions.

Another interpretation of powerlessness comes from the gendered nature of workplace behaviour and the norms surrounding the behaviour associated with promotability. McKenna (1997) refers to the world of male politics in which 'Sitting back and hoping for recognition is seen as passivity, a lack of fire, guts and ambition. Essential for success is self-promotion, and conformity to the "unwritten rules of success".' McKenna (1997, p. 51) says: '[Success is about] maintaining silence in the face of politics and backstabbing ... It has little to do with performing good work or being productive and everything to do with pecking order and egos.' We do not intend to imply here that women cannot display the political behaviour to get ahead – indeed some are very effective at it and can be just as talented or just as devious and self-promoting in organizational politics as men. But on balance there is a body of thinking that suggests they are less likely to display such behaviour – hence the imbalance.

Overall, research suggests organizational structures and processes are more influential in gender segregation than supply-side factors such as socialization and employee choice (Huffman, Cohen and Pearlman, 2010).

Activity 5.5

Think of someone whom you consider does their job very well, but has been unsuccessful in getting promotion. Assuming there is no reason why this person could not do the higher-level job (given time and training if necessary), why do you think they have not progressed?

In your analysis, draw on the concepts of power and political activity discussed above in relation to the possible lack of power of the person concerned.

National culture and powerlessness

Lien (2005) gives an interesting account of powerlessness among Taiwanese women employees and how this links directly to prevailing national culture. Feelings of powerlessness came from:

● Structural barriers such as assumptions that women leave work when married so why bother giving them opportunities to develop. Due to lack of seniority they lacked position power.

- Behavioural barriers such as bosses not 'letting go' of work and giving younger women a chance, prescribing how to do things and insisting that orders and procedures are followed without deviation. Women's talents were not called upon and bosses gave credit to others, overlooking the roles that women had played in achieving things.
- Accommodation and rationalization – this sums up the Darwinian idea of adaptation in that women tended to adapt to their work environment because if they did not they could not survive in it. However, adaptation meant surviving in a powerless niche.

Since cultural differences influence many aspects of organizational life care must be taken not to assume that practices in one culture, like Taiwan (see above), can be transferred, without question, to another. For instance, it would be unwise to assume that motivating or leadership styles that work well in a Western culture will be effective in other countries – although they might be.

The implications of these cultural differences for a discussion of power and powerlessness hinge on the very issue of difference. People from different cultures behave differently and bring different values and attitudes to the workplace. People from cultures scoring high on Hofstede, Hofstede and Minkov's (2010) high power distance dimension will expect managers to make most workplace decisions. However, in Western cultures, which characteristically score low on power distance, people who defer to others to make decisions may well be seen as lacking ambition and not ready to take responsibility. This, in turn, does not encourage people to gain power sources such as 'control of decision processes' and 'formal authority' (Morgan, 2006). Morgan also cites 'ability to cope with uncertainty' as another source of power which relates directly to another cultural dimension – uncertainty avoidance. Consequently, if a minority group's cultural upbringing is one where ambiguity must be controlled then they are less likely to demonstrate the attitudes and behaviour which could win them power of this kind.

Another example is the difference in orientation towards others that is found between different cultural groupings. The perspective of power in Western society is based mainly on the power of the individual, yet in many societies (particularly in East Asian countries) group loyalty is a virtue; it is the performance of the group that matters. Power is linked to the power of the group. Yuet-Ha (1996) points this out in her discussion of the differences between Western and East Asian work-related values and their relationship to work-related competencies. Her findings suggest that, for people from an East Asian culture, it is relatively easy to implement teamworking and shared responsibility and support. However, it is relatively difficult to implement open communication, participation, decisiveness, delegation of authority and taking leadership responsibility. Given that most of these competencies are valued in Western societies, people from minority groups that value other competencies are less likely to progress when working in the UK, the US and some European countries unless they can change others' perceptions of their differences. Their lack of power in the first place makes this difficult to achieve.

Position and powerlessness

Legislation has certainly helped to eliminate the more overt prejudices that have prevented women and minority groups from enjoying the benefits given to others, even if certain organizational and covert processes still contrive to reduce their access to power sources and influence. However, we should not simply focus on equality group membership since many employees in majority groups find themselves relatively powerless due to their position. These groups are not, as might be expected, simply those working at the lowest levels of the organization. They are powerless because of the particular positions they occupy. People near the bottom of hierarchies do not have much access to resources, information and support to get a task done or the cooperation of others to do what is necessary. Kanter (1979) identified three 'lines' of organizational power: (1) lines of supply; (2) lines of information; (3) lines of support. These have been discussed already as being basically related to resource and position power but of additional relevance here is the power that comes from *connections* with other parts of the organizational system. This derives from two sources: job activities and political alliances. Kanter says (1979, pp. 65–6):

1 Power is most easily accumulated when one has a job that is designed and located to allow *discretion* (non-routinized action permitting flexible, adaptive and creative contributions), *recognition* (visibility and notice), and *relevance* (being central to pressing organizational problems).
2 Power also comes when one has relatively close contact with *sponsors* (high-level people who confer approval, prestige, or backing), *peer networks* (circles of acquaintanceship that provide reputation and information, the grapevine often being faster than formal communication channels), and *subordinates* (who can be developed to relieve managers of some of the burdens and to represent the manager's point of view).

When people are in situations where they have strong lines of supply, information and support, their job allows them discretion and their work is recognized as being relevant to the organization's purposes, they can more easily relinquish some control and, thereby, develop their staff more effectively. In contrast to this situation:

> The powerless live in a different world. Lacking the supplies, information, or support to make things happen easily, they may turn instead to the ultimate weapon of those who lack productive power – oppressive power: holding others back and punishing with whatever threats they can muster.
>
> (Kanter, 1979, p. 67)

This situation is frequently faced by first-line supervisors. Illustration 5.8 shows how multiple causes combine to influence the attitudes and behaviour of first-line supervisors and people in similar positions and increase their feelings of powerlessness.

Illustration 5.8

First-line supervisors and powerlessness

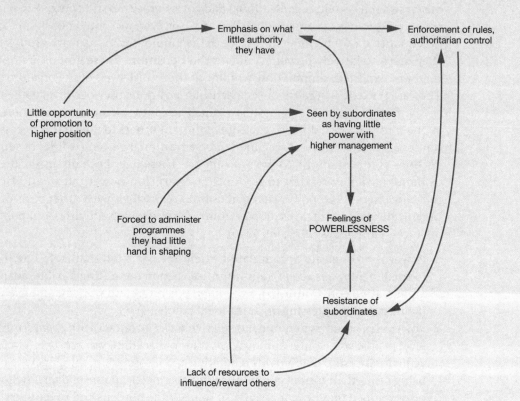

Source: Based on the description in Kanter, R.M. (1979), 'Power failure in management circuits', *Harvard Business Review*, July–August, pp. 65–75.

Support service employees are also compromised in terms of power. For example, people working in human resource departments often have little line experience and, therefore, are not involved in the mainstream organizational power networks. Being specialists, their ability to cross functions or undertake general management positions is restricted. They are, therefore, likely to get 'stuck' in a limited career structure. Having little power themselves, they cannot pass it on to others. In addition, they are vulnerable to having their work contracted to agencies or consultants outside the organization. The effect of this relative powerlessness is that they tend to become territorial, protecting their patches, drawing strict boundaries between themselves and other functional managers. These various aspects of powerlessness, collectively, lead to conservative attitudes that are resistant to change. Activity 5.6 asks you to assess a job in terms of its capacity to generate power for its occupant.

Activity 5.6

The following factors contribute to power or powerlessness. For your own job, or one you know well, consider each factor and tick the appropriate column.

Factor	Generates power when factor is:	Generates powerlessness when factor is:
Rules in the job	☐ Few	☐ Many
Predecessors in the job	☐ Few	☐ Many
Established routines	☐ Few	☐ Many
Centralized resources	☐ Few	☐ Many
Communications	☐ Extensive	☐ Limited
Task variety	☐ High	☐ Low
Physical location	☐ Central	☐ Distant
Relation of tasks to current problem areas	☐ Central	☐ Peripheral
Competitive pressures	☐ High	☐ Low
Network-forming opportunities	☐ High	☐ Low
Contact with senior management	☐ High	☐ Low
Advancement prospects of subordinates	☐ High	☐ Low
Authority/discretion in decision making	☐ High	☐ Low
Meaningful goals/tasks	☐ High	☐ Low
Participation in programmes, meetings, conferences	☐ High	☐ Low

Consider the overall picture obtained of the job. How powerful might the person occupying it be?

Source: Based on factors suggested by Kanter, R.M. (1979), 'Power failure in management circuits', *Harvard Business Review*, July–August, pp. 65–75; and Gordon, J.R. (1993), *A Diagnostic Approach to Organizational Behavior,* Needham Heights, MA: Allyn & Bacon, p. 425.

 ## Politics, power and conflict

Earlier in this chapter politics was described as the use of power. Political behaviour extends beyond formal roles and is observed in activities that are not part of someone's formal organizational role. Even in organizations which have a strong culture the experience of that culture will vary for individuals and groups who operate within their own organizational sub-cultures. What is more, a dominant culture will not solve one of the perennial issues in all organizations – the problem of scarce resources and so people more disposed towards political behaviour will use their skills to satisfy their needs at the expense of others.

As we have seen, resource power stems from scarcity and additional resource power is frequently fought over. An issue therefore arises of whether competition for resources can be beneficial or whether it is always dysfunctional. This leads to the ideas of unitarist and pluralist frames of reference. The unitary frame of reference assumes that organizations are unified around common interests and therefore conflict should not arise. Managers with pluralist views of organizations recognize that people have both common (shared) and divergent interests that will sometimes result in conflict. As such, systems and procedures are needed to manage conflict as best as possible. Unitarists consider conflict as an aberration from the normal state of affairs which recognizes only formal authority as the legitimate source of power. Thus, from a unitarist position, managers are considered as having the 'right to manage' while others are expected to subordinate their own personal interests to the good of the organization, as judged by managers. From this point of view, the only type of power recognized is formal position power. Expert power might be recognized but, in the main, only as a facet of position power.

Robbins and Judge (2013, p. 447) use the term 'traditional' to describe the unitarist view which assumes that all conflict is bad. They say: 'The traditional view ... was consistent with attitudes about group behavior that prevailed in the 1930s and 1940s'. The idea, still around, that all industrial action by workers is wrong stems from this view. The difficulty for managers, in accepting a unitary view of organizational life, is that it leaves no room for dealing with the multiplicity of interests which are now accepted as part of a democratic way of doing things; hence the concept of pluralism. Illustration 5.9 summarizes the two different views.

Illustration 5.9

The unitary and pluralist views of interests, conflict and power

	The unitary view	The pluralist view
Interests	Emphasizes the achievement of common objectives. The organization is viewed as being united under the umbrella of common goals, and striving towards their achievement like a well-integrated team.	Emphasizes the individual and group interests. The organization is regarded as a loose coalition that has a remote interest in the formal goals of the organization.
Conflict	Regards conflict as a rare and transient phenomenon that can be removed through appropriate managerial action. Where it arises it is usually attributed to the activities of deviants and troublemakers.	Regards conflict as an inherent and ineradicable characteristic of organizational affairs and stresses its potentially positive and functional aspects.
Power	Largely ignores the role of power in organizational life. Concepts such as authority, leadership and control tend to be preferred means of describing the managerial prerogative of guiding the organization towards the achievement of common interests.	Regards power as a variable crucial to the understanding of the activities of an organization. Power is the medium through which conflicts of interest are alleviated and resolved. The organization is viewed as a plurality of power holders drawing their power from a plurality of sources.

Source: Burrell, G. and Morgan, G. (2006), *Sociological Paradigms and Organisational Analysis*, London: Heinemann Educational Books Ltd, p. 195.

The unitarist frame of reference portrayed in Illustration 5.9 sits uncomfortably not only with what in many parts of the world has come to be a pluralist society, but also with the increasingly complex and sometimes chaotic circumstances that organizations deal with in the twenty-first century. In such times political behaviour is to be expected, with its associated tendency to generate both competition and cooperation (of which conflict is a part). To ignore the role of conflict as a positive force as well as a negative force in the context of organizations and change is to ignore the realities of human nature. Therefore a more detailed understanding of the nature and sources of conflict and how to manage in situations of conflict is important for anyone involved in organizational change.

Conflict in organizations

The previous section established a link between power, politics and conflict but the concept of conflict itself is by no means clear. What one person calls conflict another might see as healthy debate or competition. Definitions of conflict include:

> ... a process that begins when one party perceives that another party has or is about to affect something that the first party cares about.
>
> (Robbins and Judge, 2013, p. 446)

> Conflict is best viewed as a process that begins when an individual or group perceives differences and opposition between him/herself and another individual or group about interests, beliefs or values that matter to him or her.
>
> (De Dreu and Beersma, 2005)

Conflict must be perceived by the parties to it otherwise it does not exist. Second, one party to the conflict must be seen as about to do or be doing something that the other party (or parties) does not want – in other words there must be opposition. Third, some kind of interaction must take place. In addition, conflict can occur at a number of levels: between individuals, between groups or between organizations. We can, of course, as individuals, experience conflict within ourselves when we are wrestling with choices and decisions.

Conflict might arise because of the incompatibility of goals set for people or a confusion over the roles they are asked to play, but conflict is not a unidimensional concept. It comes in different guises according to its degree of seriousness and its capacity to disrupt or, in some cases, improve a difficult situation. Thus a different view that opens new possibilities is offered by Martin and Fellenz (2010, p. 305):

> Conflict can be considered as something that disrupts the normal and desirable states of stability and harmony within an organization. Under this definition it is something to be avoided and if possible eliminated from the operation. However, it is also possible to consider conflict as an inevitable feature of human interaction and perhaps something that if managed constructively could offer positive value in ensuring an effective performance within the organization.

This interpretation argues that being without conflict is unrealistic, and since it is inevitable, the best thing to do is manage it and use it constructively for change. This interactionist view holds that situations without conflict are prone to becoming vulnerable to threats and that conflict, within reason, will keep a group or organization more lively and alert. Conflict, therefore, can be seen as an instrument of change rather than as a breakdown of relationships. That is not to say that conflict should be encouraged as resolving it takes times and causes stress but it does suggest that good conflict resolution systems should be used by organizations.

Like so many management situations, empirical studies of conflict do not lead to the same conclusion. In some situations conflict is harmful, in others it can be beneficial. The question arises therefore, under what conditions is it harmful or beneficial? Jehn (1995) found that the level of routine mattered. When groups performed routine tasks disagreement was harmful. In contrast, in groups performing more complicated tasks, conflict was not harmful and sometimes beneficial.

Sources of conflict

A survey of UK organizations (see Table 5.3) revealed that the most often cited sources of conflict at work were personality clashes and warring egos (which probably point to power struggles behind the scenes), poor leadership from top managers, poor line management and performance management. Most blame was put on management's inability to suppress it and on confrontations

Table 5.3 Sources and solutions to conflict

Respondent ratings of the main sources of conflict		Suggested managerial interventions	
Source	% respondents	Intervention	% respondents
Personality clashes and warring egos	44	Tackle underlying tensions better	81
Poor leadership from the top	30	Have more informal discussions	67
Poor line management	29	Provide more clarity about expectations on the job	67
Poor performance management	21	Role model the right behaviour	66
Heavy workload and inadequate resources	14	Manage toxic employees firmly	64
Bullying/harassment	13	Clarify areas of responsibility	51
Lack of openness and honesty	12	Stop egos getting in the way	48
Lack of clarity about accountability	12	Improve day-to-day consultation	46
Lack of role clarity	11	Discuss conflict as part of business life	37
Clash of values and stress	10	Counsel stressed employees	23

Source: *Leadership and the management of conflict at work. Survey Report.* London: Chartered Institute of Personnel and Development (CIPD 2008), with the permission of Chartered Institute of Personnel and Development, London (www.cipd.co.uk).

between individuals. The thrust of the suggested solutions is for more information and discussion around the conflict although it is interesting to see that nearly two-thirds of people in the survey felt that 'toxic' individuals were a problem that needs managing.

Conflict also exists between organizations; for example, between corporations and activist groups such as Greenpeace, or trade unions and shareholder groups. Murphy and Dee (1992) noted that inter-organizational conflicts are often unresolved, not because the participants use different resolution strategies, but because both parties can meet their objectives by not resolving the conflict.

Other writers (e.g. Pfeffer, 1981; Mullins, 2013; Robbins and Judge, 2013) refer to the five factors described in the section below as the main sources of organizational conflict.

Interdependence

Different organizational groups depend upon each other to a greater or lesser extent, such as the interdependence between production and marketing. The balance of dependence (who depends the most) is related to power balances between groups. Conflict can also arise between two individuals whose tasks are interdependent when there are differences of opinion over priorities and procedures.

Organizational structures

Conflict can arise from the power imbalances that prevail in organizational structures. Reporting relationships in matrix structures can cause particular frustration. For example, an international subsidiary in a multinational company might report simultaneously to a regional HQ and to production division directors. In more traditional, hierarchical structures, different divisions and departments, such as sales, production and finance, can have very different orientations towards formality of dress and behaviour, interpersonal relationships and timescales. Specific problems can include delays in making decisions, power struggles for the dominant position, differing priorities between regional managers and product managers (Wolf and Egelhoff, 2013).

Rules and regulations

On the one hand, high formalization (i.e. standardized ways for people and units to interact with each other) creates fewer opportunities for disputes about who does what and when. On the other hand, where there is low formalization, the level of ambiguity is such that the potential for jurisdictional disputes increases. Robbins and Judge (2013, p. 488) maintain that conflict is more likely to be less subversive in highly formalized situations because 'rules and regulations substitute for managerial discretion'. However, in situations of over-regulation, people can become frustrated by their lack of autonomy and see rules and regulations as an expression of low trust by management.

Resource limitations

When resources are plentiful and rewards can be gained for all, the potential for conflict through competition for resources is reduced. In conditions of austerity or when redundancies are occurring the potential for conflict over resources rises. Resource conflict can also lead to increased levels of individual satisfaction and commitment. An individual's disposition towards conflict over resources is influenced by the level of self and situation preservation even though others would be adversely affected (Barsky, 2002).

Cultural differences

The previous chapter identified a number of ways in which people from different nationalities and societies differ. Therefore, it is not surprising that people from different cultures regard and resolve conflict in different ways; for example, what is just a small misunderstanding to one person can be a personal slight to another. Some nationalities prefer to avoid conflict, others are happy to confront it whilst still others favour accommodating it; each strategy depends on the different assumptions that people bring to the situation (Kim and Markman, 2013; Tinsley, 1998). Conflict can arise through misunderstandings or through inappropriate behaviour when working across national cultures. In addition, we can expect different national cultures to display different approaches to conflict resolution. For instance, people who come from a collectivist culture, such as Japan, are more likely to avoid outright confrontation than people who come from more individualistic cultures such as the United States. People from cultures scoring high on Hofstede's (2010) power distance culture are more likely to appeal to a higher authority and use bureaucratic rules and regulations to resolve conflict than people from cultures that score low on the power distance dimension.

Managing conflict

Strategies for managing conflict vary according to the managers' frame of reference. Managers who have a unitarist attitude towards those they manage will try to suppress conflict whenever possible and the dominant strategy will be to exclude the opposition from involvement in decisions. The paradox is, however, that exclusion may either cause further, more extreme, conflict behaviour or drive the expression of conflict underground. The suppression of conflict within a unitary frame of reference will be successful so long as those without power fear the consequences of conflict (e.g. being ignored, lockouts, or possibly dismissal) sufficiently to avoid it. However, when acceptable alternatives are available (e.g. alternative employment or successful industrial action), then conflict will return again thus reinforcing the view that typical business organizations cannot, in general, be managed as unitary entities. Recognition of their pluralist characteristics is required if conflict is to be managed successfully.

Conflict resolution has a big following. An influential starting point is the Conflict Management Grid (Blake and Mouton, 1970) which has been the basis of much subsequent research (Bernadin and Alvares, 1976; Van de Vliert and Kabanoff, 1990). They suggest that techniques of conflict management can be mapped on two dimensions: concern for production and concern for people. On each dimension an individual can score from low to high. The five styles are:

- Competing (high concern for production, low concern for people).
- Collaborating (problem solving) – a more constructive approach of information sharing, trying to meet both sides, represented by high scores on both dimensions.
- Compromising (moderate scores on both dimensions).
- Avoiding (low scores on both dimensions).
- Accommodating (high concern for people, low concern for production).

Each conflict-handling style has an outcome in terms of its capacity to tackle the content of the conflict and the relationship with the other party as follows:

1 *Competing*. This creates a win/lose situation and so the conflict will be resolved to suit one party only. The win/lose situation can lead to negative feelings on the part of the loser and damage the relationship.
2 *Collaborating*. This creates a win/win outcome, where both parties gain. It frequently brings a high-quality solution through the results of the inputs of both parties. Win/win outcomes result in both sides being reasonably satisfied. They require openness and trust and a flexibility of approach.
3 *Compromising*. The needs of both parties are partially satisfied. It requires a trading of resources. Openness and trust may not be as great as for collaboration but compromise might set up a relationship that, in the future, could move to collaboration.
4 *Avoiding*. This does not tackle the problem. It creates a no-win situation. It does, however, allow a cooling-off period and allows the parties to (perhaps) gather more information to begin negotiations afresh or decide there is no conflict after all. It can give rise to frustration of one party if they think the issue is important while the other side do not.
5 *Accommodating*. This can create a lose/win situation, but retains a good relationship between the parties. It involves recognizing when the other party might have a better solution than oneself. It is used when relationships are more important than the problem. It builds goodwill.

The same terminology occurs in the conflict resolution behaviour model by Thomas (1976) as shown in Figure 5.1. Here, however, each style is mapped in terms of assertiveness (a concern to satisfy one's own needs) and cooperativeness (a concern to satisfy the needs of others). Illustration 5.10 matches situations to conflict-handling styles.

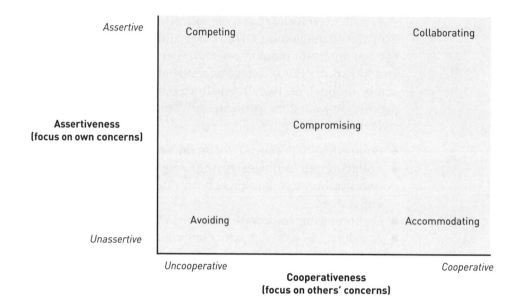

Figure 5.1 A model of conflict-handling styles

Illustration 5.10

Conflict resolution and situational appropriateness

Competing

1 When quick, decisive action is vital – e.g. emergencies.
2 On important issues where unpopular actions need implementing – e.g. cost cutting or to restore discipline.
3 On issues vital to company welfare when you think you are right.
4 Against people who take advantage of non-competitive behaviour.

Collaborating

1 To find an integrative solution when both sets of concerns are too important to be compromised.
2 When your objective is to learn, for example about complex situations.
3 To merge insights from people with different perspectives.
4 To gain commitment by incorporating concerns into a consensus.

5 To work through feelings that have interfered with a relationship.

Compromising

1 When goals are important, but the effort that would go with confrontational approaches is not worth making.
2 When opponents with equal power are committed to mutually exclusive goals.
3 To achieve temporary settlements of complex issues.
4 To arrive at expedient solutions to complex issues.
5 As a back-up when collaboration or competition is unsuccessful.

Avoiding

1 When an issue is trivial or more important issues are pressing.

2 When you perceive no chance of satisfying your concerns.
3 When potential disruption outweighs the benefits of resolution.
4 To let people cool down and regain perspective.
5 When gathering information is more important than finding a quick fix.
6 When others can resolve the conflict more effectively.
7 When issues seem tangential or symptomatic of other issues.

Accommodating

1 When you find you are wrong – to allow a better position to be heard, to learn and to show your reasonableness.

2 When issues are more important to others than to yourself – to satisfy others and maintain cooperation.
3 To build social credits for later issues.
4 To minimize loss when you are outmatched and losing.
5 When harmony and stability are especially important.
6 To allow subordinates to develop by learning from their mistakes.

Source: Thomas, K.W. (1977), 'Toward multi-dimensional values in teaching: the example of conflict behaviors', *Academy of Management Review*, 12, p. 487.

Most people have a preferred conflict-handling style, depending on their personality, culture, socialization and organizational experiences (Antonioni, 1998; Modberg, 2001). However, effective management of conflict can call upon the use of any of these styles, depending on the circumstances.

Activity 5.7

Analyze a conflict from your own organizational experience to identify which of Thomas's approaches identified in Illustration 5.10 were used?

If the conflict is still happening, which of Thomas's approaches do you think is best suited to resolving it?

Sometimes, however, conflict is on a different level altogether. A third perspective on conflict is a radicalist view which sees conflict as a result of power struggles between employers and employees who are essentially on opposite sides of a class struggle (Martin and Fellenz, 2010). Some situations are radicalized to the extent that divisions between managers and other employees are almost irreconcilable. The radical frame of reference that characterizes these situations derives from a view of society as comprising antagonistic class interests which will only be reconciled when the differences between the owners of production and the workers have disappeared. Based on a Marxist perspective, this situation is so powerful that it can cause the downfall of organizations and the social structures that support them. Usually however, in the long run the power of the owners of capital tends to prevail.

Activity 5.8

Please read the following scenario.

Raheel and Veronica both worked at the same level in the sales department of Keen Machine, a large importer of motorcycles that held the sole rights to sell one of the leading Japanese brands in Europe. They each managed a team of salespeople responsible for a different geographical area. Although the teams operated independently of each other they shared the services of two female administrators who dealt with orders, invoicing etc. The administrators also carried out typing and other administrative work for Raheel and Veronica. This work was done by whoever was available at a particular time.

Every year, all the salespeople had to undergo performance appraisals, which were performed by their manager (either Raheel or Veronica). However, the two administrators had been excluded from this process and the sales director decided that they also should be appraised as well and, to be fair to both, by the same person (either Raheel or Veronica).

Raheel's sales team had faced some difficulties on their territory recently and Raheel was having to work hard to recoup their previous good performance. The sales director, not wanting to distract Raheel from this task, asked Veronica to carry out the administrative staff appraisals.

Up to this time, Raheel had always had a good relationship with both administrators and had no complaint about their work for him. However, recently he began to notice that, if both he and Veronica gave work to the administrators at the same time, Veronica's work seemed to get done first – this was in spite of the fact that he had always thought he had a better relationship with them than Veronica. He complained to the administrators, who both declared they did not show any 'favouritism' to either himself or Veronica. He was still not satisfied but could think of no reason why their behaviour towards him should have changed.

Attempt to explain this situation using concepts and ideas related to issues of power and conflict.

 ## Power, conflict and change

Power, politics and conflict are indisputable aspects of social systems and organizational change. On the issue of power, French and Bell (1999) see it as ever-present and everywhere and that without power there would be no cooperation and no society. However, since power, conflict and political behaviour can have negative effects, the issue for managers dealing with organizational change is to use power and conflict as constructively as possible. This is, however, easier said than done.

The two faces of power

The idea that power has two faces was put forward by McClelland (1970) to explain its positive and negative aspects. In their discussion of McClelland's theories, French and Bell (1990, p. 280) remarked: 'The negative face of power is characterized by a primitive, unsocialized need to have dominance over submissive others.'

Positive power derives from a more socialized need to initiate, influence and lead and recognizes other people's needs to achieve their own goals as well as those of the organization. Negative power is about domination and control of others; positive power seeks to empower not only the self, but also others.

The terms 'constructive and destructive' can also be used in relation to different types of conflict and are clearly linked to the concepts of positive and negative power. The use of negative power almost inevitably results in destructive conflict, accompanied by a breakdown in communications and unwillingness to contemplate alternative points of view. The discontent arising tends to multiply in conditions of uncertainty that often exist when change is attempted. It is in such situations that power balances are upset and disagreements that might have been settled by compromise, escalate into destructive win/lose situations. Organizations facing conditions of change are, in many respects, at their most vulnerable to the political actions of those who stand to gain from the change as well as those who stand to lose.

The use of power

Among the cast of actors in a change process, there is generally a 'change agent'. This person has a 'special responsibility for planning, implementation and outcome of strategic change' (Lines, 2007, p. 144). Lines found that power does play a role in influencing the success of strategic implementation but the relationship between power and success is complex. Different types of power are enacted in different ways and the effects of power are mediated by the different implementation processes used.

Organizational life is full of occasions when people try to influence how others perceive the world around them. The term used to describe this is 'sensegiving' and it captures the processes that are used in efforts to help others make sense of what is going on around them (sensemaking) in an effort to reach some new, redefined, position (Drori and Ellis, 2011; Hope, 2010; Maitlis and Lawrence, 2007). Change agents with power derived from expertise are more likely to involve people and use sensegiving than change agents with low expert power (Lines, 2007). An implication is that, in organizations where participation is a strong part of the culture, expert power should be a characteristic of change agents if resistance is to be minimized.

Cynthia Hardy argues that power 'can provide the energy needed to drive the organization and its members through the strategic change process' (1996, p. 54). In addition to resource power (rewards and punishment) and process power (control of agendas and decisions) she identifies:

- *Power over meaning*: that is, attempting to alter values and norms. This involves the contemporary phenomenon of 'spin', for example, giving a set of reasons for change steeped in greater efficiency, modernization and cost savings when the real reason is to reorganize certain people out of a structure and away from positions of influence – possibly so that others more acceptable to the ruling class can be slotted in to positions of influence.
- *System power*: this is not a source that can be grasped and manipulated, rather it is a power source lying within the organization and existing by virtue of its

Table 5.4 Mobilizing the dimensions of power

	Power of resources	*Power of processes*	*Power of meaning*
Impact on actions	Principles of behaviour modification are used to influence specific actions	Confusion – focus on process without the support of resource power to direct behaviour	Confusion – focus on meaning without supporting resource power makes it difficult to influence specific behaviour
Impact on awareness	Inertia – resource power is inadequate to influence awareness	New awareness is created by the introduction of new participants, agendas and processes	Confusion – focus on meaning without the support of process power makes it difficult to translate awareness into behaviour
Impact on values	Inertia – resource power is inadequate to influence values	Inertia – process power is inadequate to influence values	Strategic change is given new meaning by influencing values and norms

Source: Hardy, C. (1996), 'Understanding power: bringing about strategic change', *British Journal of Management*, 7 (special issue), pp. S3–S16.

particular culture and structure. It is the power embedded in people's acceptance of the social conditions they work in. It is hard to change and is a backdrop to the exercise of the three other dimensions below (see Table 5.4).

Hardy argues that strategic change needs to utilize the range of dimensions to stand much chance of success. Drawing on one or two sources only will not provide the breadth of approach that is needed.

Some types of change are less problematic than others. Radical, frame-breaking change, for instance, is more likely to bring the greatest conditions of fear and uncertainty. Even so, small-scale, incremental change can upset the balance of power through small but significant redistributions of resources or changes in structure that make the skills or experience of some people more desirable than those of others. However, regardless of the content of any change it is the process that the organization must go through to get from one state to another that brings the most problems. Nadler (1988) suggests that three major problems are associated with this transition process: the problem of resistance to change; the problem of organizational control; and the problem of power.

Figure 5.2 builds on these ideas to illustrate some interconnections between power, conflict, change and political action. It also shows some possible implications for attitudes and behaviour during periods of change. Thus the transition process from one organizational state to another (desired) state, rather than being merely a series of mechanistically designed steps, is fraught with possibilities of conflict and political action.

Some types of change challenge the values and beliefs of some of the people involved and induce an internal state of conflict that, in turn, raises their resistance to change. In addition, because values and beliefs are challenged, this resistance has a moral imperative attached to it. Confusion about the means of organizational control – that is, who and what is being monitored and how – is closely associated with disturbances in the power balance which will most frequently be

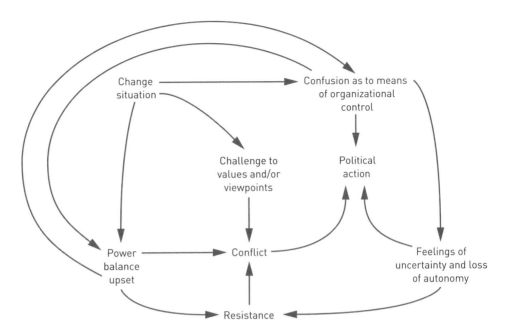

Figure 5.2 The problems of change

linked to position and resource power. During times of confusion like this opportunities present themselves for taking political action using invisible sources of power. In this context conflict, viewed as a problem, is likely to be resolved by the use of win/lose strategies.

The role of symbolic action is discussed in Chapter 4 but at this point we can note that during periods of relative stability, symbols such as stories, myths, rituals and routines and the more physical manifestations of status and power play a major part in sustaining that stability. Consequently, in periods of organizational change, these same symbols (and their relationship with symbolic power) can be used in the process of resisting change. What is more, this argument holds whether the change is incremental or is trying to shift the organizational paradigm. In addition, resistance to other than marginal changes incurs strategic drift. The process of strategic drift, if it continues without check, leads to confusion about organizational goals and the means of achieving them. This in turn lays down the conditions for conflict and political action.

Covert political action

Covert political action is a phrase used to describe actions of the most extreme kind witnessed during episodes of change. It embraces four interrelated themes: contestation of power and authority; 'perceptions of collective injury'; 'social occlusion'; and officially forbidden forms of dissent – each of which helps to explain change in organizations (Morrill, Zald and Rao, 2003). Covert political action is often not seen as organizational politics and is seen instead as criminal or deviant behaviour. However, this overlooks the underlying tensions that are causing it, since it is used by subordinated groups to display resistance and non-conformity in political struggles. Morrill and colleagues see covert political action as follows. First, it manifests in both material and symbolic forms. Sabotage and theft are explicit forms of covert action and this includes sabotage of ideas and goals, not just of machines or systems. Products can be badly assembled, production lines disrupted, machines broken or viruses released into computer systems. Some instances of whistle-blowing can be seen as attempts to sabotage an organization. Theft and misappropriation can be used to redress perceived imbalances in relations between employees and organizations.

Second, covert political action carries an element of social visibility. Organized union resistance to management plans is an example of a highly visible interest. At other times, the interests of parties to conflict may be in the open but the time and place of actions hidden (e.g. sabotage). Here, covert political action is occurring behind a veneer of conformity.

Third, covert political action can be conducted by an individual acting alone but is often undertaken in a collective and organized way, for example, workplace stoppages or refusing to cover for colleagues who are away sick. Fourth, covert action connects to change in that it challenges routines and practices that individuals or groups see as unfair. In wider society covert political action impacts on political change with an extreme example being changes won through civil disobedience or sustained terrorist activity. So why does it occur? Morrill *et al.* (2003) give the following reasons:

- *Declining control* – if control held by organizations or groups falls below a threshold level then action is taken to restore control to an acceptable level.
- *Identity* – people who identify with and who try to influence powerful groups are much less likely to engage in covert action than, say, employees who identify with each other far more strongly than they identify with the organization that is pushing for change.
- *Social networks* – the extent of social networks in an organization influences the extent of covert action since an individual is less likely to take action against a target if a friend is connected to the target. Hence the more extensive networks are, the less the climate for covert action.
- *Organization structures* – in particular how well they allow employee voice (speaking out). If people feel unable to say what they are feeling there is greater likelihood of covert action. Lack of voice is likely to foster the conditions in which grievances become long standing and eventually covert actions begin to take shape.

Covert actions should not simply be dismissed as deviant but should be recognized as a means through which individuals and groups who feel disenfranchised 'defend their dignity' and regain a level of control. It acts as a check against institutional authority.

Activity 5.9

Thinking of places where you have worked, can you identify any examples of employee behaviour that could be classed as covert political action?

The problems of change sometimes appear overwhelming. However, power, conflict and political action have both a positive and a negative aspect in the context of organizational change (De Dreu and van de Vliert, 1997).

The positive use of conflict and power

Robbins and Judge (2013) distinguish between functional or constructive conflict, and dysfunctional or destructive conflict. They regard functional conflict as a positive force that is absolutely necessary for effective performance – although functional conflict is confined to generally low-level issues. In similar vein, De Dreu and Beersma (2005) maintain that, between low conflict (a climate of complacency and apathy) and high conflict (a climate of hostility and mistrust), there is an optimal level of conflict that engenders self-criticism and innovation to increase unit performance. These theories are shown in Figure 5.3 and are expressed as a curvilinear or inverted U-shaped relationship.

Figure 5.4 illustrates the mechanisms that are assumed to be operating. It depicts a five-stage process of moving from an initial conflict situation through to alternative positive or negative outcomes. Note that stage III 'Intentions' uses Thomas's (1976) model of conflict-handling styles.

It is clear of course that organizations continue to function effectively in spite of conflicting relationships within them. There is a fine balance between conflict and

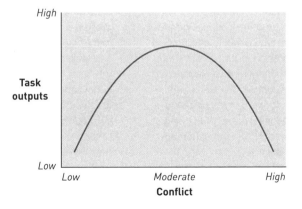

Figure 5.3 Curvilinear relationship between conflict and performance

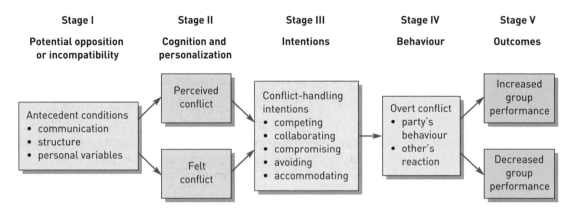

Figure 5.4 The conflict process

Source: Robbins, S.P. (2005), *Organizational Behavior: Concepts, Controversies, Applications* (11th edn), Englewood Cliffs, NJ: Prentice Hall, p. 424.

consent and studies of the relationship between job stress and performance (stress would be a logical outcome of conflict) frequently assume a curvilinear relationship although not all studies support it (Muse, Harris and Field, 2003; Onyemah, 2008). A curvilinear relationship would indicate that low levels of conflict could help to support change, but higher levels would suppress it.

Furze and Gale (1996) take an optimistic view of conflict and Illustration 5.11 lists some of their guidelines. The guidelines are general and may result in collaboration where both parties stand to win.

Illustration 5.11

Guidelines for dealing with conflict

1 *Encourage openness*. This refers to the need to explore objectives, facts, views and the assumptions that surround the issues. Openness requires statements of who benefits and how. It assumes that conflicts cannot be resolved if issues associated with them remain hidden.

2 *Model appropriate responses*. The issue here is one of role modelling. If one party is prepared to make positive responses, rather than being defensive or dismissive, this acts to encourage the other party to do likewise.

3 *Provide summaries and restatements of the position*. This helps to keep communication going and helpfully slows down the process when it becomes heated and when points that are made are in danger of being ignored and lost.

4 *Bring in people who are not directly involved*. Outsiders can act as additional information providers or take on the more process-oriented role of mediator or arbitrator. A mediator can facilitate a negotiated solution while an arbitrator can dictate one. Other possibilities are conciliators who act as communicators between the two parties (particularly if they will not communicate directly) and consultants. Instead of putting forward specific solutions, the consultant tries to help the parties learn to understand and work with each other.

5 *Encourage people to take time to think and reassess*. This means building in time for reflection. It may mean 'shelving' the problem for a while but not as a means of avoiding it.

6 *Use the strengths of the group*. This refers to taking advantage of opportunities to use non-combative members of the group to which the combatants belong. Doing this brings others into the conflict, not to take sides but to play a positive and creative role.

7 *Focus on shared goals*. Rather than concentrating from the start on differences, seek instead to identify where agreements exist – even if these are very small. These form a useful base from which to move outwards to assess just where differences exist. Parties to a conflict are often surprised at the amount of agreement present but of which they were unaware.

8 *Use directions and interests to develop areas of new gain*. Concentrating on other people's ideas can identify areas of potential gain. Then using guideline 2, summarize ideas in order to move forward.

9 *Try to build objectivity into the process*. Objectivity can be encouraged by asking those involved to express both the strengths and weaknesses of their position. What must be recognized, however, is that objectivity will always be tempered by people's value systems.

10 *Adopt an enquiring approach to managing*. This means probing through what appear to be the symptoms of conflict to understand the actual causes. Unless the fundamental cause is identified, the conflict will continue to flare up at regular intervals.

Source: Based on Furze, D. and Gale, C. (1996), *Interpreting Management. Exploring Change and Complexity*, London: Thompson International Press, pp. 312–17.

Based on their work as change consultants, Lehman and Linsky (2008) offer the following advice. Given that 'deep' change almost always throws up conflict, those leading change are encouraged to see it as a healthy sign that a journey is underway. To harness conflict to change they recommend the following practices:

- *Build a container.* The container metaphor represents a space (a padded cell perhaps) where people can 'vent their spleen'. Such a space could be off-site and allow a 'no-holds barred' approach with guarantees that there will be no repercussions for speaking out.
- *Leverage dissident voices.* Angry voices may be making some serious, if unpopular, points. Leaders of change should be open-minded about what dissidents say and not let other parties, with their peculiar political interests, suppress them.
- *Let others resolve the conflicts.* Leaders are often expected to intervene and make rulings to resolve a conflict situation. While this is something that is often needed there are times when the disputants have to be told to sort out their differences and report back to the top. Warring parties can be asked to put solutions to top management and when objections are out in the open they can be opportunities for learning.
- *Raise the heat.* Whereas leaders are often expected to maintain a climate of calm it is sometimes necessary to turn up the heat on a group to force fresh thinking. This might come from confronting a group with extensive information about its performance in an effort to force them to confront change issues.

Action on power, conflict and change

Four action steps help to shape the political dynamics of change (Nadler, 1988). The first step is to ensure or develop the support of key power groups. This involves identifying those individuals and groups who have the power either to assist change or to block it, although not all power groups have to be intimately involved in the change. However, some groups will need to be included in the planning of change to guard against them ultimately blocking it, not because it might affect them adversely, but because they had been ignored. The second step is using leader behaviour to generate energy in support of the change. Illustration 5.11 offers some guiding principles. In addition, sets of leaders working together can significantly influence the informal aspects of organizational life. The third step is using symbols and language to create energy. The fourth step for shaping the political dynamics of change is the need to build in stability. This is the use of power to ensure some things remain the same. These might be physical locations, group members, even hours of work. It is helpful to provide sources of stability like these to provide 'anchors' for people to hold on to during the turbulence of change. In addition, there is a need to let people know what will remain stable and what is likely to change.

This chapter set out to show the importance of power and conflict as elements in the politics of change. Managers who, in times of change, can reasonably assess how power is distributed and the way in which it will be used – with possible consequences for potential and actual conflict – have a good chance of implementing the change they seek. It is useful therefore to consider how to analyze individuals and groups according to their power to block change and their motivation to do so.

A first step in analyzing the potential for action is to identify who holds sufficient power to assist change or, alternatively, to work against it – that is, to carry out a 'power audit'. This can be done using a framework like that shown in Figure 5.5 based on the descriptions of the characteristics and sources of power discussed earlier. The framework should be used for each individual or group that is considered to be significant for the success or otherwise of any change process.

The second step is to compare the power of any individual or group to block change with their desire or motivation to do so. Assessing motivation to block change is not straightforward. It can be gauged, however, by considering whether the changes proposed will alter the degree of power held. As a general rule, if this is likely to be lowered then resistance to change can be expected. Figure 5.5 allows individuals or groups to be categorized according to their power to block change and their motivation to do so.

Each cell of the matrix shown in Figure 5.6 represents a different situation and strategy to deal with it. Thus, if an individual or group has little power to block change and, in addition, little motivation to do so (as represented by cell C) then no immediate action needs to be taken. However, if there is both power to block change and the motivation to do so (cell B) this represents a serious situation in terms of the need to negotiate with those concerned to reach a collaborative agreement.

Indicators of power to help or hinder change	Individual Group A*	Individual Group B*	Individual Group C*
Position 1 Status to hierarchy/formal authority 2 Power to change organizational structure, rules and regulations 3 Control of strategic decision processes 4 Control of operational decision processes			
Resources 5 Control of scarce resources 6 Control of budgets 7 Control of technology 8 Ability to reward or punish staff			
Personal characteristics 9 Involvement in interpersonal alliances and networks, with links to the informal organization 10 Able to exert 'charismatic' leadership to get others to follow 11 Able to cope with uncertainty			
Knowledge and expertise 12 Information specific to the change situation 13 Skills specific to the change situation 14 Knowledge and expertise unique to situation concerned			
Symbols 15 Quality of accommodation 16 Use of expenses budget 17 Membership of high-level decision-making committees 18 Receipt of company 'perks' 19 Unchallenged right to deal with those outside the organization 20 Access to the 'ear' of top management			

* Indicate against each indicator, the degree of power for each individual or group, according to whether it is high (H), medium (M) or low (L).

Figure 5.5 Assessing power

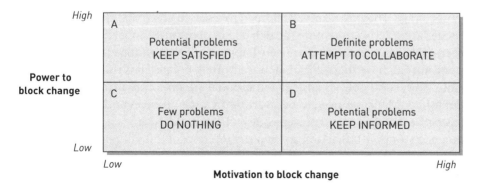

Figure 5.6 The power and motivation to block changes

A potential threat to change is represented by those who fall into cell A of the matrix – those with a high degree of power but little motivation to challenge it. This is because, if the situation itself changes, their interest may change and this might then move them into cell B. A strategy towards these groups should be one of 'keeping them satisfied'. This means maintaining their awareness of how the change might benefit them.

Cell D of the matrix represents a different kind of problem. It might be tempting to ignore this group but, because change situations are dynamic, the people in cell D might begin to gain power and thus move into the more contentious group represented by cell B. Consequently, they should be kept informed of change developments with some effort made to understand their motivations and concerns. However, people in cell D may in any radical restructuring face serious consequences, even job loss. Containment in the short term might, therefore, be the most appropriate strategy.

The axes of the matrix in Figure 5.6 are presented in negative terms in relation to organizational change, i.e. 'power to block change'. It is equally possible to label the axes positively, for example, 'power to facilitate change' and 'motivation to facilitate change'. The categorization of individuals and groups according to this framework would not necessarily be the converse of that used in Figure 5.6. Therefore, it is worth completing two matrices for a more complete analysis of power, conflict and change.

The capacity for organizations to change, both incrementally and radically depends on the multiplicity of different interests and values that are present. Power and conflict can be used to further the aims of change as well as resist them. People and groups in organizations will share some common interests and also have some conflicting ones. The style and function of leadership in the sharing or withholding of power and the management of conflict are crucial for change and this is considered in the next chapter.

Conclusions

Power and politics are driven by human differences and have become central to the study of change. They are relatively difficult to research given that they rely on deep and penetrating access to capture the rich details of organizational life. Their importance in explaining much of what really happens in organizations is now being understood although we suggest that managers often, because it is the easiest option, overlook power and politics and rely on rational arguments to explain the behaviour of others. Managers need to be aware of their own sources and levels of power and recognize the power and powerlessness of others. Managing change usually invokes a need for political action to keep the interests of individuals and groups in balance.

Buchanan and Badham (2008, pp. 47–52) define power as 'something you possess, that is a set of resources which you can accumulate'; a property of relationships between individuals or groups; and an embedded property in that it exists visibly and invisibly in the structures, regulations, relationships and norms of the organization which perpetuate existing routines and power inequalities. Power is won and lost during change, and change agents have to appreciate how and where it is being redistributed if they are to obtain a deep understanding of what they are attempting. Managers and others working with change ignore the politics of change at their peril.

Discussion questions and assignments

1 Think of people in your organization and give examples of the sources of power that they enjoy.

2 How are power relations expressed and managed, overtly and covertly, where you work?

3 Discuss the proposition: 'Conflict between individuals and groups in the workplace is inevitable.'

4 Discuss the following statement: 'If it is managed well, conflict can add substantial value to change processes'.

5 What are the main symbols of power in your organization?

Case example – Qatar 2022 ●●●

The governing body for world football, FIFA, reached a contentious decision in 2010 to hold the World Cup in Qatar in 2022. In the final round of voting, 14 votes went to Qatar and 8 to the USA. Qatar has no tradition of football, little football infrastructure and summer temperatures too severe for competitive high-quality football. Furthermore, before reaching its decision, FIFA's executive committee (exco) was briefed that Qatar was at a high risk of terrorist attack.

Investigative journalism in 2014 raised some serious concerns about the processes leading up to the Qatar decision. At the centre of the concerns and allegations were claims of bribery and corruption. Allegations were made that substantial sums of money, valuable gifts and junkets made their way from Qatari bank accounts (slush funds) into the accounts of decision makers on FIFA's exco committee that decides where future World Cup events will be staged.

A key player in the successful campaign for Qatar was BH. After the campaign, BH set out to topple the long-standing head of FIFA (JB) and take the presidency for himself. It was alleged that at a meeting of influential Caribbean football heads,

BH paid over $360,000 to cover travel and accommodation expenses and also gave each delegate $40,000 cash as a way of raising support for his presidential campaign. Very soon after, however, evidence of the cash payments was obtained and sent to FIFA's headquarters in Switzerland. A few days before the presidential ballot was due, BH was summoned to appear before FIFA's ethics committee; an event which killed any hope BH had of getting the top job. FIFA announced that both BH and a senior exco member were suspended from all activities in football pending a full investigation. FIFA's ethics committee found evidence of wrongdoing and banned BH for life. On appeal, this ban was overturned at which point BH announced his retirement from involvement in football.

Some time afterwards, following further investigations, the ethics committee banned BH again from life involvement in the game. AW, who had been president of the North, Central American and Caribbean football confederation and vice-president of FIFA, resigned in 2011 following corruption and bribery charges. Several senior figures attacked

FIFA for not representing world football, having long-standing traditions of bribery and corruption and sham investigations in which people were not properly investigated. Concerned at allegations against it, FIFA appointed a former police officer as a new security adviser. After two years, he and his team left FIFA for a new sports security post in Qatar. Their investigation of FIFA's senior officials and regional governing bodies reportedly concluded by saying:

- of the president, JB, he is ruthless, greedy, manipulative and prepared to compromise everything for personal ambition;
- of the secretary-general, he is ruthless and charmingly arrogant;
- of the head of legal services, he is consummately loyal and protective of men at the top even when he disagrees with them;
- of the European Confederation, it is historically influential but serious corruption issues exist;
- of the African Confederation, manipulated throughout for decades;
- of the Asian Confederation, marred by involvement in the Qatar bid (BH was its president for nine years);
- of the Oceania Confederation, little impact on any decisions;
- of the North and Central American Confederation, poor reputation and the Caribbean has been manipulated for decades;
- of the South American Confederation, it is led by long-serving octogenarians, will never show leadership and will be the last to change.

Further reporting claimed that after the 2010 World Cup in South Africa the 22 exco members were each given a $200,000 bonus. This was on top of their $100,000 salary for their part-time position and $750 per day allowances when working for FIFA. The money was paid into either executives' personal accounts or Swiss bank accounts. The $200,000 windfall was announced to exco the day before the Qatar decision was made. FIFA later announced that bonus payments would be stopped but at about the same time, and without saying, doubled the pay given to committee members. Later there were calls for Qatar to lose the right to hold the World Cup and for the event to switch to another country. Qatar insisted that BH, who is a Qatari, never had any official role in supporting the Qatari bid and that he always acted independently.

FIFA responded to corruption allegations from Britain by saying that they were grounded in racism and discrimination.

As we write this case (2015), at dawn on the eve of FIFA's 65th Congress in Switzerland, USA law officials have arrested seven senior FIFA officials on charges of corruption. Intimations that this was just the start were made. Speculation was that the FIFA president might lose the election the next day. However, this was not the case and he won.

Case exercise

1 What internal organizational conditions could have created a climate in which the alleged large-scale corruption and bribery took place over such a long time?

2 How were power and influence used to produce, or attempt to produce, particular outcomes for individuals?

3 What actions by FIFA could restore confidence in its integrity?

4 Assuming that external events have triggered change processes at FIFA, how would you classify these events in a PEST framework?

Sources: Information based upon:
'Mr Fixer's bid for FIFA's crown', *The Sunday Times*, 15 June 2014, p. 21.
'Bungs, junkets and the bombshell that failed', *The Sunday Times*, 15 June 2014, pp. 22–3.
'The bountiful game: FIFA's secret bonuses', *The Sunday Times*, 22 June 2014, pp. 10–11.
'From the more of corruption, a leader emerges …', *The Guardian*, 30 May 2015, pp. 1–2.
'The US has said repeatedly that it is only at the beginning of its investigation into corruption in world football and that more officials may eventually face charges', *The Daily Telegraph*, 2 June 2015.

Indicative resources

Brooks, I. (2009), *Organizational Behaviour* (4th edn), Harlow: Pearson Education. The chapter on power, politics and conflict is a useful introduction.

Buchanan, D.A. and Badham, R.J. (2008), *Power, Politics and Organizational Change*, London: Sage. This is an accessible specialist treatment of managerial life.

Clegg, S., Courpasson, D. and Phillips, N. (2006), *Power and Organizations*, Sage. A comprehensive and advanced text analyzing power in organizational, social and political theory.

Robbins, S.P. and Judge, T. A.(2013), *Organizational Behaviour* (15th edn), Englewood Cliffs, NJ: Prentice Hall. This book has an excellent section on conflict and negotiation.

Vigoda-Gadot, E. and Drory, A. (2006), *Handbook of Organizational Politics,* Cheltenham: Edward Elgar. This text contains a collection of theoretical and empirical papers on politics and power. Perspectives covered include leadership, emotions, fairness and stress.

Useful websites

www.acas.org.uk The Advisory, Conciliation and Arbitration Service (ACAS) provides advice and mediation to employers and employees. The website identifies common areas of conflict in employee relations.

www.cipd.co.uk The website of the professional body for human resource managers (Chartered Institute of Personnel and Development) contains guidance on conflict management, including a substantial downloadable guide.

www.catalyst.org Contains facts and information on women in leadership.

www.ILO.org Series of reports on labour and work throughout the world.

References

Antonioni, D. (1998), 'Relationship between the big five personality factors and conflict management styles', *International Journal of Conflict Management*, 9(4), pp. 336–55.

Barbulescu, R. and Bidwell. M. (2013), 'Do women choose different jobs from men?' *Organization Science*, 24(3), pp. 737–56.

Barsky, A. (2002), 'Structural sources of conflict in a university context', *Conflict Resolution Quarterly*, 20(2), pp. 161–76.

Barzilai-Nahon, K. (2008), 'Toward a theory of network gatekeeping: a framework for exploring information control', *Journal of the American Society for Information Science and Technology*, 59(9), pp. 1493–512.

Bernadin, H. and Alvares, K. (1976), 'The managerial grid as a predictor of conflict resolution methods and managerial effectiveness', *Administrative Science Quarterly*, 21(1), pp. 84–92.

Blake, R.R. and Mouton, J.S. (1970), 'The fifth achievement', *Journal of Applied Behavioral Science*, 6, pp. 414–26.

Blois, K. and Hopkinson, G.C. (2013), 'The use and abuse of French and Raven in the channels literature', *Journal of Marketing Management*, 29(9/10), pp. 1143–62.

Bourdieu, P. (1991), *Language and Symbolic Power*, Cambridge, MA: Harvard University Press.

Brammer, S., Millington, A. and Pavelin, S. (2009), 'Corporate reputation and women on the board', *British Journal of Management*, 20(1), pp. 17–29.

Brescoll, V.L. (2011), 'Who takes the floor and why: gender, power and volubility in organizations', *Administrative Science Quarterly*, 56(4), pp. 622–41.

Brink, M. and Benschop, M. (2014), Gender in academic networking: the role of gatekeepers in professorial recruitment, *Journal of Management Studies*, 51(3), pp. 460–92.

Brittain, V. (1964) *The Rebel Passion*, George Allen & Unwin.

Brooks, I. (2009), *Organizational Behaviour* (4th edn), Harlow: Pearson Education.

Buchanan, D. and Badham, R. (2008), *Power, Politics and Organizational Change* (2nd edn), London: Sage.

Burrell, G. and Morgan, G. (1979), *Sociological Paradigms and Organisational Analysis*, London: Heinemann Educational.

Burrell, G. and Morgan, G. (2006) *Sociological Paradigms and Organisational Analysis*, London: Heinemann Educational.

Carter, D.A., D'Souza, F., Simkins, B. and Simpson, W. (2010), 'The gender and ethnic diversity of US boards and board committees and firm financial performance', *Corporate Governance: An International Review*, 18(5), pp. 396–414.

Chartered Institute of Personnel Development (CIPD) (2015), *Gender Diversity in the Boardroom: Reach for the top* (February).

CIPD (2008), *Leadership and the Management of Conflict at Work*, Survey Report, London: Chartered Institute of Personnel and Development.

Clegg, S., Courpasson, D. and Phillips, N. (2006), *Power and Organizations*, London: Sage.

Das, H. (1988), 'Relevance of symbolic interactionist approach in understanding power: a preliminary analysis', *Journal of Management Studies*, 25(3), pp. 251–67.

De Dreu, C. and Beersma, B. (2005), 'Conflict in organizations: beyond effectiveness and performance', *European Journal of Work and Organizational Psychology*, 14(2), pp. 105–17.

De Dreu, C. and van de Vliert, E. (1997), *Using Conflict in Organizations*, Thousand Oaks, CA: Sage.

Drori, I. and Ellis, S. (2011), 'Conflict and power games in a multinational corporation: sensegiving and sensemaking as a strategy of preservation', *European Management Review*, 8(1), pp. 1–16.

French, W.L. and Bell, C.H. (1999), *Organization Development: Behavioral science interventions for organization improvement* (2nd edn), Englewood Cliffs, NJ: Prentice-Hall.

French, J.R.P. and Raven, B.H. (1959), 'The bases of social power', in Cartwright, D. (ed.) *Studies in Social Power*, Ann Arbor: University of Michigan, pp. 150–67.

Frost, D.E. and Stahelski, A.J. (2006), 'The systematic measurement of French and Raven's bases of social power in work groups', *Journal of Applied Social Psychology*, 18(5), pp. 375–89.

Furze, D. and Gale, C. (1996), *Interpreting Management: Exploring Change and Complexity*, London: Thompson International.

Gordon, J.R. (1993), *A Diagnostic Approach to Organizational Behavior*, Needham Heights, MA: Allyn & Bacon, p. 425. P32.

Handy, C. (1993), *Understanding Organizations*, Harmondsworth: Penguin.

Hardy, C. (1994), *Managing Strategic Action: Mobilizing Change: Concepts, Readings and Cases*, London: Sage.

Hardy, C. (1996), 'Understanding power: bringing about strategic change', *British Journal of Management,* 7 (special issue), pp. S3–S16.

Haslam, S., Ryan, M., Kulich, C., Trojanowski, G. and Atkins, K. (2010), 'Investing with prejudice: the relationship between women's presence on company boards and objective and subjective measures of company performance', *British Journal of Management*, 21(2), pp. 484–97.

Hofstede, G., Hofstede, J. G., Minkov, M. (2010), *Cultures and Organizations Software of the Mind.* London: Sage.

Hope, O. (2010), 'The politics of middle management sensemaking and sensegiving', *Journal of Change Management*, 10(2), pp. 195–215.

Huczynski, A. and Buchanan, D. (2007), *Organizational Behaviour* (6th edn), Harlow: Financial Times Prentice Hall.

Huffman, M.L., Cohen, P.N. and Pearlman, J. (2010), 'Engendering change: organizational dynamics and workplace gender desegregation', *Administrative Science Quarterly*, 55, pp. 255–77.

Hultin, M. and Szulkin, R. (1999), 'Wages and unequal access to organizational power: an empirical test of gender discrimination', *Administrative Science Quarterly*, 44, pp. 453–72.

Hultin, M. and Szulkin, R. (2003), 'Mechanisms of inequality: unequal access to organizational power and the gender wage gap', *European Sociological Review*, 19, pp. 143–59.

ILO (2012), *Global Employment Trends for Women*, Geneva: International Labour Organization.

Jehn, K.A. (1995), 'A multimethod examination of the benefits and detriments of intragroup conflict', *Administrative Science Quarterly,* 40, pp. 256–82.

Joecks, J., Pull, K. and Vetter, K. (2013), 'Gender diversity in the boardroom and firm performance: what exactly constitutes a critical mass?' *Journal of Business Ethics,* 118(1), pp. 61–72.

Kalantari, F. (2012), 'The influence of social values and childhood socialization on occupational gender segregation and wage disparity', *Public Personnel Management,* 41(2), pp. 241–55.

Kanter, R.M. (1979), 'Power failure in management circuits', *Harvard Business Review,* July–August, pp. 65–75.

Kim, K. and Markman, A. (2013), 'Individual differences, cultural differences and dialectical conflict description and resolution', *International Journal of Psychology,* 48(5), pp. 797–808.

King, D. and Lawley, S. (2013), *Organizational Behaviour,* Oxford: Oxford University Press.

Lawrence, T., Namrata, M. and Morris, T. (2012), 'Episodic and systemic power in the transformation of professional service firms', *Journal of Management Studies,* 49(1), pp. 102–43.

Lehman, K. and Linsky, M. (2008), 'Using conflict as a catalyst for change', *Harvard Management Update,* April, pp. 3–5.

Lien, B.Y. (2005), 'Gender, power and office politics', *Human Resource Development International,* 8(3), pp. 293–309.

Lines, R. (2007), 'Using power to install strategy: the relationship between expert power, position power, influence tactics and implementation success', *Journal of Change Management,* 7(2), pp. 143–70.

Luckerath-Rovers, M. (2013), 'Women on boards and firm performance', *Journal of Management and Governance,* 17(2), pp. 491–509.

Lunenburg, F.C. (2012), 'Power and leadership: an influence process', *International Journal of Management, Business and Administration,* 15(1).

Maitlis, S. and Lawrence, T.B. (2007), 'Triggers and enablers of sensegiving in organizations', *Academy of Management Journal,* 50(1), pp. 57–84.

Martin, J. and Fellenz, M. (2010), *Organizational Behaviour and Management* (4th edn), Andover: Cengage Learning.

McClelland, D.C. (1970), 'The two faces of power', *Journal of International Affairs,* 24(1), pp. 29–47.

McKenna, E.P. (1997), *When Work Doesn't Work Anymore: Women, Work and Identity,* New York: Hodder & Stoughton.

Modberg, P. (2001), 'Linking conflict strategy to the five-factor model: theoretical and empirical foundations', *International Journal of Conflict Management,* 12(1), pp. 47–68.

Morgan, G. (2006), *Images of Organizations,* London: Sage.

Morrill, C., Zald, M.N. and Rao, H. (2003), 'Covert political conflict in organizations: challenges from below', *Annual Review of Sociology,* 29(1), pp. 391–415.

Mullins, L.J. (2013), *Management and Organizational Behaviour* (10th edn), Harlow: Pearson Education.

Murphy, P. and Dee, J. (1992), 'Du Pont and Greenpeace: the dynamics of conflict between corporations and activists groups', *Public Relations Research,* 4(1), pp. 3–20.

Muse, L.A., Harris, S.G. and Field, H.S. (2003), 'Has the inverted-U shape theory of stress and job performance had a fair test?' *Human Performance,* 16(4), pp. 349–64.

Nadler, D.A. (1988), 'Concepts for the management of organizational change', in Tushman, M.L. and Moore, W.L. (eds), *Readings in the Management of Innovation* (7th edn), New York: Ballinger, pp. 718–32.

Nemoto, K. (2013) 'Long Working Hours and the Corporate Gender Divide in Japan' in *Gender, Work & Organization,* 20(5), pp. 512–27.

Ness, K. (2012), 'Constructing masculinity in the building trades: "most jobs in the construction industry can be done by women"', *Gender, Work and Organization,* 19(6), pp. 654–76.

O'Neill, J. (2004), 'Effects of gender and power on PR managers' upward influence', *Journal of Managerial Issues,* XVI(1), pp. 127–44.

Onyemah, V. (2008), 'Role ambiguity, role conflict and performance: empirical evidence of an inverted-U relationship', *Journal of Personal Selling and Sales Management,* XXVIII(3), pp. 299–313.

Paton, R. (1994), 'Power in Organizations', in Arson, R. and Paton, R., *Organizations, Cases, Issues, Concepts,* London: PCP.

Peiro, J.M. and Melia, J.L. (2003), 'Formal and interpersonal power in organizations: testing a bifactorial model of power in role sets', *Applied Psychology: An International Review,* 52(1), pp. 14–35.

Pfeffer, J. (1981), *Power in Organizations,* Marshfield, MA: Pitman.

Pfeffer, J. (1992), *Managing with Power: Politics and Influence in Organization,* Boston, MA: Harvard Business Press.

Pfeffer, J. (1993), 'Understanding power in organizations', in Mabey, C. and Mayon-White, B. (eds), *Managing Change* (2nd edn), London: PCP.

Robbins, S.P. and Judge, T.A. (2013), *Organizational Behavior* (15th edn), Englewood Cliffs, NJ: Prentice Hall.

Schubert, T.W. (2005), 'Your Highness: vertical position as perceptual symbols of power', *Journal of Personality and Social Psychology,* 89(1), pp. 1–21.

Schuh, S., Hernandez, S., van Quaquebeke, N., Hossiep, R., Frieg, P. and van Dick, R. (2014), 'Gender differences in leadership role occupancy: the mediating role of power motivation', *Journal of Business Ethics,* 120: pp. 363–79.

Sinai, E. Wellins, R. Ray, L. Abel, A. L. and Neal, S. (2014) *The Global Leadership Forecast 2014/15: Ready Now Leaders: Meeting Tomorrow's Business Challenges,* Pittsburgh, PA: Development Dimensions International, https://www.ddiworld.com

Singh, V., Kumra, S., and Vinnicombe, S. (2002), 'Gender and impression management: playing the promotion game', *Journal of Business Ethics,* 37(1), pp. 77–89.

Smith, A., Watkins, M., Burke, M., Christian, M., Smith, C., Hall, A. and Sims, S. (2013), Gendered influence: a gendered role perspective on the use and effectiveness of influence tactics, *Journal of Management*, 39(5), pp. 1156–83.

The Guardian (2014) 'More than 40 years after the Equal Pay Act outlawed less favourable pay and conditions in the workplace, the data shows that discrepancies in salaries widen at the higher echelons of management', 19 August 2014.

The National Management Salary Survey (2014), published by the Chartered Management Institute and XpertHR, http://www.xperthr.co.uk/salary-surveys/national-management-salary-survey

Thomas, K.W. (1976), 'Conflict and conflict management', in Dunnette, M.D. (ed.) *Handbook of Industrial and Organizational Psychology*, Chicago, IL: Rand McNally, pp. 889–935.

Thomas, K.W. (1977), 'Toward multi-dimensional values in teaching: the example of conflict.

Tinsley, C. (1998), 'Models of conflict resolution in Japanese, German and American cultures', *Journal of Applied Psychology*, 83(2), pp. 316–23.

Van de Vliert, E. and Kabanoff, B. (1990), 'Toward theory-based measure of conflict management', *Academy of Management Journal*, 33(1), pp. 199–209.

Valéry, P. (2011), taken from *Oxford Concise Dictionary of Quotations*, Oxford: Oxford University Press.

Vigoda-Gadot, E. and Drory, A. (2006), *Handbook of Organizational Politics*, Cheltenham: Edward Elgar.

Vilnai-Yavetz, I. and Rafaeli, A. (2006), 'Managing artifacts to avoid artifact myopia', in Rafaeli, A. and Pratt, M.G. (eds), *Artifacts and Organizations: Beyond Mere Symbolism*, Mahwah, NJ: Lawrence Erlbaum Associates.

Vinnicombe, S., Doldor, E. and Turner, C. (2014), *The Female FTSE Report, 2014*, Cranfield University.

Vinnicombe, S., Dolder, E., Sealey, E., Pryce P. and Turner, C. (2015), *The Female FTSE Board Report, 2015*, Cranfield University.

Wahl, A. and Hook, P. (2007), 'Changes in working with gender equality management in Sweden', *Equal Opportunities International*, 26(5), pp. 435–48.

Weber, M. (1947) *The Theory of Social and Economic Organization*, London: Oxford University Press.

Wilson, D.C. (1992), *A Strategy of Change*, London: Routledge.

Wolf, J. and Egelhoff, W. (2013), 'An empirical evaluation of conflict in matrix structure firms', *International Business Review*, 22(3), pp. 591–601.

Yuet-Ha, M. (1996), 'Orientating values with Eastern ways', *People Management*, 25 July, pp. 28–30.

Chapter 6

Leadership styles and leading change

Leadership style is often championed as one of the most significant factors in leadership success. The major theories of leadership are introduced in this chapter together with a critical summary of traditional approaches to leadership, the influence of gender in leadership and the 'dark side' of leader behaviour. We discuss 'authentic' leadership; a new and emerging theory which, it is suggested, is a 'root construct' that underpins all other positive styles of leadership. Resistance to change is also explored, as well as why change fails, organizational readiness for change and how to effectively lead and manage organizational change.

Learning objectives

By the end of this chapter, you will be able to:

- define leadership and understand how your own leadership style might influence how you would lead and manage organizational change;

- explain the similarities and differences between leadership and management;

- discuss leadership style and its relationship to situation and context;

- critically review current and historical portrayals of leaders and leadership, understanding how their leadership styles might effect and affect follower motivation and engagement.

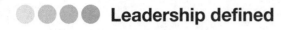

Leadership defined

Like many constructs in social sciences, the definition of leadership is subjective; some definitions are more attractive than others and there is no 'correct' definition (Yukl, 2002, pp. 4–5). Some definitions are given below to illustrate the breadth and scope of the different perspectives on leadership which exist.

> Leadership is *A process of influence leading to the achievement of desired purposes. It involves inspiring and supporting others towards the achievement of a vision ... which is based on their personal and professional values.*
>
> (Bush and Glover, 2003, p. 8)

> Leadership is *A process whereby an individual influences a group so as to achieve a common goal*
>
> (Northouse, 2013, p. 5)

> *Most definitions of leadership reflect the assumption that it involves a social influence process whereby intentional influence is exerted by one person (or group) over other people (or groups) to structure the activities and relationships in a group or organization.*
>
> (Yukl, 2002, p. 3)

> *Leadership should be defined in terms of the ability to build and maintain a group that performs well relative to its competition.*
>
> (Hogan and Kaiser, 2005, p. 172)

> *Leadership solves the problem of how to organize collective effort; consequently, it is the key to organizational effectiveness.*
>
> (Hogan and Kaiser, 2005, p. 169)

> *Great leaders are bred from great causes, but leaders, at their best, also breed great causes.*
>
> (Handy, 1996, p. 8)

> *Leadership is about results ... but it is not only about performance; it is also about meaning ... Leaders at all levels make a difference to performance. They do so by making performance meaningful.*
>
> (Goffee and Jones, 2006, p. 2)

Some of these statements and definitions of leadership might appeal to you more than others and Activity 6.1 will help you understand your own views towards the topic.

Activity 6.1

Re-read the definitions of leadership above and consider which, if any, you like or dislike. Which definitions are most meaningful to you? Next, define leadership for yourself. For you, what is leadership?

Management versus leadership

The French engineer Henri Fayol (1841–1925) was among the first to describe management as a set of processes. His Five Functions of Management are well known – *Planning, Organizing, Commanding, Coordinating* and *Controlling* – and in some respects they are still a good description of the tasks managers are expected to achieve today. Around the same time as Fayol, American industrialist Frederick Taylor introduced his principles of Scientific Management in an attempt to optimize work methods, production and efficiency through the consistent application of rigorous and measured 'scientific' approaches. However, despite an early literature on the topic, studies of what managers and leaders actually do are relatively uncommon. One of the best-known studies is Tony Watson's (1994) account of working in a British manufacturing company. He defined management as: '... organizing, pulling things together and along in a general direction to bring about long term organizational survival' (1994, p. 33).

A leading writer on management, Mintzberg (1979), studied chief executives in both large and small organizations and grouped managerial roles into three sets: three *interpersonal roles* of Figurehead, Leader and Liaison; three *informational roles* of Monitor, Disseminator and Spokesman; and four *decision-making roles* of Entrepreneur, Disturbance Handler, Resource Allocator and Negotiator. The roles highlight the ambiguity of the relationship between management and leadership; leadership appears as one aspect of a manager's job. Mintzberg did not differentiate between leadership and management in the same way as later theorists such as Kotter (1990) have done and Illustration 6.1 compares managing and leading from Kotter's perspective. Management is more concerned with the day-to-day operational detail, whereas leadership is more concerned with the longer-term strategic direction and alignment of people to the leader's organizational vision.

How leadership models have changed

Leadership theory has a long history and 'great' leaders were recognized and studied long before the relatively recent (the past 100 years) interest in managing organizations. Before we explore the major leadership style theories, Illustration 6.2 gives a condensed history of leadership through the ages and shows how thinking has changed across time.

Great Man theories

The history of the world is but the biography of great men.

(Carlyle, 1841).

Dating from the 1840s, and a series of six lectures on *The Hero* by the historian Thomas Carlyle, the thinking at the time was very much that 'leaders are born and

Illustration 6.1

Comparing management and leadership

	Management	Leadership
Creating an agenda	Planning and Budgeting – establishing detailed steps and timetables for achieving needed results, and then allocating the resources necessary to make that happen	Establishing Direction – developing a vision of the future, often the distant future, and strategies for producing the changes needed to achieve that vision
Developing a human network for achieving the agenda	Organizing and Staffing – establishing some structure for accomplishing plan requirements, staffing that structure with individuals, delegating responsibility and authority for carrying out the plan, providing policies and procedures to help guide people, and creating methods or systems to monitor implementation	Aligning People – communicating the direction by words and deeds to all those whose cooperation may be needed so as to influence the creation of teams and coalitions that understand the vision and strategies, and accept their validity
Execution	Controlling and Problem Solving – monitoring results vs. plan in some detail, identifying deviations, and then planning and organizing to solve these problems	Motivating and Inspiring – energizing people to overcome major political, bureaucratic, and resource barriers to change by satisfying very basic, but often unfulfilled, human needs
Outcomes	Produces a degree of predictability and order, and has the potential of consistently producing key results expected by various stakeholders (e.g. for customers, always being on time; for stakeholders, being on budget)	Produces change, often to a dramatic degree, and has the potential of producing extremely useful change (e.g. new products that customers want, new approaches to labor relations that help make a firm more competitive)

Source: Adapted with the permission of The Free Press, a division of Simon & Schuster Adult Publishing Group, from *A Force for Change: How leadership differs from management* by John P. Kotter. Copyright © 1990 by John P. Kotter Inc. All rights reserved.

Illustration 6.2

A brief history of leadership

1 **Great Man Theories (1840s)** – Leaders are born, not made. Leaders are heroic and charismatic. They have legitimate, expert and referent power. Examples include Winston Churchill, Bill Gates, Bill Clinton, Steve Jobs.

2 **Trait Theories (1950s)** – People inherit certain qualities and characteristics that make them much better suited for leadership. There is a perfect list of traits for leadership, and legitimate power is held by the leader.

3 **Behavioural Style Theories (1960s)** – Leadership can be learned. Leaders are made, not born; however, the focus is on a leader's actions, not their thinking.

4 **Contingency and Situational Theories (1960s)** – Particular variables in the environment or the situation will suggest the appropriate style of leadership. Legitimate and coercive power is still held by the leader.

5 **Relational and Pro-Social Theories (late 1970s onwards)** – Leadership is inter-relational and co-created between people. It can be used to transform both individuals and organizations. There is a strong ethical component to leadership. There is a shift in focus from power being the most important component to people being the most important factor to consider.

not made', i.e. not everyone can be a leader, and those people who can be leaders are genetically pre-disposed to greatness (see also Carlyle, 1907). Note also that this is a gendered view of leadership. Women were, at that time, not considered suitable for leadership roles. Rather, leaders were viewed as heroic and charismatic, who engender loyalty in their followers because of the strength of their personality and their mission.

Whilst Reich (1991) warns against the idea of reifying the leader as hero, a great leader was thought to emerge when there was a great need for followers to be saved (see Handy's 1996 definition above). It is summed up by the saying, 'cometh the hour, cometh the man', meaning that when the situation demands, someone will be found. Great Man theories remain both a popular historical and current view of leadership; from religious leaders to warrior leaders such as Genghis Khan and Marcus Aurelius, to modern political leaders such as Winston Churchill in the UK, and US presidents.

Activity 6.2

Think about 'great leaders', past and present, and list as many of them as you can. (This is great fun to do in a group, and forms the basis of a game called 'Who am I?') Next, write down those characteristics for which they were known and which characterized them as great leaders. What, if anything, do they seem to have in common?

Charismatic–visionary leadership

It is difficult to classify charismatic–visionary leadership, and this discussion might have been included in one of the later sections. However, we think it safe to assume that most, if not all 'great men *and women*' are charismatic and visionary. In addition, this concept is not new; most of us can think of historical figures that were heroic and visionary. However, it was Max Weber who contrasted charisma with bureaucratic systems of control. Charisma is about people leading not by virtue of sets of rules and procedures but through the force of their personality and the ability to create grand visions about the future. Whilst their power lasts, they are able to unify people towards that vision. Charisma comes from within the person themselves – it sets its own boundaries. Weber's original ideas illustrate it well:

> The continued existence of charismatic authority is, by its very nature, characteristically unstable; the bearer may lose his charisma ... and show himself to his followers as 'bereft of his power', and then his mission is dead, and his followers must hopefully await and search out a new charismatic leader. He himself, however, is abandoned by his following, for pure charisma recognizes no 'legitimacy' other than that conferred by personal power, which must be constantly re-confirmed. The charismatic hero does not derive his authority from ordinances and statutes, as if it were an official 'competence', nor from customary usage or feudal fealty, as with patrimonial power: rather, he acquires it and retains it only by proving his powers in real life. He must perform miracles if he wants to be a prophet, acts of heroism if he wants to be a leader in war. Above all, however, his divine mission must 'prove' itself

in that those who entrust themselves to him must prosper. If they do not, then he is obviously not the master sent by the Gods.

(Runciman and Matthews, 1978, p. 229)

Another (more mundane) definition of charismatic leaders is:

> ... charisma is a *relationship* between an individual (leader) and one or more followers based on leader behaviours combined with favourable attributes of followers. Key behaviours on the part of the leader include articulating a vision and sense of mission, showing determination, and communicating high-performance expectations ... Effects on followers include the generation of confidence in the leader, making followers feel good in his/her presence, and the generation of strong admiration or respect.

(Waldman, D.A. Ramirez, Ramirez, G.G., and House, R.J., 2001)

Belief in charismatic power revolutionizes people and channels their energies into shaping organizations. The attribute of charisma is frequently looked for in political leaders and those in positions of power. Charismatic leaders prevail in their positions as long as they are perceived to be successful. However, failure is to charisma as kryptonite is to Superman. Failure shows the charismatic leader's mortality and punctures their superhero image. In these circumstances, they are soon replaced.

Although we can describe what a charismatic leader does, we have a weaker understanding of the processes and interactions between leaders and followers, and which lead to organizational change. Research on US presidents suggests that charismatic leaders use 'consistent common strategies for breaking down, moving and re-aligning the norms of their followers' (Fiol, Harris and House, 1999, p. 450). Fiol and colleagues see change as being about changing values; championing and prioritizing one thing over and above another. It is the 'contrary of conventions' (p. 458) such that the more conventional a leader is the less charismatic they will appear. They suggest using Lewin's three-stage model to show how values can be changed. Illustration 6.3 is an example of this.

Illustration 6.3

How charisma works

Frame-breaking (unfreezing)

The charismatic leader has the job of reducing the strength of ties to existing conventions. Whatever the conventions are, the leader has to create a state of 'non-desire' for them. Non-desire can be created by arguing that adherence to convention is dysfunctional. Following the attacks on the World Trade Centre in 2001, legislation was introduced in the UK that redefined terrorism and all things connected to it and increased police powers. The government's justification (under Prime Minister Blair who many thought fitted the model of a charismatic leader) was that new legislation was essential to protect national security. Despite little evidence that existing legislation was inadequate, the message hammered out was that only greater power could protect citizens and that arguments to the contrary were dysfunctional and put the nation at risk; thus new powers of the leader were created and resistance was overcome.

Frame-moving

In stage 1, communication strategies attempt to move personal and social values from defensive positions to neutral positions (fear of change to non-fear). In stage 2, the neutral values need to be moved on to active states of desire for things. So having moved people away from wanting convention to states of not wanting convention, the next step is to create a desire for non-convention, a desire for change and a fear of not changing.

Frame-realignment (refreezing)

This phase requires acceptance (freezing) of new personal and social values which are then tapped by the leader. It should be more straightforward than stages 1 and 2 because while it tackles opposing forces, this phase gives meaning to new values. Keeping followers on board can require additional communications from leader figures. In organizations, previous leaders are 'blamed' for past actions and this is repeatedly reinforced. To support the new vision, changes to structures, processes and staff (favourable to the new leader's vision and views) are made, until the new becomes viewed as the norm.

Charismatic authority is bolstered by four additional dimensions that facilitate change (Conger, 1993, p. 279). First, charisma, being a personal characteristic, bestows on those who possess it a source of power and influence quite different to position power. Second, charismatic leadership glorifies the leader figure and their qualities and breaks with traditions. Challenges to existing social order occur since the leader's heroic attributes are championed above historic and traditional ways of doing. Third, charismatic leadership is short lived compared to rational–legal authority. In an organizational setting it exists for as long as a charismatic leader figure is present but after they have departed the changes they set in play become embedded in rational–legal structures.

> As a revolutionary force, its purpose is to bridge the transition from one existing order to the next. Its role is to create and institutionalize new order. After accomplishing this task, charisma fades or is routinized. Rules, traditions and institutions grow up to stabilize and guide the new social arrangements and to replace the charismatic leader who has departed.
>
> (Conger, 1993, p. 279)

Fourth, the commitment of followers to change is a consequence of their emotional ties with the leader figure and not through allegiance to a set of rules and structures that represent the 'organization'.

Charismatic leadership is not without its issues; for instance, the extent to which context (organizational culture, politics, organizational environment) and charisma are interrelated. Do some or all of these things need to coalesce in order for a charismatic–visionary leader to rise or is a leader charismatic anywhere by virtue of their personality and ability to convince others? Conversely, are some leaders doomed to be uncharismatic if they lack the presumed ingredients?

Landrum, Howell and Paris (2000) point out that while many writers claim that 'strong' charismatic leadership is required for strategic and 'turnaround' change, there is also a 'dark side' to charismatic leaders. They point out that charismatic leaders can lead followers in directions unhelpful to society and organizations. They also identify a possible propensity for narcissism and quote Post (1986, p. 679) who states that the charismatic leader: '... requires a continuing flow of admiration from his audience in order to nourish his famished self. Central to his ability to elicit that admiration is his ability to convey a sense of grandeur, omnipotence, and strength'. Landrum *et al.* (2000) refer to *unethical* charismatic leaders who are controlling, manipulative and self-promoting – characteristics that can jeopardize and even sabotage the turnaround efforts of the organization. To mitigate these possibilities and overcome the difficulties of leaders being all things to all people and situations, Landrum *et al.* argue for collective and distributed approaches to designing and implementing strategic change, which are discussed later in this chapter.

As you read the following discussion on trait theories of leadership, consider how much these theories might be related to the concept of charismatic–visionary leaders.

Trait theories of leadership

Originally trait theory underpinned the idea that leaders are born, not made, so the emphasis was more about *what* leaders should be like (the traits they possess) than about *how* they lead and there was a considerable amount of effort in the 1940s and 1950s in the UK and the US to identify the 'perfect' list of traits which all leaders could be said to possess. For instance, as a result of a meta-analysis of other researchers' work, carried out by Lord, De Vader and Alliger (1986), six traits of successful leaders were put forward:

- intelligence;
- an extrovert personality;
- dominance;
- masculinity;
- conservatism;
- being better adjusted than non-leaders.

A few years later, Kirkpatrick and Locke (1991) surveyed existing leadership studies and also suggested six successful leadership traits:

- *drive* – achievement, ambition, energy, tenacity, initiative;
- *leadership motivation* – personalized or socialized;
- *honesty and integrity* – the degree to which a leader can be trusted;
- *self-confidence* – including emotional stability;
- *cognitive ability* – the ability to marshal and interpret a wide variety of information;
- knowledge of the business.

In 1996, Dulewicz and Herbert reported on their research with a sample of 72 Anglo-American managers who, on the basis of several indicators of success (exceptional managerial skills in planning and organizing, managing staff and motivating others), had been identified as 'high-flyers' or 'low-flyers'. They found that high-flyers scored higher than low-flyers on the following six traits:

- risk-taking;
- assertiveness;
- decisiveness;
- achievement;
- motivation;
- competitiveness.

Comparing these three lists, we can see that intelligence, motivation and integrity feature twice whilst traits implying drive and assertiveness appear across all three lists. Northouse (2013) confined his list to those indicative of leaders in the West: *intelligence; self-confidence; determination; integrity* and *sociability*, which are similar to the other three except for *sociability*. In contrast, Shin's (1999) research into the traits of South Korean CEOs identified a substantively different list of traits to those typically proposed for Anglo-American leaders shown above. In descending order they were:

- *management respect for employees* – caring for people and developing them;
- *initiator attitudes* – solving problems and becoming involved to get things done;
- *tenacity and spirit* – not wavering in the face of adversity;
- *network-building* – developing relationships with people outside the organization yet useful to it, such as government officials and financiers;
- *emphasis on competency* – a 'Kaizen' mentality of continual improvement (see Alves, Manz and Butterfield, 2005; Heidrick and Struggles, 2004).

Top of Shin's list we find leaders showing a refreshing interest in the people they are leading in contrast to the far more egocentric traits typically found in Western studies. Clearly, culture matters when it comes to effective leadership and management.

Activity 6.3

Why do you think that the traits of successful Western and Eastern leaders appear to be so different? Or do you think that they are similar? What is it about the environment or culture which might affect how leaders behave? Reflect back to the sections on differences between national cultures in Chapter 4.

Unsurprisingly, no single list could be identified that fitted all situations, and it is interesting to note that traits such as creative thinking, charisma and intuitive reasoning (as opposed to cognitive reasoning) do not appear. Consequently, such research eventually fell by the wayside (Zaccaro, 2007). However, as a counterweight to these theories, during a similar period there was a resurgence in research following ideas in the 1960s about behaviourism which suggested that perhaps the right traits could be learned and the 'appropriate' behaviour copied by leaders.

Leadership styles and behaviour

When the original trait research struggled to explain successful leadership, researchers turned to leadership styles indicative of how leaders should behave in an attempt to understand successful leadership.

The Michigan and Ohio studies

Two influential studies of leadership (Likert, 1961; Stogdill and Coons, 1957) known respectively as the University of Michigan studies and the Ohio State studies, separately identified two independent dimensions of leadership style. The Ohio researchers named these 'consideration' and 'initiating structure'. *Consideration* is the degree to which a leader builds trust and mutual respect with subordinates, shows respect for their ideas and concern for their well-being. *Initiating structure* is the degree to which a leader defines and structures their role and the interactions within the group towards the attainment of formal goals.

The Michigan researchers used the terms 'employee-centered' and 'production-centered' leadership for these dimensions but they were virtually the same as the Ohio descriptions. The main point about these dimensions is that, because they are deemed to be independent of each other, a leader's behaviour can be categorized in four different ways. Leaders can be:

● high on consideration and high on initiating structure;
● high on consideration and low on initiating structure;
● low on consideration and low on initiating structure;
● low on consideration and high on initiating structure.

The Leadership Grid®

Building on the Ohio and Michigan studies, Blake and Mouton (1964) proposed that the most effective management style is one which is high on both the people-oriented (consideration and employee-centred) and task-oriented (initiating structure and production-centred) dimensions. Figure 6.1 gives the positions of five different styles on a later version of Blake and Mouton's managerial grid, now called the 'Leadership Grid®, (Blake and McCanse, 1991). The different combinations of concern for people and concern for production set out in Figure 6.1 result in different combinations of leadership behaviour.

The Leadership Grid® assumes that there is one best style of leadership, regardless of the situation – namely position 9,9 on the grid, the 'Team Management' style. The 9,9 style incorporates a high concern for production with a high concern for people. In contrast, position 1,9 portrays a high concern for people and low concern for production and position 9,1 portrays a high concern for production and processes and little concern for people. Activity 6.4 gives an example of a leader who lived very many years ago, but whom you might recognize in managers and leaders you encounter today.

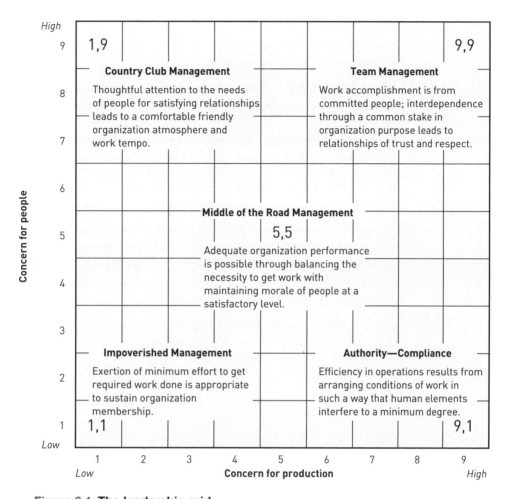

Figure 6.1 **The leadership grid**

Activity 6.4

Read the following extract from an article about Mrs Isabella Beeton, famous for her book on household management written in 1859.

Mrs Beeton: management guru

Mrs Beeton's approach can be summarized in three principles, which would certainly appear in most modern management texts: setting an example and giving clear guidance to staff; controlling the finances; applying the benefits of order and method in all management activities.

An example to staff

(In her own words.)

Early rising is one of the most essential qualities ... as it is not only the parent of health but of other innumerable advantages. Indeed when a mistress is an early riser, it is almost certain that her house will be orderly and well managed. On the contrary, if she remain in bed till a late hour, then the domestics, who ... invariably partake somewhat of their mistress's character, will surely become sluggards.

Good Temper should be cultivated ...Every head of a household should strive to be cheerful, and should never fail to show a deep interest in all that appertains to the well-being of those who claim the protection of her roof.

The Treatment of Servants is of the highest possible moment ... If they perceive that the mistress's conduct is regulated by high and correct principles, they will not fail to respect her. If, also, a benevolent desire is shown to promote their comfort, at the same time that a steady performance of their duty is enacted, then their respect will not be unmingled with affection, and they will be still more solicitous to continue to deserve her favour.

Source: Wensley, R. (1996), 'Mrs Beeton: management guru', *Financial Times*, 26 April, p. 15.

The article continues to quote from Mrs Beeton's book on the need to keep 'a housekeeping account-book ... punctually and precisely'. On the issue of order and method she says: 'Cleanliness, punctuality, order and method are essentials in the character of a good housekeeper.'

Where would you place Mrs Beeton on the Leadership Grid®?

Identify your own preferred position of leading and managing others. Why would you put yourself here and do you agree with Blake and Mouton's assertion that 9.9, 'Team Management', is the best leadership style?

The Leadership Grid® is a simplified way of categorizing different aspects of leadership behaviour. There are, however, other categories of leadership styles and behaviour that overlap with these, but which are more detailed in their descriptions; for instance, the 'powers of the person' discussed in an article by Useem (1996) who says these kinds of behaviour transcend those of particular value in particular situations. Drawing on a study of the most successful CEOs working in 48 large US firms, he condenses a long list of desirable behaviours into the following five characteristics:

- being visionary;
- showing strong confidence in self and others;
- communicating high-performance expectations and standards;
- personally exemplifying the firm's vision, values and standards;
- demonstrating personal sacrifice, determination, persistence and courage.

Contingency and situational approaches to leadership

According to these approaches to leadership, successful leadership is contingent upon situational variables; multiple stakeholders and multiple perspectives are important. The various situational variables that affect the appropriateness of leadership styles are shown in Figure 6.2.

Figure 6.2 Situational influences on leadership effectiveness

A leadership continuum

One of the best-known theories that takes situational factors into account is from Tannenbaum and Schmidt (1973) who arranged leadership behaviour along a continuum. At one end is *boss-centred leadership* which assumes a high level of authoritarian power where leaders *tell* subordinates what to do. At the other end, *subordinate-centred leadership*, leaders and subordinates *jointly* make decisions in a participative climate.

Tannenbaum and Schmidt suggest that a leader should move along the continuum, selecting the style that is most appropriate to the situation. They identify 'forces' that determine the style of leadership to use, as follows:

- The forces that determine the style of leadership emanate from the manager, for example, his or her personality and values, skills and knowledge.
- The forces in the subordinates, for example, the amount of support they need, their work experience and knowledge, commitment to the organizational goals.
- The forces in the situation, for example, the nature and urgency of the task or the problem, the constraints arising from the organization's structure, processes and culture and perhaps the organizational environment.

Given these different forces, managers/leaders might have little or a lot of room for the style of leadership they adopt (see Illustration 6.4).

Illustration 6.4

Little room to manoeuvre

Jayne was pleased that she had been put in charge of BB Company's latest building venture, the second of its kind in Japan. She had limited experience of working in this country but had talked to staff working on the other Japanese site about how to approach the management of those employed on the building works. She knew, therefore, that there were a number of factors to take into account when deciding on her own leadership approach.

The figure below illustrates the situation Jayne faced. The lengths of rules on the diagram indicate the degrees of freedom available to Jayne in the situation facing her.

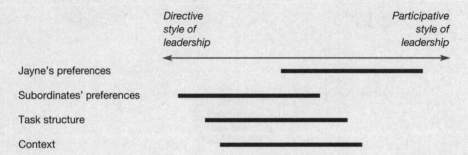

Jayne's preference was for a consultative/participative leadership style, whereas most of the Japanese employees were accustomed to a more formal management–subordinate relationship and were likely to work in this type of relationship, given the fact that Jayne was a woman. The task of building apartments was defined but unknown factors such as the weather, and possible unexpected problems with the ground, let alone any labour relations problems that could arise, contributed to there being certain unstructured elements to the situation. The BB Company prided itself on its care for its workers, so the organizational context was one that veered more towards a human relations type of approach than an authoritarian one. Even so, profit was profit and the industry was very competitive. The organization did not want anything to go wrong.

What the figure shows is that Jayne has not much room for manoeuvre in deciding what approach to take as a leader in this situation. The overlap between all the forces is not large. If she cannot influence any of the factors associated with the subordinates, the task and the context, she must make sure to adopt a leadership style that tends towards the directive end of her preferences.

Fiedler's contingency model of leadership

Like the Leadership Grid®, the task-oriented/people-oriented continuum of leadership styles is also the basis of Fiedler's (1967) Contingency theory of leadership. Here, however, three situational variables are assumed to determine the best style of leadership to adopt:

- *Leader–member relations:* the quality of the relationship between the leader and their followers and extent to which a leader has their support.
- *Task structure:* the extent to which the task or purpose of a group is well defined and the work outcomes can be judged clearly as a success or failure. This is influenced by the subjective versus objective nature of the outcomes.

- *Positional power:* the level of power, particularly reward power that the leader has over followers. Low positional power means that the leader has little authority to direct and evaluate the work of others or to reward them.

Unlike on the leadership continuum, the relationship of leadership style to the favourableness/unfavourableness of the situation is a curvilinear one. In other words, when the situation is very favourable or very unfavourable, the most effective style is said to be a task-oriented, more directive one, rather than a person-oriented one. Moderate favourability implies a person-centred approach.

Fiedler's (1967) contingency theory implies that leaders can adapt their leadership styles to the prevailing situation although Fiedler believed that this is difficult. He suggested that either leaders should be chosen so that their management and leadership style fits the situation or that elements of the situation need to be modified. It is useful, though, to note that Fielder was writing in the 1960s and that the complexities of modern organizations demand that leaders and managers are more flexible and resilient than perhaps was expected half a century ago. Whether these expectations are realistic or not is open to discussion.

Hersey and Blanchard's situational theory

One of the difficulties with situational and contingency theories is the question of how much importance should be attached to each situational or contingency factor. Clearly, both the task and goals to be achieved and the amount of power held by the leader are important, but arguably, the characteristics and expectations of group members and followers may be more important in deciding what style of leadership to adopt.

This is the central tenet of Hersey and Blanchard's (1993) situational leadership theory which puts the emphasis on the readiness of followers. According to their theory, a leader's style and behaviour should depend on the maturity and readiness of followers to undertake the task and to accept responsibility and make their own decisions. Therefore a leader's style should fall into one of four quadrants – from *telling* through *selling* and from *participating* to *delegating* (see Figure 6.3 overleaf).

In contrast to Fiedler's view that leadership styles are difficult to change, the Hersey and Blanchard model assumes that a leader is sufficiently flexible to change behaviour towards the followers depending on the situation but also on their capacity to change and mature. This proposition is also open to question.

Path–Goal theory of leadership

Originally developed by House (1971), path–goal theory maintains that the leader should use the style of leadership that is most effective in influencing followers' perceptions of the goals they need to achieve and the way (or path) they need to achieve them (Woffard and Liska, 1993). The theory relates directly to *expectancy theories of motivation* in that a leader's success is judged by whether their followers achieve their goals. In other words, effective leadership motivates and engages

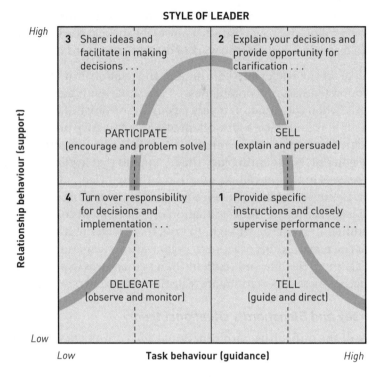

Figure 6.3 Hersey and Blanchard's theory of situational leadership

Source: Based on Hersey, P. and Blachard, K.H. (1993) *Management of Organizational Behaviour: Utilizing Human Resources* (6th edn), Englewood Cliffs, NJ: Prentice Hall, p. 197.

followers to turn effort into appropriate and high-level performance. Four leader behaviours are suggested by Path–Goal Theory:

- *Directive* – setting standards, telling followers what to do and how to do it.
- *Supportive* – being open and approachable and showing concern for followers.
- *Participative* – inviting opinions and ideas from followers and involving others.
- *Achievement-oriented* – setting challenging goals and objectives that stress improvements.

The four leadership behaviours are used, as needed, to fit the context. If followers lack confidence then supportive behaviour is called for. If the nature of the work is vague then directive leadership is needed to clarify a way forward. If work is seen as not challenging enough then achievement-oriented behaviour can be used to raise the goals for followers. If reward strategies are poor then participative leadership can help clarify what followers are seeking and change how rewards are distributed.

Two dominant situational factors are relevant to this theory. These are the characteristics of followers and the nature of the task or job and the immediate context in which it takes place. The challenge to the leader is to use a style that is congruent with the skills, motivation and expectations of followers and with the goals to be achieved, the design of the jobs and the resources and time available. Figure 6.4 shows the factors that are presumed to intervene between the effort put into doing a job and the subsequent performance.

CHARACTERISTICS OF TEAM MEMBERS

Figure 6.4 Factors intervening between effort and performance

Linked to the focus above on follower needs, Ipsos Mori (2009) polled 10,000 people to ask them what they wanted from a leader. In priority order, the research identified that followers want:

1 To be able to *trust* their leader/s.
2 *Compassion* – to feel that their leaders genuinely care about their well-being.
3 *Stability* – that change is not a constant.
4 *Hope* for the future.

Activity 6.5

The 2009 Ipsos Mori poll tried to identify the psychological needs of followers. Remembering that this research was conducted without a change environment in mind, how do you think that the desires of followers might be different in an environment of change (which is by definition, unstable)? Or do you think that their list will remain the same?

Matching organizational models and leadership roles

A number of situational or contingent factors influencing a leader's style have been discussed, one of which (not always emphasized) is the organizational context in terms of its internal environment (e.g. structure, culture, competitive position). Two different pieces of research pick up on these ideas to suggest links between different organizational models and different approaches to leadership.

Quinn (1988) proposed four organizational models distinguished on the basis of two bipolar dimensions. These are:

(a) adaptability and flexibility versus the desire for stability and control;
(b) whether organizations are outward looking (towards the environment and the competition) or internally focused towards the maintenance of systems and procedures.

Table 6.1 Summary of Quinn's four organizational models

Human relations model (adaptable and internally focused)	Open systems model (adaptable and externally focused)	Rational goal model (stable and externally focused)	Internal process model (stable and internally focused)
Towards:	Towards:	Towards:	Towards:
• Flexibility	• Flexibility	• Centralization	• Centralization
• Decentralization	• Decentralization	• Integration	• Integration
• Differentiation	• Differentiation	• Maximizing output	• Consolidation
• Maintenance of the socio-technical system	• Expansion	• Competitive position of overall system	• Continuity
	• Competitive position of overall system		• Maintenance of socio-technical systems
Values:	Values:	Values:	Values:
• Human resources	• Adaptability	• Productivity	• Information
• Training	• Readiness	• Efficiency	• Management
• Cohesion	• Growth/acquisition	• Planning	• Communication
• Morale	• External support	• Goal setting	• Stability
			• Control
THE TEAM	THE ADHOCRACY	THE FIRM	THE HIERARCHY

Source: Based on Quinn, R.E. (1988), *Beyond Rational Management: Mastering the paradoxes and competing demands of high performance,* San Francisco: Jossey-Bass, p. 48.

Table 6.1 summarizes the different characteristics of the four organizational models that result from combining these four different organizational orientations. Quinn uses the terms 'the hierarchy', 'the firm', 'the adhocracy' and 'the team' as a shorthand way of describing the internal process, rational goal, open systems and human relations organizational models respectively.

In contrast to the theories that link leadership styles to the job and task to be done and/or the followers' characteristics, Quinn proposes that different leadership styles and behaviour 'fit' the different organizational models he describes in Table 6.1. The relationship between these is shown in Figure 6.5. This framework is based on two dimensions that underpin organizational effectiveness. The horizontal dimension reflects the organizational focus varying from an internal emphasis on the workforce to an external focus on organizational survival. The vertical dimension reflects preferences for structure; in particular the choice between control and stability and between flexibility and change. Each quadrant of the framework houses one of four models of organizations namely the human relations model, the open systems model, the rational goal model and the internal process model.

The benefit of Quinn's model is that a Competing Values Organizational Effectiveness Instrument (questionnaire) has been developed and applied to identify which values model any organization reflects (e.g. Cameron, 1985; Howard, 1998). This makes it possible to consider the extent to which leadership styles are 'matched' to the organizational values, or to change the values themselves.

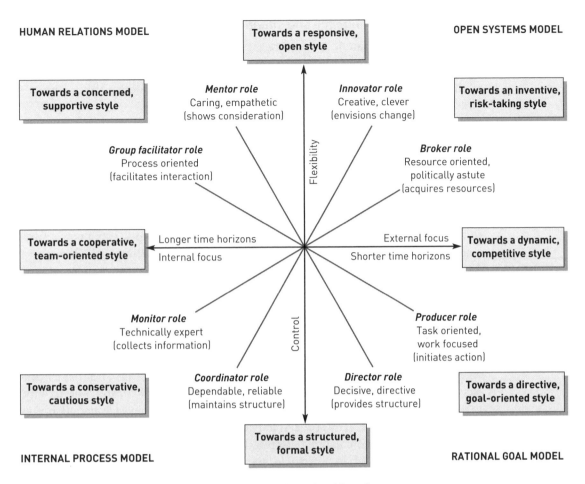

HUMAN RELATIONS MODEL

Towards a responsive, open style

OPEN SYSTEMS MODEL

Towards a concerned, supportive style

Mentor role
Caring, empathetic
(shows consideration)

Innovator role
Creative, clever
(envisions change)

Towards an inventive, risk-taking style

Group facilitator role
Process oriented
(facilitates interaction)

Broker role
Resource oriented,
politically astute
(acquires resources)

Flexibility

Towards a cooperative, team-oriented style

Longer time horizons

External focus

Towards a dynamic, competitive style

Internal focus

Shorter time horizons

Monitor role
Technically expert
(collects information)

Control

Producer role
Task oriented,
work focused
(initiates action)

Towards a conservative, cautious style

Coordinator role
Dependable, reliable
(maintains structure)

Director role
Decisive, directive
(provides structure)

Towards a directive, goal-oriented style

Towards a structured, formal style

INTERNAL PROCESS MODEL

RATIONAL GOAL MODEL

Figure 6.5 The competing values framework of leadership roles

Farkas and Wetlaufer (1996) came to similar conclusions to Quinn about the dependence of leadership style and behaviour on the needs of the organization and the business situation at hand. On the basis of interviews with 160 chief executives they found five distinctive approaches to leadership, each of which was associated with different emphases in terms of strategic planning, research and development (R&D), recruitment and selection practices, matters internal to the organization or matters external to it and with whom, and how, they spent their time. According to Farkas and Wetlaufer (p. 111) the leadership approach to be adopted depends on answering questions such as: 'Is the industry growing explosively or is it mature? How many competitors exist and how strong are they? Does technology matter and, if so, where is it going? What are the organization's capital and human assets? What constitutes sustainable competitive advantage and how close is the organization to achieving it?' To these questions one could also add: 'What kind of changes is the organization facing and what do these mean for the role of leadership?'

Problems with contingency and situational theory

Although widely researched, over time it became clear that contingency and situational theories have limitations. Parry and Bryman (2006) identified these as:

- there are simply too many contingent variables that the theory has to account for;
- disagreement regarding why some variables should be included and others excluded;
- leadership behaviours in practice were not always situationally contingent;
- most research was cross-sectional which meant that it was impossible to separate cause (leadership behaviours) from effect (performance and outcomes).

In spite of these reservations, the major contribution of contingency and situational theories, including Quinn's competing values framework, was a new understanding of the complexity of organizations and the realization that there is not 'one best way' of leading regardless of context and situation.

Relational and Pro-Social theories of leadership

Beginning in the late 1970s and overlapping with the ongoing research on trait and situational leadership, pro-social theories began to emerge that recognized that leaders and organizations had social responsibilities to their followers and that *engagement* is critical to employee motivation, retention, effort, creativity and productivity. In a more modern twist, Cunliffe (2009), describing the *philosopher leader*, advocates a 'relational' and reflexive approach to leadership and management where leadership is continually 'co-created' between the leader and their followers and where the leader is always seen in *'relation to, and ethically responsible for, others'* (p. 95). To begin this discussion, emotional intelligence is introduced which, while not a leadership style in itself, is an important influence upon leadership style.

Emotional intelligence

Emotional intelligence (EI) concerns the ability to recognize differing emotional states within oneself and others and to respond appropriately. There are three slightly different models of EI:

1 The *ability* model which concerns the processing and utilization of emotional information to navigate our social landscape (Salovey and Mayer, 1989; Salovey *et al.*, 2004);
2 Petrides and Furnham's (2001) *trait* model of EI characteristics;
3 Goleman's (1995) *mixed* model which combines both abilities and traits to drive leadership and management performance.

According to Goleman (1998, p. 93): 'Emotional intelligence is the sine qua non of leadership', meaning that it is an absolutely essential trait of a good leader. On the basis of an examination of competency models in 188 mostly large global companies, Goleman claims to have identified the personal capabilities that drive outstanding performance, suggesting that 'IQ is not enough'. Goleman grouped these capabilities into three categories: *technical skills, cognitive abilities* and the *five competencies of emotional intelligence*, which are:

- self-awareness;
- self-regulation;
- motivation;
- empathy;
- social skills.

While not decrying the need for leaders to have technical skills (such as accounting and business planning) and cognitive capabilities (such as analytical reasoning), Goleman claims these are 'threshold capabilities', that is, while being *necessary* for successful leadership they are not *sufficient* for successful leadership without the addition of emotional intelligence.

Cote and Miners (2006) describes EI as being aware of your own emotions and those of others and using these insights to lead. Bar-On (1997, p. 14) describes EI as: 'an array of non-cognitive capabilities, competences and skills that influence one's ability to succeed in coping with environmental demands and pressure'. Higgs and Dulewicz (2004, p. 175) suggest that EI is concerned with achieving one's goals through the capabilities of:

- managing one's own feelings and emotions;
- being sensitive to the needs of others and being able to influence key people;
- balancing one's own motives and drives with conscientious and ethical behaviour.

Since different leadership roles have different emotional demands it follows that jobs with high emotional content should be performed better by leaders with high emotional intelligence. Martin (2008) found a moderately strong link between EI and job performance; however, other studies have produced more mixed results (see Cote and Miners, 2006). To explain the mixed findings, Cote and Miners proposed that the relationship between EI and job performance increases as cognitive intelligence decreases. Cognitive intelligence, in other words, classic IQ, or 'general intelligence' is usually related to performance in jobs (the smarter the person, the better the performance), because more intelligent people have a better grasp of information and procedures relating to the core technical work. In this sense, EI may therefore compensate for lower general intelligence.

However, it is questionable whether components of emotional intelligence add anything new to what we already know about the psychological and social characteristics of individuals. Woodruffe (2000) thinks not and rejects claims that it does. By contrast, Barling, Slater and Kelloway's (2000) research involving 60 mixed-sex Canadian managers of varying status found no significant difference between their scores on an Emotional Intelligence Inventory and those using a measure of transformational leadership (see section below). Mandell and Pherwani (2003) found similar results from their research with 32 mixed-sex US managers.

Transactional and transformational leadership

Organizations responding to the tightening market conditions that started in the late 1970s often attempted big changes – changes that transformed structures and markets. We began to see 'hero' leaders emerge who were credited with transformational changes; transformational leaders in contrast to the less visionary *transactional* leadership style (see Illustration 6.5).

Illustration 6.5

Transactional and transformational leaders

Three dimensions of transactional leadership

- *Contingent reward:* to what extent are meaningful reward exchanges set up – exchange of rewards for effort, promise of rewards for good performance and recognition of accomplishments?
- *Management by exception (active):* to what extent do leaders anticipate problems and intervene with corrective action before problems arise?
- *Management by exception (passive):* to what extent do leaders wait for problems to arise before intervening?

Four dimensions of transformational leadership

- *Charisma*: provides vision and sense of mission for followers to follow, instils pride, gains respect and trust.

- *Inspiration*: communicates high expectations and standards, uses symbols to focus efforts, expresses important purposes in simple ways, optimistic about the future.
- *Intellectual stimulation*: challenges assumptions with fresh ideas and solicits ideas from followers.
- *Individualized consideration*: showing interest in individual followers and their development, helping them to develop. Treats employees individually, coaches, advises.

Source: Bass, B.M. (1990), 'From Transactional to transformational leadership: learning to share the vision', *Organizational Dynamics*, Winter, p. 22.

These two concepts were introduced by Burns (1978) and developed by Bass (1990). They have been influential in leadership theory and research. Transactional leadership is based on giving people rewards for doing what the leader wants. Transformational leadership, which borrows much from Weber's ideas about charisma (discussed above) relies on giving followers a purpose, a vision of something to aim for and on creating follower identification with the leader. Transactional leaders make minor adjustments to mission and the ways people are managed. Transformational leaders make big changes to mission and culture and so in theory make bigger impacts upon change. Figure 6.6 presents a model of transformational leadership that includes not only the leader's characteristics, attitudes and behaviour but also the reactions of followers.

Transformational leadership behaviours add to the two dimensions of leadership identified earlier in both the Ohio State and Michigan University studies. To summarize, in much of the leadership literature there is a general assumption now that transformational leadership is the way ahead and that where radical changes are called for it is more likely to be effective. Bass (1990, p. 20) goes so far as to say

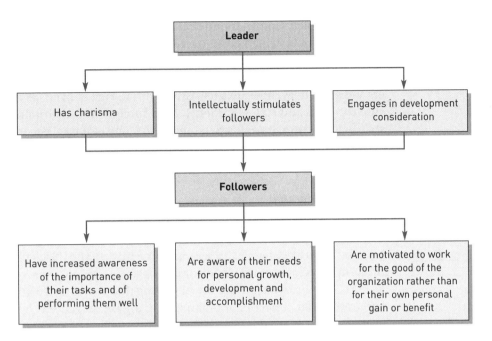

Figure 6.6 Transformational Leadership

Source: Adapted from Bass, B.M. (1990) by George, J. and Jones, G. *Understanding and Managing Organizational Behaviour* (4th edition), Harlow: Prentice-Hall, p. 394.

that transactional leadership is, in many instances, 'a prescription for mediocrity', arguing that only transformational leadership can make a difference in an organization's performance at all levels.

However, these two leadership styles are not mutually exclusive; transformational leadership is thought to complement transactional leadership by leveraging higher performance by followers (Bass and Avolio, 1993). Transactional leadership on its own will deliver a certain performance but if an overlay of transformational leadership is present then performance can be enhanced. Judge and Piccolo (2004, p. 765) found that the two styles 'are valid concepts but that they are so highly related that it makes it difficult to separate their unique effects' in studies linking leadership to performance. There is a little evidence that women display more transformational behaviours than men but the differences are small (Eagly, Johannesen-Schmidt and van Enge, 2003). However, these results are encouraging for those working to see more women in top management roles.

Researchers have looked for connections between personality traits and transformational leadership but the results are mixed. Bono and Judge (2004) found that of the 'big five' personality factors only extroversion appears to predict it, whereas Phipps and Prieto (2011), in a review of previous research on this issue, found agreeableness as a predictor of a transformational leadership style. As a result of their review, they also suggest that the skill of being able to 'politically influence' outcomes acts as a moderator between personality factors and this leadership style. The results suggest that personality (in so far as it can be assessed through questionnaires) might influence leadership behaviour but that the evidence is not yet strong enough to say how. However, Mandell and Pherwani (2003) (on their admittedly small sample) found that females rated significantly higher than males on measures of EI, which given the relationship with transformational leadership, might suggest they rate more highly in this respect also.

Although transformational leadership has captured the imagination of researchers and executives there are a few issues with it. First, it overlaps with other leadership concepts and styles. Secondly, if, as some writers maintain, it is a preferred style of leadership, it begins to resemble the 'one best way' theories of leadership, discussed earlier, that have been overtaken by later theories matching leadership to context. However, is not alone in this as some of the discussion below shows.

Servant-leadership

The term 'servant' is generally not a word one might associate with 'leader' and therein lies the paradox of the servant-leadership model. Originally coined in the 1970s by Robert K. Greenleaf, a seasoned executive of the US telephone giant AT&T, the term refers to a form of leadership that places service to others at its core. Greenleaf (1977) described a philosophy of leading that challenged conventional models and traditional concepts of organization and management by asserting that a leader must be a servant *first*. Although this concept of leadership is not entirely novel, in the context of organizational practice and research it is relatively new. Historical examples can be found in the teachings of the five major world religions (Trompenaars and Voerman, 2010) as well as in the stories of political activists such as Mother Teresa, Nelson Mandela and Gandhi. Although Greenleaf pioneered the conceptualization of 'leading through serving' in the field of management studies, some 30 years passed before management scholars began, systematically, to study, develop, and research the concept (Parris and Peachey, 2013). As such, servant-leadership is an emerging leadership theory that is gaining recognition and interest both in business practice and scholarship (van Dierendonck, 2011).

Servant-leadership is an integrative model of leadership. It can be characterized as post-heroic (Fletcher, 2004) as it de-romanticizes the image of leader as hero and figurehead while recognizing the distribution of power, the relational nature of influence throughout an organization, as well as the social and collective learning processes involved in leadership. In practice, a servant–leader integrates specific traits and behaviours, and varying styles as well as processes described in numerous leadership theories. This form of leadership differentiates itself from mainstream theories of leadership primarily through its focus (van Dierendonck *et al.*, 2014; Stone, Russell, and Patterson, 2004; Barbuto and Wheeler, 2006). More precisely, the servant–leader is concerned with the needs of others (e.g. of employees, the community, society), the desire to serve first (as opposed to lead first) and to build the leadership capacity of others (Greenleaf, 1977). In this sense, the concept challenges traditional management notions of Taylorism and Friedmanism that focus on maximizing efficiency and profit with little regard for human factors. However, in order to do servant-leadership justice in organizational practice, leaders must take care not to corrupt its integrative ideals by giving lip-service to the language while continuing to operate within old systems of domination and heroism.

Critique of servant-leadership has targeted several aspects of the theory. Characterizing it as a philosophy of leadership, Prosser (2010) makes it difficult to operationalize and measure organizational effects (Parris and Peachy, 2013). Indeed, the major criticism of servant-leadership so far has centred on its lack of conceptual development and theoretical foundation in empirical evidence (van Dierendonck and Heeren, 2006). Furthermore, its characterization as a normative theory of leadership (Johnson, 2008) has invited scepticism. Because Greenleaf occasionally made references to biblical figures, the concept has been criticized as perpetuating patriarchal systems embedded in religious doctrine (Eicher-Catt, 2005) and confusing this with in-business contexts (Hamilton and Bean, 2005). In addition, the resilience of the leader-as-hero schema and traditional notions of power-as-dominance diminish acceptance of servant-leadership and other post-heroic leadership models (Fletcher, 2004).

Although this type of leadership behaviour is a relatively new field of study with little evidence testifying to its benefits (Hunter *et al.*, 2013), there is a growing body of research supporting certain aspects of the theory. Parris and Peachy (2013) noted that a number of empirical studies produced strong evidence that servant-leadership is not only viable as a distinctive leadership construct on both individual and organizational levels, but also can be applied across cultures. Considering the factors influencing change processes discussed in the previous chapters – structure/design, culture and power – further research findings imply areas of potential for servant-leadership in change management, as they suggest which leadership styles, processes and behaviour may facilitate organizational change.

As structure and hierarchies become increasingly irrelevant due to environmental complexity and instability, modes of people-oriented leadership like servant-leadership could enhance the shift towards paradigms of flexible, post-bureaucratic organizations. Servant-leadership may support change in organizations because it presupposes contemporary designs such as the network or distributed teams forms (see Landrum, Howell and Paris, 2000), which in turn encourage both increased empowerment at all levels and more flexible communication.

Illustration 6.6

Servant-leadership and LUV: the key to minimizing resistance to change?

The term 'servant' is generally not a word one might associate with 'leader'. For Colleen Barrett, president emeritus of Southwest Airlines, America's largest low-fare domestic air carrier, the two terms are inherently linked. SWA's heart logo and listing on New York Stock Exchange as 'LUV' symbolize the company's commitment to the people-centred philosophy of management and service called *servant-leadership*. At first glance the notion of leading by serving may appear somewhat utopian. Indeed, a few aspects of the servant–leader model such as love, altruism and forgiveness seem

➡

Illustration 6.6 *continued*

quite out of place in a business context. Servant-leadership – originally described by the former AT&T executive Robert K. Greenleaf in the 1970s – is not 'soft-management' as one might assume. Servant–leaders face and manage tough decisions in volatile environments, and do so successfully. More and more servant-leadership is proving to be a viable leadership practice and potential change management catalyst. Southwest Airlines is an exemplary servant-led company who, in the face of recessions and fear of terrorism throughout the air industry, has maintained financial stability, sustained customer and employee satisfaction, and demonstrated environmental responsibility. A firm believer in the Texas-based airline's leadership model, Barrett presented the intriguing story of servant-leadership and real business at Southwest in *Leading with LUV*, the book she co-authored with management guru Ken Blanchard.

Servant-Leadership at Southwest Airlines: LUV

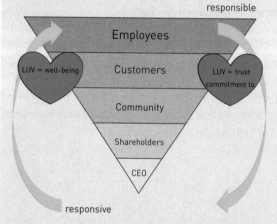

In the animated YouTube clip 'What does lead with LUV mean?' Blanchard explains the ABCs of Southwest's brand of servant-leadership: (a) acknowledge people, (b) back people up, and (c) count your people as your business partners. By sharing power and responsibility with employees and responding to the needs of employees, the benefits to customers, the community, shareholders and ultimately the CEO follow. This servant–leader model of empowerment can be visualized as an upside-down pyramid. Southwest places the base (employees) instead of the tip of the pyramid (CEO or other executives) at the top. In this way, servant-leadership puts positive relationships and people ahead of profits.

In terms of change management, this approach may be the key to minimizing resistance by enhancing employees' organizational commitment and commitment to change through improved well-being and trust. Financial data and numerous industry awards testify to the fact that Southwest's leadership practices have translated into business success and left the airline seemingly unscathed by the volatility of the industry and the aftermath of 9/11. Serving over 100 million passengers annually with some 45,000 employees, the carrier has consistently excelled in airline customer satisfaction being ranked No. 2 by *Consumer Reports*, and as an employer, having received the Glassdoor Employees' Choice Award as one of the Best Places to Work 2014. Its dedication to triple-bottom-line reporting and environmentally sound business practices also earned the company recognition as Eco Pioneer of the Year in 2012. In 43 years of service the FORTUNE 500 firm boasts 41 consecutive years of profitability with total operating revenue of $17.7 billion. Watch how servant-leadership works for Southwest Airlines in Blanchard and Barrett's 'fun-LUVing' book plug on YouTube at http://youtu.be/5Dvhca9r754.

We are grateful to Dr Kae Reynolds of the University of Huddersfield for the material used in this illustration.

Source: The Ken Blanchard Companies (2011, May 26), What does lead with LUV mean? *YouTube*, retrieved from http://youtu.be/5Dvhca9r754.
Southwest Airlines Co. (2014), Southwest Corporate Fact Sheet, *SWAmedia*, retrieved from http://www.swamedia.com/channels/Corporate-Fact-Sheet/pages/corporate-fact-sheet. Image adapted from Blanchard, K. (2012, October 13), 'Elect servant-leaders', *How we lead: Conversations on leadership with Ken Blanchard*, retrieved from http://howwelead.org/tag/servant-leadership/.

Research also suggests that an environment of servant-leadership could influence organizational change from a cultural standpoint. According to Kool and van Dierendonck (2012), servant-leadership enhances commitment to change particularly through a follower's sense of organizational justice and optimism. Several cultural factors related to the capacity to change can be linked to management communication practices such as willingness to discuss sensitive issues, openness to listen to new ideas, and attitudes of sharing information. Indeed, Kavanagh and Ashkanasy's (2006) conclusions that communication and transparency enhance organizational change processes also suggest that due to its influence on goal and process clarity servant-leadership could be an effective catalyst for change.

From a perspective of power, servant-leadership also provides an interesting model to facilitate change. Theoretically, the principle of leading by serving promotes power-sharing, distribution of power and empowerment as opposed to coercion or relying on positional power. According to van Dierendonck (2010), servant–leaders do not seek power for power's sake and have no desire to dominate others. This attitude towards power relationships in organizations may address a number of issues related to resistance to change which often arise out of a feeling of powerlessness. Servant–leaders would be expected to exercise a collaborative approach to conflict resolution based on the model's focus on serving the needs and interests of all stakeholders, including followers and communities.

From a gender perspective Eicher-Catt (2005) criticized servant-leadership's discourse for being deceptively ambiguous about the nature of power and the dynamics of gender domination. By contrast, Reynolds (2011) argued that servant-leadership offers a gender-integrative model of leadership that advocates an agenda of social change and social justice. Although empirical studies concerning these issues and servant-leadership are sparse, speculatively, servant-leadership could facilitate organizational change by virtue of its particular perspective on power.

Many of the tenets of servant-leadership, discussed above, are not dissimilar to the already established models of team and distributed leadership. For instance, distributed leadership has a positive orientation towards followers. Similar to *dispersed, devolved, democratic* or *shared* leadership, the central premise is that power is collectively shared, and leadership responsibility for decision making is collectively embedded within the combined expertise of the group rather than, as is traditionally the case, the individual responsibility of the legitimate leader. As such, distributed leadership can be considered to be collective, collaborative, dynamic, relational, inclusive and contextual (Bolden, 2007). Robbins and Coulter (2005, p. 435) argue that: 'they (the leaders) have to learn the skills such as having the patience to share information, being able to trust others and to give up authority, and understanding when to intervene.' As far back as the 1990s, Kotter (1996) was arguing for fewer bureaucratic structures with fewer rules and support systems for all.

Despite mounting evidence directly or indirectly supporting the usefulness of servant-leadership in organizational processes, there is still scepticism surrounding the theory and its effectiveness for the decision-making processes necessary, in particular, for rapid change (Hendry, 2004; Smith, Montagno, and Kuzmenko, 2004). For example, supporters appear to view servant-leadership as the ideal way of leading. However, in some cases, leaders may need to adjust leadership behaviour based on their assessment of other internal and external organizational forces such as the need for rapid and/or large-scale change.

Authentic leadership

Authentic leadership theories offer some antidote to the 'dark side' of leadership, such as anti-social traits and styles, as authentic leadership is predicated on the idea that leaders know themselves intimately, and therefore also have a greater understanding of how others are similar or different to them. They also understand how their experiences in life have made them what they are (Shamir and Eilam, 2005). Shamir, Dayan-Horesh, and Adler (2005) suggest that authentic leadership development as described by a leader's life story narratives centres around four themes, all of which, they suggest, are equally valid:

- a 'natural' leadership development process;
- development from struggle or hardship;
- leadership development from a purpose or cause;
- development as an active learning process.

The authentic leader does not try to imitate or mimic some other person or model. They are true to themselves (see Illustration 6.7), are acutely aware of their values and beliefs (Avolio and Gardner, 2005), and they understand the implications of how their leadership affects the organization and their followers. Attributes of authentic leaders (recall the traits approach at the start of this chapter) include:

- Being true to themselves (see Ilies, Morgeson and Nahrgang (2005) and their discussion of authentic leaders working in a state of eudaemonia; being self-aware, being unbiased and behaving authentically).
- Humility and modesty (Treviño, Brown and Hartman, 2003). This does not mean being weak; on the contrary it means being aware of one's limitations and

---

Illustration 6.7

An authentic leader

Michael Woodford is a British businessman who became president, chief operating officer and chief executive officer of Olympus, an optical equipment manufacturer. Having worked for the company for many years in Europe he was appointed to these roles in April 2011, and then unceremoniously sacked in October of the same year after he exposed $1.7 billion of inappropriate accounting practices aimed at hiding and concealing the true extent of corporate losses. The share price of Olympus fell by more than 80 per cent with more than $7 billion being shaved off of the value of the company. He fled in fear of his life as the Japanese Mob, the Yakuza, was also thought to be involved in the scandal. When asked why he exposed the fraud rather than accepting it, as the Olympus board expected him to, he answered that it was the right thing to do and that he could not have lived with himself if he had not done so. After an investigation, the whole Olympus board was sacked with some members going to prison.

Source: Woodford, M. (2013), *Exposure*. UK: Penguin.

mistakes, being willing to learn from them, seeing the value that others bring to situations and not being an arrogant glory seeker.

● Seeing situations from a range of perspectives, bringing out into the open the tensions and moral dilemmas existing within them.

● Knowing one's own sense of right and wrong and adhering to personal standards in decisions and relationships. When times get difficult authentic leaders display the moral courage to act consistently and not sacrifice deeply held beliefs (Verbos, Gerard, Forshey, Harding and Miller, 2007).

● Being able to manage themselves and their emotions, and being a role model to others. Having patience, resilience and flexibility.

Beddoes-Jones's (2012) research into authentic leadership, using senior Royal Air Force officers and UK business leaders, revealed that the myriad traits and styles found within the broad construct of authentic leadership sat within three factors, or 'pillars' of authentic leadership: self-awareness, self-regulation and ethics. Figure 6.7 illustrates how these sit under a canopy of relationships and on a bedrock of trust.

In our tour of leadership theories we have seen how they have evolved over time and, in a sense, we have returned to the beginning by describing characteristics

Activity 6.6

Think of the characteristics of authentic leaders and then see if you can relate them to any leaders that you know of. You may need to think of leaders of nations or social movements rather than organizations.

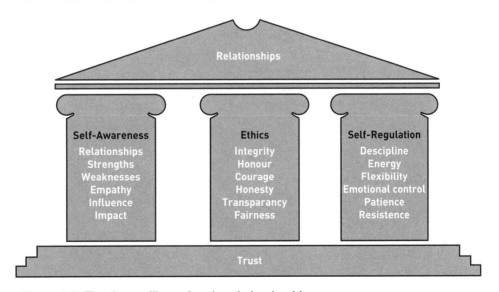

Figure 6.7 The three pillars of authentic leadership

Source: Beddoes-Jones, (2012), 'Authentic Leadership: The key to building trust', *People Management,* August, pp. 44–7.

of business leaders that are fit enough to lead organizations in the twenty-first century and fulfil the expectations of the people that work under them. Authentic leadership is a powerful theory and there are good grounds for thinking that leadership will need to move in this direction if organizations are to enjoy support from their employees as well as from government and society. Recent corporate scandals and crises blamed on poor leadership have dented public confidence in leaders who now need to work hard to recover personal and corporate reputations.

Critical approaches to leadership

Perhaps surprisingly, sometimes the very traits which support managers and leaders in their climb to the top of organizations can become their downfall (Furnham, 2010). Landrum *et al.* (2000) for example refer to *unethical* charismatic leaders who are controlling, manipulative and self-promoting – characteristics that can jeopardize and even sabotage the turnaround efforts of an organization. Hogan and Hogan (2001) investigated leadership from the reverse angle and identified the factors and traits which lead to derailment, which they termed the 'dark side' of leadership. They defined leadership as: 'the ability to build and maintain an effective team, one that can outperform its competition' (p. 40) and identified 10 dysfunctional dispositions associated with management and leadership failure (see Illustration 6.8).

Illustration 6.8

Management 'derailers'

These dispositions only become derailers when the positive elements become over-played and the manager lacks the flexibility to adapt their behaviour appropriately.

Excitable: low on emotional stability and tend to erupt into emotional displays of shouting, throwing things, slamming doors and other 'tantrum' behaviours.

Argumentative: unwilling to compromise, will challenge and argue vehemently for their position, overly alert for signs of betrayal, refusal to back down or compromise.

Cautious: fear of criticism, threatened by novelty or change, indecisive and controlling.

Detached: self-absorbed and lacking social insights, indifferent to criticism or social warmth, very focused, insensitive and poor at communicating.

Leisurely: insist on working at their own pace, retaliatory but only under conditions of high deniability, pretend to be hard-working and cooperative, very sensitive to disrespect.

Arrogant: high self-esteem and a sense of entitlement, exaggerated expectations, over-confident of success, take credit for success but deny any responsibility for failure.

Mischievous: see people as utilities to be exploited, violate expectations, confident but unpredictable, fail to deliver on commitments, manipulative, untruthful and untrustworthy.

Imaginative: eccentric and odd, changeable, self-absorbed and insensitive.

Diligent: rule-bound, over-pleasing of authority, fussy, nit-picking micromanagers who over-control people, processes and standards, unable to prioritize, poor in a crisis.

Dutiful: poor decision makers, unsupportive of staff, will not challenge authority.

Source: Hogan, R. and Hogan, J. (2001), 'Assessing leadership: a view from the dark side', *International Journal of Selection and Assessment*, vol. 9, (1–2), pp. 40–51.

Hogan, Hogan and Kaiser (2009) argued that derailed leaders are essentially deficient in one or more of four key skill areas:

1 *Intrapersonal* – self-awareness and empathy.
2 *Interpersonal* – social skills and emotional intelligence.
3 *Business* – planning, organizing and monitoring.
4 *Leadership* – team building and role modelling.

They also identify five 'early warning signs' of management derailment:

1 *Poor results*: customer complaints, cover-ups, inaccurate financial reporting, missed objectives.
2 *Narrow perspectives:* out-of-date, over-reliance on technical skills, too detail-oriented.
3 *Poor team building:* autocratic decision making, micromanagement, high turnover of staff.
4 *Poor working relationships:* insensitivity, being abrasive or abusive.
5 *Inappropriate/immature behaviour:* gossiping, poor at coping, refusal to accept responsibility.

Gender and leadership

Pertinent to this discussion is the fact that the first theory of leadership put forward in the chapter is that of the 'Great Man' theory. It is clear that these no longer relate to leadership in the twenty-first century. However, the facts are that far more men than women head up organizations and outnumber women who sit on their boards (see discussion in Chapter 5). The discussion about where to find women leaders centres around two key themes: do men and women lead similarly or differently? And if they are different, which makes the 'better' leader?

Eagly and Carli (2007) suggest that there are both similarities and differences in style between men and women leaders, but that the differences, while statistically significant, are quite small, whilst the consistency between genders is constant. Some studies indicate that women generally tend to adopt more relational, participative and transformational styles, whilst men are more likely to take a more transactional, directive style (Eagly and Johnson, 1990). This perspective is echoed by Gibson (1995) who suggests that an approach that involves a task/goal orientation and is one of assertiveness and control is most often exhibited by men; whilst women tend to take a more communal approach which is characterized by a more nurturing, caring approach with the well-being and welfare of others at its core.

By contrast, Kent and Schuele (2010) found no significant gender differences between German managers where a transformational leadership style was preferred, and Andersen and Hansson (2011) found no significant gender differences between the management and leadership styles of public-sector managers in Sweden. However, their finding raises the question as to whether leadership and management styles in Sweden may differ from UK and US norms as much as they do between the US/UK and Asia – in which case, it may not be gendered leadership which is being explored by the study, but rather cultural differences in leadership style.

Baron-Cohen's (2002) theory of *the extreme male brain* may be able to shed some light on the dichotomy between different research findings regarding gendered leadership. A specialist in the autistic spectrum of behavioural disorders, he suggests that the male brain is hard-wired for *systemizing*, whereas the female brain is hard-wired for *empathy*. Whilst Baron-Cohen's theory is completely consistent with suggestions regarding some of the studies on gendered leadership, we should be aware that the differences he describes are neuro-biological and not gendered. It is quite possible for a female to act as if she has the idealized male brain just as it is quite possible that a male may be driven to be highly empathetic and creative and display traditionally 'female' qualities. The notion of male and female brains draws on the nature–nurture theories that take no account of the influence of different child-rearing practices or social learning.

This does not stop management magazines and the business press appearing to be mesmerized by portrayals of heroic leader figures; usually men who wake at 06.00, run around the block, get to work by 07.30 and have very important meetings with very important people all day long before reading their children a bedtime story at 20.00. Portrayals of this kind have attracted a critical and rather disbelieving literature and one angle on this is through exploration of gendered narratives. Illustration 6.9 is an interesting account of a long-lived and well-known UK organization, which, incidentally, has women customers who outnumber men.

Illustration 6.9

Marks and Spencer – waiting for the warrior

Ann Rippin (2005) reinterprets the leadership history of one of the UK's best-known and perhaps best-liked retailers, Marks & Spencer. Marks & Spencer was founded in the late nineteenth century and has always been led at the highest level by men. Rippin (p. 582) points out that in histories written about M&S, 'the absence of women is exceptional'. All the top action was performed by men.

Leadership was passed initially through the male family line and when this had run its course other 'equally strong' men were brought in. She draws a parallel with the story of *Sleeping Beauty* such that the organization became, periodically, a sleeping princess waiting for a dashing and handsome prince to rejuvenate it. She allies it to 'illness narratives', i.e. 'we are sick but will be healed' (p. 584) by the arrival of Prince Charming. Later the prince displays his beautiful and fertile possession (the company, that

is). The trouble is, they don't often live happily ever after, as, when the princess falls sick again or the prince goes in search of a more beautiful princess, the search for another prince resumes.

Rippin viewed M&S as a patriarchy (actually a phallocracy) that implies that organizations are far from the rational systems we read about but can be 'locations of masculine violence' (p. 586). In M&S this violence took the form of robust exchanges between senior male managers vying for position as the alpha males. She sees M&S as gendered from birth and continuing so into its recent struggles to maintain its high-street position in a changing retail environment. The cumulative effects of men of action at the top makes change in M&S a very gendered thing and it is hard for her to imagine an alternative way of leading becoming accepted.

Activity 6.7

Can you find an organization (perhaps your own) that has a majority of women in top- and middle-level management? If so, do the management styles used in general reflect the discussions of male and female attitudes to management? Think back to the accounts of transactional and transformational leaders and any other categorizations that might be helpful in this respect. How convinced are you that men and women differ in their management styles?

Linstead, Brewis and Linstead (2005, p. 543) noted that managing change is typically 'authoritative, patriarchal, competitive, confrontational and bullying' and when managers speak and behave otherwise they are quickly labelled as going soft and losing their grip – even, horror of horrors, as acting like a woman in a masculine workplace. Studies of women as change agents are few as women are often excluded from the male social networks outside work where big decisions can be made and set in motion. So, why should gender have an influence on management theory and specifically organizational change? Most management texts present theory and best practice as gender neutral and let men and women interpret it and apply it at work. The alternative view is that since management is enacted by men and women and since the two enactors have different identities there must be some sort of interaction or influence operating (Linstead *et al.*, 2005, p. 546). Although the differences are small, studies of gender and management suggest that men are more transactional and rely more on position power to get results whereas women are more likely to be transformational and use relationships rather than power to motivate (Eagly *et al.*, 2003).

However, an additional overlay comes from the organizational context and the nature of the work. If work cultures are combative, then whether male or female the manager will have to respond with matching behaviour. Indeed, drawing on person–organization fit theory and the aim of selection processes to seek people who fit with cultures, then organizations will recruit people who appear to fit. Assuming there is no direct discrimination against women in selection then both men and women with similar characteristics will tend to be recruited.

Linstead and colleagues see Western masculinity as being focused on control: control of self, of others and of the environment. However, it is important to note that not all men are comfortable with the display of control-oriented behaviour and it is clear that some women display masculine control orientations either by nature or through conformance to a culture. The characteristics that usually accompany control such as decisiveness and quickness to punish people are, however, less acceptable in contemporary society than they once were. While these characteristics have perhaps never been suited to managing professionals who seek autonomy to use their professional knowledge rather than close direction, they are unfashionable and unwelcome to the humblest of workers who deserve, and expect, to be treated with dignity and consideration.

It is reasonable to suggest that classic masculine management styles are being challenged by a feminization of management (Kerfoot and Knights, 1993). While opening up leadership positions to women is an important social goal it is far from clear that having more women in top jobs would deliver innovation, creativity and change any better than men.

Retelling leadership stories

Collins and Rainwater (2005) offer an interesting reanalysis of a corporate transformation at giant US retailer Sears Roebuck, first told in the *Harvard Business Review* (Rucci, Kirn and Quinn, 1988). First though, we need to remind ourselves of what happened in Beijing in April 1989. This was a time of crisis for communism with huge structural changes occurring in Eastern Europe. Following the death of a pro-democracy sympathizer in China people wanted to demonstrate in Tiananmen Square, Beijing, but the Chinese government had little tolerance of demonstrations and of demonstrators. After demonstrations had taken place for some time and as numbers swelled in the square, the government sent in tanks to disperse protestors. An unknown 'rebel' stood in front of the advancing tank column and halted it – the photo of him appearing as if in conversation with the lead tank commander became an icon of resistance.

Collins and Rainwater use the Tiananmen Square 'tank man' incident to show that there are multiple ways of interpreting something like the Sears Roebuck change story. Did 'tank man' stand in front of the moving column and stop it or had it already stopped? Was he a people's hero defiant in the face of government oppression or was he an agitator who would undermine the harmonious society in which he lived? Why was he there? Was he just crossing the road with his shopping or are there more sinister explanations? Who ordered the tanks to stop advancing? Why did they stop? Had they already stopped? We don't know, but the point is that multiple stories can be written and told to explain the events that happened.

The Sears Roebuck story was written by company insiders and Collins and Rainwater criticize the paper as being an uncritical shrine to the transformational efforts of a new CEO. The new leader announced new strategic priorities and new task forces. Events were held to attune the workforce to the new position and revised 'total performance indicators' were introduced to measure performance. The paper's authors portray the transformation as an epic tale of heroic 'daring-do' with the CEO as the chief hero. It is about bringing light where there was darkness. It is *Beowulf*, it is *Biggles*.

What Collins and Rainwater then bring is a perceptive and amusing sideswipe at the paper. First, they show how the same story can be retold not as heroism but as a tragedy. What of the cast of thousands (the employees) who have only 'walk-on' parts in the play? It is a tragedy that their role, which must have been more than a little, is neglected. The CEO cast in the leading role, they argue, can just as well be seen as a villain motivated by corporate profits who manoeuvres the main characters (employees) for his own ends.

The story is also recast as a comedy. Central to the transformation was a new set of 'total performance indicators' such that, we are told, 'our model shows that a 5 point improvement in employee attitudes will drive a 1.3 point improvement in customer satisfaction, which in turn will drive a 5 per cent improvement in revenue growth … these numbers are as rigorous as any others we work with at Sears' (Rucci *et al*., 1988, p. 91). Really? Is business performance really this linear? Have we learned nothing from complexity theory? Can we not recast the main character as a fool leading willing dupes (senior management) into a Wonderland of cause and effect?

Management literature abounds with heroic stories of change. Some leaders are given nicknames to emphasize their superpowers: 'Neutron Jack' (so called because he left the buildings standing but without any people in them, rather like neutron bombs do) and 'Chainsaw Al' who was famed for cutting through organizations, slashing jobs on the way, are but two examples. We emphasize that our aim here is not to mock or deride the organizations we have used to illustrate our points, their managers who work hard to secure jobs for employees and profits for investors, or the authors of the heroic stories in which they feature. Rather it is simply to point out that stories of change are too often overly simplistic and that stories of heroism would have us overlook the true complexities and true contributions made by a largely anonymous cast.

Leadership and change

Leading change

A common theme in discussions of leadership and change is whether one style of leadership is most suited to taking organizations through periods of change, or whether different leadership approaches are required according to different change situations. Do we always need a charismatic-visionary leader or one with particular leadership traits? Alternatively, given the various types of organizational change discussed in Chapter 2, are some leadership approaches more suited to change situations than others? The discussions that follow should help answer some of these questions.

Leadership and the organizational life cycle

Greiner (1972) and Quinn (1988) proposed that different organizational life cycle stages (formation, growth, maturity and decline) need different leadership styles to take the organization forward. In the formative period when markets and structures are evolving quickly, for example, a creative and entrepreneurial style fits best. Then as the organization matures, top management styles are said to have to change. Quinn (1988), whose theories have already been discussed above (see Table 6.1 and Figure 6.5.), argues that an organization will start life positioned in the open systems quadrant requiring an innovative, risk-taking style. As it grows and develops it will include the elements of the human relations model and the rational goal model. As it reaches the stage of formalization, it will take on a more cautious stance with the internal process model. In its later life, Quinn argues that organizations might return to an open systems model but retain elements of the others. As the organization grows, matures and rejuvenates, both Greiner and Quinn argue for different leadership approaches.

This is, however, somewhat simplistic, as it is also important to differentiate change on the dimensions of large, strategic initiatives such as the embedding of a new set of organizational values, compared to the smaller, operational, ongoing and often incremental change such as procedural and process changes. In addition, in the case of large public institutions (e.g. the UK's National Health Service and education system) political issues become important, given the propensity for politicians to constantly 'tinker around the edges', therefore never allowing any changes to embed properly.

Leadership and the nature of change

Dunphy and Stace (1988, 1993) modelled approaches to change on two dimensions; the level of environmental readjustment needed to restore environmental fit and the style of leadership needed to realign it (see Figure 6.8). Their readjustment categories are:

- *Corporate transformation* – changes across the organization to business strategy, e.g. revised mission, organization-wide restructuring, new top management.
- *Modular transformation* – a major realignment of part of an organization, e.g. a major restructuring, expansion or contraction.
- *Incremental adjustment* – distinct changes but not on a radical scale, e.g. changing structure, using new production methods.
- *Fine-tuning* – typically at lower levels, e.g. clarifying goals, refining methods and procedures.

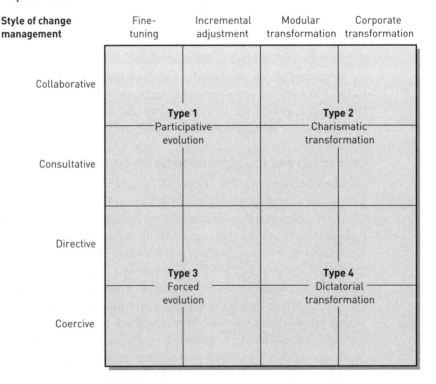

Figure 6.8 The Dunphy & Stance change matrix

Their categories of leadership are:

- *Collaborative* – wide participation of employees.
- *Communicative* – involving people in goal setting.
- *Directive* – managerial authority is the driving force.
- *Coercive* – change is forced and imposed.

Combining the environmental refitting and leadership categories above, Dunphy and Stace proposed the following approaches to managing change. When employees are in favour and support change then *participative evolution* is used when the amount of change needed is small. When environmental fit is low and when employees support radical change then *charismatic transformation* is appropriate. When employees oppose change then *forced evolution* applies when small adjustments are needed, whereas *dictatorial transformation* is needed when environmental fit is low and major realignment is needed.

A problem with typologies like this is that they imply that managers have a choice of change strategies almost as if they are selecting from a toolkit. Indeed, Dunphy and Stace claim that the model has: 'implications for the choice of strategies for managing organizational change in differing circumstances and for the training of change agents' (1988, p. 317). The model assumes that change can be planned and implemented logically and linearly, and sometimes it can. However, transformational change frequently takes place over a long period and is, or becomes, 'messy' (see Chapter 2) and more unpredictable. In these cases, managers' approaches need to vary according to the changing circumstances, not only within the organization but also in response to changes in the external environment. As Dunford (1990) says, the environment is not a fixed reality 'out there' but to some extent it is 'in here' and embodied within both the organizational culture and the thinking of the people within it.

Obstructing and facilitating change processes

Forces for and against change

Any organizational change will face forces that facilitate or obstruct it. This is particularly the case with large-scale 'frame-breaking' change or transformational change (see Chapter 2). These forces emanate from both the external and internal environments but most importantly from an organization's stakeholders and employees. Illustration 6.10 gives examples of external and internal forces that act for and against change.

Not all these forces will be present in any one change situation but it is helpful to have some reminder of these. In reality, although the external forces are important, the role of leading change is more likely to be concerned with resistance from inside the organization. In addition, some of the forces listed in Illustration 6.10 will be stronger than others. *Force field analysis* is a frequently used technique for identifying the range and strength for and against change. Developed by Kurt Lewin (1951), force field analysis is a way of identifying and bringing out into the open the forces that are impacting on a situation. It identifies power interests of actors involved and should lead to ideas about how to influence the actors to reduce the opposing forces and strengthen the driving forces.

Illustration 6.10

Forces for and against change

Driving forces for change	Driving forces against change
External forces:	*Individual resistance:*
• role of the state	• fear of the unknown
• social pressures	• dislike of the uncertainty and ambiguity
• changing technology	• surrounding change
• constraints from suppliers	• potential loss of power base
• stakeholder demands	• potential loss of rewards
• competitor behaviour	• perceived lack of skills for new situation
• customer needs	• potential loss of current skills
Internal forces:	*Organizational resistance:*
• organizational growth	• inertial forces deriving from the systemic nature of organizations
• pressures on increased performance	• interlocking aspects of structure, control systems, ritual and routines, signs and symbols
• managerial aspirations	• inertial forces deriving from group norms
• political coalitions	• potential loss of power group bases
• redesign of jobs	• entrenched interests of stakeholders
• restructuring	• lack of organizational capability
	• lack of resources
	• threat to resource allocation

Illustration 6.11

A fresh view of resistance: resistance as feedback

Managers blame resistors for not seeing the light, not being objective, being awkward. Maybe sometimes they are these things but sometimes perhaps it is the resistors who can see where plans are not joining up or see the flaws in management's assumptions. Resistance is a resource: an 'energy that can be channelled on behalf of the organization'. Ford and Ford (2009) suggest five ways of using resistance constructively:

● *Boost awareness* – top managers, having convinced themselves of the benefits, are mostly immune to how changes affect the jobs of people far below them so they should 'drop down' a few layers and talk to those who are being affected. Even emotional exchanges may add value in keeping a dialogue open.

● *Return to purpose* – communicate what needs to change and why. Middle managers need to be able to explain to their staff what needs to happen and they cannot do this unless the purpose is clear.

● *Change the change* – resistors can identify serious points about what is being proposed so do not be afraid to 'change the change' to take these points on board. Egos and positional power may impede this so it is vital that senior managers do not allow junior managers to block new insights, or allow their own prejudice or ego to get in the way.

● *Build engagement* – if communication channels are effective then worries and ideas can come to the surface. These can be managed in ways that enable individuals and groups to get involved in dealing with them and by so doing engage people in the changes.

● *Complete the past* – many people in change situations have good memories of what happened the last time change was attempted. This means that today's resistance may not be much to do with today's change but with past change. Past failures need to be acknowledged.

Source: Ford, J.D. and Ford, L.W. (2009) 'Decoding resistance to change', *Harvard Business Review*, Mar/April, pp. 99–103.

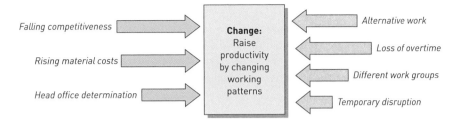

Figure 6.9 A force field diagram

Figure 6.9 is one example of forces driving for change and those restraining it. The different lengths of arrows denote the *strength of each force*: longer arrows are for stronger forces and vice versa.

Contrasting paths to change

The results of force field analyses are helpful in deciding the extent to which an organization is open or closed to change (Strebel, 1996). Figure 6.10 depicts Strebel's model of 'change paths' to show the different approaches to change depending on the levels of resistance to change and their strength. He offers the following advice on this (Strebel, 1992, p. 67):

1 Look for closed attitudes by examining what processes are in place for bringing new ideas into the sector, company or business unit.
2 Look for an entrenched culture by examining what processes are in place for reflecting on values and improving behaviour and skills.
3 Look for rigid structures and systems, by examining when the organization, business system, the stakeholder resource base and the industry last changed significantly; and by enquiring to what extent the structures and systems are capable of accommodating the forces of change.

Resistance	PROACTIVE	REACTIVE	RAPID	
Closed to change	Radical leadership	Organizational realignment	Downsizing and restructuring	Discontinuous paths
Can be opened to change	Top-down experimentation	Process re-engineering	Autonomous restructuring	Mixed paths
Open to change	Bottom-up experimentation	Goal cascading	Rapid adaptation	Continuous paths
	Weak	Moderate	Strong	**Change force**

Figure 6.10 Contrasting change pathways

Source: Strebel, P. (1996) Choosing the Right Change Path, *Mastering Management*, Part 14, Financial Times, pp. 5–7, © The Financial Times Limited. All Rights Reserved.

4 Look for counterproductive change dynamics by examining whether historical forces of change are driving the business and by enquiring to what extent these have become the new force of resistance.

5 Assess the strength of the overall resistance to change by examining to what extent the various forces of resistance are related and the extent to which power and resources can deal with them.

Both Dunphy and Stace's, and Strebel's models, however, offer prescriptions for matching leadership styles to levels of change in highly formulaic and prescriptive ways and tend to ignore those things which followers have themselves identified as highly desirable, such as the trust, compassion, stability and hope as identified by Ipsos Mori in 2009. The high failure rate of mergers and acquisitions and other strategic change initiatives alert us to just how difficult it is to lead and manage change. Dealing with resistance to change is one of the most important things in leading change.

Resistance to change

'Resistance to change' is a widely used phrase which captures a broad range of meaning. It is frequently associated with changes in employees' terms and conditions and their working practices; that is the legal contract they have with their employer. However, there is another type of *psychological* contract based on unwritten expectations and assumptions, that, when threatened, can also lead to resistance. Piderit (2000) identifies three different kinds of resistance: behavioural, affective and cognitive. Behavioural resistance could manifest as non-compliance or disruption to planned changes such as industrial action, which is usually the result of threats to employees' legal contracts. Alternatively, others might resist by using logic to defend and argue for the preservation of their preferred routines or by arguing that a similar change was tried historically which also failed. Other people may stay silent and comply with change but with their feelings and their emotional state not conducive to genuine acceptance of the change initiative.

This latter resistance could relate to what people *feel* as a change to their psychological contract, even though they might not consciously recognize this as such. Guest and Conway (2002) and Conway and Briner (2002) define the psychological contract as: '... the perceptions of the two parties, employee and employer, of what their mutual obligations are towards each other'. Note the term 'perceptions' which implies that this is based on 'understandings' which are assumed implicitly between the parties, rather than recognized openly. Resistance to change is often seen as a negative thing that management should try to eradicate; however this overlooks the fact that those doing the resisting might have a good logical reason to do so (which might be able to be resolved), but may also have a, somewhat unrecognized, emotional reaction that is likely to involve what is perceived as changes to their psychological contract. This latter feeling could provide a 'sticking' point and therefore, management should look beyond what appears to be obvious.

Resistance, whatever its cause, is generally seen as a negative outcome but, looked at another way, it can be a source of ideas and energy. Ford and Ford (2009) for instance, recommend that resistors should not be overlooked but that resistance should be seen as a form of valuable feedback that can support and ultimately enhance the change initiative.

Cynicism and scepticism

Cynicism and scepticism are two concepts which are quite closely related but also quite different. Stanley, Meyer and Topolnytsky, (2005, p. 436), consider that scepticism towards change is: 'doubt about the viability of a change for the attainment of its stated objective'. Cynicism towards change differs in that it is a: 'disbelief about a management's implied or stated motives for a specific organizational change'. In other words, cynicism indicates a lack of trust and is likely to be associated with disturbance of the psychological contract. Stanley *et al.* (2005) found that cynicism was a moderate predictor of resistance to change. This link implies that change agents should work on overcoming cynical reactions in communication strategies. If employees are disbelieving and distrusting of management in general then the ingredients of a problem are in place and cynical reactions can spiral out of control, as shown in Figure 6.11.

Illustration 6.12 shows how communication and building engagement, as well as recognizing other's feelings paid dividends in helping staff accept their new boss. It also shows how recognizing possible sources of cynicism can assist strategies for overcoming such resistance in the future.

Illustration 6.12

Mr Cathode

Jayne was pleased that the change management consultancy company she worked for had promoted her and given her a project of her own to manage. It was with a small manufacturing company which made and mixed tins of paint to resell to some of the large DIY stores. The workforce had all been there for many years; however, new management had been brought in to 'shake things up a bit' and increase productivity. In her promotion interview, Jane's boss had said to her: 'We're promoting you because we love the results that you get. We don't know how you get them, but the clients love you.'

On the first day on the project, Jayne made sure that she met every employee, not just the management, but everyone on the shop floor. She knew that they would be feeling insecure and that they wouldn't trust her (how could they,

they didn't know her), so she was polite and friendly, cheerful and positive. She paid particular attention to identifying any 'Mr Cathodes'. In her experience, every organization has one or two, and they are usually a fulcrum point in the business. They are often well respected, and as they influence a lot of people, Jayne knew that if she could turn them round and get them on board they would be the key to a successful or unsuccessful project.

So that's how she did it; through transformational leadership at an operational level. She focused on developing good-quality relationships with both the management, and the employees, especially with the 'cathodes' in the organization. Over the years, Jayne learned much from them. The 'cathode', of course, is the negative pole of a battery.

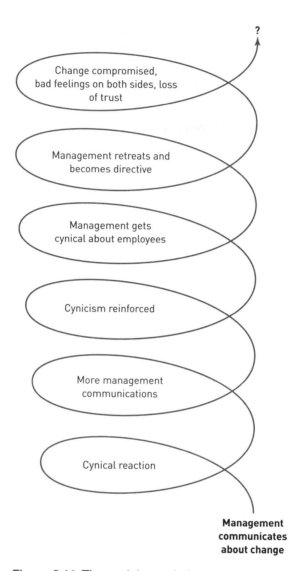

Figure 6.11 The cynicism spiral

Readiness for change

Readiness for change helps facilitate change. It is an important precursor to coping with resistance according to Armenakis, Harris and Mossholde (1993). Readiness involves shaping and conditioning attitudes and beliefs to be favourable for change. As such, communication strategies need to emphasize two key messages:

- *Urgency* – The need for change, i.e. explaining the gap between what the organization needs to be doing in the future compared to what it is currently doing, and the critical time available before the change must occur.
- *Readiness* – Employees ability to change and their ability to do it well. This is important because if employees think they cannot achieve the required changes, then they will avoid any 'discretionary effort' into achieving it.

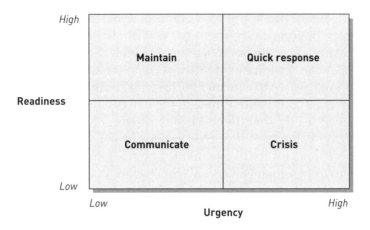

Figure 6.12 Organizational readiness for change

Combining the two concepts of urgency and readiness generates the typology shown in Figure 6.12. These are, together with the responses suggested on how to cope with the four states of change:

- *Low readiness/low urgency* – calls for a communication strategy to enhance readiness. This could involve opinion forming and active participation of employees in events that raise readiness. This might be the least problematic state of change.
- *Low readiness/high urgency* – this is a crisis situation which may need a rapid injection of new personnel and reassignment of people to new tasks.
- *High readiness/low urgency* – the priority here is to keep messages about the discrepancy current with frequent communications about progress.
- *High readiness/high urgency* – a quick response scenario exists in which high energy for change needs to be maintained. The change here could happen smoothly, but vigilance for unexpected 'glitches' is needed.

Leader–member exchange

Leadership cannot be studied in isolation, but should always be viewed in the societal and cultural context within which it takes place and with followership in mind. For example, leaders may perceive their activities as arising from a specific leadership approach. However, their attitudes and the way they behave are interpreted by different followers in different ways (Dobrosavljev, 2002). Leaders also behave differently with different people.

For instance, some followers are held in high esteem and included in what goes on, others are treated with respect but perhaps not involved much, others may be ignored, or worse, treated with disdain. This observable feature of organizational life led Graen and colleagues (Graen and Scandura, 1987; Graen and Uhl-Bien, 1995) to develop what has become known as leader–member exchange (LMX) theory, with *members* in this context being those people who are working with the leader.

Graen argued that the different types of leader–member relationships fall into two types: in-group and out-group. People in the in-group are involved in decision making and might be given projects to lead. Their opinions will be sought and the leader may well share confidences about other people and plans with them. They are well placed to influence the leader regarding their own tasks, assignments and career advancement. People in the out-group are kept at a distance and are only given the information needed to do their job. Their ideas are not sought and if they volunteer ideas, they may struggle to be taken seriously. In-group members are likely to believe that they have better knowledge and competencies than out-group members and may believe that this justifies their inclusion in the in-group. They may put down out-group members whom they perceive as being less capable. Out-group members may look at the in-group and think they are favoured not because of enhanced competencies, but because they are good at influencing upwards and impression management or because they have some other hold or influence over the leader. The dynamics of an 'us and them' such as this culture is invariably fundamentally damaging, both to relationships and also to organizational achievement. It is this which has led at least one major global organization, BP, to include the concept of 'One Team' into its five core organizational values (www.bp.com).

The effects of LMX relationships are felt, particularly, when organizations want to change, either in large or small measure, because this is when leaders need to persuade followers to move in a particular direction and to change their thinking and behaviour. While in-group members, who have been communicated with more effectively, may be keen to implement the changes, the out-group typically takes much more convincing and could be an important source of resistance. Consequently, the quality of the leader–member relationship seems likely to have a big influence on how communications about change are interpreted by others. For instance, leader communications to members of the in-group are likely to be received positively whilst those with the out-group are as likely to be received negatively. In other words, the in-group 'attributes' positive motivations to the leader but the out-group does the opposite (Furst and Cable, 2008). In some cases, leaders may not even bother to try and explain to someone what they need from them and why because they have already categorized them as a resistor.

In a study of Dutch employees during a merger (Van Dam *et al.*, 2008) found that employees who reported high-quality leader–member exchanges also reported low resistance to change. They also found that providing information openly, giving people opportunities to participate, and having trust in the people managing the change were all (as you would expect) related to lower resistance. This suggests that bottom-up approaches to change in which employees interact directly with leaders and change agents are likely to be more effective than top-down approaches characterized by remoteness and impersonal, autocratic, management dictates. Moreover, it is not enough to seek high-quality leader–member exchange relationships only when change is needed; it should be sought routinely so that it is in place to support change when the requirement to change comes along, as it inevitably will in our modern world and global society. Good-quality relationships need to be a part of daily work routines (Van Dam, Oreg and Schyns, 2008). Following Van Dam *et al.*'s advice could help avoid the formation of out-groups in the first place and their behaviour when attempting organizational change; even though this is, in some cases, not easy to do.

Conclusions

Leadership theory began with trying to understand Great Man theories and a subsequent search for their universally applicable leadership traits and styles, but increasingly recognized that leadership approaches need to be flexible to fit organizational culture, contexts and complexities. Transactional and transformational approaches were heralded, but with leadership scandals such as Enron in 2001, Lehman Brothers in 2008, Olympus in 2011 and Volkswagen in 2015, it became clear that leadership has a dark side. Such political and corporate mismanagement has led to a new emphasis on the ethical, self-regulatory and psychological self-awareness inherent within authentic leadership, which is suggested to be a root construct underpinning all other positive styles such as distributed and servant-leadership (Avolio and Gardner, 2005, p. 315). Leadership theory has changed as society has changed, reflecting the higher emphasis now given to ethics and responsibility.

Resistance to change, previously often seen as a challenge to the power and authority of leaders, is now better understood from a psychological perspective. Whilst good communication is recognized as one of the best strategies for dealing with it, learning how to manage change is one of the biggest challenges leaders in organizations face today. With the context now in place, in Part Three we look at the more practical considerations of how to plan, design and implement change.

Discussion questions and assignments

1 Drawing on your own experience of organizational change, describe a situation where the leader was seen as, or styled themselves as, an 'heroic' figure.

2 In the context of the discussion of different types of change in Chapter 2, and the idea that organizations must be alert to their ever-changing environments, debate the advisability of seeking managers at all levels who can act as transformational leaders.

3 Examine the concept of 'leaders of change' as it might apply across different societies and organizations.

4 Think of a change situation that you have been in. What were the sources of resistance? How did management try to combat them?

5 If you wanted to develop your own leadership skills/style what would you prioritize? What do you need to be better at? How might you begin to develop leadership qualities?

Case example ●●●

Leadership: collective failure across several agencies

This case illustrates leadership failure in public service organizations. In August 2014 an independent report into child sexual abuse in Rotherham, England, revealed that 1,400 children had been victims of organized sexual violence and abuse over a 15-year period and raised the most serious concerns about leadership in the local council and the behaviour of the regional police force (Hay, 2014).

The revelations were not new. Back in 2002, it was claimed that senior staff at Rotherham council sanctioned a 'raid' on one of its own offices to locate and remove files containing details of the scale and seriousness of the abuse. This happened after council staff realized that a draft report investigating abuse allegations was about to reveal evidence of a widespread system of abuse. There were strong suspicions that the removal of case reports (detailed investigations into specific abuse cases) was an outcome of collusion and cover-up. Furthermore, investigations in 2002, 2003 and 2006 made by front-line youth workers were suppressed or ignored by people in leadership positions. Rotherham council had tried to prevent the publication of a 2010 report into the murder of a 17 year-old girl; even taking the case unsuccessfully to the High Court.

In the years covered by the case it was claimed that 'community leaders' in Rotherham knew about the scale of abuse but were unable to stop it. After the highly critical report came out in 2014 the government ordered inspections of children's services in the town. The Independent Police Complaints Commission said that the report's findings raised 'serious and troubling concerns' about the involvement of the police in the scandal. The regional police and crime commissioner (a new role supposedly created to oversee the police and ensure they are answerable to the local community) had previously had a position of responsibility for children's and young people's services in Rotherham council. It was reported that council workers had been reluctant to pursue repeated claims of abuse and violence because they were scared of being seen as racist and of damaging 'community cohesion'.

Suppression and disregard of evidence was aggravated by political sensitivities. Some council workers clearly believed that revelations could attract the attention of extremist political groups. Political tensions in the local region skirted around a 'politically inconvenient truth' that people in leadership roles were keen to hide.

This distressing case draws attention to the interplay between leadership, culture and politics across a range of organizations and agencies. The official report (Hay, 2014) concludes that over the 12 years covered by the enquiry, 'the collective failures of political and officer leadership were blatant' (p. 1) and that, 'it is hard to believe that any senior officers or members [of Council] from the leader and Chief Executive downwards, were not aware of the issue. Most members showed little obvious leadership or interest in CSE [child sexual exploitation] ...' (p. 101).

It is perhaps relevant to this case that from 1997 there had been five chief executives of the council plus one acting chief executive and there had also been regular staff turnover in a 'director of safeguarding' role. Responding to questioning during the inquiry, former chief executives claimed that their 'overriding priority' had been economic regeneration; which might indicate that other problems, even of the most serious kind, were given a lower priority. Organization culture also fuelled this particular fire. Some senior councillors were described as aggressive and intimidating and the 'overall culture' was described as 'macho' and sexist to the extent that the culture probably impeded any efforts that council workers made to tackle a problem that was grounded in sexual abuse.

As of 2014, no past or present officer or official had been disciplined even though misconduct in public office is a criminal offence in the UK. Only five men had been convicted of offences relating to this case. When the Hay report came out, the initial response of people who had been in positions of leadership was a robust denial that they had done anything wrong, although they were all very sorry for what had happened.

Case exercise

1 Why do people in leadership positions sometimes resort to covering up sensitive information rather than act on it to change and improve?

2 Why do people in leadership positions sometimes fail to take responsibility for their past actions – often in the face of damning criticism?

3 To what extent might frequent changes of leadership in senior posts have contributed to the failure to stop wrong-doing in this case?

4 Under what conditions might frequent leadership changes be beneficial to organizations?

Sources:

Hay, A. (2014), *Independent Inquiry into Child Sexual Exploitation in Rotherham (1997–2013)*.
The Times, 27 August 2014, pp. 1, 8–9.
The Times, 28 August 2014, pp. 1, 8.

Indicative resources

Harvard Business Review (2011), *HBR's Ten Must Reads on Leadership*, Boston, MA: Harvard Business School Press. This book is a selection of the top ten most influential papers on leadership published in the HBR.

Useful websites

http://www.nhs.leadershipacademy.nhs.uk This site provides information on how the National Health Service sees leadership and describes the behaviour that the NHS seeks in its present and future leaders.

http://www.i-l-m.com This is the website of the Institute for Leadership and Management and contains research and comment in the field.

http://www.cipd.co.uk See the Chartered Institute of Personnel Development for factsheets and research reports on leadership and change.

http://www.vectorstudy.com/management-topics/laissez-faire-leadership This site summarizes leadership theory.

http://www.youtube.com/watch?v=XKUPDUDOBVo Summarizes 10 leadership theories in five minutes. See YouTube for a range of short videos explaining core concepts of leadership.

●●●● References

Alves, J. C., Manz, C. C. and Butterfield, D. A. (2005), 'Developing leadership theory in Asia: The role of Chinese philosophy', *International Journal of Leadership Studies*, 1(1), pp. 3–27.

Andersen, J. A. and Hansson, P. H. (2011), 'At the end of the road? On differences between women and men in leadership behavior', *Leadership and Organization Development Journal*, 32 (5), pp. 428–41.

Armenakis, A., Harris, S.G. and Mossholde, K.W. (1993), 'Creating readiness for change', *Human Relations*, 46(6), pp. 681–704.

Avolio, B.J. and Gardner, W.L. (2005), 'Authentic leadership development: getting to the root of positive forms of leadership', *Leadership Quarterly*, 16(3), pp. 315–38.

Barbuto, J. E., and Wheeler, G. T. (2006), 'Scale development and construct clarification of servant-leadership', *Group and Organization Management,* 31(3), 300–26.

Barling, J., Slater, F. and Kelloway, E.K. (2000), 'Transformational leadership and emotional intelligence: an exploratory study', *Leadership and Organization Development Journal*, 21(3) 157–61.

Baron-Cohen, S. (2002), 'The extreme male brain theory of autism', *Trends in Cognitive Sciences*, 6(6), pp. 248–54.

Bar-On, R. (1997), *Emotional Quotient Inventory: Technical Manual*, Multi-Health Systems, Toronto.

Bass, B.M. (1990), 'From transactional to transformational leadership: learning to share the vision', *Organizational Dynamics*, Winter, pp. 19–31.

Bass, B.M. & Avolio, B.J. (1993), Transformational leadership: a response to critiques, in M.M. Chemers, & R. Ayman. (eds), *Leadership Theory and Research,* London: Academic Press.

Beddoes-Jones, F. (2012), 'Authentic leadership: the key to building trust', *People Management*, August, pp. 44–7.

Blake, R.R. and McCanse, A.A. (1991), *Leadership Dilemmas: Grid Solutions*, Houston, TX: Gulf Publishing.

Blake, R.R. and Mouton, J.S. (1964), *The Managerial Grid*, Houston, TX: Gulf Publishing.

Blanchard, K. (2012, October 13), 'Elect servant-leaders', *How we lead: conversations on leadership with Ken Blanchard,* retrieved from http://howwelead.org/tag/servant-leadership/.

Bolden, R. (2007), *Distributed Leadership*, in A. Marturano, and J. Gosling (eds), *Leadership, The Key Concepts*, Abingdon: Routledge.

Bono, J.E. and Judge, T.A. (2004), 'Personality and transformational and transactional leadership: a meta analysis', *Journal of Applied Psychology,* 89(5), 901–10.

Burns, J.M. (1978), *Leadership*, New York: Harper & Row.

Bush, T. and Glover, D. (2003), *School Leadership: Concepts and Evidence*, Nottingham: National College for School Leadership.

Cameron, K.S. (1985), *Cultural congruence, strength and types: relationships to effectiveness*, Working Paper, University of Michigan, Ann Arbor: MI.

Carlyle, T. (1841), *On Heroes, Hero-Worship and the Heroic in History,* NY: Fredrick A. Stokes & Brother.

Carlyle, T. (1907), *Heroes and Hero Worship*, Boston: Adams.

Collins, D. and Rainwater, K. (2005), 'Managing change at Sears: a sideways look at a tale of corporate transformation', *Journal of Organizational Change Management*, 18(1), pp. 16–30.

Conger, J. (1993), 'Max Weber's conceptualization of charismatic authority: its influence on organizational research', *Leadership Quarterly*, 4(3), pp. 277–88.

Conway, N. and Briner, R.B. (2002), 'A daily diary study of affective responses to psychological contract breach and exceeded promises', *Journal of Organizational Behavior,* 23(3), 287–302.

Conway, N. and Briner, R.B. (2005), *Understanding Psychological Contracts at Work*, Oxford: Oxford University Press.

Cote, S. and Miners, C. (2006), 'Emotional intelligence, cognitive intelligence and job performance', *Administrative Science Quarterly*, 51, pp. 1–28.

Cunliffe, A. L. (2009), 'The philosopher leader: on relationalism, ethics and reflexivity – a critical perspective to teaching leadership', *Management Learning*, 40(1), pp. 87–101.

Dobrosavljev, D. (2002), 'Gadamer's hermeneutics as practical philosophy', *Philosophy, Sociology and Psychology*, 2(9), pp. 605–18.

Dulewicz, V. and Herbert, P. (1996), 'Leaders of tomorrow: how to spot the high-flyers', *Financial Times*, 20 September, p. 16.

Dunford, R. (1990), 'Strategies for planned change: an exchange of views between Dunford, Dunphy and Stace', *Organization Studies*, 11(1), pp. 131–5.

Dunphy, D. and Stace, D. (1988), 'Transformational and coercive strategies for planned organizational change: beyond the OD model', *Organization Studies*, 9(3), pp. 317–34.

Dunphy, D. and Stace, D. (1993), 'The strategic management of corporate change', *Human Relations,* 46(8), pp. 905–20.

Eagly, A. H. and Carli, L.L. (2007), *Through the Labyrinth: the Truth about how Women Become Leaders.* Boston, MA: Harvard Business School Press, pp. 130–1.

Eagly, A.H. and Johnson, B.T. (1990), 'Gender and leadership style: a meta-analysis', *Psychological Bulletin*, 108(2), pp. 233–56.

Eagly, A.H., Johannesen-Schmidt, M.C. and van Enge, M.L. (2003), 'Transformational, transactional and laissez-faire leadership styles: a meta-analysis comparing men and women', *Psychological Bulletin,* 129(4), pp. 569–91.

Eicher-Catt, D. (2005), 'The myth of servant-leadership: A feminist perspective', *Women and Language,* 27(1), 17–25.

Farkas, C.M. and Wetlaufer, S. (1996), 'The Ways Chief Executive Officers Lead', *Harvard Business Review*, May–June, pp. 110–22.

Fiedler, F.E. (1967), *A Theory of Leadership Effectiveness,* New York: McGraw-Hill.

Fiol, C.M., Harris, D. and House, R. (1999), 'Charismatic Leadership: strategies for affecting social change', *Leadership Quarterly*, 10(3), pp. 449–82.

Fletcher, J.K., (2004), 'The paradox of postheroic leadership: An essay on gender, power, and transformational change', *Leadership Quarterly* 15(5), 647–61.

Ford, J.D. and Ford, L.W. (2009), 'Decoding resistance to change', *Harvard Business Review*, Mar/April, pp. 99–103.

Furnham, A. (2010), *The Elephant in the Boardroom: The Causes of Leadership Derailment*, UK: Palgrave McMillan.

Furst, S.A. and Cable, D.M. (2008), 'Employee resistance to organizational change: managerial influence tactics and leader-member exchange', *Journal of Applied Psychology*, 93(2), pp. 453–62.

Gibson, C. (1995), 'An investigation of gender differences in leadership across four countries', *Journal of International Business Studies*, 26(2), pp. 225–79.

Goffee, R. and Jones, G., (2006), *Why should anyone be led by you? – What it takes to be an authentic leader,* Boston: Harvard Business Press.

Goleman, D. (1995), *Emotional Intelligence*, New York, NY: Bantam Books, Inc.

Goleman, D. (1998), 'What makes a leader? IQ and technical skills are important, but emotional intelligence is the *sine qua non* of leadership', *Harvard Business Review*, November–December, pp. 93–104.

Graen, G.B. and Scandura, T.A. (1987), 'Toward a psychology of dyadic organizing', *Research in Organizational Behaviour*, 9, pp. 175–208.

Graen, G.B. and Uhl-Bien, M. (1995), 'Relationship-based approach to leadership: development of leader-member exchange (LMX) theory of leadership over 25 years', *Leadership Quarterly*, 6, pp. 219–47.

Greenleaf, R. K. (1977), *Servant-leadership*, Mahwah, NJ: Paulist Press.

Greiner, L. (1972), 'Evolution and revolution as organizations grow', *Harvard Business Review*, July–August, pp. 37–46.

Guest, D.E. and Conway, N. (2002), *Pressure at Work and the Psychological Contract*, London: CIPD.

Hamilton, F., and Bean, C. J. (2005), 'The importance of context, beliefs, and values in leadership development', *Business Ethics: A European Review,* 14 (4), 336–47.

Handy, C. (1996), 'The new language of organising and its implications for leaders', in F. Hesselbein, M. Goldsmith, and R. Beckhard (eds), *The Leader of the Future*. The Drucker Foundation Future Series. San Francisco: Jossey-Bass.

Heidrick & Struggles (2004), *The Heidrick & Struggles Leadership Capital Series: 'The Asian Perspective',* Chicago, IL: Heidrick & Struggles International, Inc.

Hendry, J. (2004), *Between enterprise and ethics: business and management in a bimoral society*, New York, NY: Oxford University Press.

Hersey, P. and Blanchard, K.H. (1993), *Management of Organizational Behavior: Utilizing Human Resources* (6th edn), Englewood Cliffs, NJ: Prentice-Hall.

Higgs, M. and Dulewicz, V. (2004), 'The emotionally intelligent leader', in Rees, D. and McBain, R. (eds), *People Management: Challenges and Opportunities,* London: Palgrave-MacMillan.

Hogan, R. and Hogan, J. (2001), 'Assessing leadership: a view from the dark side', *International Journal of Selection and Assessment,* 9(1-2), pp. 40–51.

Hogan, R., Hogan, J. and Kaiser, R. (2009), 'Management derailment', In S. Zedeck, (ed.) *American Psychological Association Handbook of Industrial and Organizational Psychology*. NY: APA.

Hogan, R. and Kaiser, R. B. (2005), 'What we know about leadership', *Review of General Psychology*, 9(2), pp. 169–80.

House, R.J. (1971), 'A path–goal theory of leader effectiveness', *Administrative Science Quarterly*, 16, pp. 321–38.

Howard, L.W. (1998), 'Validating the competing values model as a representation of organizational cultures', *International Journal of Organization Analysis,* 6(3), pp. 231–50.

Hunter, E.M., Neubert, M.J., Perry, S.J., Witt, L.A., Penney, L.M., and Weinberger, E. (2013), 'Servant leaders inspire servant followers: Antecedents and outcomes for employees and the organization', *Leadership Quarterly*, 24, 316–31.

Ilies, R., Morgeson, F.P. and Nahrgang, J.D. (2005), 'Authentic leadership and eudaemonic well-being: understanding leader-follower outcomes', *Leadership Quarterly*, 16(3), pp. 373–94.

Ipsos Mori (2009), http://businessjournal.gallup.com/content/113542/what-followers-want-from-leaders.aspx accessed 3 August 2014.

Jay, A. (2014), *Independent Inquiry into Child Sexual Exploitation in Rotherham (1997-2013)*, Rotherham: Rotherham Metropolitan Borough Council.

Johnson, C. E. (2008), *Meeting the Ethical Challenges of Leadership: Casting Light or Shadow,* Thousand Oaks, CA: Sage.

Judge, T. A. and Piccolo, R. F. (2004), 'Transformational and transactional leadership: a meta-analytic test of their relative validity', *Journal of Applied Psychology,* 89(5), 755–68.

Kavanagh, M. H. and Ashkanasy, N. M. (2006), 'The impact of leadership and change management strategy on organizational culture and individual acceptance of change during a merger', *British Journal of Management,* 17, 81–103.

Kent, T. W. and Schuele, U. (2010), 'Gender differences and transformational leadership behavior: do both German men and women lead in the same way?' *International Journal of Leadership Studies,* 6(1), pp. 52–66.

Kerfoot, D. and Knights, D. (1993), 'Management, masculinity and manipulation: from paternalism to corporate strategy in financial services', *Journal of Management Studies,* 30(4), 659–77.

Kirkpatrick, S.A. and Locke, E.A. (1991), 'Leadership: do traits matter?' *Academy of Management Executive,* May, pp. 48–60.

Kool, M., and van Dierendonck, D. (2012), 'Servant-leadership and commitment to change, the mediating role of justice and optimism', *Journal of Organizational Change Management,* 25(3), 422–33.

Kotter, J.P. (1990), *A Force for Change: How Leadership Differs from Management*, New York: Free Press.

Kotter, J.P. (1996), *Leading Change*, Boston, MA: Harvard Business School Press.

Landrum, N.E., Howell, J.P. and Paris, L. (2000), 'Leadership for strategic change', *Leadership and Organization Development Journal,* 21(3), pp. 150–6.

Lewin, K. (1951), *Field Theory in Social Science,* New York: Harper & Row.

Likert, R. (1961), *New Patterns of Management,* New York: McGraw-Hill.

Linstead, S., Brewis, J. and Linstead, A. (2005), 'Gender in change: gendering change', *Journal of Organizational Change Management,* 18(6), pp. 542–60.

Lord, R.G., De Vader, C.L. and Alliger, G.M. (1986), 'A meta-analysis of the relation between personality traits and leadership perceptions: an application of validity generalization procedures', *Journal of Applied Psychology*, 71, pp. 402–10.

Mandell, B. and Pherwani, S. (2003), 'Relationship between emotional intelligence and TL style: a gender comparison', *Journal of Business and Psychology,* 17(3), 387–404.

Martin, C.M. (2008), 'A meta-analytic investigation of the relationship between emotional intelligence and leadership effectiveness', Unpublished D. Ed. dissertation, East Carolina University.

Mintzberg, H. (1979), *The Nature of Managerial Work*, Englewood Cliffs, NJ: Prentice-Hall.

Northouse, P. G. (2013), *Leadership: Theory & Practice*, (6th edition) Thousand Oaks, CA: Sage.

Parris, D. L., and Peachy, J. W. (2013), 'A systematic literature review of servant-leadership theory in organizational contexts', *Journal of Business Ethics, 113*, 377–93.

Parry, K.W. and Bryman, A. (2006), 'Leadership in organizations', in Clegg, S.R., Lawrence, T.B. and Nord, W.R. (eds) *The SAGE Handbook of Organization Studies*, London: SAGE, pp. 447–67.

Petrides, K. and Furnham, A. (2001), 'Trait emotional intelligence: psychometric investigation with reference to established trait taxonomies', *European Journal of Personality*, 15, 425–48.

Phipps, S.T.A and Prieto, L.C. (2011), 'The influence of personality factors on transformational leadership', *International Journal of Leadership Studies*, 21(3), 430–47.

Piderit, S.K. (2000), 'Rethinking resistance and recognizing ambivalence: a multidimensional view of attitudes toward an organizational change', *Academy of Management Review,* 25(4), pp. 783–94.

Post, J.M. (1986), 'Narcissism and the charismatic leader-follower relationship', *Political Psychology*, 7(4), 675–88.

Prosser, S. (2010), *Servant-leadership: More philosophy, less theory* [Essay], Westfield, IN: The Greenleaf Center for Servant-leadership.

Quinn, R.E. (1988), *Beyond Rational Management: Mastering the Paradoxes and Competing Demands of High Performance*, San Francisco, CA: Jossey-Bass.

Reich, R.B. (1991), 'The team as hero', in J. Henry and D. Walker, (eds) *Managing Innovation*, London: Sage.

Reynolds, K. (2011), 'Servant-leadership as gender-integrative leadership: paving a path to gender-integrative organizations through leadership education', *Journal of Leadership Education,* 10(2), 155–71.

Rippin, A. (2005), 'Marks and Spencer – waiting for the warrior', *Journal of Organizational Change Management*, 18(6), pp. 578–93.

Robbins, S.P. and Coulter, M. (2005), *Management*, (8th edn), Eaglewood Cliffs, NJ: Prentice Hall.

Rucci, A., Kirn, S. and Quinn, R. (1998), 'The employee-customer profit chain at Sears', *Harvard Business Review,* January–February, pp. 82–97.

Runciman, W.G. and Matthews, E. (1978), *Max Weber: Selections in Translation*, Cambridge: Cambridge University Press.

Salovey, P., and Mayer, J.D. (1989), 'Emotional intelligence', *Imagination, Cognition, and Personality*, 9(3), pp. 185–211.

Salovey, P., Mayer, J., Caruso, D. (2004), 'Emotional intelligence: theory, findings, and implications', *Psychological Inquiry, 15,* 197–215.

Shamir, B., Dayan-Horesh, H. and Adler, D. (2005), 'Leading by biography: toward a life-story approach to the study of leadership', *The Leadership Quarterly*, 1(1), pp. 13–29.

Shamir, B. and Eilam, G. (2005), 'What's your story? A life-stories approach to authentic leadership development', *The Leadership Quarterly*, 16(3), pp. 395–417.

Shin, Y.K. (1999), 'The traits and leadership styles of CEOs in South Korean companies', *International Studies of Management and Organization*, 28(4), pp. 40–8.

Smith, B.N., Montagno, R.V., and Kuzmenko, T.N. (2004), 'Transformational and servant-leadership: content and contextual comparisons', *Journal of Leadership and Organizational Studies*, 10(4), 80–90.

Southwest Airlines Co. (2014), Southwest Corporate Fact Sheet, *SWAmedia,* retrieved from http://www.swa-media.com/channels/Corporate-Fact-Sheet/pages/corporate-fact-sheet.

Stanley, D.J., Meyer, J.P. and Topolnytsky, L. (2005), 'Employee cynicism and resistance to organizational change', *Journal of Business Psychology*, 19(4), 429–59.

Stogdill, R.M. and Coons, A.E. (1957), *Leader Behavior: Its Description and Measurement*, Columbus, OH: Ohio State University Bureau of Business Research.

Stone, A.G., Russell, R.F. and Patterson, K. (2004), 'Transformational versus servant-leadership – A difference in leader focus'. *Paper presented at the Servant-leadership Roundtable*, Regent University, Virginia Beach, VA.

Strebel, P. (1992), *Breakpoints: How Managers Exploit Radical Business Change*, Cambridge, MA: Harvard Business School Press.

Strebel, P. (1996), 'Choosing the right change path', *Mastering Management*, Part 14, *Financial Times*, pp. 5–7.

Tannenbaum, R. and Schmidt, W.H. (1973), 'How to choose a leadership pattern', *Harvard Business Review*, 51, May–June, pp. 162–80.

Treviño, L.K., Brown, M. and Hartman, L.P. (2003), 'A qualitative investigation of perceived executive ethical leadership: perceptions from inside and outside the executive suite', *Human Relations*, 56, pp. 5–37.

Trompenaars, F. and Voerman, E. (2010), *Servant-leadership Across Cultures: Harnessing the Strengths of the World's Most Powerful Management Philosophy*. New York, NY McGraw-Hill.

Useem, M. (1996), 'Do leaders make a difference?' *Mastering Management*, Part 18, *Financial Times*, pp. 5–6.

Van Dam, K., Oreg, S. and Schyns, B. (2008), 'Daily work contexts and resistance to organizational change: the role of leader-member exchange, development climate and change process characteristics', *Applied Psychology: An International Review*, 57(2), pp. 313–34.

van Dierendonck, D. (2011), 'Servant-leadership: a review and synthesis', *Journal of Management,* 37(4), 1228–61.

van Dierendonck, D., and Heeren, I. (2006), 'Toward a research model of servant-leadership', *International Journal of Servant-Leadership,* 2(1), 147–64.

van Dierendonck, D., Stam, D., Boersma, P., de Windt, N. and Alkema, J. (2014), 'Same difference: exploring the differential mechanisms linking servant-leadership and transformational leadership to follower outcomes', *The Leadership Quarterly, 25*, 544–62.

Verbos, A.K., Gerard, J.A., Forshey, P.R., Harding, C.S. and Miller, J.S. (2007), 'The positive ethical organisation: enacting a living code of ethics and ethical organisation identity', *Journal of Business Ethics*, 76, pp. 7–33.

Waldman. G.A., Ramirez, G.G., House, R.J., and Puranam, p. (2001), 'Does leadership matter? CEO attributes under conditions of perceived environmental uncertainty.' *Academy of Management Journal*, 44, 134–43.

Watson, T. (1994), *In Search of Management*, London: Routledge.

Wensley, R. (1996), 'Mrs Beeton, management guru', *Financial Times*, 26 April, p. 15.

Woffard, J.C. and Liska, L.Z. (1993), 'Path–goal theories of leadership: a meta-analysis', *Journal of Management,* 19, pp. 857–76.

Woodford, M. (2013), *Exposure,* London: Penguin.

Woodruffe, C. (2000), 'Emotional intelligence: time for a time-out', *Selection and Development Review*, 16(4), pp. 3–9.

van Dierendonck, D. 'Servant Leadership: A Review and Synthesis', *Journal of Management*, July 2011 37: 1228-1261, first published on September 2, 2010

Yukl, G. (2002), *Leadership in Organizations* (5th edn), Englewood Cliffs, NJ: Prentice-Hall.

Zaccaro, S.J. (2007), 'Trait-based perspectives of leadership', *American Psychologist*, 62(1), pp. 6–16.

Part Three

STRATEGIES FOR MANAGING CHANGE

Two major themes have emerged from the discussions in Parts One and Two of the book that have a bearing on the practical issues of preparing for, designing and implementing change in organizations: the context for, and content of, change.

Part Three turns to the practicalities of *doing* change in the sense of designing, planning and implementing change – in other words concentrating on the processes through which change happens. Two different approaches to managing change processes, each encompassing various methodologies, are discussed in Chapters 7 and 8. These approaches relate directly back to the types of change discussed in Chapter 2, in particular, the concepts of hard and soft problems, difficulties and messes. Chapter 7 concentrates on change approaches that are based on rational–logical models of change which are most appropriate for situations of hard complexity where the 'people' issues are low. In contrast, Chapter 8 recognizes that many change situations involve issues of organizational politics, culture and leadership that dictate an approach to change which can deal more easily with situations characterized by soft complexity.

Finally, Chapter 9 considers issues that will affect work and organizations in the future and trends in researching change.

Chapter 7

Hard systems models of change

There are a number of models for handling change in situations of hard complexity. This chapter describes one and, in order to demonstrate its use, applies it to a particular change situation. The limitations of this type of model are discussed.

Learning objectives

By the end of this chapter you will be able to:

● recognize change situations (problems/opportunities) characterized mainly by hard complexity, where the use of hard systems methodologies are appropriate;

● describe the main features of hard systems methodologies for defining, planning and implementing change;

● explain the hard systems model of change (HSMC) as representative of hard systems methodologies of change;

● discuss the limitations of hard systems methodologies of change and, therefore, the need for other change methodologies more suited to situations of soft complexity.

Situations of change

In Chapter 2 a number of different ways of categorizing organizational change were discussed, from incremental to radical, frame-breaking or discontinuous changes. As Chapter 2 showed, expectations with respect to the ease with which change happens vary according to its perceived complexity. Consequently, change in situations that are characterized by hard complexity is more likely to be enacted easily and speedily than change in situations which show soft complexity, that is, where issues are contentious and there is a high level of emotional involvement on the part of those likely to implement the change and those who will be affected by it.

There are many approaches to planning and implementing change. Some are more appropriate to situations of hard complexity while others are more appropriate to situations of soft complexity or, as Chapter 2 characterized them, 'messy' situations. Flood and Jackson (1991), using a systems perspective, classify various methodologies in a similar way but use the terms 'simple system' and 'complex system' instead of difficulties and messes. What is of more interest, though, is that Flood and Jackson also classify these methodologies according to their appropriateness of use in situations characterized by different ideological viewpoints. Three ideological viewpoints, representing three types of relationships between people, are defined. Two of these (the unitary and pluralist viewpoints) have been discussed already in Chapter 5 (see Illustration 5.9); all three are described in Illustration 7.1.

Illustration 7.1

Characteristics of unitary, pluralist and coercive relationships

Unitary

People relating to each other from a unitary perspective:

- share common interests;
- have values and beliefs that are highly compatible;
- largely agree upon ends and means;
- all participate in decision making;
- act in accordance with agreed objectives.

Pluralist

People relating to each other from a pluralist perspective:

- have a basic compatibility of interest;
- have values and beliefs that diverge to some extent;

- do not necessarily agree upon ends and means, but compromise is possible;
- all participate in decision making;
- act in accordance with agreed objectives.

Coercive

People relating to each other from a coercive perspective:

- do not share common interests;
- have values and beliefs that are likely to conflict;
- do not agree upon ends and means and 'genuine' compromise is not possible;
- coerce others to accept decisions.

Source: Based on Flood, R.L. and Jackson, M.C. (1991), *Creative Problem Solving: Total systems intervention*, Chichester: Wiley, pp. 34–5.

Using an extensive list of different methodologies for problem solving and change, Flood and Jackson suggest which are most appropriate in situations characterized as simple or complex systems but modified by whether relationships between people tend to be of a unitarist, pluralist or coercive nature. It is not the intention here to consider all the possibilities. What is important is to note that different logics dominate each possibility in terms of suggesting a particular approach to change. Consequently, in situations of hard complexity (e.g. where simple systems and a unitarist ideology of relationships prevail), a particular type of change approach will be appropriate, whereas in situations of soft complexity (e.g. where complex systems and a pluralist ideology of relationships prevails), a different type of change approach should be used. This chapter concentrates on the first of these situations, to describe an approach to change that is representative of those approaches which are best applied in the relatively bounded situations described variously as difficulties, simple/unitarist systems or, in more straightforward terms, 'hard' situations.

Systematic approaches to change

Most people have the capacity to think logically and rationally. Indeed, some would say this is the only way to approach problem solving or respond to opportunities and, therefore, there can be one basic way of planning and implementing change. It is upon this premise that the more systematic approaches to managing change are based. Derived from earlier methods of problem solving and decision making such as systems engineering methods and operational research (Mayon-White, 1993), these 'hard' approaches rely on the assumption that clear change objectives can be identified in order to work out the best way of achieving them. What is more, a strict application of these approaches dictates that these objectives should be such that it is possible to quantify them, or at least be sufficiently concrete that one can know when they have been achieved. For instance, consider the situation described in Illustration 7.2.

Illustration 7.2

Dissatisfaction with the system for providing IT support services

Susan, a member of staff of the Faculty of Art and Design at Northshire University, was making a telephone call to the office of the IT support service to report that the computer link from her office to the resource centre was not working. As usual, there was no one there – she supposed the staff employed in the office were somewhere in the faculty fixing someone else's computer. She decided, therefore, to send an email but knew that because of the time it took to respond to individuals, it would not be dealt with by the IT support team before the next day. Even then, from past experience, she suspected that when it was received she would not get a response without at least one reminder and perhaps two. Overall she took a particularly dim view of the quality of IT support service provided and was sure that, if she were responsible for this service, she could improve its effectiveness without too much effort or many more resources.

Illustration 7.2 provides an example of what appears to be a difficulty about which most people could agree – it appears to have fairly defined boundaries. There are clearly some problems with the way IT faults are reported to the IT support service and the way they are responded to when they are received. It is also clear that some quantitative indices could be devised on which to judge the system and that might give evidence of improvement if this were to take place. What follows is, first, a generalized description of a model of change which is most suited to situations such as this – that is, in situations which are more of a difficulty than a mess and, second, a more fully worked-out example of its use to plan and implement change in the Beautiful Buildings Company.

The hard systems model of change

The methodology for change described here draws on a range of sources (Open University, 1984, 1994, 2000; Flood and Jackson, 1991; Paton and McCalman, 2008). To avoid confusion with the Open University's model, the 'systems intervention strategy' (SIS), and Paton and McCalman's 'intervention strategy model' (ISM), the approach described here is referred to simply as the 'hard systems model of change' (HSMC).

Change in three phases

The HSMC is a method that has been developed for designing and managing change. Its roots lie in methods of analysis and change associated with systems engineering, operational research and project management, that is, where there is an emphasis on means and ends – in other words, on the means with which particular set goals are to be achieved. The HSMC is especially useful when dealing with situations that lie towards the 'hard' end of the hard–soft continuum of change situations. It provides a rigorous and systematic way of determining objectives (or goals) for change; this is followed by the generation of a range of options for action; the last step is testing those options against a set of explicit criteria. The method is also useful where quantitative criteria can be used to test options for change. However, it is also possible to use qualitative criteria – a possibility that is discussed later in the chapter. The process can be thought of as falling into three overlapping phases:

1 The *description* phase (describing and diagnosing the situation, understanding what is involved, setting the objectives for the change).
2 The *options* phase (generating options for change, selecting the most appropriate option, thinking about what might be done).
3 The *implementation* phase (putting feasible plans into practice and monitoring the results).

Within these three phases a number of stages can also be identified. These are shown in Illustration 7.3. What follows describes the stages in more detail.

Illustration 7.3

Stages within the hard systems methodology of change

Phases	Stages	Actions appropriate for each stage
Description	1 Situation summary	Recognize need for change either to solve a problem or take advantage of an opportunity Test out others' views on the need for change Using appropriate diagnostic techniques, confirm the presence of hard complexity and a difficulty rather than a mess
	2 Identify objectives and constraints	Set up objectives for systems of interest Identify constraints on the achievement of the objectives
	3 Identify performance measures	Decide how the achievement of the objectives can be measured
Options	4 Generate options	Develop ideas for change into clear options for achievement of the objectives Consider a range of possibilities
	5 Edit options and detail selected options	Describe the most promising options in some detail Decide, for each option, what is involved, who is involved and how it will work
	6 Evaluate options against measures	Evaluate the performance of the chosen options against the performance criteria identified in Stage 3
Implementation	7 Develop implementation strategies	Select preferred option(s) and plan how to implement
	8 Carry out the planned changes	Involve all concerned Allocate responsibilities Monitor progress

The stages

Illustration 7.3 shows how the stages relate to the phases and provides an indication of likely actions at each stage. An important point to note, however, is that although Illustration 7.3 presents the phases and stages as a series of sequential steps that follow on logically one from another, this rarely happens so neatly in reality. Nor is it desirable, as Paton and McCalman (2000, p. 84) make clear when they say of their version of this approach: 'Iterations will be required at any point, within or between phases, owing to developing environmental factors.' There will, therefore, be times when there is a need for iteration, or 'backtracking', from one stage/phase to earlier stages/phases, as insights generated at later stages reveal the requirement for modifications to previous ones.

Phase 1: Description

Stage 1: Situation summary

The basic idea in Stage 1 is to start by describing the system within which change is going to be made. This is an important stage in the change process and should not be rushed. People who are centrally concerned with the change (those sponsoring it and those who will carry it out) should be consulted. Unless the specification of the problem and description of the situation are done carefully, the subsequent change objectives and process will be flawed. This stage includes the following:

- Stating the commitment to the analysis and the reason for doing it. For example, statements such as the following might be made:

  - commitment to ensuring the current product range is maintained after the takeover;
  - a commitment to developing new markets while maintaining market share for existing services;
  - a commitment to reducing the amount of floor space occupied by merchandise not achieving at least a 25 per cent profit margin;
  - a commitment to moving to another site or offices.

- Describing, in words and with diagrams, the situation within which changes will be set.

At the end of this stage the scope of the study will be defined, as will the range of problems and issues to be addressed. Try to defer, until Stage 4, thinking about *how* the change(s) will be brought about.

Stage 2: Identification of objectives and constraints

In the context of Stage 2, an objective can be defined as something that is desired; a constraint is something which inhibits or prevents achievement of an objective. In reality, objectives are likely to be things over which members of organizations may have some control. Constraints are frequently things in an organization's environment (whether this is internal or external to the organization) over which it has little control. This stage addresses both objectives and constraints. It involves being clear about where the decision makers want to go and which ways might be impassable or perhaps temporarily blocked. This stage involves the following:

- Listing objectives that are consistent with the themes which emerged from the diagnostic stage.
- Arranging the objectives into a hierarchy of objectives – an objectives tree. An example of a generalized objectives tree is shown in Figure 7.1. This shows how the high-level objective comes at the top, with lower-level objectives (sub-objectives) arranged in descending order. Lower-level objectives 'lead to' or help the achievement of higher-level objectives.
- Listing constraints in terms of those that (a) are inviolable and (b) may be modified.

Stage 3: Identification of performance measures

The question here is: 'How will I know whether or not I have achieved my objective?' If at all possible, use quantifiable measures, e.g. costs (in monetary terms), savings (in monetary terms), time (years, days, hours), amount of labour, volume etc. This stage includes the following:

● Formulating measures of performance, which can be put against the objectives on the objectives tree.

It is possible that some objectives cannot be quantified. In this case, some form of rating or ranking can be used as a measure of performance. Figure 7.2 is an example of an objectives hierarchy for improving the effectiveness of an organization's IT support service. The measures of performance for each of the main objectives are in brackets.

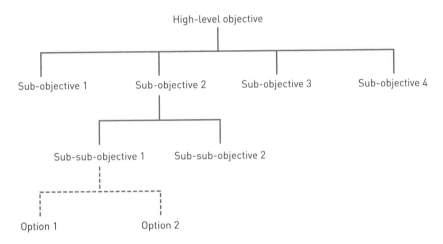

Figure 7.1 The structure of an objectives tree

Note: Some objectives may not be compatible – achieving one may mean sacrificing another. In other cases, some objectives may be linked to others – achieving one or more may be necessary in order to achieve another.

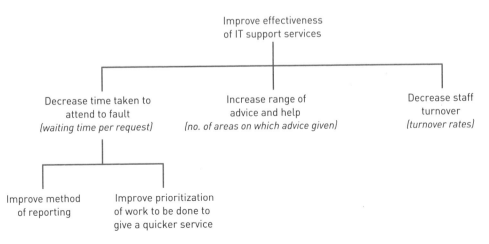

Figure 7.2 An objectives tree for improving the IT support services

Phase 2: Options

Stage 4: Generation of options (routes to objectives)

The setting of objectives to be achieved is based on the concept of *what* needs to be done to bring about change. By contrast, the generation of options stage is the stage of finding out *how* to achieve the objectives. If the objectives tree is well developed, as Figure 7.1 shows, some of the lower-level objectives may actually be options. There will, however, almost certainly be more. In addition, therefore, to any options that 'creep into' the objectives tree, this stage involves the following:

- Drawing up a list of options. This can be done by making use of any number of creative thinking techniques such as:

  - brainstorming;
  - ideas writing;
  - questioning others;
  - focus groups;
  - interviews;
  - research;
  - meetings;
  - organizational comparisons/benchmarking;
  - gap analysis.

At the end of this stage a set of specific ideas should have been generated which will help the problem or opportunity – in the sense that they will further the achievement of the objective(s), rather than that they will break the constraints, and lead to beneficial changes to the situation described in Stage 1. Figure 7.3 gives a list of options for the sub-sub-objective of 'improve prioritization of work to be done to give a quicker service' – which is one of the objectives in an objectives hierarchy for improving the effectiveness of the service given by an organization's IT department in support of those who use computer-based programs to help with their work.

Stage 5: Editing and detailing selected options

At the stage of editing and detailing some options, it may be necessary to sort the options, in terms of those that are likely to be feasible given the particular situation described in Stage 1 and the constraints identified in Stage 2. The selected options should then be described in more detail – or 'modelled' – in terms of what is involved, who is involved and how it will work. It may be that some options cluster together and are better considered as a group. Other options will stand independently and must, therefore, be considered in their own right. There are many ways of testing how an option might work. The following are some possibilities drawn from a comprehensive list produced by the Open University (1994, pp. 35–6):

(a) Physical models (architectural models, wind-tunnel test pieces etc.).
(b) Mock-ups (make mock-ups of new products – sewing machines, aircraft, clothes dryers etc.).

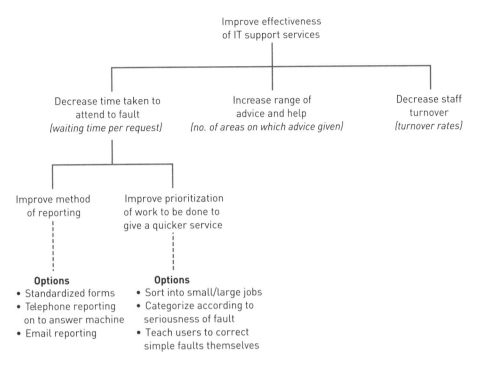

Figure 7.3 An objectives tree for improving the IT support services, with options generated for the two sub-sub-objectives

(c) Computer simulation models (for complex production systems, financial systems etc.).

(d) Cashflow models (either manually produced or computer driven).

(e) Experimental production lines, or laboratory-scale plant.

(f) Scale plans and drawings (alternative office layouts, organizational structures etc.).

(g) Cost/benefit analyses (as models of the likely trade-offs that would take place if a particular option were exercised; can be qualitative as well as quantitative).

(h) Corporate plans or strategies (any one plan or proposal represents a 'model' of how the corporation or organization could develop its activities in the future).

(i) Organization structure plans and proposals (for example, a chart of a new organization structure would show how the formal communication links or reporting channels would work if the structure were adopted).

(j) Organizational culture analyses (methods of describing organizational cultures as the means of identifying effects of different options on the culture of the organization).

Clearly, some of these processes can be time consuming and expensive. However, many options can be described or modelled through the use of diagrams (e.g. of different organizational structures, of input–output processes) or some form of cost/benefit analysis.

It is at this stage of the HSMC that each of the options generated for the objectives in Figure 7.3 would be explored in more detail, using the questions listed earlier about who would be involved, how it would work and what financial and other resources would be required for it to work. Some form of cost/benefit analysis could be used with costs and benefits being those of time as well as money.

Stage 6: Evaluating options against measures

The evaluation stage of the change process is a decision area. It allows choices of options to be made against the criteria identified in Stage 3. Figure 7.4 shows a generalized evaluation matrix that compares one option against another on the basis of the measures set during Stage 3.

Before making your recommendation, you should complete the following:

- Check that the model you have used is an accurate representation of the system.
- Consider whether the model seems to contain any bias or mistaken assumptions.
- Evaluate each option, or combination of options, according to how well it meets the performance measures. Rating the options overall on a scale (say of 1 for very good and 5 for very bad) is a useful guide.

Figure 7.5 is a rough estimate of the desirability of some of the options generated from the objectives in Figure 7.3.

A more detailed examination of each option in Figure 7.5 would show more precisely the impact, in terms of the performance criteria, on each objective listed. For the purposes of this example, however, an estimate has been made. On the basis of these, it is clear from the evaluation matrix in Figure 7.5 that some of these options could be combined. For instance, the best method of reporting should be combined with the best method for prioritizing work to be done. On this basis, option 2 combined with option 3 seem to contribute most to the main objective. However, if an email standard format of reporting were to be used, this would also help speed and accuracy in reporting faults. It could also include space for indicating urgency in terms of lack of access to the particular program affected. The only

Objectives and related measures of performance	Option A	Option B	Option C	Option D
Objective 1, measure 1				
Objective 2, measure 2				
Objective 3, measure 3				

Figure 7.4 An evaluation matrix

Objectives and related measures of performance	Options			
	Telephone reporting on to answer machine	*Email reporting*	*Categorization according to seriousness of fault*	*Use of written standardized reporting form*
Sub-objective Decrease time taken to attend to fault *(waiting time per request)*	Low cut in waiting time	Medium cut in waiting time	High cut in time for serious faults; low cut for simple faults	Low cut in time – delays through need to post
Sub-sub-objective Improve method of reporting *(fault reporting received more quickly and accurately)*	High increase in speed of reporting	High increase in speed and some increase in accuracy of reporting	No effect	High increase in accuracy of reporting
Sub-sub-objective Improve prioritization of work to be done *(serious faults dealt with first)*	Difficult to estimate	Small improvement	Great improvement	Some improvement

Figure 7.5 An evaluation matrix for some options to improve the effectiveness of the IT support services

problem with an email solution is it relies on this function not being the one at fault! If this is the case, written or telephone communication must be resorted to.

Phase 3: The implementation phase

Stage 7: Implementation

In problems of a definite 'hard' nature, implementation will rarely be a problem. With problems tending towards 'softness', implementation will be a test of how much people involved in the change have participated in its design.

There are three strategies for implementation:

1 Pilot studies leading to eventual change.
2 Parallel running.
3 Big bang.

Pilot studies help sort out any problems before more extensive change is instituted, but they can cause delay – a factor that is particularly important in a fast-moving, dynamic situation.

Parallel running applies most frequently to the implementation of new computer systems, but can be applied to other kinds of change. The new system is run, for a time, alongside the old system, until confidence is gained that the new system is reliable and effective.

Big bang implementation maximizes the speed of change, but can generate the greatest resistance. Big bang implementations carry a high risk of failure unless planned very carefully.

Implementation often involves a blend of all three strategies.

Stage 8: Consolidation – 'carry through'

It takes time for new systems to 'bed in'. It is at this stage that there tends to be a decline in concentration on the need to support the change, and nurture both it and the people involved. Yet this is one of the most crucial stages if the change is to be accepted and successful. Even after the implementation process further changes can be forced on the situation at any time if the imbalance between the system and the environment becomes too great. There is no justification for 'sitting back'.

Using the hard systems model of change

Illustration 7.4 describes concerns about the way large plant and machinery is acquired and maintained for use on the building sites of the Beautiful Buildings Company. What follows is a description of the process Gerry Howcroft went through to identify a number of options for improving this situation to put before the senior managers' meeting. The description takes the form of notes made by Gerry, interspersed with comments on the method he used.

Illustration 7.4

Financial savings on the provision and maintenance of plant for use on building sites

'The next item on the agenda is the issue of the increasing costs of providing and maintaining major items of plant on the UK building sites. At our last meeting we saw an earlier draft of this paper. We must now come to some decision as to which option to follow and how it will be implemented.'

So spoke Gillian Lambeth, the managing director of the Beautiful Buildings Company, at one of its regular senior managers' meetings. The next item on the agenda was the increasing costs of purchasing and maintaining large items of plant (such as cranes, diggers and earth-moving equipment) used on the various UK building sites. The item had come to the fore because of the latest rises in the cost of purchasing and maintaining some of these large items of plant, which were necessary components in any building project. What was more, in the case of plant breakdowns, getting the specialist maintenance services to effect speedy repairs was always problematical.

Gerry Howcroft, who was responsible for overseeing management of all the UK sites, had prepared a number of options for change that he believed would reduce these costs and improve the maintenance problems. These had already been discussed in rough form at a previous meeting. He had now gained more information on the costs etc. of following the different options and had distributed the latest version of these to the managers before the meeting. The meeting now settled down to discuss what to do.

Change at the BB Company

Gerry Howcroft's Note 1   21 May

Need to think back to that course on managing change.

Is this a difficulty or a mess?

Application of criteria discussed in the book they gave us (Senior, 'Organizational Change' – Chapter 2 – Illustrations 2.12 and 2.13) … situation is: bounded in terms of problem definition, people involved, timescale and resources available.

Plus – situation is like Stacey's conditions of 'close to certainty' rather than conditions of 'far from certainty' (also mentioned in Senior's book – Chapter 2).

Think, therefore, that this is more of a difficulty than a mess.

So – think will have a go at using the HSMC.

Stage 1: Summarizing the BB Company's concerns

As overall sites manager, Gerry was responsible for the acquisition and maintenance of plant and equipment deemed necessary for carrying out the complex activities that take place on any building site. In this role, he had to make sure that large plant such as cranes and diggers were fit to carry out the required work. This entailed his finding the best suppliers in terms of cost and service back-up and ensuring proper maintenance of the plant. Recently, however, the costs of maintaining two large cranes and a digger, which were currently being used on two different sites, had begun to escalate and it seemed as if costs generally for using plant such as this were rising. Gerry wondered whether the equipment had been ill-used or not well maintained or whether it was simply beginning to wear out. As part of the first stage of applying the HSMC he decided to visit the sites in question and talk to the site manager and any others who had views about the provision, use and maintenance of this type of plant. On his return he summarized his findings in another note (see Note 2).

Gerry Howcroft's Note 2   19 May

Visited Karen (site manager) at the Three Towers site. She said cranes such as these should last 'forever' if looked after. Think this far-fetched given the way the guys use them. Didn't seem to be anyone personally responsible for servicing and maintaining them – one of the men got some overtime each week to hose them down – if they broke down and the operator couldn't fix it, the service agent was sent for. On the other hand, Jed (who operated the crane all the time at the Riverside site) said his crane was just so old that, in spite of good maintenance it had 'had its day' – this in spite of Jed's obvious feelings of 'ownership' towards the crane!

Think there are many contributions to rising costs – a couple of diagrams might help – see Note 3.

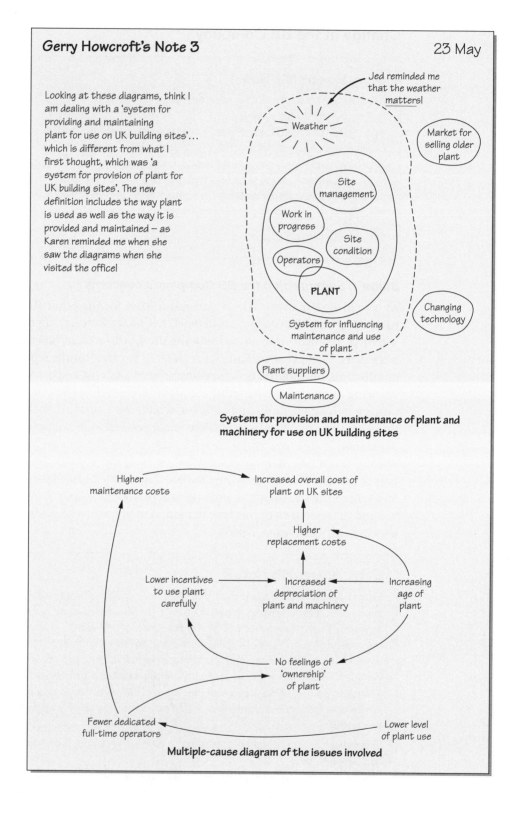

Gerry Howcroft's Note 3   23 May

Looking at these diagrams, think I am dealing with a 'system for providing and maintaining plant for use on UK building sites'... which is different from what I first thought, which was 'a system for provision of plant for UK building sites'. The new definition includes the way plant is used as well as the way it is provided and maintained – as Karen reminded me when she saw the diagrams when she visited the office!

Jed reminded me that the weather matters!

Weather

Market for selling older plant

Site management

Work in progress

Site condition

Operators

PLANT

Changing technology

System for influencing maintenance and use of plant

Plant suppliers

Maintenance

System for provision and maintenance of plant and machinery for use on UK building sites

Higher maintenance costs

Increased overall cost of plant on UK sites

Higher replacement costs

Lower incentives to use plant carefully

Increased depreciation of plant and machinery

Increasing age of plant

No feelings of 'ownership' of plant

Fewer dedicated full-time operators

Lower level of plant use

Multiple-cause diagram of the issues involved

Stage 2: Setting up objectives to be achieved and recognizing constraints

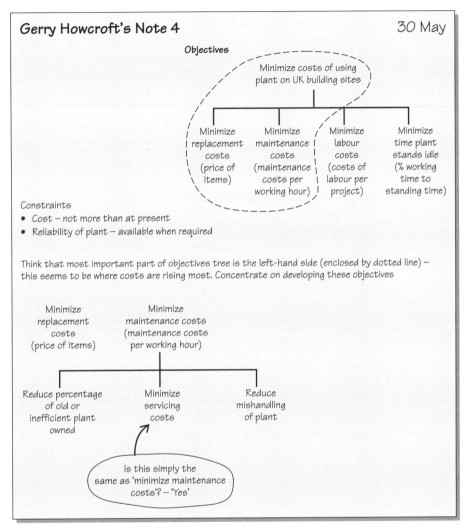

Having summarized the situation regarding the issue of plant costs, Gerry's next step was to build a hierarchy of quantifiable objectives. His Note 4 shows the results of this activity. Gerry did not find this activity particularly easy, given the requirement of the HSMC methodology that lower-level objectives should logically contribute to higher-level objectives and contribute overall to the top objective, in this case of 'minimizing the costs associated with the use of plant on UK building sites'. However, he recognized that some confusion of objectives was inevitable before a clear system of objectives began to emerge. Even so, he reminded himself that the characteristics of a good objective are as follows:

1 It should address the problem to be solved.
2 It must be relevant to the issues identified.
3 It should provide a guide on what needs to be done to make the change from the current situation to the desired situation.
4 It must be something that can feasibly be acted upon.

It can be seen from Gerry's Note 4 that he did not develop all the higher-level objectives into more detailed sets of sub-objectives. Given his knowledge of his management colleagues and their way of thinking, he made a decision to concentrate on the objective 'Minimize maintenance costs' to develop sub-objectives for further consideration, but also to consider the objective 'Minimize replacement costs'. With regard to the objectives 'Minimize labour costs' and 'Minimize time plant stands idle', he kept these 'in reserve' in case of need for further exploration of the issue.

Having developed his objectives hierarchy as far as he could in a direction thought feasible and achievable, the next step for Gerry was to develop further the measures of performance for the objectives identified (encircled) in Note 4.

Stage 3: Identify performance measures

Gerry Howcroft's Note 5	2 June
Objective	**Measure**
1. Minimize replacement costs	Cost of replacing item of plant over a specified period of time averaged out per year (assume cost of new plant for now).
2. Minimize maintenance costs	Cost of maintenance (includes servicing and repair) averaged out on a working hourly basis – i.e. does not include time standing idle.
3. Reduce percentage of old/ inefficient plant	Say no plant to be more than eight years old.
4. Reduce mishandling of plant	Difficult to measure. May have a look at training given – assuming training improves standard of plant handling. Another measure might be cost of maintenance per operator – easier to do when operator full time on plant. For now using a scale of 1 (low) to 5 (high) according to effect on plant might be okay.

Note 5 shows the table Gerry compiled to ensure he had some idea of how he would tell if and when an objective had been achieved. From Gerry's Note 5, it can be seen that some objectives are more difficult to quantify in *practice*, even if, theoretically, measures can be put upon them. In addition, the simple measure of 'price of items' for the objective 'Minimize replacement costs' was not sufficient. The cost needed to be expressed for a certain period of time, which could be related either to (say) a number of years or the period of a particular project. The measure for reducing mishandling of plant could, perhaps, have been formulated in monetary terms but, for the present, Gerry decided to use a scale to judge the likely effects of any option on this objective.

Stage 4: Generate options for change

Having set up some objectives to be achieved – hopefully, to improve the situation – Gerry's next step was to generate a range of options that would enable the objectives to be achieved. He did this by asking Kerry, one of the site managers, and the accounts manager to help in 'brainstorming' ideas for change. The results of this brainstorm are shown in Note 6.

Gerry Howcroft's Note 6   6 June

Options for change

Objective:	Minimize replacement costs
Options:	Find cheapest supplier
	Stop buying plant
	Increase replacement time
	Get someone else to replace the plant
	Hire not buy
	Lengthen life of plant
	Buy second-hand
Objective:	Reduce percentage of old/inefficient plant owned
Options:	Sell everything over a certain number of years old
	Sell everything not used on a regular basis and hire occasionally as required
	Replace old plant with new plant more frequently
	Don't own any plant
	Borrow plant from others
Objective:	Minimize servicing costs
Options:	Reduce number of services per period of time (say operating hours)
	Obtain cheaper provision of services
	Don't service at all
	Operators do all servicing rather than just basics
	Use other people's plant, which they service
	Contract out servicing to lowest bidder
Objective:	Reduce mishandling of plant
Options:	Train operators in plant handling
	Institute operator gradings (linked to pay) based on handling performance
	Contract out operating to operators employed by specialist agencies

---

Stage 5: Edit options and detail selected options

Gerry considered all these options in the light of the constraint of maintaining a high level of reliability of plant. It seemed that the options might reduce to a few main themes. At this point Gerry decided to try out the options list on a couple of colleagues (one of whom was the company accountant) to see which they thought might be feasible. He also used his own judgement. He eventually arrived at a list that included some options as they stood, amalgamated others and eliminated yet others (see Note 7).

Gerry Howcroft's Note 7   9 June

Themes emerging from options list

- Finding a cheaper source for buying plant (either new or second-hand)
- Don't buy plant – hire or borrow
- Use only plant which is less than eight years old (or whatever period seems appropriate considering rise in repair and maintenance as age increases)
- Increase the period of time before replacement
- Service plant less frequently than at present
- Train operators to do all servicing and maintenance
- Contract out operating to specialist firms
- Offer incentives for better operating practices

Comments

Some of these options contradict each other, so if one is taken up another might be automatically cancelled – e.g. 'Increase time before replacement' conflicts with 'Use plant eight years old or younger'.

Given the importance the MD attaches to safety on sites, I am going to go for options that are in line with her concerns and which meet the constraint of 'reliability of plant'.

For the time being, therefore, I am going to turn an objective into a constraint and work to have plant that is no older than eight years.

Within these constraints, the following seem worthy of further consideration.

1 Continue buying own plant (search for cheapest deals) with maintenance outsourced.
2 Continue buying own plant with maintenance done by own staff.
3 Continue buying plant that is used continuously and hire other for occasional use: maintenance of own plant done by own staff.
4 Continue buying plant that is used continuously and hire otherwise but outsource maintenance of own plant.
5 Hire all plant with maintenance as part of the deal.
6 Offer incentives for good performance in plant handling.

I guess there are more permutations but, depending on how the costings come out on these, we can look at those later.

As Note 7 indicates the options available seemed to range from, at the one extreme, the BB Company's owning and maintaining all plant to, at the other extreme, hiring (or leasing) plant that was maintained entirely by the suppliers. A number of possibilities were clearly possible between these two. The options listed as 1 to 5 are a mix of these. What is evident from the range of possible options is that some quite detailed information is required before one option can be evaluated against another. In addition, option 6 might only be relevant if one of options 1 to 4 were chosen. If option 5 were chosen, incentives to operate the plant well might not be thought relevant if all maintenance costs were included in the hire contract.

Stage 6: Evaluate options against measures

The method of evaluating options against the measures of performance associated with each of the objectives to be reached varies according to the type of options generated. For example, if the options are different production systems, not only would these have to be evaluated on cost measures, but they might also involve evaluation through building some simulations of the different systems. These could, of course, be physical models but they could also be computer models. For Gerry's purposes, it was possible to construct an evaluation matrix that allowed comparison of options one against another in terms of the measures of performance for the defined objectives. Note 8 is a record of Gerry's first attempt, on very limited information, at an evaluation matrix.

Gerry Howcroft's Note 8   16 June

Objectives and related measures of performance	Options					
	1 Continue buying own plant with maintenance outsourced	**2** Continue buying own plant with maintenance by own staff	**3** Continue buying continuously used plant and hire plant that is used only occasionally: maintenance of own plant done by own staff	**4** Continue buying continuously used plant and hire otherwise: outsource maintenance of own plant	**5** Hire all plant with maintenance as part of the deal	**6** Offer incentives for good plant-handling performance
Minimize replacement costs (£ per year)	High cost	Medium cost	Medium cost	Medium cost	Medium cost	Low cost
Minimize maintenance costs (£ per working hour)	High cost	Medium cost	Medium cost	Medium–high cost	Medium cost	Low cost
Reduce mishandling of plant (scale of 1 to 5 – 1 being least effective, 5 being most effective)	1	3	2	1	1	4

Need to give some information on this to the senior managers' meeting on 23 June – only a week away!
Have got only limited information on options – still, can make some guesses at this point and will take the views of colleagues as to which options to pursue – then must get better information on hiring etc.

Gerry took copies of the first draft of the evaluation matrix to the senior managers' meeting. The outcome of the discussion of what he had prepared was that he should get more information on options 3, 4 and 5, which involved different levels of hiring plant instead of purchasing it. What Gerry had to do, in effect, was to go back to Stage 5 to get more detail about these options before preparing a final evaluation matrix. This took some time, what with getting information from the finance department (only to discover that it was not kept in a 'user-friendly' form!) and from companies that hired out plant and equipment. Eventually, however, having gathered as much information as he could, he prepared a final evaluation matrix for discussion at the meeting referred to in Illustration 7.4.

The outcome of that discussion is recorded in Gerry's Note 9.

Gerry Howcroft's Note 9   5 August

What a long discussion, which went round and round in circles – difficult to decide between one option and another – the evaluation matrix was very helpful but then decisions are not always perfectly logical!

Eventually, decided on the hiring option with maintenance all-in – however we could not change overnight to this from where we are at present – just purchased a new digger on the Blackton site.

Will need to do a thorough survey of the state of plant on all the sites to determine when to make the changeover to hiring.

Interesting that the meeting decided to retain our own operators for now (even though could get an agency to supply these) – so will start talks with Personnel as to how we might give extra training and/or offer incentives to improve operator performance – after all, the maintenance costs part of the hiring contract is dependent on the amount of maintenance needed – large repairs will incur extra cost.

Seems an implementation strategy is required!

Stage 7: Develop implementation strategy

Gerry realized that the 'big bang' strategy for implementing change was not viable for his situation. Some of the plant had only recently been purchased, while other items were some years old. Overall, plant on the various sites was in different states of repair. Gerry therefore decided to go for the 'parallel running' implementation strategy where older and/or poorly maintained plant was replaced first. This would also offer the opportunity of monitoring the costs of hiring against owning *in reality* as against the theoretical case that the options had presented. If, after all, the savings proved negligible or negative, another evaluation of options could be done.

One good thing about retaining the company's own operators was that there were likely to be few problems from the workforce on the changeover. What might happen, however, was the occasional hiring of plant plus operator when it was required for a limited, short period. This would give a chance to see how such hirings were received generally.

Stage 8: Carrying out the planned changes

For Gerry and the other senior managers the changes, when implemented, will need monitoring. Changing from purchasing plant to hiring it may not mean much change in the way plant is operated on the building sites. However, the changes in the way maintenance and repairs are carried out will require operators and site managers to learn a new system of reporting and getting these done.

One of the benefits of going through the processes involved in applying the HSMC methodology was that Gerry realized how little monitoring of the costs of plant usage had been done up to the change. When trying to obtain the costs of the different ways of providing and maintaining plant, he became very much aware of the diffuse nature of much of the information he wanted. From now on, he was going to make sure that the finance department arranged its systems so that the commitment of large expenditure such as this could be monitored. This would, of course, mean yet more change, but in a different part of the organization.

Further uses for the hard systems model of change

The HSMC has been posed as a methodology for change that is most appropriately used in situations of hard complexity, or what have been termed difficulties. The case study involving Gerry Howcroft and the BB Company illustrates this use. In Gerry Howcroft's case, there is reason to believe that resistance to the planned changes will not be high. However, this is not always the case, as the discussion in Chapter 6 showed. Whenever and wherever possible, therefore, those people who are likely to be affected by the change should be consulted as early as possible. In addition, support from senior management is essential for any but the most localized, operational types of change.

It was clear that, in Gerry's case, the information he needed to construct an informative evaluation matrix was not easily obtainable – particularly with regard to that which he required from his own organization. This stage of the methodology can, therefore, be quite long if a realistic evaluation of options is to be done. By the same token, it is possible to go through the stages of the methodology quite quickly to address key factors associated with the change situation. A small group of people could quickly drive a way through this methodology to suggest at least a tentative solution in a situation requiring change. In addition, as Paton and McCalman (2008, pp. 121–22) point out:

> A Q & D (quick and dirty) analysis can be a useful starting point for the change agents tackling a more complex problem. It will indicate key factors and potential barriers to change, it will highlight the principal players and give an indication of resource requirements. Such an analysis will at an early stage set the scene for things to come and provide the change agents with a valuable insight into the complexities of the transition process.

An example of using the HSMC in this 'quick and dirty' way, that is as a starting point to an analysis of more messy situations, is given in Illustration 7.5 and Figures 7.6 and 7.7. These demonstrate the early stages in considering how to expand the provision and delivery of open and resource-based learning in the further education colleges run by the local education authority of 'Shire County'.

Illustration 7.5

Change in the further education colleges of Shire County

The question of how to expand the position and delivery of learning brought forth the following commitment statement:

In an environment of decreasing numbers of 16–19-year-olds and limited numbers of adults participating in further education, the aim for the future is to make it possible for more people to participate in education and training through the expansion of open and resource-based learning (O&RBL) both as an integral part of mainstream provision as well as an alternative but equally credible way of facilitating and accrediting learning.

A causal-loop diagram (see Figure 7.6) was constructed to provide further information about the forces operating for and against the desire to expand O&RBL. From this a range of objectives were formulated, together with a list of possible measures of performance.

An initial attempt at an objectives hierarchy is shown in Figure 7.7.

Possible measures of performance (not particularly attached to specific objectives):

- Establish O&RBL centres by ? (date).
- Extend availability of provision to 48 weeks per year by ? (date).
- Achieve x% of open and resource-based learners by ? (date).
- ? (number) of companies using O&RBL by ? (date).
- ? (number) of staff trained in the delivery of O&RBL by ? (date).
- ? (number) of students gaining qualifications through O&RBL by ? (date).
- Complete changeover to providing mathematics instruction in modules by ? (date).
- ? % increase in use of O&RBL in all mainstream provision by ? (date).

Existing state of affairs

- Falling numbers of 16–19 year olds coming into further education (FE)
- Only small percentage of adults participating in FE
- Current FE provision not always accessible to needs of adults in terms of content, qualifications and mode of delivery

GAP

Desired state of affairs

- Increase proportion of 16–19 year olds in FE
- Significant increase in number of adults in FE
- Improve accessibility for all learners, but for adults in particular, i.e. greater choice of content, qualifications and mode of delivery relevant to educational and training needs

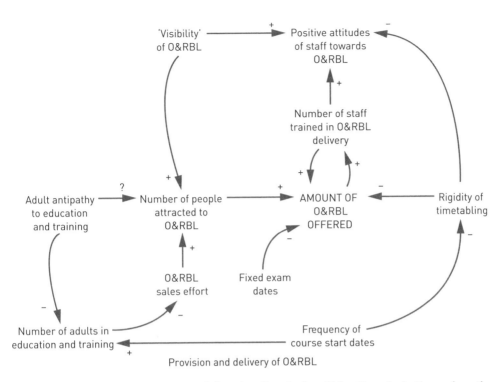

Figure 7.6 Causal-loop diagram of the situation facing Shire County further education services

Note: The + signs denote a causal relationship in the same direction. The − signs denote a causal relationship in opposite directions

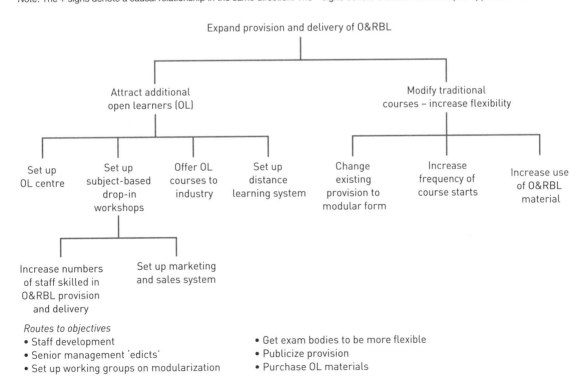

Figure 7.7 Hierarchy of objectives for expanding O&RBL provision in Shire County

Conclusions

The hard systems model for change provides a practical approach designed to be applied to situations – such as the Beautiful Buildings Company example – of low to medium complexity (difficulties). It is particularly useful when an area of the organization may need to be changed but may not infringe on other areas and when choices based on rational decision making can be made (see March's 1984 theories of choice and decision making).

The HSMC can also be effective to begin to diagnose a change situation (see Illustration 7.5) before categorizing it into more simple or more complex change. For instance, using the HSMC in the case of Shire County was useful for setting out the commitment to change, carrying out (with the help of diagrams) a situational analysis of the forces for and against the change and formulating some objectives and measures of performance in preparation for planning and implementing the change. What this methodology was less good at doing was identifying the political and moral issues surrounding the implementation of radical change of this kind. In addition, current organizational, professional and institutional cultures were clearly going to make changes of this kind difficult.

This was a case where the changes desired would take some time to come to fruition and would involve changes not only to the buildings and teaching areas (i.e. physical changes) but also to attitudes and behaviour – changes that would include both staff and students (present and potential students). The changes proposed here were more in line with what has been described as 'organizational development', that is, change that is ongoing, which involves most parts of the organization and most of its members and that will not succeed without the involvement of all concerned at all stages in the change process. The next chapter describes in more detail a change process more relevant to situations of soft complexity – in other terms, messes.

Discussion questions and assignments

1 Can you think of a time at work when a change that would be considered 'hard' or 'difficult' was not implemented as effectively as planned? If you were to apply the HSMC approach could you identify where things went wrong?

2 Can you think of change situations within your organization that are more difficult than messy, where the HSMC would be both appropriate and effective? What factors would you need to consider in order to ensure effective planning, decision making, implementation and review?

3 Considering issues raised in this chapter, under what circumstances might the HSMC not be appropriate and why? Could some of these issues be overcome so as to be able to use this phased approach?

 Indicative resources

March, J.G. (1984), 'Theories of choice and making decisions', in Paton, R., Brown, R., Spear, R., Chapman, J., Floyd, M. and Hamwee, J. (eds), *Organisations: Cases, Issues, Concepts*: London: Harper & Row. This text offers a critique of models for change which assumes that the process of choice is a rational one, based on having complete, or almost complete, knowledge of the alternatives which are generated. They argue that choices frequently involve moral as well as cognitive issues and that decisions about action, once made, are then overtaken by events which make implementation difficult if not impossible.

Open University (2000), *Managing Complexity: A Systems Approach*, Course T306, Milton Keynes: Open University, http://www3.open.ac.uk/courses/bin/p12 .dll?C01T306. This is an Open University course that draws on and extends a range of approaches to managing complexity which have been developed by internationally recognized systems practitioners. They include the soft systems method, the viable systems model and the hard systems method. Of particular relevance to the material in this chapter is Block 2, which discusses the hard systems approach.

Paton, R.A. and McCalman, J. (2008), *Change Management: A Guide to Effective Implementation* (3rd edn), Sage: London. This text reinforces the approach to change discussed in this chapter (see Chapter 5) and also discusses two more change approaches: 'Total project management' and 'The organization development model' (the latter of which is the subject of the next chapter). Particularly helpful is Chapter 4, 'Mapping change', which 'teaches' how to use diagrams effectively in diagnosing and implementing change.

Pollack, J. (2007), 'The changing paradigms of project management', *International Journal of Project Management*, 25(3), pp. 266–74. This paper offers a critical review of the literature that confirms strong links between the hard paradigm and project management. However, it also demonstrates that undercurrents exist in the literature, which suggest a growing acceptance of the soft paradigm. Models of the field are presented through which the influence of these paradigms on the field can be understood, and a way is suggested in which further developments in the use of the soft paradigm in project management could be progressed.

Useful websites

www.open.ac.uk This is the Open University website. There are links from here to information about all the courses it offers.

http://www.ukss.org.uk/ The UK Systems Society (UKSS) website. The UKSS is a non-profit-making, professional society registered as an educational charity. The Society is committed to the development and promotion of 'systems' philosophy, theory, models, concepts and methodologies for improving decision making and problem solving for the benefit of organizations and the wider society.

●●●● References

Flood, R.L. and Jackson, M.C. (1991), *Creative Problem Solving: Total Systems Intervention*, Chichester: Wiley.

March, J.G. (1984), 'Theories of choice and making decisions', in Paton, R., Brown, R., Spear, R., Chapman, J., Floyd, M. and Hamwee, J. (eds), *Organisations: Cases, Issues, Concepts*: London: Harper & Row.

Mayon-White, B. (1993), 'Problem-solving in small groups: team members as agents of change', in Mabey, C. and Mayon-White, B. (eds), *Managing Change (2nd edn)*, London: PCP.

Open University (1984), Block III, 'The hard systems approach', Course T301, *Complexity, Management and Change: Applying a Systems Approach*, Milton Keynes: Open University Press.

Open University (1994), 'Managing the change process', Course B751, *Managing Development and Change*, Milton Keynes: Open University Press.

Open University (2000), *Managing Complexity: A Systems Approach*, Milton Keynes: Open University Press.

Paton, R.A. and McCalman, J. (2000), *Change Management: A Guide to Effective Implementation* (2nd edn), London: Sage.

Paton, R.A. and McCalman, J. (2008,) *Change Management: A Guide to Effective Implementation* (3rd edn), London: Sage.

Chapter 8

Soft systems models for change

Through a revision of the concept of soft complexity, this chapter begins by challenging the notion of rationality as applied to organizational change. This is followed by a short description of Lewin's three-phase model of change as a prelude to a more detailed description and discussion of organizational development (OD) as an approach to change. Some limitations of organizational development as a change philosophy and as a change approach are discussed.

Learning objectives

By the end of this chapter you will be able to:

- recognize that some change situations (problems/opportunities), by nature of their complexity and particular characteristics, require soft rather than hard systems approaches to change;

- consider the philosophy, value orientation and theoretical underpinnings of OD as a generalized example of soft systems models for change;

- outline and describe the processes and practices that comprise most OD approaches to designing and implementing organizational change;

- critically review the limitations of OD approaches to managing change.

 ## Managing change in situations of soft complexity

The previous chapter ended with an example of the need for change for which the hard systems model for change (HSMC) had limited applicability. This was because the situation that gave rise to the requirement to expand open and resource-based learning in further education colleges in Shire County was characterized by both hard and soft complexity. As Chapter 7 highlighted, it was possible, using the HSMC, to build an objectives hierarchy with measurable performance criteria and to generate some options for bringing about the necessary changes. However, while this was fine in theory, other factors – the organizational culture, entrenched power bases and established leadership styles, as well as the simultaneous reorganization of the county education service that was driving the change – combined to make the process of change much more complex, diffuse and confused than it appeared at first sight. In summary, what faced those charged with bringing about the changes was much more of a mess than a difficulty, what Checkland and Poulter (2006) term 'problematic' (as opposed to problem), implying that a different approach to planning and implementing change was required.

In a chapter aptly named 'The art and science of mess management', Ackoff (1993) identifies three different 'kinds of things' that can be done about problems. He says (p. 47): 'They can be *resolved, solved or dissolved.*'

According to Ackoff: 'To resolve a problem is to select a course of action that yields an outcome that is good enough, that *satisfices* (satisfies and suffices).' This is an approach that relies on common sense, based on previous experience as to what might work or not and, to some extent, on trial and error. People who use this approach (and Ackoff says most managers are problem resolvers) do not pretend to be objective in their decision making. They use little especially collected data, either of a quantitative or qualitative nature, justifying their conclusions by citing lack of time or lack of information or too complex a situation for anything other than minimizing risk and maximizing the likelihood of survival. Ackoff calls this the 'clinical' approach to dealing with messes, a metaphor that emphasizes different people preoccupied with different aspects of the problem situation, but coming together to reach some consensus on how to proceed with resolving the problem. However, while this approach is likely to keep most people satisfied and 'on board' with the change, a major criticism is that, because of its commitment solely to qualitative thinking based on past experience and hunch, it lacks analytical rigour in its formulation of objectives and the means of evaluating them. Therefore it is never quite clear how far the objectives of the change have been met.

This criticism can certainly not be levelled at the 'solvers' of problems. By contrast with resolvers of problems, rather than using simple common sense and what might have been successful in the past, solvers of problems use approaches to problems that are much more heavily reliant on research-based scientific methods, techniques and tools. This means they eschew qualitative models in favour of quantitative models in their aspirations to be completely objective. Ackoff calls this the 'research' approach to mess management. It is much more likely to be used by management scientists and technologically oriented managers. This approach is akin to hard systems models of change in its emphasis on quantitative methods of analysis, objective setting and generation of options for change as demonstrated in the description of the HSMC in the previous chapter. However, while addressing the lack of 'hard' data in the clinical approach to mess management, the research approach is limited in that its techniques are more applicable to mechanistic systems (which lend themselves to performance definition and measurement) than to purposeful human behaviour (which includes many immeasurable elements). In addition, given that a mess is not just one problem but a complex set of problems interacting one with another, decomposing the mess to deal with one problem at a time (as this approach would suggest) loses the essential properties of the larger, more complex, whole. This is summarized well by Ackoff (p. 51):

> Therefore, when a research-orientated planner decomposes a mess by analysis, he loses its essential properties ... As a consequence, what he perceives as the hard facts of the mess are really soft fictions of his imagination, abstractions only loosely related to reality.

From this it seems that both resolvers, with their clinical approaches to bringing about change, and solvers of problems, with their research approaches to change, are limited in their capacity to plan and implement change in unbounded soft situations characterized as messes. Consequently Ackoff suggests a third approach, based on the concept of *dissolving* problems. Of this approach to problem solving he says (p. 48):

> To *dissolve* a problem is to change the nature, and/or the environment, of the entity in which it is embedded so as to remove the problem. Problem dissolvers *idealize* rather than satisfice or optimize because their objective is to change the system involved or its environment in such a way as to bring it closer to an ultimately desired state, one in which the problem cannot or does not arise.

He calls this approach the 'design' approach in that problem dissolvers, in addition to using the methods and techniques of problem resolvers and problem solvers, seek to redesign the characteristics of the larger system containing the problem (for instance changing the organizational culture, structure, systems and/or processes). Thus they look for dissolution of the problem in the wider containing system rather than looking for solutions in the contained parts. Ackoff (p. 48) maintains that only a minority of managers use this approach and they are those 'whose principal organizational objective is *development* rather than growth or survival, and who know the difference'. Of the concept of development he says (pp. 48–9):

> To develop is to increase and desire to improve one's quality of life and that of others. Development and growth are not the same and are not even necessarily related.

As an example of this he refers to the fact that a heap of rubbish can grow without developing and a person can develop without growing.

As the situation for change unfolded in the further education system in Shire County, it became evident that this was not a problem to be resolved or solved, but a complex set of problems that was likely to require the wider system containing it to be redesigned. In effect, what this system faced was not a problem in the 'something has gone wrong' sense, but a web of issues of interconnected parts that are likely to change and develop over time, frequently, depending on whose point of view is current. Even the objectives themselves were somewhat unclear and by no means shared by all.

It is not usual to find reference to 'dissolving' problems in the literature on change. Yet most of the change models associated with 'soft' situations and systems (i.e. those characterized by soft complexity) imply a need for redesigning systems at many levels of the organization. These include issues associated with individuals and the groupings they form, as well as with organizational strategy, structure and processes. This means not only an emphasis on the *content* and *control* of change (as the hard systems models of change dictate), but also an emphasis on the *process* by which change comes about, or as Buchanan and Boddy (1992, p. 27) maintain, a need for 'backstaging' as well as 'public performance'. In other words, there is a need to be concerned with what Buchanan and Boddy (p. 27) call 'the exercise of "power skills", with "intervening in political and cultural systems", with influencing negotiating and selling, and with "managing meaning".'

The consequences of this are that designing change in messy situations must also include attention to issues such as problem ownership, the role of communication and the participation and commitment of the people involved in the change process itself. It also means, as evidenced in the following section, challenging the notion that planning and implementing change can be wholly rational, a notion that the majority of hard systems models of change assume.

The challenge to rationality

For some time the literature on corporate strategy and strategic change (for example Balogun and Hope Hailey, 2008; Carnall, 2007; Stacey, 2008) has put forward arguments challenging the idea that people make decisions and choices according to some rational model of decision making. For example, rational models of change, with their associated scientific management techniques, overlook the significance of the cultural, political and cognitive dimensions of organizational life.

This is not to say, however, that people do not act rationally. It is to say (Carnall, 2007, p. 126) that they act according to their own view of what is rational for them. Carnall uses the example of 'clinical' rationality in healthcare, where rationality is apparent in the decisions of doctors that govern the pattern of care provided and the use of resources. This, however, does not mean that all doctors have the same views, beliefs or attitudes or that they would argue for the same vision of healthcare. This will include their particular perspective of the causes, consequences and need for change, moulded by their values, culture, attitudes and political position within the organization. Any case for change will not, therefore, be accepted according to some (supposedly) objective rational analysis. Change, in this scenario, will only be possible and effective if it is accompanied by processes that address, in particular, the feelings, needs and aspirations of individuals, the group processes that bind them together and the structures and systems that are forces for stability rather than change. Added to these are the cultural, political and symbolic processes that act to maintain the current organizational paradigm, or 'the way things are done around here'.

Given all this, it appears that hard systems models of change, although necessary in some defined and agreed situations, are not sufficient to explain organizational messes and are extremely limited in providing a model for planning and implementing change in these situations. For instance, hard systems approaches to change require the setting of quantifiable objectives against which they can be judged. This assumes that there is little argument about *what* the change objectives are. These approaches are useful in situations where change is sought to the *means* whereby things are done and where a problem can be *solved* in the terms discussed by Ackoff in the previous section. By contrast, one of the distinguishing features of organizational messes is that there is no agreement on what constitutes the problem, let alone what changes are required. Consequently it is more likely that those involved in these types of situations are looking to challenge not just the *means* of doing things, but also the *purposes* and *why* things are done and even if they should be done *at all*. In other words, they are searching for ways to *dissolve* rather than just *solve* problems, in Ackoff's terms. In summary, therefore, what this latest discussion leads to is an argument for an approach to change that can cope more effectively with situations of soft complexity – in other words some type of soft systems model for change.

There is neither the space nor the necessity to illustrate here all the different variants of models for bringing about change in soft, messy situations. What follows, therefore, is a generalized description of 'organizational development' (more commonly known as the OD approach) – an umbrella term for a set of values and assumptions about organizations and the people within them that, together with a range of concepts and techniques, are thought useful for bringing about long-term, organization-wide change; that is, change which is more likely to dissolve problems than resolve or solve them.

Organizational development – philosophy and underlying assumptions

According to French and Bell (1999, pp. 25–6) organization development is:

a long-term effort, led and supported by top management, to improve an organization's visioning, empowerment, learning and problem-solving processes, through an ongoing, collaborative management of organization culture – with special emphasis on the culture of intact work teams and other team configurations – using the consultant–facilitator role and the theory and technology of applied behavioral science, including action research.

Cummings and Worley (2013, p. 1) see organization development as:

A process that applies behavioural science knowledge and practices to help organizations build the capacity to change and achieve greater effectiveness, including increased financial performance and improved quality of work life. OD differs from other planned change efforts, such as project management or product innovation, because the focus is on building the organization's ability to assess its current functioning and to achieve its goals. Moreover, OD is oriented to improving the total system – the organization and its parts in the context of the larger environment that affects them.

More succinctly, they offer the following (Cummings and Worley, 2013, p. 2):

Organizational development is a system wide and transfer of behavioural science knowledge to the planned development, improvement, and reinforcement of the strategies, structures and processes that lead to organizational effectiveness.

An examination of these definitions confirms some distinguishing characteristics of the OD approach to change:

1 It emphasizes goals and processes but with a particular emphasis on processes – the notion of organizational learning (Senge, 1990; Pedler, Boydell and Burgoyne, 1991; Argyris and Schön, 1996) as a means of improving an organization's capacity to change.
2 It deals with change over the medium to long term, that is, change that needs to be sustained over a significant period of time.
3 It involves the organization as a whole as well as its parts.
4 It is participative, drawing on the theory and practices of the behavioural sciences.
5 It has top management support and involvement.
6 It involves a facilitator who takes on the role of a change agent (Buchanan and Boddy, 1992; French, Bell, and Zawacki, 2005).
7 It concentrates on planned change but as a process that can adapt to a changing situation rather than as a rigid blueprint of how change should be done.

In addition, French and Bell (1999, p. 29) give the following 10 OD principles:

1 OD focuses on culture and processes.
2 OD encourages collaboration between organization leaders and members in managing culture and processes.
3 Teams of all kinds are particularly important for accomplishing tasks and are targets for OD activities.
4 OD focuses on the human and social side of the organization and in so doing also intervenes in the technological and structural sides.
5 Participation and involvement in problem solving and decision making by all levels of the organization are hallmarks of OD.

6 OD focuses on total system change and views organizations as complex social systems.

7 OD practitioners are facilitators, collaborators and co-learners with the client system.

8 An overarching goal is to make the client system able to solve its problems on its own by teaching the skills and knowledge of continuous learning through self-analytical methods. OD views organization improvement as an ongoing process in the context of a constantly changing environment.

9 OD relies on an action research model with extensive participation by client system members.

10 OD takes a developmental view that seeks the betterment of both individuals and the organization. Attempting to create 'win/win' solutions is standard practice in OD programmes.

The discussion that follows develops these definitions and underlying philosophy and assumptions.

The significance of people in organizations

Employees have a large interest in learning within an organization. According to Argyris and Schön (1996), employees are an organization's building blocks and they provide an overview of the organizational memory. Argyris and Schön argue that there is a gap between what employees say they do (espoused theory) and what they do (theory in use). This concept is useful for understanding human behaviour when a situation changes. In single- and double-loop learning employees are notified of changes through orders, memos and directives issued by authorities. Unfortunately, this often leads to cynicism, de-motivation and defensiveness, which in turn lead to reduced cooperation.

The OD approach to change is, above all, an approach that cares about people and which believes that people at all levels throughout an organization are, individually and collectively, both the drivers and the engines of change. Consequently one underlying assumption is that people are most productive when they have a high quality of working life. In addition there is an assumption that, in many cases (and perhaps the majority), workers are under-utilized and are capable, if given the opportunity, of taking on more responsibility for the work they do and of contributing further to the achievement of organizational goals.

Paton and McCalman (2008, p. 166) offer three 'fundamental' concepts with respect to the management of people and gaining their commitment to their work and organization:

1 Organizations are about people.

2 Management assumptions about people often lead to ineffective design of organizations and this hinders performance.

3 People are the most important asset and their commitment goes a long way in determining effective organization design and development.

These assumptions are not new. Even so, many managers continue to practise Taylorism and scientific management – which in Matsushita's (1988) words means: 'executives on one side and workers on the other, on one side men [sic] who think and on the other men [sic] who can only work'. Yet Matsushita, drawing on his experience as head of the Sony organization, went on to say:

> We are beyond the Taylor model; business, we know, is so complex and difficult, the survival of firms so hazardous in an environment increasingly so unpredictable, competitive and fraught with danger, that their continued existence depends on the day-to-day mobilization of every ounce of intelligence.

The OD approach to change is entirely in line with these sentiments. What is more, these sentiments extend to a number of assumptions regarding people in groups. The first of these is that people are in general *social* beings. They will, therefore, form groups – whether these are legitimized by the organization in terms of formal work teams or whether they are the more 'informal' groupings that form part of every organization's functioning. French and Bell (1999, p. 68) reinforce this assumption by saying that: 'One of the most psychologically relevant reference groups for most people is the work group, including peers and boss.' Consequently the work group becomes increasingly important in any attempt at change. Yet in many cases work groups do not effectively utilize resources for collaboration. For instance, the formal leader of any group cannot perform all the leadership functions at all times and in all situations. Thus, for a group to become effective, all group members must share in problem solving and in working to satisfy *both* task and group members' needs. If work groups are managed in such a way as to engender a climate of mistrust and competition between participants, then any change will be seen as a threat rather than an opportunity and all the negative aspects of group functioning will come to the fore to work against the change. OD approaches to change assume, therefore, that work groups and teams are an essential element in the process of designing and implementing change. However, as individuals interact to form groups and other collective working relationships, so do groups interact and overlap to form larger organizational systems that, in their turn, influence an organization's capacity to learn and change.

The significance of organizations as systems

One of the characteristics of OD approaches to change mentioned earlier in the chapter is that it involves the organization as a whole as well as its parts – a characteristic exemplified by Pugh (1993, p. 109) when he refers to organizations as 'coalitions of interest groups in tension'. Chapter 1 introduced the idea that organizations are systems of interconnected and interrelated subsystems and components that include more formal organizational structures and processes as well as culture, politics and styles of leadership which are closely bound up with the values and attitudes people bring to their workplaces.

This idea is one of the most important assumptions of OD as a process of facilitating change. This is because, first, it reinforces the systemic nature of organizational life and the fact that changes in one part of the organization will inevitably impact on operations in another part. For instance, the multiple-cause diagrams used in previous chapters to depict a number of different change situations are good illustrations of the *interconnectedness* of causes and consequences of complex messy situations.

Second, and related to this, OD challenges the assumption that a single important cause of change with clear effects can be found, as well as the assumption that any cause and its effects are necessarily closely related in space and time. This is most clearly stated by Carnall (2007, p. 131):

> [The] causes of a problem may be complex, may actually lie in some remote part of the system, or may lie in the distant past. What appears to be cause and effect may actually be 'coincidental' symptoms.

Third, any organization is a balance of forces built up and refined over a period of time. Consequently, proposed change of any significance will inevitably change this balance and will, therefore, almost certainly encounter resistance. Consequently, OD approaches assume that no single person or group can act in isolation from any other. For instance, if win/lose strategies are common to the behaviour of management then this way of dealing with conflict will permeate other workers' attitudes to settling disputes and disagreements. By way of contrast, if managers openly discuss problems and take views on how these might be addressed, then this culture of trust and cooperation will reach into other parts of the organization's functioning – hence the belief that OD activities need to be led by top management if they are to succeed in bringing about successful change.

Fourth, because organization development as a concept is assumed to operate throughout an organization, the OD process is most definitely not a 'quick fix' to the latest management problem. This is articulated by French and Bell (1999, p. 75), who say that change 'takes time and patience, and the key movers in an OD effort need to have a relatively long-term perspective'.

Finally, OD approaches to change are essentially processes of facilitating *planned* change. Consequently, an effective manager of change:

> *anticipates* the need for change as opposed to reacting after the event to the emergency; *diagnoses* the nature of the change that is required and carefully considers a number of alternatives that might improve organizational functioning, as opposed to taking the fastest way to escape the problem; and *manages* the change process over a period of time so that it is effective and accepted as opposed to lurching from crisis to crisis.
>
> (Pugh, 1993, p. 109)

The significance of organizations as learning organizations

The ideas in the previous two sections (the significance of people in organizations and the significance of organizations as systems) come together in the assumptions that, for organizations operating in increasingly complex and turbulent environments, the only way to survive and prosper is to be a *learning organization*. For instance, most employees, if given the opportunity, have a large interest in learning within an organization, and it is through this that an organization can become a learning organization.

The concept of a learning organization is built upon the proposition that there is more than one type of learning. In support of this proposition Argyris (1964, 1992) and Argyris and Schön (1996) distinguish between *single-loop* and *double-loop* learning or, as Senge (1990) terms them, *adaptive* and *generative* learning. The concepts of single- and double-loop learning can be explained in terms of systems for change that are either goal oriented or process oriented (Open University, 1985). In brief, a goal-oriented approach to change is directed towards changing the means by which goals are achieved. By contrast, those who subscribe to a process-oriented approach to change, while still concerned with goals, focus more on fostering a change process that enables the goals to be challenged. In other words, goal-oriented approaches are concerned with doing things better, while process-oriented approaches are concerned with doing the right things.

With a goal-oriented approach, the problem or issue is likely to be seen as an interesting, though possibly substantial *difficult;* that is, it is perceived primarily as a technical and financial matter with a specific time horizon and hence fairly well bounded. The main focus is on increased efficiency of goal achievement. Management of this type of change is frequently done through a project team led by more senior managers concerned primarily with cost/benefit aspects (goals and constraints). A goal-oriented approach is analogous to thermostatically controlling the temperature of a heating system. The temperature is predetermined and the thermostat merely alters the means through which the temperature is maintained. In essence, what is not questioned is the initial setting of the goal. It is not difficult to see that goal-oriented approaches to problems, issues and change are basically congruent with hard systems models of change. Once the objective is identified, then the issue that remains is to establish the most efficient means of achieving it – hence the function of objectives trees as described in the previous chapter.

By contrast, within a process-oriented approach the problem is likely to be seen as distinctly *messy*. The changes might have long-term and, as yet, unforeseen ramifications, which make the formulation of goals and constraints problematic. The problem is much more concerned with changing the behaviour of people and the structures and cultures within which they work. A process-oriented approach starts by identifying who must be involved in the process, what sort of issues should be addressed and how all this can be facilitated. The phases of the project are by no means as clearly defined as in a goal-oriented approach. It may take some time before the problem itself is agreed, which will most likely challenge the goal itself. In these situations single-loop learning is necessary as a means of monitoring the performance of organizational systems and subsystems in relation to the objectives set for them. However, single-loop or adaptive learning, which depends mainly on individualistic learning, is not sufficient in situations that require creative thinking to develop new visions and ways of doing things.

Elkjaar (1999, pp. 86–7) speaks of 'social learning' and that it is necessary to participate and be engaged in organizational projects. In a good exposition and critique of the learning organization, Paton and McCalman (2008, pp. 296–7) summarize the views of double-loop or generative learning as expressed by the main writers on learning organizations/organizational learning as follows:

> They emphasize a collaborative, participative approach centred on team processes. They demonstrate a commitment to the creation of a shared vision of the future direction of the company and the necessary steps, structural and behavioural, to achieve that vision. They stress a proactive approach to learning, creating new experiences, continuous experimentation and risk-taking. Finally, they each emphasize the role of leaders to facilitate the change process and to foster a commitment to learning.

This quotation indicates that process-oriented/double-loop/generative learning involves issues associated with organizational structures, cultures and styles of leadership in terms of the capacity of these aspects of organizational life to

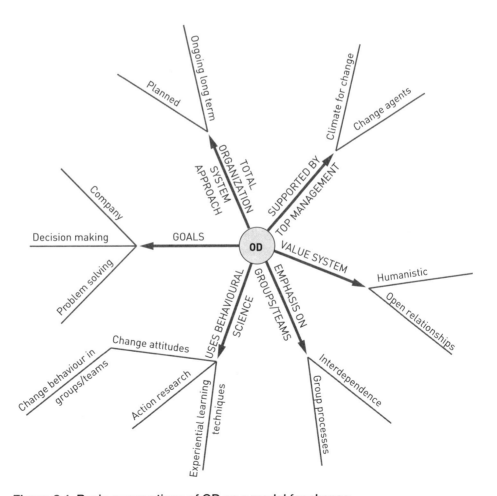

Figure 8.1 Basic assumptions of OD as a model for change

support and facilitate this type of learning. It certainly draws attention to many of the issues discussed in Part Two, the importance of people and the concepts associated with organizations as collections of subsystems interacting and reflecting the organizational system as a whole – concepts that are wholly in line with the organizational development approach to change.

Figure 8.1 summarizes the philosophy and underlying assumptions of OD as a process for facilitating organizational change. The remainder of this chapter attempts to spell out in more detail the nature of the OD process itself.

The OD process

OD is at heart a process of facilitation of organizational change and renewal. It operates at all levels of the organization – individual, group and organizational. It is a relatively long-term process for initiating and implementing planned change. It takes into account the messy nature of many organizational problems, which involve unclear goals and differing perspectives on what constitutes the problems, let alone how to solve them. It recognizes organizations as social entities where political as well as intellectual responses to change can be expected. What is important to remember is that although the stimulus for change in organizations generally comes from the external environment, the primary motivator for *how* change is accomplished resides with the people in the organization.

On the basis of these assumptions, organization development as a process for instigating, and implementing, change has two important characteristics. The first is that it is a process of change which has a framework of recognizable phases that take the organization from its current state to a new, more desired future state. Second, within and across these steps, the OD process can be perceived to be a collection of activities and techniques that, selectively or accumulatively, help the organization and/or its parts to move through these phases. The idea of phases can be most clearly demonstrated through a consideration of Lewin's (1951) three-phase model of change. This is followed by a more detailed description of OD as it has developed in more recent times.

Lewin's three-phase model of change

Most OD models of change consist of a series of phases or steps, although these probably do not happen as neatly as they are described. One of the earlier and most influential models of planned change that is still referred to extensively in the literature on change is Lewin's (1951) model of the change process, as mentioned in Chapter 6. What follows is a more detailed description of the three phases of *unfreezing, moving* and *refreezing*.

Unfreezing

The first of these phases – unfreezing – concerns the 'shaking up' of people's habitual modes of thinking and behaviour to heighten their awareness of the need for change. According to Cummings and Worley (2013, p. 22), this implies disturbing the status quo by either strengthening the forces that could *push* for change and/or weakening the forces which are maintaining the situation. This is likely to include the introduction of information showing discrepancies between desirable goals and modes of operating and what is currently happening. According to Goodstein and Burke (1993), it might even include selectively promoting employees or terminating their employment. For instance, in the case of Pitford College in Shire County (see Chapter 7, Illustration 7.5) a member of staff was promoted to director of open and resource-based learning (O&RBL). Other staff had their responsibilities changed to include 'tutoring' (rather than teaching) students working mainly in a self-service type of learning environment. All staff received news that a new O&RBL centre was to be built and that the timetables of all full-time students would be altered so that at least 20 per cent of their time would be spent learning in the new centre, using multimedia materials on a 'pick and mix' basis according to their needs. Part of this unfreezing process was the extensive consultation with heads of departments and other decision makers to discuss the new developments – which were seen as challenging the prevailing wisdom of how education and training in the further education sector should happen.

Another example of the application of OD to a 'frame-breaking' or 'transformational' change occurred when the 'Regional College', a student nurse training establishment, was forced to change the way it operated. Illustration 8.1 describes the beginnings of this process.

Illustration 8.1

Change at the Regional College of Psychiatric Nursing

Lewin's unfreezing process was evident in the environmental pressures which caused a school of nursing to review its entire mode of operation when the whole system of education for trainee nurses was changed. The courses leading to graduate status were to be centralized in another institution. Instead of simply allowing this school to close down, the director set out a case, to the relevant authorities, for the development of courses that would lead to the award of postgraduate masters level degrees, allowing the undergraduate level courses to move to the central institution. Her case was accepted which meant she had to set about the task of convincing her staff of the benefits of what was essentially 'frame-breaking/transformational' change. She recognized what the unfreezing phase of change

would entail. Staff would be 'shaken up' and their professional roles changed. Although some individuals might look forward to the change, others might not, fearing the additional training they would have to do to bring themselves up to a standard to teach at postgraduate rather than undergraduate level. All members of staff were to have their roles and terms of employment changed. She had to face the fact that some staff might leave or be 'persuaded' to do so. During the unfreezing process staff were likely to grieve for what they were losing in spite of those who might welcome the change.

Source: Grateful thanks go to Esther Warnett of the Berufsschule für Pflege, Switzerland for allowing us to draw on her experiences whilst researching and preparing her Doctorate in Education thesis.

Moving

The second phase of Lewin's change process – moving – is essentially the process of making the actual changes that will move the organization to the new state.

As well as involving new types of behaviour by individuals, this includes the establishment of new strategies and structures, with associated systems to help secure the new ways of doing things. In Shire County this involved a number of different activities. First, a series of staff seminars on the concept and operation of O&RBL were carried out. As a result staff were concerned with redesigning their courses to include at least 20 per cent delivery of learning on O&RBL principles. In fact, some staff planned to deliver certain learning programmes as *predominantly* O&RBL programmes.

In addition, in Pitford College and one of the other two colleges in Shire County, large new O&RBL centres were built with multimedia teaching and learning facilities. Dignitaries representing education, industry and commerce were invited to the opening ceremonies, which were used as a symbol for change as well as advertising the facilities to those who might support them. The inclusion of local employers' representatives emphasized the importance of providing for the needs of adult learners as well as those of the youngsters who had, traditionally, been the main 'customers' of these colleges. What is more, in the redefinition of teaching as 'facilitating learning' it was recognized that the managers of these new O&RBL centres did not necessarily have to be academics. This was further reinforced by associating the new centres very closely with existing library and computer services whose staff were not classed as academics.

Refreezing

Lewin's final phase in the change process – refreezing – involves stabilizing or institutionalizing the changes. This requires securing the changes against 'backsliding' and may include recruitment of new staff who are 'untainted' by the old habits. The continuing involvement and support of top management is crucial to this step. All of the elements of the cultural web (see Chapter 4) are important in establishing new ways of doing things. Once strategy, structure and systems have been changed it is equally important to reinforce the changes through symbolic actions and signs such as a change of logo, forms of dress, buildings design and ways of grouping people to get work done. The use of continuous data collection and feedback is essential to keep track of how the change is progressing and to monitor for further change in the light of environmental changes.

In the case of the colleges in Shire County, although the move to a culture of open and resource-based learning continued to some degree, it was constrained by a slackening off of commitment from top management as the environment in which the colleges operated changed yet again and brought new imperatives. Included in this were changes in the economic environment that brought changes in the political environment. These were increasing unemployment rates among young people and, as a result, a commitment on the part of government to increase training opportunities through funding full-time education provision for the 16–19 age group. In addition, there was an increase in training opportunities for adults. These opportunities frequently operated outside the further education system in the private sector, thereby, perhaps, lessening the requirement for more flexible provision within the further education colleges themselves.

Consequently the phase of 'moving' the current situation to the desired future one was never fully completed and the follow-through of refreezing – absorbing the change into the culture of the organization – was put in jeopardy.

Lewin's three-phase model of organizational change can be criticized mainly for its concept of refreezing, that is, the idea of cementing the changes in place to create a new organizational reality. While this aim to prevent the backsliding mentioned earlier is laudable, it tends to ignore the increasingly turbulent environment within which many modern organizations operate and the need for *continuous* change. In addition, Burnes (2004, p. 997), in his critique of the model, said that it assumed organizations operate in a stable state, it was only suitable for small-scale change projects, it ignored organizational power and politics, and was top-down management driven.

This should not, however, detract from the debt that current OD approaches owe to the work of Lewin and his colleagues. This debt is summarized by French and Bell (1999, p. 44) when they say: 'Lewin's field theory and his conceptualizing about group dynamics, change processes, and action research were of profound influence on the people who were associated with the various stems of OD.' This remains the case today.

Lewin's concept of organizational change as a *process* dominates much of OD theory, a view supported by Burnes (2004) in his recognition of Lewin's contribution to understanding group behaviour and the roles groups play in organizations and society. In addition, there is widespread recognition that organizations must carry out an assessment of where they are now, where they want to be in the future and how to manage the transition from the one state to the other. Where current theories of OD are leading, however, is to a realization that change is a process that is not linear and is itself complex and messy, including many loops back and forth from one stage in the process to another. The following description tries to capture the essence of this. However, because of the limitations in describing something that is so dynamic, the process may appear more mechanistic than it is in reality. It should be remembered that what is being proposed is only a framework within which many variations may occur.

OD – an action research-based model of change

According to Paton and McCalman (2008, p. 217), 'change is a continuous process of confrontation, identification, evaluation and action'. They go on to say that the key to this is what OD proponents refer to as an action research model. Coghlan and Brannick (2014) and Cummings and Worley (2015) give detailed descriptions of action research. Succinctly, it is a *collaborative* effort between leaders and facilitators of any change and those who have to enact it. It involves the following steps:

1 Management and staff perception of problem(s).
2 Data gathering and preliminary diagnosis by those concerned with leading the change (who can be internal and/or external to the organization).
3 Feedback to key people, management and those involved in the change.

4 Joint agreement of the problem(s).
5 Joint action planning.
6 Implementation of the change.
7 Reinforcement and continuous assessment of the change, which could lead to
   further data collection, rediagnosis and further action.

Therefore action research is, as its name suggests, a combination of research and
action. This means collecting data relevant to the situation of interest, feeding back
the results to those who must take action, collaboratively discussing the data to for-
mulate an action plan and, finally, taking the necessary action. Figure 8.2 shows
the action research cycles in their relationship to the main stages of the OD process.

A number of elements distinguish this approach from the hard systems model
of change discussed in Chapter 7. First, it is not a 'one-off' event, which ends when
a change has been completed. In describing the application of OD in a US electricity utility, Alpander and Lee (1995) illustrate this by saying: 'Organizations which
are successful in maintaining their competitiveness have learned to view change
not as a one-time event, but an ongoing process necessary to remain on the cutting edge in meeting customer needs.' This includes the ideas within the concept
of a learning organization discussed earlier. Second, it is an iterative or cyclical process that is continuous and which, if OD is taken as part of an organization's philosophy of action, continues as part of everyday organizational life. Third, each of
the components of the model (diagnosis, data gathering, feedback to the client
group, data discussion and work by the client group, action planning and action)
may be used to form each of the major phases that make up a typical OD process.

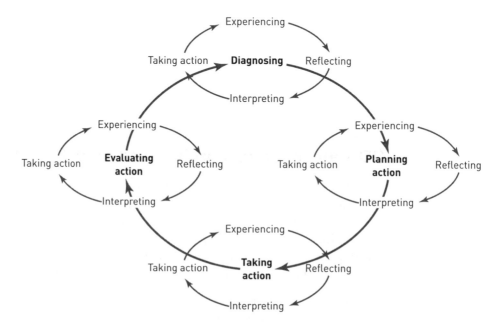

Figure 8.2 The General Empirical Method in Action Research projects

Source: Coghlan, D. and Brannick, T. (2014), *Doing Action Research in Your Own Organization* (4th edn), London:
Sage, p. 30.

Furthermore, as Figure 8.2 shows, these components may, collectively, form cycles of activity *within* each phase of the OD process.

Finally, the OD approach to change is firmly embedded in the assumption, that all who are or who might be involved in any change should be part of the decision-making process to decide what that change might be and to bring it about. It is not, as some hard systems models of change suggest, a project planned and implemented by senior managers or some designated project manager, with the assumption that other workers in the organization will automatically go along with it.

Building on the concept of action research, Figure 8.3, illustrates the major stages of the OD model. These are now described in more detail. It is important to note that change on the scale involved in most OD efforts does not succeed without some established facilitation function. Hence the emphasis on the role of the facilitator, or as termed here the *change agent*, as evidenced by positioning this person or group in the centre of the diagram. The role of the facilitator or change agent, who can be internal or external to the organization, is discussed later in the chapter. What follows first is a more detailed description of the stages that make up the OD model itself.

Stages 1a and 1b: The present and the future

An examination of Figure 8.3 shows two stages strongly linked together in a symbiotic relationship. Hence the labelling of them as 1a and 1b – that is, two processes that are, in effect, intertwined and which could be regarded as one. The reason for this is that it is never clear whether a change process should start with the development of a vision for change (that is, where the organization wants to be), followed by a diagnosis of where the organization is at present; or whether a start should

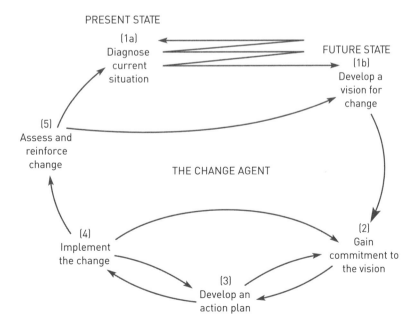

Figure 8.3 The OD model for change

be made with diagnosing 'what is', followed by statements about 'what could be'. For instance, Buchanan and McCalman (1989, p. 12), in their four-step model of perpetual transition management (trigger layer, vision layer, conversion layer, and maintenance and renewal layer) pose the 'trigger layer' (which examines environmental opportunities and threats) before the 'vision layer' (which defines the future). In contrast, Mabey and Pugh (1995) put as the first stage the process of agreeing the organization's purpose/mission. This is followed by an assessment of the organization's external and internal environments.

Coghlan and Brannick (2014, p. 10) refer to the need for a 'pre-step', which firstly examines the context of the change and its purpose. They ask the questions: 'Why is the change necessary or desirable?'; 'What are the economic, political and social forces driving change?'; 'In terms of the internal forces, what are the cultural and structural forces driving change?' By attempting to answer these questions, an assessment can be made as to their potency, and the nature of the demands they make on the organizational system. This helps to assess the degree of choice the organizational system, and those who work in it, have.

In reality, as the zigzag arrow in Figure 8.3 shows, the processes of diagnosis of the current situation and developing a vision for change, act in parallel. However, for ease of description, Stages 1a and 1b are discussed separately.

Activity 8.1

Compare the OD model for change shown in Figure 8.3 with the action research model shown in Figure 8.2.

What differences are there between the two?

Can you see how the small cycles within each major of Coghlan and Brannick's major phases might relate to the major stages of the OD model?

Stage 1a: Diagnose current situation

This stage is where an environmental analysis is carried out. In addition, as Chapter 1 discussed, the temporal and internal environments must be assessed. In an ideal world this would be done on an ongoing basis: (a) to detect strategic drift; and (b) to gather data on the organization's capacity to respond to a change in direction or ways of operating. However, sometimes it takes a crisis to trigger this type of diagnosis.

Diagnostic processes such as these clearly call upon the data-gathering component of the action research aspects of the OD model and the feedback of the results for discussion and verification by those concerned with, and involved in, the subsequent change. As mentioned earlier, in addition to data gathering about the organization's external environment, there is also a need for an examination of one or more things such as:

● organizational purposes and goals;
● organizational structure and culture;
● prevailing leadership approaches and styles;

- recruitment practices, career paths and opportunities;
- reward structures and practices;
- individuals' motivation and commitment to their work and organization;
- employee training and development provision;
- intra- and inter-group relationships.

The diagnostic stage forms the foundation for all the subsequent stages of the OD cycle. It is the beginning of the data collection process that will continue throughout the change process. It should provide information about the 'total system'. Data gathering, therefore, is done at the individual, group and organizational levels and should include those things that form barriers to organizational performance as well as those which contribute to organizational success. Table 8.1 provides a comparison of different methods of data collection. The data collected, particularly from carrying out interviews, making observations and engaging in other unobtrusive methods of data collection can be put together in a 'rich picture' (see Checkland's (1981) and Checkland and Poulter's (2006) description of soft systems). This can be constructed by the change leader or change agent but, as importantly, should also include those involved in the change. Rich pictures are particularly useful in gaining an understanding of a complex system from the

Table 8.1 Comparison of different methods of data collection

Method	Major advantages	Potential problems
Questionnaires	1 Responses can be quantified and easily summarized 2 Easy to use with large samples 3 Relatively inexpensive 4 Can obtain a large volume of data	1 No empathy 2 Predetermined questions/ missing issues 3 Over-interpretation of data 4 Response bias
Interviews	1 Adaptive – allows data collection on a range of possible subjects 2 Source of 'rich' data 3 Empathic 4 Process of interviewing can build rapport	1 Expense 2 Bias in interviewer responses 3 Coding and interpretation difficulties 4 Self-report bias
Observations	1 Collects data on behaviour, rather than reports of behaviour 2 Real time, not retrospective 3 Adaptive	1 Coding and interpretation difficulties 2 Sampling inconsistencies 3 Observer bias and questionable reliability 4 Expense
Unobtrusive measures	1 Non-reactive – no response bias 2 High face validity 3 Easily quantified	1 Access and retrieval difficulties 2 Validity concerns 3 Coding and interpretation difficulties

Source: Nadler, D. (1977), *Feedback and Organization Development: Using Data-based Methods*, Reading, Mass: Addison Wesley, pp. 156–8. Reprinted in Cummings and Worley (2009, p. 159) by permission – Pearson Education, Inc., Englewood Cliffs, NJ.

viewpoints of the people involved in the change situation. They are helpful in identifying issues regarding how people *think*, *feel* and *what they do* in terms of the *tasks* they perform, their *ways of working* and the *relationships* they have with each other.

The director of the college referred to in Illustration 8.1 worked with her staff to create a rich picture of the college systems and the staff's fears and hopes as the change began. The picture was displayed in the staff room and various members of staff added to it and changed it as the change process evolved. New rich pictures emerged along this process. These pictures acted as powerful tools to depict scenarios that would have been difficult to put into words. Many of the illustrations and activities in the chapters in Part Two are useful diagnostic tools for use at this stage in the change process.

Illustration 8.2 is a summary of the context for change at the Hardwater Mineral Water Company. This is also depicted in Figure 8.4 as a rich picture. From looking at the rich picture it can be seen that much more can be displayed than is evident in the account. However, this picture is a single person's first reaction to the situation they found themselves in. Rich pictures are typically drawn by more than one person in change contexts and, from these, a composite picture will emerge.

Illustration 8.2

The Hardwater Mineral Water Company Ltd

Part 1: The context of the change situation
The Hardwater Mineral Water Company Ltd (HMWC) was a regional bottler of mineral water located in an English region. The company was formed in the early 1990s and grew steadily and profitably over the ensuing 10 years under the ownership of the founders. Although it had some sales across the UK, the HMWC was essentially a regional company having the majority of its sales within a single region. In 2001, the HMWC was acquired by the 'Fishy Group', since when it consistently failed to make a profit. At the time of the acquisition, the Fishy Group was a well-established family business that for many years had been prominent in the regional fishing industry. As this industry declined, the company had diversified into the business of ice production and was one of the largest suppliers of ice-cubes in the UK, supplying most of the major retailers. It was the increasing demand for mineral water ice-cubes that led to the acquisition of the HMWC.

At the time of this acquisition, the Fishy Group owners, and family members and friends who were also employed, knew nothing about the UK bottled-water industry and market. Consequently,

the chairman brought in a new managing director and sales director (at very high salaries) with the task of bringing in new business and returning the company to a profitable trading situation. However, these two directors were nearing the end of their working careers and were more interested in the title of 'director' and associated salary and fringe benefits than working to develop the business.

Meanwhile, whilst the ice-cube business continued to operate profitably, the HMWC's products of flavoured water, which contained additives including preservatives and sweeteners, were losing market share fast. This was exacerbated by consumers and schools (where products with additives were banned) increasingly demanding additive-free products, but which the company had failed to introduce. The lack of effort on the part of the directors meant that much of the responsibility for bringing in new business fell on the sales manager with little support from those at a senior level. The sales manager's situation was not helped by the chairman's threats to close the business down unless it could generate a profit. Even if the HMWC had won a national contract, it would not have had the economies of scale necessary to compete on pricing, particularly given market competition from national and multinational brands.

By 2006, the chairman had sold off all the Fishy Group's fishing vessels and was spending most of his time aboard his private yacht. He effectively handed over the day-to-day control of the HWMC business to his daughter, who took over the role of managing director whilst still employing the 'other' managing director and the sales director, as well as the several family members and friends. In spite of now having three directors, HMWC had no sales and marketing strategy nor did it conduct market research to establish why sales and profitability were down. Instead they blamed the situation on the

sales manager and sacked him. Not long after that the original managing director and sales director left the company and the chairman's daughter, as the new managing director, took over management of the sales staff. This certainly lowered some costs. However, without a realistic sales strategy based on the changing market demands for additive-free products, together with a competent sales manager and 'field'-based sales executives experienced in the industry, sales continued to decline.

Figure 8.4 is a rich picture of the diagnosis of the 'messy' situation facing the HMWC, its managing director and staff.

Source: We are grateful to Andrew Cressey for this summary account and for the rich picture shown in Figure 8.4.

A more self-explanatory rich picture is that shown in Figure 8.5. This rich picture was the result of a group of people working together to depict how they perceived their situation at the start of a process of change.

Activity 8.2

Go back to Part Two of the book and, in conjunction with the list in Table 8.1, list those illustrations and activities you think might be useful for the process of carrying out a diagnosis of the current state of your organization or one with which you are familiar. On the basis of what you know about your place of work or one familiar to you, and if necessary in consultation with others, attempt to construct a rich picture. If this is not possible, imagine you are one of the sales staff at the Hardwater Mineral Water Company Ltd and use the account in Illustration 8.2 to construct a rich picture from your point of view.

It is clear that data collection and analysis are crucial to this stage in the OD process. It is important to note, however, the necessity for giving feedback on the findings to those from whom the data came, for further discussion and verification – a process particularly important in the case of data gained from the administration of questionnaires and through observation, where there is little interaction between questioner and questioned. This feedback process also serves the purpose of developing a vision for change – that is, where the organization wants to be in the future. Illustration 8.3 describes the techniques of data collection and feedback used by the director of the Regional College as she carried out the diagnostic phase of the change with her staff.

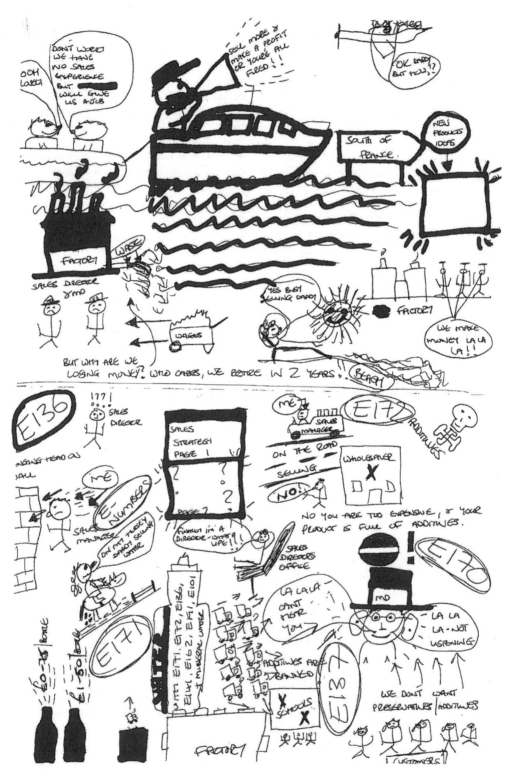

Figure 8.4 Rich picture of the Hardwater Mineral Water Company

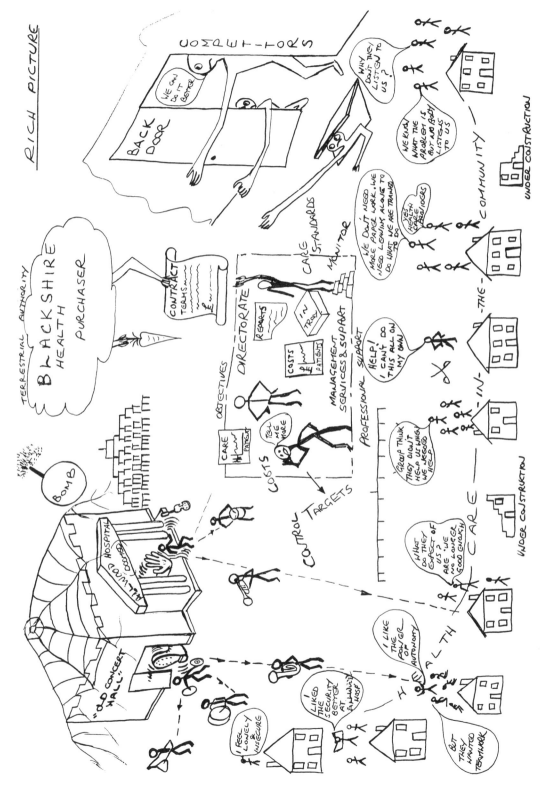

Figure 8.5 Rich picture of changes in the organization of services for people with learning disabilities

Illustration 8.3

Diagnosing the situation facing the Regional College of Psychiatric Nursing

In order to diagnose the situation facing the Regional College, the director undertook a series of exercises with her staff. First, she met with her four departmental heads (who, with the director, formed the School Committee) to analyze the external context for the change. Secondly, she used the concepts of 'difficulties' and 'messes' to identify those issues (difficulties) that were more easily managed and those (messes) that would be more problematical both for themselves and particularly for the other staff members. A month later, she called together all the 20 members of staff for a team day. She showed and discussed with them the results of the PEST analysis and shared and received their perceptions of the implications of the 'mess' they faced. In particular the staff agreed that they faced a situation that had: 'serious and worrying implications for all concerned' (see Chapter 2, Illustration 2.12). Most importantly, she was able to agree with the staff that the nature of change is sometimes perceived subjectively, as more 'frightening' than it is in reality.

Two months after she started the diagnostic stage, the director brought her heads of department together to take part in an exercise similar to constructing a 'rich picture', except this exercise used objects that could be arranged and rearranged to depict, in a three-dimensional way, what the group thought and felt about the problems and issues in which they were and would be involved. The fact that the objects could be picked up and moved about, allowed the group participants to change their representations and those of others and build on each other's ideas. In addition to these meetings and group exercises the director carried out one-to-one interviews with members of staff. She also had the results of an official questionnaire showing the staff's and students' perception of the learning climate and the strategy and leadership of the College.

The diagnostic stage of this first cycle in Regional College's change process ended with a meeting of the director and heads of departments to carry out a SWOT analysis (see Johnson, Scholes and Whittington, 2008): that is, an exploration of the organization's external environment for Opportunities and Threats and the internal environment for Strengths and Weaknesses. This process took account of the results of the meetings, exercises, interviews and the results of the questionnaire.

As the arrows in Figure 8.3, between the diagnosis and developing the vision stages, show, during these three months the vision for the college of becoming a postgraduate institution was accepted even though, as the director's reflections on this process show: 'the workload at the moment seems almost insurmountable'.

Source: Grateful thanks go to Esther Warnett of the Berufsschule für Pflege, Switzerland for allowing us to draw on her experiences whilst researching and preparing her Open University Doctorate in Education thesis

Stage 1b: Develop a vision for change

An organization's sense of what needs to change comes out of the process of organizational diagnosis and creative thinking. However, as we have already seen, this does not happen only when the diagnosis is complete. As the diagnosis proceeds and problem and success areas emerge, theories of what should be changed begin to form. These, in turn, bring demands for new information that will eventually move the process towards some definition of what the future should look like.

One way of looking at this stage of activity is to perceive it as a *creative* phase, in the sense that 'something or some process that is new' is being looked for. This might imply a different strategy in terms of products, services or markets. It might also imply a change in structure and culture – including the way people are managed and led. Flood and Jackson (1991) and Morgan (2006) suggest the use of metaphors as organizing structures to help people think about their organizations. The examples given are: organizations as machines, organisms, brains, cultures, teams, coalitions, prisons, instruments of domination and organizations in flux and transformation. Thus, Stage 1a would be concerned with identifying which metaphor best matched the current organization and Stage 1b would identify a metaphor to which its members might aspire. One implication of course is that the aspired to metaphor would likely imply a change to the underlying values of the organization.

Cummings and Worley (2015, pp. 184) say that:

> The vision describes the core values and purpose that guide the organization as well as an envisioned future towards which a change is directed. It provides a valued direction for designing, implementing and assessing organizational changes. The vision can also energize commitment to change by providing members with a common goal and a compelling rationale for why change is necessary and worth the effort.

Rather more picturesquely, Burnside (1991, p. 193) said:

> A vision can be described as a living picture of a future, desirable state. It is living because it exists in the thoughts and actions of people, not just in a written document. It is a picture because it is composed not of abstractions but of images.

On the concept of 'images', Burnside quotes Lievegoed (1983, p. 75) as saying: 'Images are more meaningful than abstract definitions. Images always have a thought content, an emotional value, and a moral symbolic value' and goes on to say: 'A vision is thus integrative because it brings these dimensions together.' According to Burnside there are two main aspects to visions: the strategic picture, which he calls the 'head' side, and the relational picture, which he calls the 'heart' side. Illustration 8.4 refers to a company that, when it was created, conformed closely to these ideas.

Illustration 8.4

The Body Shop's values

In 1976 reflecting the principles and vision of its main creator, Anita Roddick (now deceased), the first Body Shop, a retailer of skin care and fragrance products was opened. From this small beginning the company grew to its present size (as a manufacturer as well as retailer) of over 2,500 stores in over 60 markets worldwide.

The website (www.thebodyshop.com) sets out the company's values, which are: *'activate self-esteem'*;

'against animal testing'; *'protect our planet'*; *'support community trade'*; and *'defend human rights'*, *'The Body Shop Foundation'*, the latter of which gives financial support to organizations (frequently in developing countries) working in areas of human and civil rights, environmental and animal protection that otherwise have little hope of conventional funding.

Based on: The Body Shop, www.thebodyshop.com

Activity 8.3

Have a look at the Body Shop web site which elaborates on the list of values below, and consider how far you think these values meet the definitions of a vision as given above?

THE BODY SHOP'S VALUES

- Against animal testing business to the pursuit of social and environmental change
- Support community fair trade
- Activate self-esteem
- Defend human rights
- Protect the planet
- Ethical trade
- The Body Shop Foundation

This example of employee involvement in the development of an organization's vision underlines the close linking of Stages 1a and 1b and their combined outputs in identifying an organization's present and desired states in terms of two aspects of its functioning. These outputs are: first, the gap that represents the difference between an organization's current strategy and goals and those to which it must aspire in order to respond to the forces and circumstances of changing internal and external environments; second, the gap between what Benjamin and Mabey (1993, p. 182) call: 'the core values as they are related internally to the ethos of the organization'.

Stage 2: Gain commitment to the vision and the need for change

It is at the second stage of the OD process that feedback from the results of Stages 1a and 1b is most important. Unless those concerned and involved with the change have been consulted and have participated in the process to this point, there will be little incentive for them to 'buy into' the new vision and the change process that will follow it.

This stage is akin to the 'conversion layer' in Buchanan and McCalman's (1989) model of perpetual transition management – the one that follows the trigger and vision layers which were mentioned earlier. However, gaining recruits for the change is not easy, as Pugh's (1993) four principles for understanding the process of organizational change show (see Illustration 8.5 and Activity 8.4). These principles in turn draw attention to the need for managers to use many different and interacting ways to gain the commitment and involvement of all concerned in the change programme.

Pugh's four principles draw attention to the need for not just two-way but many-way communication as part of the process of gaining commitment to the vision and the need for change. This is one of the reasons why most descriptions of OD-type models of change emphasize the importance of managing resistance

---

Illustration 8.5

Pugh's principles and rules for understanding and managing organizational change

Principle 1: Organizations are organisms
This means the organization is not a machine and change must be approached carefully, with the implications for various groupings thought out. Participants need to be persuaded of the need for change and be given time to 'digest' the changes after implementation.

Principle 2: Organizations are occupational and political systems as well as rational resource-allocation ones
This means that thought must be given to how changes affect people's jobs, career prospects, motivation and so on. It also means paying attention to how change will affect people's status, power and the prestige of different groups.

Principle 3: All members of an organization operate simultaneously in the rational, occupational and political systems
This means that all types of arguments for change must be taken seriously. It is not sufficient merely

to explain different points of view. Rational arguments for change are as important as those which involve changes in occupational and political systems.

Principle 4: Change is most likely to be acceptable with people who are successful and have confidence in their ability and the motivation to change
This means ensuring an appropriate place (or set of people) from which to start the change and to ensure the methods used are relevant to those who are 'first in line' in accepting the change.

Source: Based on Pugh, D.S. (1993), 'Understanding and managing change', in Mabey, C. and Mayon-White, B. (eds), *Managing Change* (2nd edn), London: PCP, pp. 109–10.

Activity 8.4

Identify a major change in an organization with which you are familiar – preferably one in which you have been involved.

   Consider each of Pugh's principles and make notes regarding the following in terms of gaining people's commitment to the need for a new vision and associated change.

Principle 1

- *Were the implications for different groupings thought out?*
- *What (if any) methods were used to persuade people of the need for change?*

Principle 2

● *Was thought given to how the changes might impact on people's:*
  – positions and prospects?
  – status?
  – power?

Principle 3

● *Were the comments (supportive or otherwise) of different people and groups taken seriously and acted upon?*

Principle 4

● *How much effort was made to increase people's confidence in the new vision?*
● *How much effort was made to identify those people and groups who were most likely to 'spearhead' the change?*

through discussion, negotiation and active participation of those likely to have to make the changes. Established work groups and teams become particularly important at this stage, as is evidenced by French and Bell's (1999, p. 155) statement that:

> Collaborative management of the work team culture is a fundamental emphasis of organization development programmes. This reflects the assumption that in today's organizations much of the work is accomplished directly or indirectly through teams. This also reflects the assumption that the work team culture exerts a significant influence on the individual's behaviour ... Teams and work groups are thus considered to be fundamental units of organizations and also key leverage points for improving the functioning of the organization.

Consequently the process of gaining commitment to change must include working at the group level of the organization and recognizing the strength of influence of both formal and informal group leaders. In addition, it is more efficient of time and effort to communicate with individuals as groups than with them solely as individuals – even though this should not be the only means of communicating with them. It is not, however, sufficient merely to inform people of the vision and the necessity for change. This is because visions for change are rarely so clearly structured that information from all levels of the organization can be ignored. As Smith (1995, p. 19), writing on the realities of involvement in managing change, says: 'No top manager can know at the outset [of any change] exactly what needs doing, what information is needed, or where it is located.'

Jones (1994, p. 49), in his aptly named paper titled 'Which lever do I pull now?', talks of 'listening to the organization'. Reporting research with top management on the reasons why large-scale programmes of change often fail, Smith (1995) says that nearly all the managers interviewed reported on how much they had underestimated the importance of communication. However, as Jones says, this is not simply a question of senior management shouting louder from the top. This will not identify and bring to the surface the doubts that people have and their fears of what change might mean for them. Neither will it bring to the surface any problems with implementing the vision that top management may not be able to see for themselves.

Far from shouting from the top, the action research cycle of collecting and analyzing data and feeding back the results should be maintained here, as in the previous stages, to avoid widespread alienation of the workforce from the need to change and the vision to which it relates. Lloyd and Feigen (1997, p. 37) neatly summarize the dangers of not doing this when they say: 'Vision statements only work when the needs of those at the bottom of the organization are integrated upwards with the needs of the market.' Accomplishing this means being sensitive, not only to people's worries about the way tasks and structures may be affected by the change, but also to what Mabey and Pugh (1995, p. 36) term the 'emotional readiness for change, the quality of existing relationships and the latent commitment to new ways of working'. Otherwise, any plan for action has little chance of being successfully implemented.

Stage 3: Develop an action plan

The development of an action plan can be thought of as beginning the phase of managing the transition from an organization's current state to its desired future state, as shown by the 'journey to the future' zigzag in Figure 8.3. However, it also continues the process of gaining commitment to the vision but with a somewhat changed emphasis on *how* that vision can come about.

A number of issues are important in this stage of the OD process. One is the issue of *who* is to guide the planning and, later, the implementation of the change. Another is the issue of precisely *what* needs to change to achieve the vision, while a third is *where* any intervention should take place. The following explores these issues in more detail.

The role of a change agent

The success of using an OD approach to facilitate change rests on the qualities and capabilities of those who act as the facilitators of change. Moving organizations from current to future changed states is not easy and requires knowledge and skills that some managers might not possess. In addition, many managers are often so close to the day-to-day issues and problems of managing that they find it difficult to stand back from the current situation of *managing* to take on the role of change agent as well. For these and other reasons, such as the need for managers, themselves, to learn how to manage change, many writers on change advise that a change agent, who is external to the organization, is necessary. However, the change agent as facilitator of change does not necessarily have to be from outside the organization, as the director of the Regional College of Psychiatric Nursing (see Illustrations 8.1 and 8.3) demonstrates. She was the director of the organization and the change it had to make, as well as the change agent within an OD process. Coghlan and Brannick (2014) discuss the issues involved in a single person occupying dual organizational and change agent roles. They discuss how internal change agents' existing relationships with others will alter alongside changes in the agents themselves. Whilst Figures 8.2 and 8.3 do not explicitly demonstrate the role of reflection in each stage of the process, both external and internal change agents should keep a reflective diary that records their thoughts and emotions as well as actions proposed during the change cycles.

Apart from engaging an external change agent or using an internal change agent, it is not unusual to involve someone from another part of the organization, not the one that is the focus of the change. Indeed some large organizations have departments or divisions that are specifically set up to act as OD consultants to the rest of the organization. What should also be borne in mind is that all the skills and competencies required of a change agent might not reside in one individual. It might, therefore, be preferable to use more than one person or, in the case of large-scale change, a team of people.

Buchanan and Boddy (1992) give a helpful list of the competencies of effective change agents, based on research on how managers deal with change (see Illustration 8.6) which is reminiscent of the characteristics of 'transformational' leaders (see Chapter 6). However, this list must be considered in the context of how it came about. The evidence for constructing the list came mainly from questioning project managers – that is *internal* change agents who were concerned with changes in their own project areas. Perhaps, because of this, it emphasizes more the *content* of the change and how to get ideas accepted, rather than the *process* skills of consultation and participation which form an essential part of the facilitation role. In this respect it can be compared with Paton and McCalman's list of the roles taken on by effective change agents (Paton and McCalman, 2008, p. 232):

1 To help the organization define the problem by asking for a definition of what it is.
2 To help the organization examine what causes the problem and diagnose how this can be overcome.
3 To assist in getting the organization to offer alternative solutions.
4 To provide direction in the implementation of alternative solutions.
5 To transmit the learning process that allows the client to deal with change on an ongoing basis by itself in the future.

Illustration 8.6

Competencies of an effective change agent

Goals

1 Sensitivity to changes in key personnel, top management perceptions and market conditions, and to the way in which these impact the goals of the project in hand.
2 Clarity in specifying goals, in defining the achievable.
3 Flexibility in responding to changes outwith the control of the project manager, perhaps requiring major shifts in project goals and management style and risk taking.

Roles

4 Team-building activities, to bring together key stakeholders and establish effective working groups and to define and delegate respective responsibilities clearly.

5 Networking skills in establishing and maintaining appropriate contacts within and outside the organization.
6 Tolerance of ambiguity, to be able to function comfortably, patiently and effectively in an uncertain environment.

Communication

7 Communication skills to transmit effectively to colleagues and subordinates the need for changes in project goals and in individual tasks and responsibilities.
8 Interpersonal skills, across the range, including selection, listening, collecting appropriate information, identifying the concerns of others and managing meetings.
9 Personal enthusiasm, in expressing plans and ideas.
10 Stimulating motivation and commitment in others involved.

Negotiation

11 Selling plans and ideas to others, by creating a desirable and challenging vision of the future.
12 Negotiating with key players for resources or for changes in procedures and to resolve conflict.

Managing up

13 Political awareness, in identifying potential coalitions and in balancing conflicting goals and perceptions.
14 Influencing skills, to gain commitment to project plans and ideas from potential sceptics and resisters.
15 Helicopter perspective, to stand back from the immediate project and take a broader view of priorities.

Source: Buchanan, D. and Boddy, D. (1992), *The Expertise of the Change Agent*, Hemel Hempstead: Prentice Hall, pp. 92–3.

In contrast to the concept of a change agent, Kotter (1996) uses the concept of a 'guiding coalition' and suggests four key characteristics as being essential for it to be effective:

1 *Position power*: Are enough key players on board, especially the main line managers, so that those left out cannot easily block progress?
2 *Expertise*: Are the various points of view – in terms of discipline, work experience, nationality etc. – relevant to the task at hand adequately represented so that informed, intelligent decisions will be made?
3 *Credibility*: Does the group have enough people with good reputations in the firm so that its pronouncements will be taken seriously by other employees?
4 *Leadership*: Does the group include enough proven leaders to be able to drive the change process? (Kotter, 1996, p. 57).

It is clear, however, that the guiding coalition cannot, by itself, cause widespread change to happen. What it can do is to set targets for change that, collectively, will move the organization and its members much closer to realizing the vision which was developed in Stage 1b and further refined in Stage 2. Having done this, the issue becomes: '*Who is to do what, with what kind of involvement by others?*'

Responsibility charting

Beckhard and Harris (1987, pp. 104–8) developed a technique called 'responsibility charting' that assesses the alternative behaviours for each person or persons involved in a series of actions designed to bring about change. They describe the making of a responsibility chart as follows:

> Responsibility charting clarifies behaviour that is required to implement important change tasks, actions, or decisions. It helps reduce ambiguity, wasted energy, and adverse emotional reactions between individuals or groups whose interrelationship is affected by change. The basic process is as follows:
>
>> Two or more people whose roles interrelate or who manage interdependent groups formulate a list of actions, decisions, or activities that affect their relationship (such as developing budgets, allocating resources, and deciding on the use of capital) and record the list on the vertical axis of a responsibility chart [see Figure 8.6]. They then identify the people involved in each action or decision and list these 'actors' on the horizontal axis of the form.

The actors identified can include:

R = the person who has the *responsibility* to initiate the action and who is charged with ensuring it is carried out.

A = those whose *approval* is required or who have the power to veto the decision. This could be the responsible person's superiors.

S = those who can provide *support* and resources to help the action to take place.

I = those who merely need to be *informed* or consulted but who cannot veto the action.

Certain ground rules are set out when making a responsibility chart. French and Bell (1999, pp. 172–3) summarize these as follows:

1 Assign responsibility to only one person. That person initiates and then is responsible and accountable for the action.

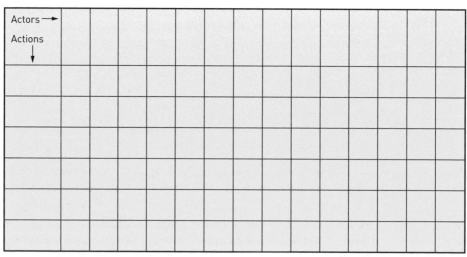

Key :
R = Responsibility (not necessarily authority)
A = Approval (right to veto)
S = Support (put resources towards)
I = Inform (to be consulted before action but with no right of veto)

Figure 8.6 Example of a responsibility chart

2 Avoid having too many people with an approval–veto function on an item. That will slow down task accomplishment or will negate it altogether.

3 If one person has approval–veto involvement on most decisions, that person could become a bottleneck for getting things done.

4 The support function is critical. A person with a support role has to expand resources or produce something that is then used by the person responsible for the action. This support role and its specific demands must be clarified and clearly assigned.

5 Finally, the assignment of functions (letters) to persons at times becomes difficult. For example, a person may want A–V (approval–veto) on an item, but not really need it; a person may not want S (support) responsibility on an item, but should have it; or two persons each want R (responsibility) on a particular item, but only one can have it.

This discussion of responsibility charting illustrates the 'chicken and egg' nature of planning organizational change. While it is right to consider who will lead and participate in implementing change, this has to be done in conjunction with what needs to change.

Activity 8.5

Identify a change initiative in which you have been involved (or one with which you are familiar). You may find it helpful to use the example identified in completing Activity 8.4.

To give you practice in using a responsibility chart, list some of the actions associated with that change and assign the people involved according to their responsibility role(s).

Consider whether Beckhard and Harris's ground rules for assigning roles were adhered to. If not, did this cause confusion of responsibilities and/or impede action?

The what and where of change

Pugh (1986) devised a matrix of possible change initiatives based on the different issues that can hamper change and the level at which they occur. Figure 8.7 is a reproduction of what has become known as the 'Pugh OD matrix'.

The matrix can be used to help with action planning (as represented by the initiatives listed in italics) about: (a) the type of intervention required to facilitate change in line with the organization's vision (represented by the columns); and (b) the level at which it should take place (represented by the rows). For instance, at the level of the individual, problems may be occurring because there are few opportunities for promotion from the job of factory-floor supervisor to higher levels of management, salespeople see no reason to change given their current bonus plan, and many middle managers have made their jobs to suit their own needs rather than those of the organization. Problems at the inter-group level might include marketing and production arguing about the feasibility of setting up a new production line to satisfy what the marketing staff consider to be a market opportunity. Intervention is frequently required at the organizational level when

	Behaviour (What is happening now?)	**Structure** (What is the required system?)	**Context** (What is the setting?)
Organizational level	General climate of poor morale, pressure, anxiety, suspicion, lack of awareness of, or response to, environmental changes *Survey feedback, organizational mirroring*	Systems goals – poorly defined or inappropriate and misunderstood; organization structure inappropriate – centralization, divisionalization or standardization; inadequacy of environmental monitoring – mechanisms *Change the structure*	Geographical setting, market pressures, labour market, physical condition, basic technology *Change strategy, location, physical condition, basic technology*
Inter-group level	Lack of effective cooperation between sub-units, conflict, excessive competition, limited war, failure to confront differences in priorities, unresolved feelings *Inter-group confrontation (with third-party consultant), role negotiation*	Lack of integrated task perspective; sub-unit optimization, required interaction difficult to achieve *Redefine responsibilities, change reporting relationships, improve coordination and liaison mechanism*	Different sub-units' values, lifestyle; physical distance *Reduce psychological and physical distance; exchange roles, attachments, cross-functional groups*
Group level	Inappropriate working relationships, atmosphere, participation, poor understanding and acceptance of goals, avoidance, inappropriate leadership style, leader not trusted, respected; leader in conflict with peers and superiors *Process consultation, team building*	Task requirements poorly defined; role relationships unclear or inappropriate; leader's role overloaded, inappropriate reporting procedures *Redesign work relationships (socio-technical systems), self-directed working groups*	Insufficient resources, poor group composition for cohesion, inadequate physical set-up, personality clashes *Change technology, layout, group composition*
Individual level	Failure to fulfil individual's needs; frustration responses; unwillingness to consider change, little chance for learning and development *Counselling, role analysis, career planning*	Poor job definition, task too easy or too difficult *Job restructuring/modification, redesign, enrichment, agree on key competencies*	Poor match of individual with job, poor selection or promotion, inadequate preparation and training, recognition and remuneration at variance with objectives *Personnel changes, improved selection and promotion procedures, improved training and education, bring recognition and remuneration in line with objectives*

Figure 8.7 The Pugh OD matrix

Source: From Course P679 'Planning and Managing Change', Block 4, Section 6. Copyright © The Open University.

an organization's structure prevents the emergence of, let alone action upon, initiatives that could be beneficial to the organization as a whole.

Beckhard and Harris (1987, p. 73) suggest the following organizational subsystems – any of which can be considered as a starting point for change:

- *Top management:* the top of the system.
- *Management-ready systems:* those groups or organizations known to be ready for change.
- *'Hurting' systems:* a special class of ready systems in which current conditions have created acute discomfort.
- *New teams or systems:* units without a history and whose tasks require a departure from old ways of operating.
- *Staff:* subsystems that will be required to assist in the implementation of later interventions.
- *Temporary project systems:* ad hoc systems whose existence and tenure are specifically defined by the change plan.

Activity 8.6

What similarities and differences can be found between Pugh's levels of analytical focus and Beckhard and Harris's list of subsystems for intervention?

In addition to the issue of where change interventions might take place, the planning of OD interventions must also take account of the degree of change needed that is the scope of the change activities. In terms of Pugh's OD matrix, this means considering whether:

(a) people's *behaviour* needs to change; and/or
(b) the *organization's structure and systems* need to change; and/or
(c) the *context or the setting* needs to change.

According to Mabey and Pugh:

> The first (left-hand) column is concerned with current behaviour symptoms which can be tackled directly. Since it suggests methods and changes which address the symptoms without intervening into the required system or setting, this column comprises the least radical of the development strategies. Indeed in some cases the results may not be recognized as change at all – merely as overcoming some difficulties in the proper workings of the current system. Thus in one application, as the result of a team-building exercise with a Ward Sister and her staff, the functioning of the ward, the morale of staff, and the standard of patient care all improved. The Hospital Management Committee regarded this process not as a change, but one of getting the organization to work properly.
>
> But it may be that this degree of intervention is not sufficient to achieve the required aims. It could be that, however improved the group atmosphere and

leadership style, the group will not function well because it is not clear what the organization requires of it, adequate information to carry out the group task is not available at the appropriate time, and the tasks are inappropriately divided and poorly allocated to the members of the group. In these circumstances, the second column, concerned with organizing the required system, is the appropriate degree of intervention. This is a greater degree of intervention because it may require change in the structure, systems, information flows, job design etc., which inevitably affects a much wider range of the 'organizational environment' of the particular group.

Even this degree of intervention may be insufficient. The problems may lie in the contextual setting (changing market pressures, physical distance, poor group composition, poor promotion procedures etc.). Then the degree of intervention in the third (right-hand) column is appropriate. This is a still greater degree of intervention requiring strategy changes, considerable expenditure of resources (both financial and human), and carrying with it greater likelihood of disruption with its attendant costs. It is not, therefore, to be undertaken lightly.

(Mabey and Pugh, 1995, pp. 40–1)

Mabey and Pugh go on to say that, as action moves from the left- through to the right-hand column, a greater degree of intervention and commitment is required. Consequently, they suggest starting at the left column of the matrix and moving towards the right only as it becomes necessary because of the dictates of the problem. Activity 8.7 offers an opportunity to become more familiar with the content of the matrix and how it might be used in planning change.

Activity 8.7

The best way to understand the Pugh OD matrix is to apply its different 'cells' to a real organizational example.

Choose a situation from your own experience where a need for change has been established.

Go through the matrix and note which cells are appropriate for starting interventions that will help in the change process.

If you find this too difficult to start with, look at the following list of organizational problems and activities and note in which of the Pugh matrix cell(s) you would place them.

1 *The accounts department who 'lived' on the top floor always seemed to be at loggerheads with the research and development team who were 'housed' in an outside annex.*
2 *Since the redundancies, which were mentioned wherever you went in the organization, people were moaning about the amount of work they had to do and the lack of recognition of this by senior management.*
3 *The staff in the post-room appeared bored with their jobs. Admittedly, the work was rather repetitive.*
4 *It took too long to get an answer to queries, because the boss had always to be informed.*
5 *The members of the project group felt abandoned and without leadership.*

As stated earlier, the process of developing an action plan for change should be done through consultation and collaboration with those who will implement the change, thus reinforcing commitment to change. Beckhard and Harris's (1987, p. 72) concept of the action plan being a 'road map' for the change effort is a useful one. In addition, they say that an effective action plan should have the following characteristics:

- *Relevance*: activities are clearly linked to the change goals and priorities.
- *Specificity*: activities are clearly identified rather than broadly generalized.
- *Integration*: the parts are closely connected.
- *Chronology*: there is a logical sequence of events.
- *Adaptability*: there are contingency plans for adjusting to unexpected forces.

The last of these characteristics is particularly important. As anyone knows, it is all well and good setting out on a journey with the route well defined beforehand. However, because of the many things that exist to thwart the best-laid plans (in the case of the journey: traffic, passenger sickness, road works, accidents and so on), the plan must be flexible enough to adapt to the changing circumstances of not only *what* needs to change, but also possible changes in the transition process itself. Consequently, as Figure 8.3 shows, the development of an action plan must always be linked closely to its subsequent implementation.

Stage 4: Implement the change

Any text dealing specifically with organization development as a change methodology contains details of different techniques and methods for initiating and implementing change (see, for instance, French and Bell, 1999; Cummings and Worley, 2015). For the present purposes, the activities in italics in the Pugh OD matrix in Figure 8.7 can be used to illustrate ways of initiating organizational change. As the matrix illustrates, these relate to the different levels of analytical focus and the scope of the change activities. The following gives additional details of those activities. It should be noted, however, that because these activities are mainly concerned with the behaviour column of the matrix, it *does not mean* that they are, necessarily, any more important than the activities concerned with structure and context. They are selected for further explanation simply because they may not be as familiar as some of the others.

Survey feedback

Surveys can be used to assess the attitudes and morale of people across the organization and are used at different stages in the OD process. At the implementation stage they are important for the effective management of the change. Feedback from surveys of those involved in the change activities helps stimulate discussion of what is working and what is not and should result in modifications to the action plan or the way it is being implemented or, sometimes, to a reorientation of the vision.

For example, Lloyd's of London, one of the City's prestigious financial institutions, carried out an employee opinion survey on the progress of a large-scale change programme, the results of which were fed back to the staff involved for further discussion and appropriate action. Clarke, Hooper and Nicholson (1997, p. 29), writing about this, say:

> The process was designed to demonstrate to people that the corporation was not just saying: 'Your views are important', but that it actually meant it. Not only was the management team prepared to listen, it would also distribute the results openly and honestly. More importantly it would act on the views expressed. Sophisticated timetabling, communications, objective setting and measurement ensured that this happened.

The survey was repeated 18 months later to identify progress on actions resulting from the first survey.

Organizational mirroring

'The organization mirror is a set of activities in which a particular organizational group, the host group, gets feedback from representatives from several other organizational groups about how it is perceived and regarded' (French and Bell, 1999, p. 186). Organizational mirroring is different from interventions at the inter-group level, being concerned with relationships between three or more groups. It is a technique that benefits from the services of a change consultant who is not connected with any of the groups involved in the process. A 'fishbowl' technique is frequently used as part of organizational mirroring. This is where the group asking for feedback (the host group) first sits and listens to what the other group representatives have to say (without interruption). The representatives of the host group and the other group then exchange places to allow the host group to have their say (ask for clarification, information etc.) without interruption. Finally, the representatives of both groups are divided into small sets to work together on problems that emerge before all coming together to devise action plans, assign people to tasks and set target dates for improvements to be completed.

The techniques of survey feedback are most frequently associated with gaining information on people's attitudes and behaviour. It should not be forgotten, however, that other types of information gathering will be just as important – for instance with regard to progress against financial and other quantifiable measures of organizational performance.

Inter-group confrontation (with third-party assistance)

Although a technique of 'confrontation' sounds alarming it enables two groups, which have their unique specialties, to confront organizational issues that go beyond their particular expertise. Mabey and Pugh suggest that an exercise such as this might require a day or so away from distractions and be helped by a 'neutral' facilitator. The objective is to help the members of the two groups increase their awareness of the importance of each other's activities to the overall organizational performance and thus reduce a sense of 'them and us'.

French and Bell, and Mabey and Pugh, suggest a process where each group is asked to produce two lists. The first is the complaints 'we' have against 'them'. The second is the complaints that 'we' think 'they' would have about 'us'. Lists are then shared between the two groups. According to Mabey and Pugh, two characteristics usually emerge. First, some of the complaints can be dissolved fairly quickly, being the result of simple misunderstandings or lack of communication. Second, the lists of both groups show a surprising degree of congruency; in other words 'we' know what they think about 'us' and 'they' know what we think about 'them'. The lists form the basis for further discussion and exploration of how conflict can be resolved and more positive working relationships established. Reference back to Illustration 5.10, in Chapter 5, which lists explanations of the different types of conflict, might help with the process of inter-group confrontation.

Role negotiation

Role negotiation is a technique developed by Harrison (1972). Basically it involves individuals or groups negotiating to 'contract' to change their behaviour on a *quid pro quo* basis. In general it requires the help of a facilitator and (typically) during a day's workshop session, each set of participants is asked to say what they want the others to *do more of, do less of* or *maintain unchanged*. A follow-up meeting a month or so later assesses progress and, if necessary, renews or sets up new contracts. It is important to note that this *does not* involve probing people's likes and dislikes about each other. It concentrates solely on the roles they play and their behaviour as part of these.

Process consultation

Schein (1998) regards process consultation (PC) as a central part of organizational development. According to French and Bell (1999, p. 164): 'The crux of this approach is that a skilled third party (consultant) works with individuals and groups to help them learn about human and social processes and learn to solve problems that stem from process events.' The kinds of interventions that are part of process consultation are: agenda-setting; feedback of observational data; coaching and counselling of individuals and suggestions about group membership; communication and interaction patterns; allocation of work, responsibilities and lines of authority. French and Bell say (p. 163):

> The process consultation model is similar to team-building interventions and inter-group team-building interventions except that in PC greater emphasis is placed on diagnosing and understanding process events. Furthermore there is more emphasis on the consultant being more nondirective and questioning as he or she gets the groups to solve their own problems.

French and Bell imply, in this discussion, that the consultant is someone external to the organization. This process, however, is also essential for internal change agents with the recognition that greater effort might be needed in order to undertake 'nondirective questioning'.

Team building

Team building is an essential part of the OD process. Individuals working together do so in many different ways – not all of which contribute to team effectiveness. Consequently issues such as the overall size of the team, the characteristics of its members, the focus and direction of the team and its role within the organization are important. In situations of change any or all of these might also need to change. Team-changing and team-building techniques can help in this.

Team-building techniques can be used for established long-term groups as well as for special, shorter-term project groups. Processes included in team building are:

(a) diagnosis of the task together with individuals' and group needs;
(b) diagnosis and negotiation of roles;
(c) responsibility charting;
(d) understanding and managing group processes and culture.

Usually a change agent or independent consultant/facilitator is used to help in team building.

Life and career planning

There are a number of exercises that can help in career planning, which is part of life planning. One is to draw a lifeline representing the past, present and future. Past events are positioned according to important things that have happened in life, including things done well and things done not so well – 'ups' as well as 'downs'. Future desired events are also recorded on the line, and some indication is given of time of achievement. Another exercise is to write one's obituary as if death were to occur now and then as if death were some years in the future. The last exercise is intended to give some idea of what is hoped for in the near and far future. The use of a life coach or mentor can be helpful in the application of these techniques.

Activity 8.8

Think back to the change which you identified for Activity 8.5. Which of the techniques (at any level or scope) in Pugh's OD matrix were used as the change was implemented? Were they appropriate?

The role of short-term wins

Implementing change that will ultimately transform an organization is a *long-term process* and it is understandable if commitment to the vision becomes somewhat weakened on the way. Consequently the achievement of 'short-term wins' (Kotter, 1996) is important, both as a motivating factor and as a mechanism for tracking the progress towards the longer-term goals. However, Kotter (1996, p. 123) goes further than this in identifying six ways in which short-term wins can help organizational transformations. These are:

● *Provide evidence that sacrifices are worth it:* wins greatly help justify the short-term costs involved.

- *Reward change agents with a pat on the back:* after a lot of hard work, positive feedback builds morale and motivation.
- *Help fine-tune vision and strategies:* short-term wins give the guiding coalition concrete data on the viability of their ideas.
- *Undermine cynics and self-serving resistors:* clear improvements in performance make it difficult for people to block needed change.
- *Keep bosses on board:* provides those higher in the hierarchy with evidence that the transformation is on track.
- *Build momentum:* turns neutrals into supporters, reluctant supporters into active helpers etc.

Short-term wins do not, however, happen automatically as part of the change process. They have to be planned *deliberately* so that they become much more probabilities than possibilities. According to Kotter (pp. 121–2), a short-term win has three characteristics:

1 It is visible: large numbers of people can see for themselves whether the result is real or just hype.
2 It is unambiguous: there can be little argument over the call.
3 It is clearly related to the change effort.

An example of a short-term win is when a company reduces delivery time on one of its main products by a predetermined percentage in a predetermined time; or when the number of customer complaints reduces by (say) 50 per cent during the first half of the year; or when the jobs of a group of employees become easier to do because they are getting more relevant information in a more timely way. Short-term wins are not targets; for example, 'We expect to increase our sales in the next couple of months'. Neither is the fact that two previously sworn enemies are now talking pleasantly to each other a short-term win, unless the outcome is some further improvement in morale and organizational performance.

The setting and assessment of short-term wins links the implementation stage of the OD process to the more all-embracing assessment of the organization's progress towards its vision and the continuing reinforcement of the change process itself.

Stage 5: Assess and reinforce the change

Assessing change

In organizational situations of hard complexity it is relatively easy to assess the extent to which change has been achieved. So the setting of 'hard' objectives and quantifiable performance measures makes this a more straightforward process. However, in the softer, more 'messy' situations where change methodologies of the OD type tend to be used, change is an evolving process concerned not only with changes in quantifiable performance objectives, but more frequently with changes in attitudes, behaviours and cultural norms where measurement is bound to be less precise. Even so, measurement of these things is possible. It is also desirable in terms of its role in providing positive feedback that the change process is 'working' and in testing how far the organization has moved towards achievement of its vision.

A number of ways are available for measuring the softer issues associated with change:

1 *A survey or cultural audit*, which can potentially cover all staff. Its results can be quantified and quickly disseminated. The audit can be done at regular intervals to provide repeated snapshot measures of an organization's progress towards its change objectives. The Nationwide Building Society is an example of an organization that uses such a system as part of its commitment to continuous improvement.

2 *Interviews with individuals or focus groups*, which allow the collection of more qualitative, in-depth information. An example of testing what a company's vision and values statement meant to staff was the exercise carried out by The Body Shop just after a public challenge to its integrity regarding its stance of being socially responsible in its policies and practices. The Body Shop called it 'gazing into the mirror'. It consisted of 44 meetings, each with 20 different staff and managers from all parts of the organization. All the meetings were attended by a board member and a moderator who later summarized the discussions to produce a report of the main themes arising and subsequent recommendations for action.

3 *An examination of turnover and absenteeism rates* as an indication of general morale and well-being.

4 *An analysis (through observation or questionnaire) of group performance* in terms of task achievement, but also in terms of the quality of meetings (including number of meetings and length) and leader performance.

5 '*Re-picturing the organization*', that is, asking staff to re-draw any rich pictures that they might have produced at Stages (1a)/(1b) of the OD process (see Figure 8.3). Re-picturing might also include the use of metaphors in line with those suggested by Morgan (2006) (see Stage 1b earlier in this chapter). In contrast to the pictures and metaphors that depict the pre-change situation, the rich pictures that are drawn at this stage in the change process should relate more closely to the change vision. If this proves to be so, then management can have some confidence that the change has been successful in respect of how employees feel about it.

Reinforcing and consolidating change

Farquhar, Evans and Tawadey (1989, p. 49) noted that:

> A real danger in the process of organizational change is the failure to carry it through sufficiently far. Companies may be tempted to relax when the immediate crisis recedes while they still have not addressed the deeper organizational problems which generated the crisis.

The lesson from this is that the new order resulting from any change needs to be institutionalized. This is well put by Mabey and Pugh (1995, p. 50):

> Individuals need to be held personally accountable for prescribed initiatives; new working relationships and boundaries between different working groups need to be negotiated; ways of recognizing and rewarding desirable behaviours and attitudes need to be devised to demonstrate that the organization is serious about the change strategies that have been set.

It is pointless expecting people's behaviour to change if this is not reinforced by concomitant changes in personnel policies and practices, including appraisal, career development and reward systems. In addition, staff training and development needs to reorient itself to the needs of the new vision and the changes that help guide its attainment. According to Farquhar *et al.* (1989), this is particularly important with regard to middle managers. While change can happen fast at the top (often through bringing in new people) and be accepted at the lower levels of an organization (particularly if the rewards for change are clear), middle managers, who perform the bridging function between the two, may be slower to accept new cultures, policies and practices. Yet it is middle management that must make change work. They must, therefore, be given the new skills they will need – particularly when structures and cultures are expected to change.

More generally, the action research model of data collection, data analysis and feedback for action is just as important at this stage of OD as at any other. Any change programme is stressful, but if employees continue to *own* change this stress will become not negative stress but, rather, positive pressure to accept that change can be the norm, with the adoption of innovative, change-oriented behaviour.

An assessment of the OD model for change

The model of OD presented here departs to some extent from early OD models that emphasized mainly the attitudinal and behavioural aspects of organizational life and gave insufficient attention to aspects such as strategy, structure, technology and, in particular, the needs of customers or clients, let alone shareholders, and the financial environment within which most organizations operate. Not only has it drawn from these earlier models, but it has used elements of other, more directive change models such as Kotter's (1996, Part 2) eight-stage change process and Paton and McCalman's (2008, p. 12) reproduction of Buchanan and McCalman's (1989) model of perpetual transition management.

Even so, organization development as a philosophy and a process can be critiqued according to a number of criticisms. The following are examples.

OD does not always face up to harsh realities of change

Almost all models of change include, in one form or another, the underlying concept of unfreezing. From an OD point of view this would be achieved through a typical action research process of data collection, analysis and feedback as part of a participatory process of education for change. Yet authors such as Clarke (1994) and Johnson (1990) describe this process of unfreezing in much harsher terms.

Clarke (pp. 147–8) talks of 'speeding up the unfreezing process' through *destabilizing* people to detach them from the old order. She quotes the example of Centraal Beheer, an insurance company in the Netherlands: 'creating an anxiety greater than the risk of doing something different'. She goes on to say (p. 149): 'Pent-up anger and discontent are the motivators for change; no significant change is possible without them.' Clarke talks the language of crisis and even of engineering a crisis in order to speed up the unfreezing process.

Johnson (p. 190) goes further than Clarke with his talk of 'symbolic acts of questioning or destruction' to start the unfreezing process. He gives examples of John de Lorean trying to change his division of General Motors by promulgating stories to ridicule the dominant culture and of Lee Iacocca firing 33 out of 35 vice-presidents within three years of taking over at Chrysler. Johnson continues this line of thinking by saying (p. 190): 'As conflict and debate grows, managers may actually foster it by symbolic acts of conflict, destruction and degradation.'

However, care must be taken that crisis is not seen merely as a threat and, as Ferlie and Bennett (1993) point out, paradoxically reduces energy, creativity and flexibility. From an OD point of view crisis would be seen as an opportunity that, in Ferlie and Bennett's (p. 270) words:

> forces awkward issues up the agendas [when] we are likely to see continuing pressure from pioneers, the formation of special groups who evangelize the rest of the organization, high energy and commitment levels, and a period of organizational plasticity in which anything seems plausible.

Alternatively, as Farquhar *et al.* (1989, p. 37) point out: 'Not all companies see crisis as a prerequisite for major organizational change.' Triggers for change could come from the aspirations of top management, perhaps through anxiety about an uncertain future including a downturn in results or fear for their own positions. Monitoring the internal and external organizational environments on a regular basis can detect potential crises in their early and most treatable phases. What needs to be recognized is that change without crisis is most frequently incremental and time is needed to build the momentum for larger-scale, more radical change.

OD is limited when change situations are 'constrained'

OD has been promoted as a change model for coping with situations of soft complexity where goals and also the means of achieving them are unclear. However, there are situations which have many of the characteristics of soft complexity yet are constrained in the sense that the goals are predetermined and the means of achieving them are to some extent set. In other words change is dictated by top management or the precise requirements of some part of the organization's external environment. For instance, healthcare is proscribed by the need to safeguard the public against malpractice and legislation regarding the use of treatments and drugs. Setting up a new doctor's practice must adhere to many different forms of regulatory requirement. Franchisees must often run their businesses according to the dictates of the franchiser.

It may be, of course, that, when change is desirable, a hard systems model of change is most appropriate. However, 'dictated' or 'forced choice' change is likely to bring resistance from those who must implement it. Therefore, although the earlier stages of the OD model may not be applicable, there is still the requirement to develop an action plan, and implement, assess and reinforce change. In addition, gaining commitment to and participation in this part of the change process by those who must make the change is of the utmost importance. Consequently, even in highly constrained situations of change, implementation must be as collaboratively executed as in any other OD process.

OD requires 'out of the ordinary' leadership

Over many years of teaching MBA students and asking them to identify what leadership style they use or aspire to use, transformational leadership (see Chapter 6) is the one that gets named most often. Very few said they aspired to be authoritative, coercive or directive. However, the culture of many organizations makes it difficult to involve others continuously whilst trying to manage medium- and large-scale change. Some leaders do not have the attitude or persistence that prepares them for the 'long haul' of frame-breaking change. Couple this with what Coghlan and Brannick (2014) term *denial* that change is required or relevant, and *dodging*, which is an effort to divert the change, then an argument could be made that a more directive style of leadership is needed.

In her account of leading the change in the Regional College of Psychiatric Nursing, the director comments that her original plan to be a distributive leader (see Chapter 6) had to be reassessed as her staff went through a period of resistance to what they envisaged happening to their roles and identities. Leading change is itself a complex process and the skill is not always to be a transformational leader but to know when to use one style of leadership compared to another.

OD fits uneasily with the structures and culture in the public sector

In general, organic organizational structures (see Chapter 3) rather than mechanistic ones are more suited to organizations embracing an OD model of change. Consequently the application of OD in organizations with multilevel accountability and reporting relationships can be a problem. Coupled with this are the added pressures from politicians (local and national) as well as appointed officials.

However, as the public sector has moved towards market principles, OD models for change become more realistic and easier to apply. Indeed, because of the extreme complexity of these organizations and the massive changes they have to face, change models that do not take account of the soft, messy situations they face have little likelihood of succeeding.

Illustration 8.7 is an extract from the 'Employers' Organization for Local Government' website where it makes the case for the use of OD in the context of the large-scale changes faced by institutions of local government in the United Kingdom.

Illustration 8.7

Making sense of change – saying goodbye to 'initiative fatigue'

Why should we be interested in organisation development?

Councils are facing unrelenting pressure to provide better quality services at a time when they are under unprecedented scrutiny. The introduction of the corporate governance and capacity assessment presents a further challenge, not least because it comes on top of other government initiatives, such as best value.

Change initiatives often fail because organisations try to implement a number of activities too quickly and without proper coordination or thought about the implications for people management. This leads to 'initiative fatigue' where staff become disillusioned and more resistant to change.

Many authorities are beginning to consider the importance of Organisation Development as part of preparing for e-government. So far, there has generally been more emphasis on ICT, systems and the use of technical experts, yet more than 50 per cent of ICT projects fail because of cultural or organisational problems. E-government will demand support at the top and people with organisational development expertise helping to plan and implement ICT and related changes strategically throughout the local authority.

During recent years 'Oganisation Development' (OD) has re-emerged as a key element in the strategic management of change, providing a focus for the cultural and organisational change needed for continuous improvement, aligning systems, culture and activities to the achievement of organisational goals. It enables better use of financial, human and technological resources, fosters a greater sense of organisational purpose and it is therefore more likely to deliver the required performance improvement.

What sorts of activities are integral to Organisation Development?

These include linking OD with council objectives, finding and developing staff with the right skills to help champion OD throughout the organisation and encouraging wide participation and ownership of the continuous improvement process among staff and elected members. Building in this perspective at the beginning will mean that changes are grounded and sustainable, with people management considerations integrated into the process.

Where is Organisation Development located within local authorities?

In principle OD can be located anywhere in an authority structure, though recent research shows that where posts are located within the chief executives' department there is closer liaison and a more flexible organisational response to wide-ranging demands. But wherever the function is located there are a wide range of behaviours, skills and knowledge that will be needed across the organisation.

Taking it forward – What next for you?

● Have you got commitment and involvement at the top of the organisation?
● Is there someone in your organisation who is coordinating OD activities?
● Have you got a 'map' of the OD activities happening in your organisation?

Source: This is an extract from the Local Government Employer's Organization website that appeared in 2006. The site address is no longer available. However, the sentiments expressed appear to be relevant to organizations in the public sector now.

More recently, Parkes (2008, p. 44), director of HR and OD at Croydon Council, discussed how the council's human resources OD consultancy team brought about change to reduce sickness levels across the council workforce. Parkes notes that what was then a newly formed team learned a number of lessons for the future. These include:

- make sure you have a strong leadership from the top;
- involve managers in setting the policy – don't just impose it upon them;
- be consistent in your approach right across the organization;
- train everyone you need to in what is expected from them;
- deliver accurate, timely communications so people understand what you are trying to achieve;
- stick at it and don't give up.

A further example of the issues concerned with change in the public sector is discussed by Crawford, Costello, Pollack and Bentley (2003).

OD does not 'work' in all cultures

This chapter and Chapter 7 have described at least three ways of designing and implementing organizational change and ways of dealing with resistance and conflict have been addressed. What must be recognized, however, is the predominantly Western bias of much that is written about organizations and change. Consequently, not all change methods and techniques are transportable across national boundaries or even to different ethnic groupings within single countries (Adler, 2007; Jaeger, 1986). This is particularly the case with the range of techniques associated with OD as a philosophy and a methodology for bringing about change.

In an extensive discussion of organizational development and national culture, Jaeger linked typical OD values with each of Hofstede's (1980) dimensions of culture and concluded that they have a low correspondence with high power distance, high uncertainty avoidance, high masculinity and moderate individualism. Consequently, some OD-type interventions will struggle to be accepted in societies that score highly on these dimensions.

For instance, although Jack's article 'Caste in stone' with his comment, 'Challenge French corporate at your peril', was written in 1997, it appears still to be current. The Expatica website (http://www.expatica.com/fr/employment/Business-culture-in-France_102491.html), a website for people working abroad, says: 'In France both business and political life are characterized by a strong hierarchical structure in large companies. Positions and the corresponding power are clearly defined. And when dealing with the French, you should stick to formal etiquette'. Compared to France, doing business in India is more relaxed, time keeping more variable and discussions at meetings allowed to go off track. Even so, it is important to observe protocol regarding hierarchy and treat superiors with respect.

In spite of national cultural differences, many large multinational organizations employ similar strategies, operations and staffing policies regardless of where in the world they do business. Other organizations might want to take advantage of the knowledge and experience of people from the localities. Whichever stance is taken, Cummings and Worley's (2015) extensive discussion of the application of OD in different parts of the world demonstrates how the cultural context in which organizations exist has to be considered when any change process is proposed.

Having said this, there are many OD techniques that can be used in spite of the existence of less than propitious attitudes and beliefs on the part of those involved. French and Bell (1999) use the concept of 'depth of intervention' to distinguish those techniques that interact mainly with the more formalized organizational systems (such as job enrichment, management by objectives, role analysis and attitude surveys) and those that go deeper into exploring the informal and more personal organizational systems – for instance team building, encounter groups and interpersonal relationship explorations. Depth of intervention is a useful concept for deciding how 'deep' to go in the use of OD-type interventions as part of the process of change that involves people from different cultures. It is particularly relevant for those organizations that operate outside their home country environment.

Conclusions

Soft systems models for change, of which OD is a well-known example, contrast with hard systems in being able to address the issues of soft complexity inherent in 'messy' situations. Soft systems approaches to change emphasize not just the content and control of change but also the *process* by which change comes about. They require consideration of the cultural and political aspects of organizations as much as the structure and systems. 'Change agents' facilitating change using these approaches require influencing skills and the skills of negotiation. Because different individuals respond to their different *perceptions* of events, which will differ one from another, change agents need to understand the aspirations and feelings of those working in change situations as well as the group processes that bind them together.

Soft systems models of change are, essentially, *planned* approaches to change. This does not mean, however, that they cannot account for unexpected and surprising events. Indeed the requirement to iterate frequently around and across the different phases and stages of the model takes account of the probability that there will be 'changes within changes' occurring. Taken together, hard and soft systems models of change offer those working with change ways of addressing issues in their simplicity and complexity to enhance the work of organizations and the lives of those working in them.

Discussion questions and assignments

1 Debate the pros and cons of using external change agents compared to internal ones.

2 Compare and contrast the HSMC and OD approaches to change. Give examples of types of change situations where each may be appropriate.

3 To what extent do you consider Lewin's three-phase model is appropriate for today's organizations?

4 Draw a rich picture of life as experienced by you in your organization.

5 If your manager is looking for a 'quick fix' to manage a change process, how might you justify using an OD approach to change?

Case example ●●●

Implementing a new patient information system at a major teaching hospital trust

Technological developments and increasing demand on the current ageing computerized patient administration system at a large teaching hospital trust led to the decision to implement a change project to replace the existing system with a newer, up to date system and roll out throughout all departments within the Trust.

The information technology (IT) department was given the responsibility for the project, and allowed to select the members of the project team that was formed. This consisted primarily of internal and external (from the software supplier) IT experts, with the inclusion of planning, contracting and finance staff. Other departments (such as training) were delegated specific tasks but were not included in the project team.

The project team began by conducting a review of the current system and a scoping exercise for the new system. Of particular importance was to ensure that the new system was technically capable of linking to external NHS computer systems used by general practitioners and primary healthcare providers, that it was technically robust enough to deal with projected increase in demand, and could as a minimum provide the same level of functionality as the old system. The project was viewed as being primarily a technical exercise, with the focus being on the technical functionality of the new system and the ease of transfer of existing records.

The project was centrally driven from the IT department and a single Trust-wide announcement was made to inform staff of the upcoming change. The only other involvement that the majority of the primary users of the patient administration system had with the project was when they were invited to attend compulsory training on the new system three to six months before the expected 'go live' date of the new system. This training was designed to inform them of the differences with the new system and equip them with the new skills, procedures and expertise to use it. The training was not designed to allow feedback on the new system, despite the strong opinions that

some members of staff held and wanted to feed into the project.

The project was managed through monthly project team meetings that focused on the development of software, the testing of the new system, planning and installing the new IT equipment that was necessary, the financial cost of the project, and the projected cost savings associated with the benefits from the successful delivery of the project and how these would help the Trust meet its financial performance targets.

At one of the project team meetings it was discovered that minute technical changes to the new system, which affected how it was to be used, would require the user training material to be re-written, and those staff who had already been through the original training would need to be re-trained. This new training programme would increase significantly the training costs for the project and threatened to put the entire project over budget. As this had not been raised as a potential risk to the project at the project initiation and planning stage (part of the 'develop an action plan' stage of the OD model for change on p. 307), there was no ready prepared contingency in place. Due to the difficulty designing, and delivering this training at very short notice the training programme had not been completed before the 'go live' date.

The new patient administration software had been successfully developed and tested by the project 'go live' date, and the decision was taken that, as the roll-out of the training had not been successfully completed, the old system would run in parallel for a period of time. The IT department and project team considered the project to be successfully delivered – the new system was able to go live on the target date and although there was still training to complete there were no major technological issues that needed addressing. The project was considered closed and the audit department were tasked to carry out a follow-on audit to reinforce the successful delivery of the project.

Nine months after the 'go live' date and more than six months after the completion of the training, staff were audited to assess the compliance with using the new system. Only 32 per cent of staff were found to be exclusively using the new system, 14 per cent of staff were using the new system for some tasks, and the old system for others. The remainder (54 per cent) were not using the new system at all. The audit was followed by a survey to learn why the usage rates for the new system were so poor. The reasons given were varied (as you would expect), but several key themes were identified:

- 'The new system makes it harder to do my job than the old system.'

- 'I never had the training for the new system.'
- 'I was confused by the multiple training courses and so have kept using the old system as it is easier.'
- 'I already know how to use the old system so why would I change?'
- 'There is no incentive to use the new system (and no penalty for using the old system).'
- 'The old system works perfectly well for what I need it to do.'

A workgroup was formed to look into the 'delayed delivery' of the expected benefits from the new patient administration system, its membership was taken from the original project team.

(*Source*: Grateful thanks go to Jim Bamford of Huddersfield University, UK for the material contained in this case study.)

Case exercise

- Considering the OD model for change in Figure 8.3 (p. 307) and the stages that it proposes are necessary for the successful implementation of change:
  - Which stages were done well?
  - Which stages could have been done better?
  - What could have been done to improve the potential for successful delivery of the project?
  - Were any stages missed out entirely?

- What lessons could the Trust learn from this change project?

- What would you recommend to the executive board to ensure the ultimate success of the new patient administration system?

Indicative resources

Buchanan, D.A. and Badham, R.J. (2008), *Power, Politics and Organizational Change: Winning the Turf Game* (2nd edn), London: Sage.

Checkland, P. (2000), 'Soft-systems Methodology: a thirty-year retrospective', *Systems Research and Behavioural Science*, 17, pp. 11–58.

Checkland, P. and Poulter, J. (2006), *Learning for Action: A Short Definitive Account of Soft Systems Methodology and its Use, for Practitioners, Teachers and Students*, Chichester: John Wiley and Sons Ltd. This is a more detailed account of soft systems methodology. It has several appendices discussing creative thinking techniques and the theory underlying soft systems approaches to change.

Coglan, D. and Brannick, T. (2014), *Doing Action Research in Your Own Organization* (4th edn), London: Sage.

Cummings, T. and Worley, C. (2015), *Organization Development and Change* (10th edn), Mason, OH: Thomson South-Western. Part of this is dedicated to the effective implementation of OD and how it can be used in both public and private sectors. There are numerous case studies as examples of issues associated with OD and applications of it in a variety of organizations.

French, W.L., Bell, C.H. and Zawacki, R.A. (2005), *Organization Development and Transformation: Managing Effective Change* (6th edn), McGraw-Hill. French *et al.* have dedicated much of their time to promoting and educating in the field of OD. This text offers a good introduction to OD and guidance in using this approach.

Reynolds, M. and Holwell S. (2010) (eds), *Systems Approaches to Managing Change: A practical guide*, Milton Keynes. This is a book of chapters by different writers. It is helpful in giving different views on approaches to managing change.

Whitney, D. and Trosten-Bloom, A. (2003), *The Power of Appreciative Inquiry*, San Francisco, CA: Berrett-Koehler. Based on the principles of OD (people and their potential) this book in particular supports the ideas and concepts associated with learning organizations.

Useful websites

www.actionlearningassociates.co.uk This site is helpful for those who have further interest in action learning. It provides a working definition, offers examples of how action learning can be used, how the groups operate and how to use 'in-house' sets for the purposes of OD.

www.ifal.org.uk This is the UK's official action learning site.

www.open.edu/openlearn This is a site for many short, non-qualification courses offered free by the Open University, Milton Keynes, UK. Section 4 of the course 'Management: Perspective and Practice' contains units of learning material relevant to tackling 'messy' problems.

References

Ackoff, R.L. (1993), 'The art and science of mess management', in Mabey, C. and Mayon-White, B. (eds), *Managing Change*, London: PCP.

Adler, N.J. (2007), *International Dimensions of Organizational Behavior*, Cincinnati, OH: South-Western College Publishing, ITP.

Alpander, G.G. and Lee, C.R. (1995), 'Culture, strategy and teamwork: the keys to organizational change', *Journal of Management Development*, 14(8), pp. 4–18.

Argyris, C. (1964), *Integrating the Individual and the Organization*, New York: Wiley.

Argyris, C. (1992), *On Organizational Learning*, Oxford: Blackwell.

Argyris, C. and Schön, D. A. (1996), *Organizational Learning II*, Reading, MA: Addison-Wesley.

Balogun, J. and Hope Hailey, V. (2008), *Exploring Strategic Change* (3rd edn), Harlow: Financial Times Prentice Hall.

Beckhard, R. and Harris, R.T. (1987), *Organizational Transitions: Managing Complex Change* (2nd edn), Reading, MA: Addison-Wesley.

Benjamin, G. and Mabey, C. (1993), 'Facilitating radical change: a case of organization transformation', in Mabey, C. and Mayon-White, B. (eds), *Managing Change* (2nd edn), London: PCP.

Buchanan, D. and Boddy, D. (1992), *The Expertise of the Change Agent: Public Performance and Backstage Activity*, Hemel Hempstead: Prentice Hall.

Buchanan, D. and McCalman, J. (1989), *High Performance Work Systems: The Digital Experience*, London: Routledge.

Burnes, B. (2004), *Managing Change: A Strategic Approach to Organisational Dynamics* (4th edn), Harlow: Financial Times Prentice Hall.

Burnside, R.M. (1991), 'Visioning: building pictures of the future', in Henry, J. and Walker, D. (eds), *Managing Innovation*, London: Sage.

Carnall, C. (2007), *Managing Change in Organizations* (5th edn), Harlow: Pearson Education.

Checkland, P. (1981), *Systems Thinking, Systems Practice*, Chichester: Wiley.

Checkland, P. and Poulter, J. (2006), 'Learning for action: a short definitive account of soft systems methodology, and its use for practitioners, teachers and students', in Reynolds, M. and Holwell S. (eds), *Systems Approaches to Managing Change: A practical guide*, Milton Keynes: The Open University.

Clarke, J., Hooper, C. and Nicholson, J. (1997), 'Reversal of fortune', *People Management*, 20 March, pp. 22–6, 29.

Clarke, L. (1994), *The Essence of Change*, Hemel Hempstead: Prentice Hall.

Coghlan, D. and Brannick, T. (2014), *Action Research in Your Own Organization* (3rd edn), London: Sage.

Crawford, L. Costello, K. Pollack J. and Bentley L. (2003), 'Managing soft change projects in the public sector', *International Journal of Project Management*, 21(6), pp. 443–8.

Cummings, T.G. and Worley, C.G. (2009), *Organization Development and Change* (9th edn), Mason, OH: South-Western.

Cummings, T.G. and Worley, C.G. (2013), *Organization Development and Change* (10th edn), Stamford, CT: Cengage Learning.

Cummings, T. and Worley, C. (2015), *Organization Development and Change* (10th edn), Mason, OH: Thomson South-Western.

Elkjaar, B. (1999), 'In search of a social learning theory', in Easterby-Smith, M., Burgoyne, J. and Araujo, L. (eds), *Organizational Learning and the Learning Organization: Development in Theory and Practice*, London: Sage, pp. 75–91.

Farquhar, A., Evans, P. and Tawadey, K. (1989), 'Lessons from practice in managing organizational change', in Evans, P., Doz, E. and Laurent, A. (eds), *Human Resource Management in International Firms: Change, Globalization, Innovation*, London: Macmillan.

Ferlie, E. and Bennett, C. (1993), 'Patterns of strategic change in health care: district health authorities respond to AIDS', in Hendry, J., Johnson, G. and Newton, J. (eds), *Strategic Thinking, Leadership and the Management of Change*, Chichester: Wiley.

Flood, R.L. and Jackson, M.C. (1991), *Creative Problem Solving: Total Systems Intervention*, Chichester: Wiley.

French, W.L. and Bell, C.H. (1999), *Organization Development: Behavioural Science Interventions for Organizational improvement* (6th edn), Upper Saddle River, NJ: Prentice.

French, W.L., Bell, C.H. and Zawacki, R.A. (2005), *Organization Development and Transformation: Managing Effective Change* (6th edn), McGraw-Hill.

Goodstein, L.D. and Burke, W.W. (1993), 'Creating successful organization change', in Mabey, C. and Mayon-White, B. (eds), *Managing Change*, London: PCP.

Harrison, R. (1972), 'When power conflicts trigger team spirit', *European Business*, Spring, pp. 27–65.

Hofstede, G. (1980), *Culture's Consequences: International Differences in Work-related Values*, London and Beverley Hills, CA: Sage.

Jack, A. (1997), 'Caste in stone: challenge to French corporate hierarchies at your peril', *Financial Times*, 10 April.

Jaeger, A.M. (1986), 'Organization development and national culture: where's the fit?' *Academy of Management Review*, 11(1), pp. 178–90.

Johnson, G. (1990), 'Managing strategic action: the role of symbolic action', *British Journal of Management*, 1, pp. 183–200.

Johnson, G., Scholes, K. and Whittington, R. (2008), *Exploring Corporate Strategy: Texts and Cases* (8th edn), Harlow: Financial Times Prentice Hall.

Jones, P. (1994), 'Which lever do I pull now?: the role of "emergent planning" in managing change', *Organisations and People*, 1(1), January, pp. 46–9.

Kotter, J.P. (1996), *Leading Change*, Boston, MA: Harvard Business School Press.

Lewin, K. (1951), *Field Theory in Social Science*, New York: Harper & Row.

Lievegoed, B. (1983), *Man on the Threshold*, Driebergen: Hawthorne Press.

Lloyd, B. and Feigen, M. (1997), 'Real change leaders: the key challenge to management today', *Leadership and Organization Development Journal*, (1), pp. 37–40.

Mabey, C. and Mayon-White, B. (1993) (eds), *Managing Change* (2nd edn), London: PCP.

Mabey, C. and Pugh, D. (1995), Unit 10, 'Strategies for managing complex change', Course B751, *Managing Development and Change*, Milton Keynes: Open University Press.

Matsushita, K. (1988), 'The secret is shared', *Manufacturing Engineering*, March, pp. 78–84.

Morgan, G. (2006), *Images of Organization*, London: Sage.

Nadler, D. (1977), *Feedback and Organization Development: Using Data-based Methods*, Reading, MA: Addison Wesley, pp. 156–8. Reprinted in Cummings and Worley (2009, p. 159) by permission – Pearson Education, Inc., Englewood Cliffs, NJ.

Open University (1985), Unit 8, 'Process', Course T244, *Managing in Organizations*, Milton Keynes: Open University Press.

Parkes, P. (2008), 'How I make a difference at work', *People Management*, August, p. 44.

Paton, R.A. and McCalman, J. (2008), *Change Management: A Guide to Effective Implementation* (3rd edn), London: Sage.

Pedler, M., Boydell, T. and Burgoyne, J. (1991), *The Learning Company*, London: McGraw-Hill.

Pugh, D. (1986), Block 4, 'Planning and managing change', *Organizational Development*, Milton Keynes: Open University Press.

Pugh, D. (1993), 'Understanding and managing change', in Mabey, C. and Mayon-White, B. (eds), *Managing Change* (2nd edn), London: PCP, pp. 108–12.

Schein, E. (1998), *Process Consultation Revisited: Building the Helping Relationship*, Reading, MA: Addison-Wesley.

Senge, P. (1990), *The Fifth Discipline: The Art and Practice of the Learning Organization*, New York: Doubleday Currency.

Smith, B. (1995), 'Not in front of the children: the realities of "involvement" in managing change', *Organisations and People*, 2(2), pp. 17–20.

Stacey, R. (2008), *Strategic Management and Organisational Dynamics: The Challenge of Complexity* (5th edn), Harlow: Financial Times Prentice Hall.

Whitney, D. and Trosten-Bloom, A. (2003), *The Power of Appreciative Inquiry*, San Francisco, CA: Berrett-Koehler.

Chapter 9

Future directions
and challenges

Change exists at both macro levels such as restructuring a multinational
organization and at micro levels such as when individuals see their jobs
being redesigned. This chapter identifies the key trends that will continue to
prompt macro- and micro-level changes in organizations and at the effects
they are having. It also looks at the act of changing and introduces the idea
of organizational capacity for changing and at how people make sense of the
changes going on around them.

Learning objectives

By the end of this chapter, you will be able to:

- identify and discuss the contemporary economic and social forces that
  are pressuring organizations to change;

- analyze the extent to which organizations will need to innovate more
  frequently in the future;

- identify and discuss organizational capacity for change;

- evaluate the concept of a psychological contract and apply it to your
  own situation;

- discuss the main challenges facing change researchers.

Introduction

Part One examined the way organizations and the context in which they operate have changed throughout time and discussed how political, economic, social and technological forces impact on the way that organizations operate. The concept of organizational change was shown to be heterogeneous in that there are many types of change occurring both sequentially and simultaneously, sometimes predictable and sometimes unexpected.

Part Two elaborated on this by addressing aspects of organizational life that influence change outcomes in one way or another. Part Three introduced two major methodologies for change. Given all this it would be ideal if the overall outcome was an all-embracing, widely accepted theory of change with agreed guidelines on 'how to do it'. However, the issues discussed and models of change given in the previous chapters do give us guidelines on how to proceed in these times of organizational uncertainty.

The purpose of this final chapter is to look to the future in terms of some of the major trends that are likely to influence industry, lifestyles and social structures and which, in turn, will affect organizations – their strategies, structures, how they are led, employment practices and the need to work with change. We also consider more closely the act of changing and recent thinking on how it happens and how best to catalyze it.

Current and future business environments

As we saw earlier there are many triggers of change that emanate from both the internal and external organizational environments. Many of these will affect an organization directly such as the appointment of a new top manager or falling organizational competitiveness. Others, however, will exert influence more indirectly, such as changing demographics, lifestyles, social structures, working patterns and levels of employment/unemployment. Prevailing political ideologies, government priorities and world events are also amongst these.

Social structures

Social class

In 2013, on the basis of a survey of 162,426 people across the UK (161,400 web and 1,026 face-to-face survey), Savage *et al.* (2013), in collaboration with the British Broadcasting Corporation (BBC), reported research resulting in a new way of measuring class. This doesn't define class just by the job that individuals do, but by the different kinds of economic, cultural (cultural and leisure time 'tastes') and social (the extent to which people of other employment classes are known) resources or 'capitals' that people possess. Named 'The Great British Class Survey', the report proposes the following new social classes:

- **Elite** *(6 per cent sample)* – the most privileged group in the UK, distinct from the other six classes through its wealth. This group has the highest levels of all three capitals (household income £89,082; savings £142,458).
- **Established middle class** *(25 per cent sample)* – the second wealthiest, scoring highly on all three capitals. The largest and most gregarious group, scoring second highest for cultural capital (household income £47,184; savings £26,090).
- **Technical middle class** *(6 per cent sample)* – a small, distinctive new class group which is prosperous but scores low for social and cultural capital. Distinguished by its social isolation and cultural apathy (household income £37,428; savings £65,844).
- **New affluent workers** *(15 per cent sample)* – a young class group which is socially and culturally active, with middling levels of economic capital (household income £29,252; savings £4,918).
- **Traditional working class** *(14 per cent sample)* – scores low on all forms of capital, but is not completely deprived. Its members have reasonably high house values, explained by this group having the oldest average age at 65 (household income £13,305; savings 9,500).
- **Emergent service workers** *(19 per cent sample)* – a new, young, urban group which is relatively poor but has high social and cultural capital (household income £21,048; savings £1,138).
- **Precariat, or precarious proletariat** *(15 per cent sample)* – the poorest, most deprived class, scoring low for social and cultural capital (household income £8,253; savings £793).

It is interesting to note the predominance of the middle class (even though still only 25 per cent), who have good incomes, are socially connected and have 'highbrow' cultural tastes. The much smaller distinctive elite category is in stark contrast to the precariat grouping, whilst the traditional working class (which has an average age of 65) is in decline. This new categorization of seven classes, differentiated by amount of economic, social and cultural capital, gives helpful information to organizations and their managers making decisions on whether to refocus or change their products and who to employ to deliver them, which in turn might signal changes in the way they do things. However, as time goes on, the relative sizes of these different social classes could change in the light of changing demographics.

Demographic changes

Population predictions for the future Illustration 9.1 shows the structure of the UK population in 2012 and as it is predicted to be in the periods to 2035.

Illustration 9.1

UK national population projections 2012 onwards

- The UK population is projected to increase at a steady rate, from an estimated 63.7 million in mid-2012 to:
  - 68.0 million by mid-2022;
  - 70 million in 2027;
  - 73.3 million over the 25-year period to 2035.
- The number of people of pension age is projected to remain stable until around 2020, then will increase (despite increases in the state pension age) from 12.2 million to 16 million in 2034.

- The number of people of working age will grow from 39.7 million in 2013 to 42.1 million in 2020 and then at a slower rate to 44.1 million in 2037.
- In 2013, there were 3.4 people of working age for every person of pensionable age. This ratio is expected to fall to 2.8 in 2033.
- The number of children under five will continue to grow slowly from 4 million in 2013 to 4.1 million in 2021 and then will decrease back to 4 million in 2033.

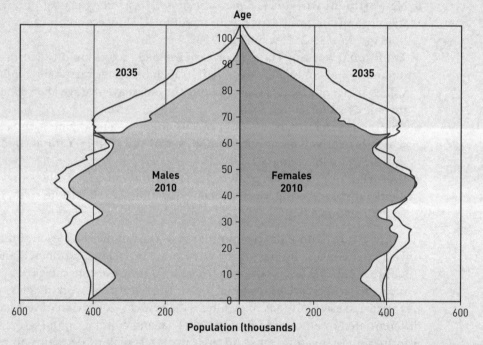

Estimated and projected age structure of the United Kingdom population mid-2010 and mid-2035

Source: http://www.ons.gov.uk/ons/rel/npp/national-population-projections/2010-based-projections/sum-2010-based-national-population-projections.htm

The ageing population and decreasing proportion of young people   From the statistics above, it is clear that the UK population is getting older, given the low birth rate and people living longer. This is also the case in the European Union (see Figure 9.1). For instance, between 1992 and 2012, the proportion of working-age population (15–64 years) across the EU increased by 0.5 per cent whilst the proportion of older people (aged 65 and above) increased by 3.7 per cent. This increase came at the expense of a decrease of 3.5 per cent in the proportion of younger people aged 0–14 years (European Union, 2013).

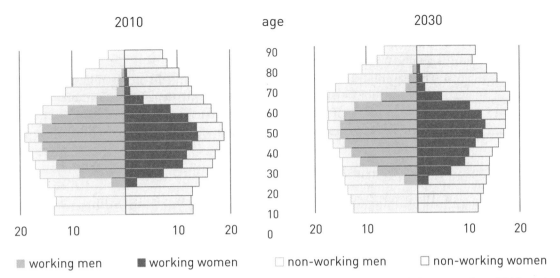

Figure 9.1 Population by sex, age, group and employment for the EU 27 countries, 2010 and 2030 (million)

Source: EU Employment and Social Situation Quarterly Review: Special Supplement on Demographic Trends, March 2013

This trend is producing an older workforce, on average, with an increasing number of older people being able to, and often needing to, work past normal retirement age as pension schemes are feeling the pressure of increasing numbers of retirees, with some schemes now closed to new employees.

All this has consequences for organizations providing public services – housing, education, health. There are also implications for the creation of new products and services for an ageing but relatively active population and for those who will require services in their home that might not yet have been thought of.

Changing lifestyles

Household composition and ownership   According to the UK Office for National Statistics, average household sizes have changed little over the decade to 2014. There were 26.7 million households in the UK in 2014, with the following characteristics:

Households

- The number of households has increased by 22.6 million (7 per cent) since 2004, similar to the growth in the UK population during this period.
- The average number of people per household was 2.4, the same as the European average.

Living alone

- A total of 7.6 million (28 per cent) people lived alone, a similar percentage to the European average.
- Residents of 59 per cent of single-person households were 85+ years old.

Lone parents

- UK households containing one lone parent family increased from 2.6 million in 2004 to 2.8 million a decade later.
- There were 2 million lone parents with dependent children in the UK; women accounted for 91 per cent of lone parents with dependent children.
- The proportion of lone parents with dependent children, living in the UK, is much higher than the European average; only two countries (Iceland and Norway) have a higher proportion.

Owner-occupiers and renters

- The percentage of owner-occupiers in 2014 was 63 per cent, a reduction from 71 per cent in 2003.
- In 2013–14, two-thirds (14.3 million) of householders had bought their own house. Of these, 33 per cent (14.3 million) owned outright, whilst 31 per cent had a mortgage. For the first time, the number of people owning their own house outright was larger than that for owners with a mortgage.
- In 2013–14, the UK private rented sector was growing, and had already over-taken the social rented sector. In 2013–14, 19 per cent of households were rent-ing privately, up from 18 per cent in 2012–13, while the proportion of social housing remained steady at 17 per cent.

Young people still 'at home'

- In 2014, 3.3 million (26 per cent of this age group) young adults aged 20–34 were living with parents in the UK, a rise of 0.6 million since the economic downturn in 2008. This was mainly the result of a large rise in the numbers of 20- to 24-year-olds.

Marriage and co-habiting   In 2014 there were 18.6 million families in the UK. Of these, 12.5 million were married-couple families, the most common family type in the UK. Cohabiting-couple families grew by 29.7 per cent between 2004 and 2014.

Cohabiting couples

- Cohabiting-couple families are the fastest-growing family type in the UK. In 2014, there were nearly 3 million opposite-sex cohabiting-couple families and 84,000 same-sex cohabiting-couple families in the UK.
- Cohabiting-couple families account for 16.4 per cent of all families in the UK.
- A bill which addresses the rights of cohabiting couples is in the early stages of passing through the UK parliament.

In the UK, a shortage in the supply of housing has become an issue, because of a number of factors, such as the growth in numbers of single parents needing homes, people living longer, the increase in single households and shortage of affordable rented properties. This is good news for the construction industry and allied trades. However, any expansion of this, either to build private or social hous-ing, will require larger numbers of workers from the skilled and semi-skilled trades. This will, in turn, mean an expansion of apprentices and training courses, which will involve government and training organizations as well as employers.

The future of work

The United Kingdom

The collapse of the Lehman Brothers bank in 2008 was the start of what became a worldwide recession that lasted for the next five years and from which the UK, EU and other countries have only relatively recently begun to recover. It is in this context that in May 2014 the UK Commission for Employment and Skills published a report titled 'Working Futures 2012–2022: Introduction and Commentary' (Wilson *et al.*, 2014). This document is the fifth in a series of decade-long projections of the UK's labour market and is based on what the authors say is 'a rigorous, evidence-based projection covering the entire UK labour market' (p. 1). What follows is a summary of the main predictions made. These are:

- An increase of 1.8 million (6 per cent) in the number of people employed.
- Economic output set to expand over the period by 20 per cent.
- An additional 12.5 million job openings from replacing workers leaving the workforce.
- Business services will be the driving sector of economic growth, adding 28 per cent in output and more than 1.1 million jobs.
- IT will see the fastest growth, at 31 per cent (280,000 jobs).
- Health and social work will add nearly 450,000 jobs to the economy.
- Care workers (nearly 600,000), corporate managers (nearly 500,000) and STEM (science, technology, engineering, mathematics) professionals (over 350,000 workers) will see the largest jobs growth. Business, public service, education and health professionals will account for another 820,000 net new jobs.
- Intermediate skill level roles are in overall decline, with the task of replacing those exiting the workforce ensuring that large numbers of job openings will exist across skill ranges, including in manufacturing industries and skilled trade occupations.
- Continued improvements in gender balance will be seen, with large shares of new professional and associate professional jobs going to female employees; female employees will also dominate the expanding care sector.

In addition:

- The UK is becoming a more ethnically diverse country, mainly as a result of the free movement of workers across the EU, as well as immigrants (including students) coming from other countries. If immigration of certain classes of workers is curtailed, this could result in a dearth of certain skilled workers.
- Technological change is becoming a feature of economic life affecting low-skill jobs whilst increasing the number of highly skilled ones. New developments through increased automation or biotechnology will transform jobs and ways that work is organized even though precise effects may not yet be known. A cash-free economy is developing with implications particularly for retail organizations.

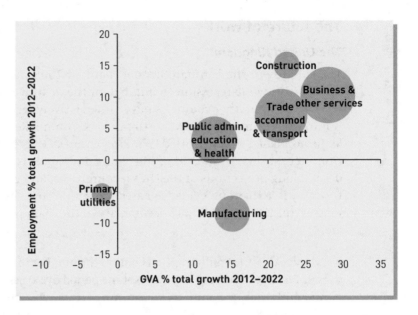

Figure 9.2 Projected output and employment growth by sector group, 2012–2022

Source: Wilson *et al.* (2014). *Working Futures 2012–2022: Introduction and Commentary*, UK Commission for Employment and Skills (p. 11).

Figure 9.2 shows the trend for six broad sector groups.

From this it can be seen that manufacturing will decline in its share of output and employment, but will move away from low-value-added industries to a growing emphasis on high-value-added industries such as car manufacturing and processes that feed the growth of maintenance and support services to customers who have already bought the manufactured goods. There is evidence from the US that 14 per cent of the increased service-sector share of the workforce can be attributed to the reorganization of work from manufacturers to outsourced service providers (Berlingieri, 2013).

Fewer, but more highly skilled, employees will be required and particularly those with IT and technology skills. For instance, product designers and consulting engineers will be required and found in a larger variety of workplaces. Care workers might have to become skilled in assisting with home-based diagnostic and monitoring devices. The projection of continued expansion in the number of science, research, engineering and technology professionals – from 1.35 million to 2.1 million in 2022 – implies that advanced technical skills retain a critical place in the UK economy. These workers are unlikely to appear without collaboration with government and training institutions and, if in short supply, will command premium pay.

The share of the workforce made up of public administration, education and health services will fall back as fiscal consolidation continues to limit the opportunity for expansion. However, organizations in the private sector could see opportunities to replace capacity in these areas with implications for training and development of their new and existing employees. Construction, which in many ways relies on its workforce (even with advances in industrial-type processes), is projected to grow somewhat, recovering the ground lost during the recession.

The changing age structure of the workforce is much more likely to lead to a shift in the gender balance, with consequences for how workforces are managed. As the projected reduction in secretarial and administrative work continues, increasingly more educated women (who work predominantly in these occupations) will look for higher-level work opportunities.

The structure of the workforce is changing, with increasing part-time and flexible working as well as self-employment. This might be by worker's choice but could be a result of employers not wishing to have the constraints of employing workers full-time. Workplaces will be four-generational (4G) with four generations working side by side. Traditional notions of hierarchy and seniority will become less important. Facilitating collaboration across multiple generations, and their values, will be in increasing demand.

Global outlook

The European Union   The economic recovery which started in the EU in the spring of 2013 remains subdued and recent GDP forecasts for the EU have been revised downwards. However, despite the weak macro-economic background, employment has shown a small but consistent growth in the EU since mid-2013, in the large majority of EU Member States, and across the large majority of sectors. Many challenges remain in the EU, with important social consequences, in particular long-term unemployment and low employment opportunities for youth (15–24) and young adults aged 25–39.

The European Commission (2015) has focused on three mutually reinforcing pillars that apply to all 27 countries:

- pursuing fiscal responsibility and boosting investment;
- improving employment policy and social protection;
- implementing structural reforms.

The first two of these are clear in their implications for governments, financial institutions as well as business. It is the third 'implementing structural reforms' in product, service and labour markets which will impact on business. The aim here is to help raise productivity, competitiveness and investment, thus boosting job creation and growth and contributing to prosperity and greater social fairness. Currently, uncertainty exists as to whether the relationship between the UK and the EU countries will change and how, and whether fragmentation of the EU will occur with one or more countries leaving. Much of this will be decided at government levels but the results could have far-reaching effects for UK business in whatever sector, given the amount of trade to and from the UK.

Other parts of the world   The rise of major emerging economies, such as the BRICS (Brazil, Russia, India, and China), means greater opportunity for UK exports, but also greater competition. The UK has benefited from global competition as countries such as China expanded the supply of low-cost manufactured goods, which lowered prices in the UK (Wilson *et al.*, 2014). However, the situation then changed as costs rose for imported commodities and in China economic growth slowed down. Even so, Illustration 9.2 shows that there are opportunities in Asia (especially for internet-based companies).

In the USA, the economy continues to struggle. However, as it climbs out of recession, it has seen its manufacturing growth outpace that of other advanced

Illustration 9.2

On the rise: female consumers in Asia

A survey of urban women across eight markets finds nearly half are joint or sole breadwinners.

- Nearly half of urban women prefer shopping on-line rather than offline.
- Majority of women browse online at least once a day.
- The younger generation are mobile and find independence appealing.

A detailed survey of 5,500 women across Asia's major urban areas conducted by The Economist Intelligence Unit finds that they are increasingly empowered financially and they are driving the explosive growth of e-commerce in the region. The survey results are published in a report entitled *On the rise and online: Female consumers in Asia*. The report was commissioned by VIPSHOP.

Across the eight markets covered, 41 per cent of the women surveyed say they are joint breadwinners in their household and another 8 per cent say they are sole breadwinners. The trend is particularly pronounced in mainland China, where 62 per cent of women describe themselves as joint breadwinners. Women are also showing increasing independence in handling finances – just over two-thirds report having their own bank accounts (76 per cent in mainland China) and 48 per cent hold their own credit cards.

Nearly half of women polled (49 per cent) say they prefer shopping online to doing so in stores. The figure is as high as 69 per cent in mainland China. There are several reasons why women prefer online shopping. Most women point to cost savings (62 per cent) and time savings (60 per cent), but they also feel that online retailers can be relied upon to have the products they want to buy in stock (59 per cent) and that online shopping offers a broader range of choices (56 per cent). Nearly half of the women (48 per cent) say they feel pressured and stressed in traditional shops (more than 50 per cent of women in Macau, South Korea, India and mainland China feel this way), and 27 per cent feel store staff talk down to them because they are women (a sentiment that is most pronounced in Macau, India and mainland China).

For many women, online shopping has become a favourite pastime. Among the survey respondents, 63 per cent say they browse the Internet for products and services at least once per day, with nearly 30 per cent doing so twice or more per day. Nearly 90 per cent of the women surveyed buy some clothing and accessories online (39 per cent buy the majority of their clothing this way) and 83 per cent buy some cosmetics (29 per cent buy the majority of their cosmetics online).

Many of the trends uncovered in the research are driven by the younger generation, suggesting that the move towards online shopping in general, the shift to shopping on mobile devices and a preference for being addressed on a personal level by marketers are likely to intensify. Among 18- to 29-year-olds, 53 per cent prefer shopping online rather than offline, compared to 48 per cent among 30- to 49-year-olds and 42 per cent for those between 50 and 60 years of age. Similarly, 58 per cent of 18- to 29-year-olds shop on their phones, compared to 38 per cent of 40- to 49-year-olds.

nations with some 500,000 jobs created in the years 2012–15. However, according to Michael Theis, writing for the Austin Business Journal (http://www.bizjournals. com/austin/news/2015/02/24/hispanics-projected-to-dominate-us-employment. html), after a rise in the USA's overall labour force over the next few years, a period of slow growth is expected as the 'baby boom' generation (which occurred later than in the UK) retires, leading to growth at only 2.6 per cent per year from 2020 to 2034.

It is interesting that a good proportion of this growth will be fuelled by Hispanic employment because Hispanics are a younger and faster-growing segment of the population. Using conservative assumptions, Theis's analysis predicts that the proportion of Hispanic workers will rise to 23 per cent of the US workforce in 2034 – an addition of 2.4 million Hispanic workers. The different demographic characteristics of Hispanic workers, particularly in their continued use of Spanish

(65 per cent of them used Spanish as their main language in 2013) and culture, could impact on the way some businesses operate.

In general, though, given that roughly half of all US companies get some of their revenue from outside the country, a slowing global economy could translate into slowing global sales and fears of a stock-market correction in the US (Profit Confidential, 2015).

Uncertainties and the longer term

On the basis of evidence gained from literature, expert interviews, high-level workshop discussions, and analysis of trends and what might disrupt them, a report by

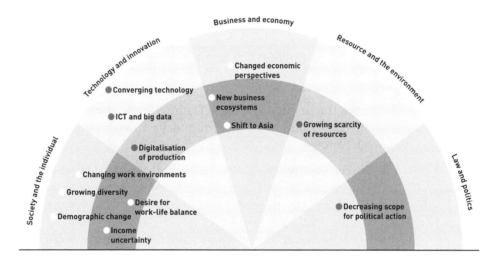

Figure 9.3 Trends shaping future UK jobs and skills to 2030

Source: Based on University of Wales and Z-punkt (2014), *The Future of Work, Jobs and Skills in 2030*, UK Commission for Education and Skills, Wath upon Dearne, South Yorkshire, pp. 8–11.

the UK Commission for Education and Skills (UKCES) in collaboration with the University of Wales and Z-punkt (2014) titled *The Future of Work, Jobs and Skills 2030* identified 13 trends which it considers most influential on UK jobs and skills to 2030. Figure 9.3 depicts these categorized into five groups.

These trends are considered to be relatively stable until 2030, in the main describing the current situation – what they term the 'business-as-usual' scenario. However, on the basis of a literature review, expert interviews and analysis of the central and common drivers underlying the trends and disruptions, UKCES then considered what might happen if developments occurred to disrupt this scenario, causing deviations from it. From this, it identified 10 key disruptions on the basis of their plausibility to the UK context in 2030 and judgement of the severity of their impact on jobs and skills if they were to occur. Figure 9.4 depicts these disruptions in a similar format to that of Figure 9.3, which allows a comparison between the two.

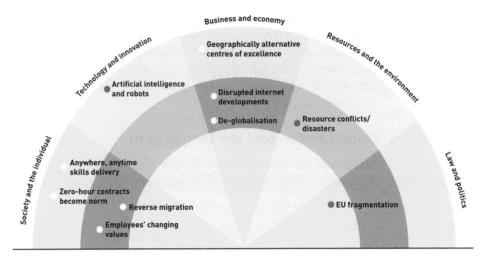

Figure 9.4 Disruptions that could radically change the nature of work

Source: Based on University of Wales and Z-punkt (2014), *The Future of Work, Jobs and Skills in 2030,* UK Commission for Education and Skills, Wath upon Dearne, South Yorkshire, pp. 14–15.

From the trends depicted in Figure 9.3 and the possible disruptions to these shown in Figure 9.4, four different development paths or scenarios were developed. These are:

- **Forced Flexibility** – greater business flexibility, incremental innovation, modest economic growth and weakened job security.
- **The Great Divide** – informed by employees' changing values and zero-hours contracts become the norm.
- **Skills Activism** – informed by artificial intelligence and robots everywhere and anywhere/anytime skills and delivery.
- **Innovation Adaptation** – informed by geographically alternative centres of excellence, reverse migration and anywhere/anytime skills and delivery.

Illustration 9.3 gives more details of these.

Illustration 9.3

Summary of scenarios for work, jobs and skills in 2030

	Scenario One Forced Flexibility (Business as usual)	Scenario Two The Great Divide	Scenario Three Skills Activism	Scenario Four Innovative Adaptation
Economic conditions	Moderate economic growth in the context of a world economy	Sturdy UK recovery fuelled by high-tech and innovative businesses	Slow recovery following prolonged crisis	Stagnant economy within a turbulent international environment
Social conditions	Widening income gap, low-skilled workers are the most vulnerable	Two-tiered society with deep division between the economic 'haves' and the 'have-nots'	Automation of professional work has hit medium-income groups hard	Decrease in income inequality as financial sector struggles to compete internationally

	Scenario One Forced Flexibility (Business as usual)	Scenario Two The Great Divide	Scenario Three Skills Activism	Scenario Four Innovative Adaptation
Labour market context	Hourglass shaped – ferocious competition for low-skilled positions and a hollowing out of the middle of the workforce	Competitive and attractive marketplace for high-skilled jobs, poor opportunities for the low-skilled	Significant disruption to medium- and highly skilled work. Jobs are mainly project-based with high turnover	Growing virtual workforces as a strategy for productivity in a low-growth environment, increased work intensity
Policy context	Easing of employment regulation and focus on job quality. Reduced public funding available for training and skills due to fiscal constraints	Liberal immigration policies and labour regulation create a supportive environment for business. Minimal public funding available for training and skills	Extensive government-driven skills programme and investment to facilitate reskilling, supportive government regulation strengthens employee position	Commitment to skills development despite deficit reduction, government drive to re-engineer training and skills content and delivery to best fit need
Uptake of innovation	Focus on incremental innovation in UK businesses, across almost all UK sectors	Radical innovation in life and material sciences driving economic growth	Disruptive IT automation restructures professional tasks	Wide integration of cost-efficient ICT technologies to enable business survival
Education and training context	Greater commercial focus and responsiveness to employer needs, although fees are higher	Highly competitive and efficient but also expensive which reduces access	Reform of system and expansion of access to all socio-economic backgrounds	Significant increase in online provision as a cost-effective option

Source: Based on University of Wales and Z-punkt (2014), *The Future of Work, Education and Skills in 2030*, UK Commission for Education and Skills, p. 17.

The different futures, depicted in Illustration 9.3, may not come to pass and be something different, or the future might be a mixture of them. Nevertheless, they give 'food for thought' to organizations in what appears to be becoming an uncertain world. Whatever happens, the relationship between employers and managers is likely to be more fluid, which puts pressure on the legal agreements between them as well as the more informal and imprecise 'psychological contract'.

The changing psychological contract

The term 'psychological contract' can be traced back to the 1960s and interest in social exchange theory. As a framework to analyze the non-formal relationship between an employee and their employer it was first used, in its current form, in the early 1960s but became more popular following the economic downturn in the early 1990s (CIPD, 2014). At this time, the concept attracted attention as it offered a powerful way of analyzing the perceptions of, and feelings and reactions of the victims of mergers, takeovers, redundancies, downsizing and sometimes aggressive employer behaviour witnessed at the time. These corporate changes often led to new terms and conditions of employment, and Cooper (1998, p. 98) remarked that in total they added up to 'the most profound changes in the workplace since the industrial revolution'.

Rousseau and Parks (1993, p. 19) define the psychological contract as representing 'an individual's beliefs regarding terms and conditions of a reciprocal exchange agreement between that person and another party'. Arnold *et al.* (2005) talk about 'mutual obligations' between employer and employee. For most of the time, as employees perform their normal routines, the contract remains hidden. However, it quickly becomes visible and expressed when it is broken or when one side feels that a breach of contract has been attempted (Sparrow, 2000, p. 171), often when change is attempted or forced upon employees.

The recession of the 1990s and the continuing impact of globalization are alleged to have destroyed the basis of the traditional deal since job security is no longer on offer (CIPD, 2014). Changes currently affecting the workplace include:

- increasing numbers of employees on part-time, flexible and 'zero-hours' work;
- organizations downsizing and delayering, meaning remaining employees have to do more;
- markets, technology and products constantly changing;
- organizational structures becoming more fluid and geographically dispersed.

It is possible that employees, in particular younger ones, no longer expect job security, or to receive anything over and above their legal contract of employment and some commitment to fairness in everyday relationships. The shrinking of the public sector, where formal employment contracts (with holiday and retirement entitlements) exist, and the growth of the private sector, is changing the nature of relationships between those employed and their employers.

The nature of the psychological contract is particularly important for managers involved with change. They need to be alert to not only the effects of changing legal employment contracts (for instance in takeovers or as delayering or job changes occur) but also to how changes in processes, management style, forms of communications and organizational culture will influence the psychological contracts, frequently built up over many years.

For new employees the contract begins to be formed early in recruitment when they interact with organizational literature and websites and then later in selection processes when they interact with the people they will work with in interviews or assessment centres. In the first few weeks and months of working in a new place the new employee's experiences will shape the contract they are building; the behaviour of co-workers and the stories they tell are influential.

They see the performance of others and hear stories of what to do and what not to do. Performance management systems have a big impact upon expectations of work and rewards. Issues of how the organization distinguishes between poor, average and top performers and how are they rewarded differently become important.

The psychological contract therefore has a big influence on employee acceptance of change, such that managers need to be alert to how employees will perceive it. Given the pervasiveness and urgency of change today there are implications for how organizational practices act to shape contracts. While it is far too simple to suggest that organizations can put into place experiences that will shape psychological contracts so that employees will readily accept change, it is clear that certain organizational actions do act to shape contracts. Careful management of selection and socialization procedures could be used to set expectations of working life that are at least conducive to change.

Innovation and creativity

In many cases, the trends for the future, shown in Figures 9.3 and 9.4, emphasize creativity and innovation, influenced by employers and employees changing values and attitudes to work and living. There is also an emphasis on new technologies, which in turn lead to new ways of organizing. These changes could benefit both organizations and those who work in them. They could also lead to splits in the structure of society: those who enjoy high standards of living and are able to move between well-paid jobs; and those who also change jobs, but not out of choice, and who have much more precarious lifestyles as a result of job insecurity and low pay. However, in a global world, without creativity and innovation we will, as a whole, stagnate as a society and organizations will not evolve.

Creativity and innovation are not, though the same thing. Aubke (2014), drawing on the work of Amabile (2000), says that although creativity is a necessary component of innovation, it is not sufficient in itself. She maintains that in order to be creative a person requires some creative thinking skills, a sound field-specific expertise (knowledge) and lastly some intrinsic motivation. It is only then that creativity may transform into an idea, product or process, which changes the existing organizational environment, which in turn depends on the 'organizational resources available, the organizational motivation and openness to promote innovations and whether or not management practices are conducive to fostering innovations' (p. 5). The impact of the organizational environment on creativity, and vice versa, is illustrated in Figure 9.5.

This model is helpful in identifying the organizational elements that support creativity. However, it focuses on the individual as the source of creativity. This is not always what happens as Aubke recognizes when she refers to as 'creativity in networks' and the process of maintaining ties of different strengths to diverse others. In this way knowledge passes from one person to another and changes in the process.

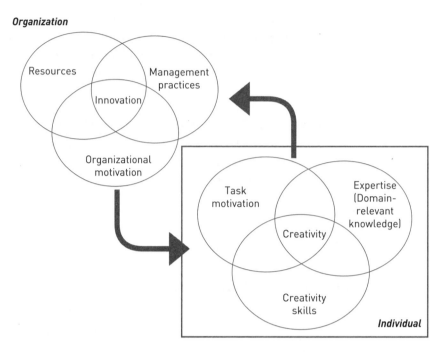

Figure 9.5 Impact of organizational environment on creativity

Source: Aubke, F. (2014), 'Creative hot spots: a network analysis of German Michelin-starred chefs', *Creativity and Innovation Management*, 23(1), pp. 3–14.

Miles, Snow and Miles (2000) say that knowledge is a key asset when innovating. They also emphasize the role of the organizational environment when they say that approaches to facilitating innovation require organizational resources and investments. For example, they say (p. 301): 'Innovation cannot be managed hierarchically because it depends on knowledge being offered voluntarily rather than on command.' Furthermore, they maintain that approaches to facilitating innovation require investments that often appear to be unjustified within current organizational accounting systems.

Their argument is that models of organizing that involve standardization and, more recently, customization which have required, respectively, 'meta-capabilities' of coordination and delegation, are no longer sufficient for innovation to flourish. This is because organizations of the future need not just knowledge but knowledge generation and transfer, which in turn require social interaction and exchange between organizational members and with those outside the organization. The logical outcome of this, they argue, is that *collaboration* is the key to innovation – what Miles *et al.* call the new 'meta-capability'. Acknowledging that collaboration is not entirely natural in many organizational cultures, they suggest three conditions for collaboration to happen:

1 People need *time* to discuss ideas, reflect, listen and engage in a host of activities that might produce fresh ideas.
2 They need to develop strong bonds of *trust* between each other – a willingness to expose one's views without the fear of being exploited and to probe more deeply for new insights and perspectives.

3 People need a sense of *territory* marking one's place in the outcomes of the collaborative process. These visible stakes might be stock ownership, stock options, visible awards and collegial recognition amongst others.

All these conditions are dependent on managers creating the organizational conditions for innovation to flourish. Pearson (2002, p. 1), in his article 'Tough-minded ways to get innovative', says that most chief executives want their companies to be more competitive, not just on one or two dimensions but across the board. He goes on to identify two basic principles for this:

First they understand that consistent innovation is the key to the company's survival. Being innovative in one or two areas just won't work. Second, they know that the most powerful changes they can make are those that create value for customers and potential customers.

Disruptive innovation theory

The theme of creating value, for potential customers in particular, is addressed by Anthony and Christensen (2005, p. 38) with their concepts of 'disruptive change' and 'disruptive innovation theory'. This theory holds that:

Existing companies have a high probability of beating entrant attackers when the contest is about sustaining innovations with radical or incremental improvements that target demanding customers at the high end of the market who are willing to pay premium prices for better products. [However] established companies tend to lose to attackers with disruptive innovations, cheaper, simpler, more convenient products or services that start by meeting the less-demanding customers.

An example of this is the Hudl tablet that was launched by Tesco supermarket in 2013 as a low-cost basic tablet retailing at £119. A report on this tablet at the time (*The Independent*, 15 October 2013) quoted Tesco's chief marketing officer Matt Atkinson as saying: '… the Hudl launch is about making technology more accessible and experts believe it is largely aimed at first-time tablet users who are naturally less tech-savvy'. Two years later, Hill reviewed the Hudl 2 tablet versus the Apple iPad mini and concluded:

While both these slates are at the more affordable end of the market there is still quite a difference in their prices. The Tesco Hudl 2 is just £99, while the iPad mini is a pricier £199. So you're paying at least £70 extra, which is quite a chunk of change when the difference between the two isn't huge in day to day use.

(Hill, 2015)

Another example is the introduction and success of discount retailers Aldi and Lidl, who offer basic food and clothing products at prices that significantly undercut the 'big four' supermarkets (Sainsbury, Morrisons, Tesco and Asda). What is more, in May 2015, Quinn, writing in *The Grocer*, reported that Aldi and Lidl were moving to the front with their plans to open far more stores, over a much wider geographical area, than any of the leading four supermarkets.

At the time, neither the creation of the Hudl nor the appearance of the retail discounters, as well as other examples given by Anthony and Christensen, was predicted. Even so, these authors maintain that, by using 'disruptive innovation theory', organizations have the best chance of creating new growth by bringing disruptive innovations into a marketplace. Regarding this they say that the principle at the core of the disruptive innovation theory is that companies innovate faster than customers' lives change. This leads to companies ending up producing products that are too good, and too expensive for many customers. Consequently, there are market segments that have been overlooked. Thus an opening has been created for someone else (perhaps unencumbered by expensive managements, infrastructure and staff) to fill the gap. So, the question is: How can anyone spot potentially transforming innovations? One answer is to recognize three different customer types:

- *Undershot customers* are customers for whom existing products are not good enough. Signals of undershot customers include customers eagerly snatching up new products, steady or increasing prices and the struggles of organizational specialists to continue to meet their needs. Undershot customers look for sustaining innovations that close the gap between what is available and the job they are looking to get done.
- *Overshot customers* are customers for whom existing products are too good. Signals of overshot customers include customer reluctance to purchase new products and declining prices. Overshot customers welcome low-end disruptive innovations that offer good enough products and performance at low prices.
- *Non-consumers* are customers that lack the skills, wealth or ability to buy many products or processes for themselves.

All these three customer groups offer opportunities to apply disruptive innovation theory. For example, someone must have spotted a group of people (non-consumers) for whom (a) the idea of needing a tablet was absurd, and (b) did not have the money to purchase one of the existing tablets that were perhaps in any case thought 'too complicated' to understand – hence the idea of the Hudl, offered not by specialist retailers but by an organization that they already shopped at and trusted.

It could be argued that the emergence of discounting food retailers such as Lidl and Aldi met the needs of the overshot customers, and disrupted the assumption that only 'hard-up' people would use basic, warehouse-type food stores. For the undershot customers, the lack of being able to sleep properly on long-haul flights led to airlines firstly introducing seats that turned into beds and then suites containing both chair and bed, with separate restaurant. We might ask ourselves what airline accommodation will be like in the future. By contrast, budget airlines innovated to disrupt the conventional belief that people of low income had no need/desire to fly.

Leading innovation

Miles *et al.* (2000) assume a style of leadership that is participative, caring of followers, and which recognizes the role of everyone in the efforts to make any organization successful. This is exemplified by Bennis (2000) and McGill and Slocum (1998) who argue for the demise of 'top-down' leadership. Bennis (p. 73) says: 'The most urgent projects require the coordinated contributions of many talented people working together' and (p. 74): 'No change can occur without willing and committed followers.'

He maintains that it is only in the solving of relatively simple technical problems that top-down leadership is effective. For the resolution of 'adaptive', complex, messy problems many people at all levels of the organization must be involved and mobilized. Two further quotations (Bennis, 2000, p. 76) suffice to make the point:

> Post-bureaucratic organization requires a new kind of alliance between leaders and the led. Today's organizations are evolving into federations, networks, clusters, cross-functional teams, temporary systems, ad hoc tasks, lattices, modules, matrices – almost anything but pyramids with their obsolete top-down leadership.

The new reality is that intellectual capital, brain power, know-how and human imagination have supplanted capital as the critical success factors and leaders have to learn an entirely new set of skills.

Amabile and Khaire (2008, pp. 103–4), drawing on contributions at a colloquium on leading creativity, maintain that the first priority of leadership is to engage people who can undertake creative work. This implies people who can not only do the everyday tasks allotted to them, but who can also contribute imagination. This might be easier said than done. However, Amabile and Khaire offer the following advice to managers (p. 106–7):

> If you're trying to enhance creativity ...
> - remember you are not the sole fount of ideas;
> - enable collaboration;
> - enhance diversity;
> - map the stages of creativity and tend to their different needs;
> - accept the inevitability and utility of failure;
> - motivate with intellectual challenge.
>
> (Amabile and Khaire, 2008)

A paradox

A look back at the list of general trends posed at the beginning of this chapter and a summary of the discussion so far paints the following scenario. On the one hand there is a picture of people becoming more individualistic, independent and living for some of their adult lives alone, and communicating increasingly through ICT and with more choice in respect of their lifestyle. This attitude to life and work is reinforced by the increase in 'non-standard' working that is frequently insecure and which does not engender commitment to any particular organization and its goals. On the other hand there are business thinkers arguing for more organic, network and virtual organizations that require collaborative attitudes and behaviour so that innovation can flourish. So we appear to have a paradox: are changing career patterns undermining the key attitudes and behaviour that employers need?

Empowerment is part of the answer but in spite of the emphasis put on empowering employees to work in organic, network and virtual forms of organizations, many large organizations continue to conform to hierarchical principles of structure and accountability. The skills that managers need to be successful in this type of organization are not those which comfortably agree with the principles of empowering subordinate levels of staff. Even if empowering abilities are developed, they are unlikely to be rewarded or acknowledged. Behaving in empowering ways does not support the culture and processes that make these managers successful. Many of the characteristics – such as showing determination, drive/energy, leading from the front, objective decision making and personal achievement – are not among the key empowering characteristics.

Chapter 8 discussed the significance of organizations as learning organizations. However, according to Schein (1999), requiring individuals to learn to think and behave in these ways is essentially asking them to put themselves through transformational culture change – coming as they frequently have from organizational cultures more suited to traditional bureaucratic norms of command and control – not least because these types of systems discourage creativity and innovation. He goes on to say (p. 7): 'But paradoxically, when we speak of "culture change" in organizations we are typically demanding levels of cognitive redefinition that can probably only be achieved by some version of coercive persuasion.' This is because these individuals are being asked to *disconfirm* what they have believed is *right* – what they have been used to doing for much of their organizational life.

This seems a worrying scenario given the belief, as Miles *et al.*, Bennis and others assert, in alternative, more satisfying and effective ways of running organizations. One relatively recent method that overcomes these concerns and which builds on the approaches to change discussed in Chapter 8 is *appreciative inquiry*.

Appreciative inquiry

Appreciative inquiry (AI) is an organizational change methodology that takes a different view from traditional approaches, being a more holistic and humanistic method that focuses on the 'positive psychology' generated by asking positive questions rather than concentrating on negative questions and solving problems. The basic idea is that asking positive questions creates a positive atmosphere that is more likely to generate fresh ideas and employee engagement towards solutions.

Introduced by David Cooperrider, AI is a search for the best in people and what is happening in their organizations (Cooperrider and Whitney, 2005). It is about capturing their imagination of what is most effective and of using that imagination to create possible futures. The notion of 'generativity' is ingrained in AI since it is more concerned with discovering new possibilities and energizing people around those possibilities rather than focusing on working within existing patterns of behaviour (Zandee, 2015). Eight principles serve to explain how AI should be implemented (Dunlap, 2008):

1 *The constructionist principle* – this maintains that reality is constructed through social interactions. An individual or group in a workplace will experience a countless number of interactions and these interactions create a particular reality for that person or group. This reality then becomes institutionalized and reproduced through action. Reality, therefore, is only one possible reality; it is socially constructed.

2 *Simultaneity* – in contrast to the normal approach of analyzing data and then deciding what to do, simultaneity expresses the idea that inquiry and change occur together. When people are involved in thinking about positive questions, the ensuing discussions and stories begin to change their attitudes and behaviour.

3 *The poetic principle* – this expresses the notion of organizations as narratives, continually being co-authored by the people in them together with outsiders who work with them. The past is written and shapes what is to be written but what is written next (metaphorically speaking) is open and depends on what is inquired about and what stems from the inquiry. The language of the inquiry also influences future outcomes.

4 *Anticipation* – the images (anticipations) of the future that people create begin to shape their constructions and discourses about the future. Imagine, for instance, how anticipation of a stormy meeting with your boss might influence your behaviour compared to anticipation of an upbeat meeting. A gloomy future makes for a gloomy present; a positive future makes for a positive present.

5 *Being positive* – positive climates create conditions for change far more than negative climates. Healthy social relationships between people create atmospheres of trust and support and are therefore important to underpin positive interactions relating to work.

6 *Wholeness* – all groups and stakeholders connected to a change should be involved to maximize the capacity for creative outcomes. If some stakeholders are excluded then the whole story is not narrated.

7 *Enactment* – individuals and groups must enact changes that they want to see. It is about living the future in the present.

8 *Free choice* – people should not be constrained in terms of how they contribute to an inquiry. They need to be free to decide how they will contribute as free choice will raise commitment and creativity. Suppression of the ways in which people might contribute is also assumed to suppress commitment and creativity.

Appreciative inquiry is a form of action research (Gold, 2014; Zandee, 2015) that can involve large numbers (potentially thousands) of participants to create a learning community and shape possible futures. It is suited to situations where large numbers of participants are involved in working across an organization(s) that needs to innovate its way towards some new reality. AI is more likely to be used in public services and not-for-profit sectors such as healthcare, education and religion and has been applied to a wide range of change situations including transforming a nursing culture (Moody *et al.*, 2007), improving services in healthcare (Baker and Wright, 2006), cultural change (Van Oosten, 2006), and to create a shared meaning of organizational ethics (van Vuuren and Crous, 2005). The tendency of AI to be used in non-profit contexts may reflect its soft systems characteristics and, arguably, a better fit with organization cultures characterized by cooperation, humanism and democracy (Drew and Wallis, 2014). The relative absence of AI in the for-profit sector may reflect a general lack of confidence in its assumptions and 'positive' inquiry movement in organizational theorizing and has been criticized for being too evangelical and uncritical (Fineman, 2006)

The eight principles of AI are used to underpin a four-stage (4-D) cycle to engage people. The first stage is *Discovery* of what is done well in the group or organization and what makes it happen. The second stage is *Dreaming* of possible futures based on the exceptional experiences identified in Discovery. The third is *Designing* what should be done to implement the shared view of the future, and the fourth stage is *Destiny*, which is a collective agreement on the systems to support the desired future state (Watkins and Mohr, 2001).

Although it has an intuitive appeal stemming from its inclusive and democratic ethos, AI is not a panacea and does have some limitations; being labour intensive is among them. Evaluating AI as a way of raising citizen participation in local government uncovered the following issues (Schooley, 2012).

- Very skilful facilitators are required to accentuate the positive and prevent regression to negative thinking.
- The overt focus on the positive could suppress the voices of people with genuine grievances.
- Some decisions and intentions would need referral back to the council who could quash the ideas generated by AI processes.

Despite the popularity of AI, little research has evaluated how effective it is. Little is known about how people participating in AI feel about it although recent research has shown that participation satisfies basic psychological needs for competence, autonomy and relatedness and therefore can impact on individual psychological capital (Verleysen *et al.*, 2015). As such, AI has the potential to enhance human potential through working and learning with others.

At the collective level, an evaluation of 20 cases where AI had been used found that 7 were judged to have produced transformational outcomes although not all cases had intended to be transformational (Bushe and Kassam, 2005). Where transformational change was observed, Bushe and Kassam suggested that two qualities of AI were instrumental in the process:

- the focus on changing how people think and not what they do;
- the focus on creating an environment in which ideas lead to self-organizing change.

However, this meta-analytic approach to AI implies that it is possible to evaluate AI in some objective sense in that there is some reality out there to be found (i.e. that AI is or is not effective). Since AI is based on principles of social constructionism, that is what is positive is a social construction, it follows that whether it is successful or not in a particular setting is also a social construction. Evaluation of AI is an ongoing part of an AI intervention.

Illustration 9.4

Using AI in a multicultural change setting

Refugees and asylum seekers looking to settle in a new country confront problems such as discrimination, accessing education, finding employment and cultural adaptation. It makes sense for agencies dealing with migrants to be staffed by people who understand the backgrounds of the people they are helping. However, culturally diverse work settings can create additional perspectives and complexities in change situations because of wide-ranging cultural values and attitudes towards work held by employees.

A US organization (the Agency) dealing with refugees and asylum seekers had found that change interventions by managers had 'met lukewarm responses and passive resistance' thought to be rooted in the cultural sensitivities of staff, e.g. doing something that others might judge to be inappropriate. An AI approach at the Agency first engaged all employees (40) in an 'appreciative discourse' around strategic planning and then engaged them in a reflective evaluation of their attitudes towards change. The 4-D model was used and questions posed included:

- Describe a time when you were proud to be with the Agency. What was the situation? Who was involved and what made you proud? (Discovery)
- Imagine yourself and the Agency in five years' time. What does it look like? What resources are needed to get there? (Dream)
- What will the ideal organization structure look like? How would that affect decisions and what is needed for staff to flourish? (Design)

- What actions are needed to create the Agency of the future? What needs to happen to create the organization that you described in the Discovery and Dream phases? (Destiny)

The AI approach used in the Agency avoided conversations fixated on issues, problems and concerns and created an environment comfortable with discussing ideas without upsetting others; psychological safety was increased. Usually reticent employees contributed more and personal relationships improved. AI was credited with creating an emotionally safe place in what was previously sometimes a hostile and tense working environment.

Source: Based on Rao, M. (2014), 'Cultivating openness to change in multicultural organizations: assessing the value of appreciative discourse', *Organization Development Journal*, Autumn, pp. 75–88.

This summary of AI presents a view of the process of changing that is capable of getting people engaged in shaping their futures. However, one issue is whether all organizations have the capacity for change and whether some are more ready than others.

Capacity for change

We can see by looking at organizations in the same sector that although they face similar pressures for change they embark on different change programmes, have different journeys and arrive at different destinations and have different experiences of success and failure. Some organizations may evolve into market leaders whereas others wither and die. The different ways in which organizational leaders interpret environmental signals offer one explanation for this, but so does the idea that organizations have different capacities to change (Meyer and Stensaker, 2006). This refers to their ability to undertake 'large-scale changes without compromising daily operations or subsequent change processes' (p. 218); that is, the positive effects of change outweigh the negative effects. If the idea that organizations carry a certain change capacity is accepted, then it makes sense to ask how that capacity can be expanded. The following offers some possibilities:

- *Framing* communication of the reasons for change, including use of symbols and metaphors to reinforce and simplify messages. Open, honest and transparent communication amongst and with staff is critical for success (Ace and Parker, 2010; Meyer and Stensaker, 2006).
- *Participation* of employees in the design and implementation of change is now accepted as inescapable. This ensures commitment by sharing decision-making power, fostering interdependence and building a collective identity. However, employees must see that this is genuinely wanted and has an impact in the workplace (Ace and Parker, 2010; McPhee, 2007).

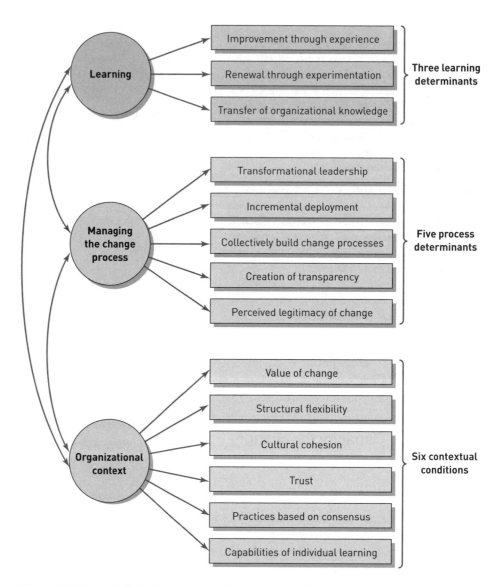

Figure 9.6 A model of change capacity

Source: Based on Klarner, P., Probst, G. and Soparnot, R. (2008), 'Organizational change capacity in public services: the case of the World Health Organization', *Journal of Change Management*, 8(1), pp. 57–72.

- *Pacing and sequencing* refers to the tempo and timing of change. Continuous implementation of initiatives requires team members to adapt work routines, processes and social interactions with other team members. Slow change gives opportunities to learn about what is happening but slowness could be seen as lack of urgency and it gives resistors the best chance to mount a defence. Fast change can accelerate the benefits but could crash and burn if poor decisions are made. Getting the pace and sequencing (the timing of different interventions) right is a key challenge for management (Meyer and Stensaker, 2006; Carter, Armenakis, Field and Mossholder, 2012).

- *Change fatigue* is passive resignation. It is not the acceptance or rejection of change. Instead, it is a general sense of apathy towards the organizational change(s). Continuous change is also tiring, so pacing and sequencing change will help. Explaining the change goals and processes and intended benefits helps, along with frequent briefings on progress towards the goals (Turner, 2012).
- *Routinizing* new routines, structures and processes so as to create a sense of trust and predictability, whilst changing only what is necessary because these are the things that connect people, and offer support and understanding (McCann, Seisky and Lee, 2009).
- *Recruiting* people specifically to help implement changes: consultants, change agents or perhaps new appointments to key positions. There are also implications for the organization's general approach to selection and in particular the competences that it seeks in new appointments (Lengnick-Hall, Beck and Lengnick-Hall, 2011; Meyer and Stensaker, 2006).

Focusing on these issues will help the organization's capacity for change to increase. Change capacity is a dynamic capability that underpins the ability to manage change over a period of time (Meyer and Stensaker, 2006; Klarner, Probst and Soparnot, 2008). Klarner *et al.* (2008) offered a model of change capacity as shown in Figure 9.6.

Change capacity is conceptualized as comprising three correlated dimensions: learning, change process and organizational context. These dimensions are thought to mutually reinforce each other and each dimension is assessed through the determinants or conditions shown in Figure 9.6. The basic idea is that change agents can assess each of the 14 determinants and conditions to see how far they are present in the organization as a forerunner to intervening and strengthening where there are weaknesses – see Illustration 9.5.

Illustration 9.5

Dr WHO?

The model of change capacity shown in Figure 9.1 has been applied to the World Health Organization (WHO) (Klarner *et al.*, 2008). The WHO was on a mission to see that people the world over enjoy the best possible health, but in the face of new health problems (HIV/AIDS) and funding issues it had become somewhat too bureaucratic. A new director general set out on a drive to make the WHO more flexible and responsive. A classic case of realigning with the environment, it seems. A programme of change was evaluated after 18 months using a case study methodology.

Klarner and colleagues judged that all three learning dimension determinants were present in full measure. However, the organizational context dimension was judged lacking on structural flexibility, practices based on consensus and

individual learning capabilities. The change process dimension was found wanting on incremental deployment, building change processes and creating transparency. Despite some rather big omissions in relation to the model, they say the changes intended had been mostly met and overall were thought to have had a 'positive impact' and concluded that the WHO's capacity for change was 'moderate'.

Models of this type are limited in that we cannot escape having to reach some rather judgemental conclusions about the extent to which the proposed catalysts of change are present. Nevertheless, they can act as useful templates to stimulate thinking around some important factors that influence the success of change initiatives.

There are various theories on the extent to which employees can cope with change and whether this increases or otherwise employees' capacity for change. For example, one theory maintains that experience of change breeds further capacity for change. Another theory argues for the opposite; for instance, once change is achieved there should be no necessity for more change and that capacity for change is reduced. Carter *et al.* (2013) tested the first theory in circumstances where transformational leaders operated to bring about continuous incremental organizational change at lower hierarchical levels. They found that, within the teams they led, the frequency with which change occurred moderated the link between workplace relationships and performance. The nature of this moderation effect showed that this link was stronger when change frequency was high.

By contrast, on the basis of their research in the context of episodic change, Beck, Brudel and Woyode (2008) refute the 'change breeds change' hypothesis and support a deceleration hypothesis in which change leads to less change.

In conclusion it appears, unsurprisingly, that the capacity for change differs depending on previous experience of the type of change, how it is led, and the context.

Challenges for future research on change

Despite being among the most studied aspects of organizations, there is much more to understand about change and organization development. Much of the earlier theorizing led to prescriptive 'how to' models that neglect crucial aspects of context such as micropolitics and workforce skills. As this book nears an end, therefore, it is worth looking at some of the gaps and limitations in change research as a way of understanding where research is needed.

1 *Multiple contexts and levels of analysis.* Early studies were typically of one-off change events but these overlooked the contextual factors that were influencing particular episodes. More recently, there has been more focus on change contexts and on the changing process than on finding out what can be understood by researching single change events. The emphasis is moving to exploring change while it is happening, to detect the complex nature of historic, political and environmental factors on change outcomes and the way these interact with actions within organizations.

2 *Time, history, process and action.* Most studies of management are cross-sectional. They are snapshots of situations and as such they are incapable of separating cause from effect. Many organizations have existed for a long time, so any snapshot study excludes the past and how it shaped the situation captured in the photograph. However, history is not just a chronological sequence of events; it is powerful in shaping prevailing and future processes and needs to be examined in this context. Implications therefore are for the inclusion of time in understanding of change and this can be achieved by historical studies of sectors and organizations or by research programmes that follow change over time.

3 *Change processes and organizational performance.* Whereas many studies of change unravel the processes going on, more need to take account of the link between capacity for change and success or failure of change programmes themselves. This poses considerable challenges to researchers, however, as measures of capacity for change as well as the change outcomes are called for. Easy quantitative measures may not be available and so more qualitative judgements may have to be made.

4 *International comparative research.* Most change research takes place in single organizations or at best in a few organizations in the same country. For understandable practical reasons the field lacks studies of change on a cross-national scale although these are needed to help understand innovation, new ways of organizing, the influence of national cultural differences and the limitations of normative theory.

5 *Reciprocity, customization, sequencing and pace.* While there is much theory and advice available to change agents, deciding where and how to start a change initiative is difficult. How receptive will people be? What change approach should they use in what context? What advice is there on when and how to sequence events and interventions? How much urgency and pace can be injected into proceedings? Answers to some of these questions would help inform this under-researched area.

6 *Scholar–practitioner engagement.* Management research is often carried out by a lone researcher, maybe a small team of researchers, conceptualizing and designing studies in the first place, gathering and analyzing data. There is little interaction with the research setting, other than acquiring permissions, until the research process starts. However, the study of change needs research strategies that engage with participants in agreeing how problems are described, what data is needed, how it should be collected and interpreted and what kind of process will be used to feedback results to organizational personnel? Teams of researchers working alongside organizations over a long time frame will be needed.

7 *Political influences.* Most organizations exist in political environments – local, national and international. These may facilitate or constrain what changes organizations can or cannot make, overtly or not. This is a sensitive area for researchers but, nevertheless, needs recognizing when appropriate.

The classic approach to management research, including change and organization development, relies upon positivistic approaches to defining and investigating research questions. From the 1980s onwards alternative ways of seeing change have emerged and are captured in Table 9.1.

The classical approach perceives change situations as possessing a single truth and reality which needs to be discovered and then told to the waiting world. Ways of discovering the true situation rely on objective methods of collecting data (e.g. top managers know best, management information is valid). Data analysis shows the way forward to a new organizational position. Change, like TV shows, occurs as episodes and in between the episodes there are periods of no change.

Table 9.1 Trends in organization development

Classic organization development	New organization development
• Based in classical science and modern thought and philosophy	• Influenced by the new sciences and postmodern thought and philosophy
• Truth is transcendent and discoverable; there is a single objective reality	• Truth is immanent and emerges from the situation; there are multiple, socially constructed realities
• Reality can be discovered using rational and analytic processes	• Reality is socially negotiated and will, almost certainly, involve power and political processes
• Collecting and applying valid data using objective problem-solving methods leads to change	• Creating new mindsets or social agreements, sometimes through explicit or implicit negotiation, leads to change
• Change is episodic and can be created, planned and managed	• Change is continuous, and can be self-organizing
• Emphasis on changing behaviour and what one does	• Emphasis on changing mindsets and how one thinks

Source: Marshak, R.J. and Grant, D. (2008), 'Organizational discourse and new organization development processes', *British Journal of Management*, 19, Special Issue, p. S8. Reproduced with permission.

In contrast to the classical approach, new perspectives drawing on postmodernism have emerged (Marshak and Grant, 2008). Rather than seek to understand a simple objective reality, multiple realities are recognized – for example, appreciating the ways different groups of actors involved in a situation will differ and that each interpretation has its own validity. Power and the exercise of political energy are used to shape reality. Change is seen as a continuous phenomenon (not episodic) and is grounded in changes to how people think, as well as how they behave.

This thinking is reflected in modernist, sophisticated modernist or postmodernist views of change (Kirkbride, Durcan and Obeng, 1994). A *modernist* view of the world sees change as incremental, evolutionary, constantly developing, following a linear path and worked out according to a known recipe about what should change and how. Thus modernists tend to believe in change models based on simple cause and effect: if the right levers are pulled in relation to desired outcomes, those outcomes should surely follow.

A *sophisticated modernist* view of the world would see change as transformational, revolutionary, periodic, following a circular path (i.e. 'moving in a complex and dynamic fashion from emerging strategy to deliberate strategy and back again' (p. 157)) and one where the end point can change as the change process unfolds. As a result, this view recognizes that the world does not stand still for long. The *postmodernist view* of change is summed up as follows (Kirkbride *et al.*, pp. 158–9):

> The post-modern world can ... be seen as one characterized by randomness and chaos, by a lack of certainty, by a plethora of competing views and voices, by complex temporalities, and where organizations are unable to produce recipes for dealing with the unstable environment.

A cursory examination of some of today's organizations will show that there is 'truth' in all these views of change – the 'trick' is to know when and where one or the other is current. For instance, in limited, constrained situations, a modernist view of change may be most appropriate and might loosely be linked to the hard systems model of change, which implies transition rather than transformation and planned rather than emergent change.

The version of an OD model of change presented in the previous chapter is more congruent with a sophisticated modernist view of the world – provided the presence of continuous feedback loops is stressed and it is recognized that the vision and its associated change goals are not fixed – in the sense that the change process is never complete.

The postmodernist view does not easily attach itself to any recognizable model of change. What it does point towards, however, is a model of organization that is organic, flexible, niche market-oriented, where jobs are highly de-differentiated, de-demarcated and multi-skilled in a context of employment relationships based on subcontracting and networking. Change, in this context, could take on any number of faces and forms.

Conclusions

Understanding change and changing have become one of the biggest preoccupations for management theory reflecting the situation now that change, and changing, exercise the minds of most managers most of the time. Whether planned or emergent, change takes a number of different forms, each of which requires a different type of action. Building capacity to change and using collective methods of action research and appreciative inquiry to involve people in changing are promising approaches that appear to offer more than conventional approaches.

While there is no one best way to achieve successful organizational change, making efforts to understand the wide variety of change situations and to be familiar with the different characteristics of change itself will help organizations and their members negotiate appropriate paths to change and face the future with some confidence. There are key areas that should be considered in relation to the diagnosis, implementation and review of change situations:

1 *Multiple paths to change*:

- continuous environmental scanning (internal and external) to get early warning of change triggers;
- understanding the different types of change;
- adopting a contingency approach to developing plans for managing change based on an understanding of the change scenario being faced.

2 *The challenge of diversity*:

- regarding differences between people as something to be valued;
- recognizing that interacting with people across different cultures is essential to effective organizational effectiveness;

3 *Empowerment and control*:

- change is more likely to be a success if those it affects are willing collaborators;
- the effective collaboration of employees/stakeholders is more likely if they are involved at all stages of the change process and not just its implementation;
- behaviour linked to empowerment should be reinforced through appropriate reward mechanisms.

4 *Creativity and innovation*:

- creative and innovative approaches to change are more likely to flow from a diverse workforce;
- creativity and innovation require a creative organizational climate if they are to flourish;
- the organization and its managers need to foster structures and processes that facilitate creativity.

Change calls for high levels of persistence. This means persisting in the face of an ultra-unstable environment; persisting in the face of systems that are built for stability rather than change; persisting in the face of plans which are out of date as soon as they are formed. It means recognizing that nothing is perfect and that people will act in infuriating and annoying ways but that, when necessary, will bring the genius of their humanity to solve apparently insoluble problems. For organizations, it is learning that change is necessary and often very effective, even when business is good. Change is not easy but it can be interesting. It is certainly worth the journey, even if the place we arrive at is surprising.

Discussion questions and assignments

1 What do you think the future holds for your organization or one of which you have experience? How would you plan for this?

2 What is the capacity for change in an organization you know well? Consider how an organization's capacity for change would influence its approach to change in the future.

3 How would you describe the psychological contract you have with an organization you know?

Indicative resources

Arnold, J. with Silvester, J., Patterson, F., Robertson, I., Cooper, G. and Burnes, B. (2005), *Work Psychology* (4th edn), Harlow: Pearson Education. This book is extremely useful when focusing on present and future trends that employers and managers are facing given its emphasis on behaviour in the workplace and change.

Whitney, D. and Trosten-Boom, A. (2003) *The Power of Appreciative Inquiry*, San Francisco, CA: Berrett-Koehler.

Useful websites

http://www.technobility.com/docs/article036.htm This is a consultant's site which contains views and thoughts on managing change.

http://www.ons.gov.uk/ons/interactive/uk-national-population-projections—dvc3/index.html This is from the UK Office for National Statistics which offers predictive interactive graphs for different sections of the population.

http://changefatigue.weebly.com/change-capacity.html An interesting unusual presentation (with lists of resources) of capacity to change, resilience and change fatigue.

https://www.gov.uk/government/uploads/system/uploads/attachment_data/file/303340/the_future_of_work_slide_pack.pdf University of South Wales/Z-punkt (2014), 'The Future of Work, Education and Skills in 2030', UK Commission for Education and Skills.

References

Ace, W. and Parker, S. (2010), 'Overcoming change fatigue through focused employee engagement', *OD Practitioner*, 42(1), pp. 21–5.

Anthony, S. A. and Christensen, C. M. (2005), 'How you can benefit by predicting change', *Financial Executive*, 21(2), pp. 36–41.

Amabile, T. (2000), A Model of Creativity and Innovation in Organizations. In Staw, B. and Sutton, R. (eds.), *Research in Organizational Behavior*, Vol. 22.Elsevier Science, Amsterdam.

Amabile, T. M. and Khaire, M. (2008), 'Creativity and the role of the leader', *Harvard Business Review*, 86(10), pp. 100–9.

Arnold, J., Silvester, J., Patterson, F., Robertson, I., Cooper, C. and Burnes, B. (2005), *Work Psychology: Understanding Human Behaviour in the Workplace*, Harlow: Pearson Education.

Aubke, F. (2014), 'Creative hot spots: a network analysis of German Michelin-starred chefs', *Creativity and Innovation Management*, 23(1), pp. 3–14.

Baker, A. and Wright, M. (2006), 'Using Appreciative Inquiry to Initiate a Managed Clinical Network for Children's Liver Disease in the UK', *International Journal of Health Care Quality Assurance*, 19(7), pp. 561–74.

Beck, N., Bruderl, J. and Woyode, M. (2008), 'Momentum or deceleration? theoretical and methodological reflections on the analysis of organizational change', *Academy of Management Journal*, 51(3), pp. 413–35.

Bennis, W. (2000), 'The end of leadership: exemplary leadership is impossible without the full inclusion, initiatives, and cooperation of followers', *Organizational Dynamics*, pp. 71–80.

Berlingieri, G. (2013), 'Outsourcing and the rise of services', CEP Discussion Paper No. 1199, *Centre for Economic Performance*, LSE, April.

Bushe, G.R. and Kassam, A.F. (2005), 'When is Appreciative Inquiry Transformational? A Meta Case Analysis', *Journal of Applied Behavioral Science*, 41(2), pp. 161–81.

Carter, M.Z., Armenakis, A.A., Field, H.S. and Mossholder, K.W. (2012), 'Transformational leadership, relationship quality, and employee performance during continuous incremental organizational change', *Journal of Organizational Behaviour,* 34(7), 942–58.

CIPD (2014), *The Psychological Contract*, London: CIPD.

Cooper, C. (1998), 'The changing psychological contract at work', editorial, *Work and Stress*, 12(2), pp. 97–100.

Cooperrider, D.L. and Whitney, D. (2005) 'A Positive Revolution in Change: appreciative inquiry, in Cooperrider, D.L., Sorenson, P.F., Whitney, D. and Yaeger, T.F. (eds) *Appreciative Inquiry: Rethinking Human Organization Toward a Positive Theory of Change*, Champaign, IL: Stipes.

Dunlap, C.A. (2008), 'Effective Evaluation through Appreciative Inquiry', *Performance Development*, 47(2), pp. 23–29.

Drew, S. and Wallis, J.L. (2014), 'The use of appreciative inquiry in the practices of large-scale organizational change: a review and critique', *Journal of General Management,* 39(4), pp. 3–26.

Economist Group (2014), *On the Rise: Female Consumers in Asia,* http://going-global.economist.com/en/2014/12/15.

European Commission (2015), *Country Specific Recommendations 2015: Further efforts needed to support a robust recovery*, http://ec.europa.eu/social/main.jsp.

European Union (2013), *EU Employment and Social Situation Quarterly Review: Special Supplement on Demographic Trend*, Luxembourg: Publications Office of the European Union.

Eurostat News Release, 8 June, 2011, http://ec.europa.eu/eurostat/web/products-press-releases/-/3-08062011-BP.

Fineman, S. (2006), 'On being positive: concerns and counterpoints', *Academy of Management Review*, 31(2), pp. 270–91.

Gold, J. (2014), 'Revans reversed: focusing on the positive for a change', *Action Learning: Research and Practice*, 11(3), pp. 264–77.

Hill, S. (2015), 'Tesco Hudl 2 Review', *Techradar*, http://www.techradar.com/reviews/pc-mac/tablets/tesco-hudl-2-1267726/review/820, 20 April.

Kirkbride, P.S., Durcan, J. and Obeng, E.D.A. (1994), 'Change in a chaotic world', *Journal of Strategic Change*, 3, pp. 151–63.

Klarner, P., Probst, G. and Soparnot, R. (2008), 'Organizational change capacity in public services: the case of the World Health Organization', *Journal of Change Management*, 8(1), pp. 57–72.

Lengnick-Hall, C.A., Beck, T.E. and Lengnick-Hall, M.L. (2011), 'Developing a capacity for organizational resilience through strategic human resource management', *Human Resource Management Review*, 21, pp. 243–55.

Marshak, R.J. and Grant, D. (2008), 'Organizational discourse and new organization development processes', *British Journal of Management*, 19, Special Issue, S7–S19.

McCann, J., Selsky, J. and Lee, J. (2009), 'Building agility, resilience and performance in turbulent environments', *People and Strategy*, 32(3), pp. 44–51.

McGill, M. E. and Slocum, J.W., Jr (1998), 'A little leadership, please?' *Organizational Dynamics*, 26(3), pp. 39–49.

McPhee, M. (2007), 'Strategies and tools for managing change', *The Journal of Nursing Administration*, 37(9), pp. 405–13.

Meyer, C.B. and Stensaker, I.G. (2006), 'Developing capacity for change', *Journal of Change Management*, 6(2), pp. 217–31.

Miles, R.E., Snow, C. and Miles, G. (2000), 'The Future.org', *Long Range Planning*, 33, pp. 300–21, Office for National Statistics, http://www.ons.gov.uk.

Moody, R.C., Horton Deutsch, S. and Pesut, D.J. (2007) 'Appreciative Inquiry for Leading Complex Systems: supporting the transformation of an academic nursing culture', *Journal of Nursing Education*, 46(7), pp. 319–24.

Pearson, A. E. (2002), 'Tough-minded ways to get innovative', *Harvard Business Review*, 80(8), pp. 117–25.

Profit Confidential: *Stock Market Forecasts, Financial and Economic Analysis since 1986*, http://www.profitconfidential.com, accessed 19 May 2015.

Rao, M. (2014), 'Cultivating openness to change in multicultural organizations: assessing the value of

appreciative discourse', *Organization Development Journal*, Autumn, pp. 75–88.

Rousseau, D.M. and Parks, J.M. (1993), 'The contracts of individuals and organizations', in *Research in Organizational Behavior*, Greenwich, CT: JAI Press, 15, pp. 1–43.

Quinn. I (2015), 'Aldi and Lidl move to the front in distribution space race', *The Grocer*, 22 May, http://www.thegrocer.co.uk/stores/property-and-planning/aldi-and-lidl-move-to-front-in-distribution-space-race/.

Savage, M. (2013), 'A new model of social class? Findings from the BBC's Great British Class Survey experiment', *Sociology*, 0(0), pp. 1–32.

Schein, E. (1999), 'Empowerment, coercive persuasion and organizational learning: do they connect?' *The Learning Organization*, 6(4), pp. 1–11.

Schooley, S.E. (2012), 'Using appreciative inquiry to engage the citizenry: four potential challenges for public administrators', *International Journal of Public Administration*, 35(5), pp. 340–51.

Sparrow, P.R. (2000), 'The new employment contract: psychological implications of future work', in Burke, R.J. and Cooper, C.L. (eds), *The Organization in Crisis: Downsizing, Restructuring and Privatisation*, London: Blackwell, pp. 167–87.

Turner, D.M. (2012), 'Change fatigue: Is your organization too tired to change?' Retrieved from http://www.thinktransition.com/articles/change-fatigue-is-your-organization-too-tired-to-change/

University of Wales and Z-punkt (2014), *The Future of Work, Jobs and Skills in 2030*, Wath upon Dearne: UK Commission for Education and Skills, pp. 8–11, pp. 14–15, p. 17.

Van Vuuren, L.J. and Crous, F. (2005), 'Utilising Appreciative Inquiry (AI) in creating a shared meaning of ethics in organizations', *Journal of Business Ethics*, 57, pp. 399–412.

Verleysen, B., Lambrechts, F. and Van Acker, F. (2015), 'Building psychological capital with Appreciative Inquiry: investigating the mediating role of basic psychological need satisfaction', *Journal of Applied Behavioural Science*, 51(1), pp. 10–35.

Watkins, J.M. and Mohr, B.J. (2001) *Appreciative Inquiry: Change at the Speed of Imagination*, San Francisco: Jossey Bass.

Wilson, R., Beaven, R., May-Gillings, M., Hay, G. and Stevens, J. (2014), *Working Futures 2012-2022: Main Report*, Evidence Report 83, UK Commission for Employment and Skills, Wath upon Dearne, March.

Zandee, D.P. (2015), 'Appreciative Inquiry research review and notes', *AI Practitioner*, 17(1), pp. 61–5.

Name index

Subject Index